Interpersonal Communication Theory:

A Reader

Sheryl A. Friedley
George Mason University

The chapter titles originally appeared in Relational Communication: Continuity and Change in Personal Relationships, 2nd ed.
Wadsworth Publishing Company - Belmont, CA

Printed in the United States of America.

ISBN: 1-933005-33-5

59 Damonte Ranch Parkway, #B284 • Reno, NV 89521 • (800) 970-1883

www.benttreepress.com

Address all correspondence and order information to the above address.

Interpersonal Communication Theory: A Reader

PART I: Conceptual Foundations for Studying Personal Relationships

Chapter 1—Communication and Personal Relationships 3

Reading: **The Postulate of Interpersonal Needs: Description**
**William C. Schutz*

Chapter 2 – Theoretical Insights into Personal Relationships . . 27

Reading: **Relationship Awareness: Crossing the Bridge Between Cognition and Communication**
**Linda K. Acitelli*

Chapter 3 – Communication: The Central Dynamic in Personal Relationships 49

Reading: **Theoretical Foundations**
**L. Edna Rogers and Valentin Escudero*

Chapter 4 – Relational Culture: The Nucleus of Intimacy 69

Readings: **The Dark Side of Jealousy and Envy: Desire, Delusion, Desperation, and Destructive Communication**
**L. K. Guerrero and P. A. Andersen*

Communication in Intercultural Relationships
**Ling Chen*

Chapter 5 – The Social Context of Personal Relationships . . . 129

Readings: **Cultural Contracts Theory: Toward an Understanding of Identity Negotiation**
**Ronald L. Jackson II*

Different Standpoints, Different Realities: Race, Gender, and Perceptions of Intercultural Conflict
**Mark P. Orbe and Kiesha T. Warren*

PART II: The Evolution of Personal Relationships

Chapter 6—Launching Personal Relationships 153

Reading: **Communicating Under Uncertainty**
**Charles R. Berger*

"Becoming a Family": Developmental Process Represented in Blended Family Discourse
**Dawn O. Braithwaite, Loreen N. Olson, Tamara D. Golish, Charles Soukup and Paul Turman*

Chapter 7—Committing to Personal Relationships 211

Readings: **Love and Commitment**
**John H. Harvey and Ann L. Weber*

The Unacknowledged Role of Emotion in Theories of Close Relationships: How Do Theories Feel?
**Sally Planalp*

Chapter 8—Maintaining and Repairing Personal Relationships 259

Readings: **The Everyday Accomplishment of Work and Family: Exploring Practical Actions in Daily Routines**
**C. E. Medved*

When Partners Falter: Repair After a Transgression
**Tara M. Emmers-Sommer*

Chapter 9—Transforming and Ending Personal Relationships 303

Readings: **Holding On by Letting Go/Letting Go by Holding On: Approaches to Grief**
**Christine B. Smith*

Negotiation of Dialectical Contradictions by Parents Who Have Experienced the Death of a Child
**Paige W. Toller*

INTRODUCTION

Welcome to this advanced course in interpersonal communication. As such, this course is specifically designed to introduce you to the terminology, key concepts, and theoretical approaches used to study the nature of human relationships. Because communication is a broad-based discipline, I realize that not all of you are naturally drawn to study interpersonal communication; nevertheless, I firmly believe that this area of communication pervades every facet of your personal and professional lives. How you use interpersonal communication skills to create, sustain, re-define, and perhaps terminate any of these everyday relationships will have a profound impact on the quality of your own lives.

As a professor who has pursued a life-long interest to study interpersonal communication, I already know the value of this course and the subject matter it explores. Since the study of interpersonal communication as a part of the broader communication discipline is still relatively new, I know too that to study its roots will lead to you literature in such related disciplines as psychology, linguistics, sociology, and anthropology. Although the writings in some of these disciplines are challenging, they are essential to understand our discipline's history; as such, I believe it is important for you to read some original works from both classic and contemporary writers who explore specific issues in greater depth. A basic text that only summarizes and integrates this work, no matter how well it is written or how complete, is simply not sufficient to appreciate the foundations of interpersonal communication. As a result, I have selected this set of readings to supplement specific topics covered by Julia Wood in her text, *Relational Communication: Continuity and Change in Personal Relationships*, 2nd ed.

The first half of this course will focus on the conceptual foundations for studying personal relationships; it will include the first five chapters of the Wood text as well as the first seven articles in this supplemental reader. The second half of this course will then focus on the development of personal relationships; it will include the final five chapters in the Wood text as well as the final eight articles in this supplemental reader. I have written a brief "Introduction" for each reading to provide a "frame" from which to view the reading's focus as it specifically relates to the chapter. In addition, I have concluded each reading with a section entitled, "Consider This…" As you reflect on what you have learned from the reading, I hope you will find these questions useful as you consider how to apply this knowledge to your everyday lives

.As noted earlier, I already know the value of studying communication in human relationships – the challenge may be to convince you of its merits. Since we've all communicated in relationships from birth, it's easy to believe there's nothing new to learn. Unfortunately, there are times when all of us (including your professor), need to develop new insights and new skills for managing these relationships. As you explore the topics of this course, I hope you will have many "lightbulb" experiences – those magic moments when the "light" in your head goes on and you say to yourself, "Oh, now I know why I felt or behaved that way – I get it!" If you have even one "lightbulb" experience during this course and, with this new insight improve the quality of just one relationship, then I believe this course will have been meaningful for you.

Sheryl A. Friedley, Ph.D.
Professor of Communication
George Mason University

CREDITS

Acitelli, L. K. (2002). Relationship awareness: Crossing the bridge between cognition and communication. *Communication Theory. 12(1),* pp. 92-112.

Braithwaite, D. O., Olson, L. N., Golish, T. D., Soukup, C. & Turman, P. "Becoming a family": Developmental processes represented in blended family discourse. (August, 2001). *Journal of Applied Communication Research. 29(3),* 221-247. Reprinted by permission of Taylor & Francis, Ltd., http://www.tandf.co.uk/journals.

Emmers-Sommer, T. M. (2003). When partners falter: Repair after a transgression. In D. J. Canary & M. Dainton (Eds.), *Maintaining Relationships through Communication.* Mahwah, NJ: Lawrence Erlbaum Associates.

Escudero, V. & Rogers, L. E. (2004). Theoretical foundations. In L. E. Rogers and B. Escudero (Eds.), *Relational Communication*, Mahwah, NJ: Lawrence Erlbaum Associates.

Guerrero, L. K. & Andersen, P. A. The dark side of jealousy and envy: Desire, delusion, desperation, and destructive communication. In B. H. Spitzberg and W. R. Cupach (Eds.), *The Dark Side of Close Relationships*, Mahwah, NJ: Lawrence Erlbaum Associates.

Harvey, J. H. & Weber, A. L. (2002). Love and Commitment. In *Odyssey of the Heart.* Mahwah, NJ: Lawrence Erlbaum Associates.

Jackson, R. L. (2002). Cultural contracts theory: Toward an understanding of identity negotiation. *Communication Quarterly. 50(3&4),* 359-367. Reprinted by permission of Taylor & Francis, Ltd., http://www.tandf.co.uk/journals.

Medved, C. E. (Spring, 2004). The everyday accomplishment of work and family: Exploring practical actions in daily routines. *Communication Studies. 55(1),* pp. 128-145. Reprinted by permission of Taylor & Francis, Ltd., http://www.tandf.co.uk/journals.

Orbe, M. P. & Warren, K. T. (2000). Different standpoints, different realities: Race, gender, and perceptions of intercultural conflict. *Communication Quarterly. 48(1),* 51-57. Reprinted by permission of Taylor & Francis, Ltd., http://www.tandf.co.uk/journals.

Planalp, S. (2003). The unacknowledged role of emotion in theories of close relationships: How do theories feel? *Communication Theory. 13(1),* 78-99.

Schutz, W. C. (1966). The postulate of interpersonal needs: Description. In *The Interpersonal Underworld.* Science and Behavior Books. Palo Alto, CA: pp. 13-33.

Smith. C. B. (unpublished). Holding on by letting go/letting go by holding on: Approaches to grief.

Toller, P. W. (February, 2005). Negotiation of dialectical contradictions by parents who have experienced the death of a child. *Journal of Applied Communication Research. 33(1),* 46-66. Reprinted by permission of Taylor & Francis, Ltd., http://www.tandf.co.uk/journals.

PART 1

CONCEPTUAL FOUNDATIONS FOR STUDYING PERSONAL RELATIONSHIPS

CHAPTER 1

Communication and Personal Relationships

Imagine that you've been asked to work as part of a team to complete an assigned course project. As the team convenes for the first time, you warily begin to assess the team members individually. Who seems to be energized by the prospect of a team project and who would much rather work alone? Who prefers to lead and who prefers to follow? Who is motivated by the approval of other team members and who has little concern for the feelings of other team members? As these team members come together to create personal relationships, each of them (and you) bring individual biological, psychological, and emotional characteristics to the relationship.

In Chapter 1 of her text, *Relational Communication*, Julia Wood begins by defining personal relationships, providing initial insights into those personal relationships, and discussing several factors that influence personal relationships. Among those influences, Wood notes that individuals enter relationships as active participants – we "assume agency" in our relationships. The qualities and characteristics that we, as individuals, bring to the relationship provide a critical starting point for understanding our personal relationships. To gain new insight into some of the intrapersonal characteristics that define who we are in our personal relationships, let's examine the work of William C. Schutz.

William C. Schutz, a psychologist who received his Ph.D. from the University of California – Los Angeles, is considered a founding father of humanistic psychology. In his 1966 book, *The Interpersonal Underworld*, Schutz made the observation that "people need people—but in what ways?" From his research, Schutz identified three specific interpersonal needs that each of us use in ways that influence how we relate to others: 1) our need for inclusion, 2) our need for control, and 3) our need for affection. As you read his work, Schutz clearly defines each of these needs; he discusses feelings often associated with these needs and goes on to explain how these needs influence our self-concept. Schutz then provides some powerful examples of how these needs, in various forms, influence our behavior in personal relationships throughout our lives.

From the postulates presented in this reading, Schutz eventually developed his theory of interpersonal needs. To test his theory, he created a questionnaire that could be used to assess how these needs influence individual behavior in relationships. This tool is known as the FIRO-B (Fundamental Interpersonal Relations Orientation—Behavior); it assesses the three interpersonal needs (inclusion, control, and affection) both in terms of our desire to receive these qualities from others as well as our desire to express these qualities to others. As he refined his theory, Schutz later redefined the need for affection as a need for openness, and while he initially believed individual predispositions on these needs were relatively stable over the life span, he came to believe that situations and circumstances over a lifetime could account for individual changes on these dimensions. Though his theory may be considered simplistic in the study of human relationships today, it was instrumental in identifying three important dimensions that influence individuals as they develop personal relationships.

The Postulate of Interpersonal Needs: Description

William C. Schutz

Postulate 1. The Postulate of Interpersonal Needs.

(a) Every individual has three interpersonal needs: inclusion, control, and affection.

(b) Inclusion, control, and affection constitute a sufficient set of areas of interpersonal behavior for the prediction and explanation of interpersonal phenomena.

Explanation: In studying interpersonal behavior it is important to isolate the relevant variables. "People need people" serves as a good starting point; but, if the frontiers of knowledge are to recede, the next question must be investigated: "in what ways do people need people?"

The literature is not lacking in contestants for the mantle of "basic interpersonal variables." French[1] in a recent report summarizes the factors found in the factor analysis of various personality tests; he was able to reduce the number of apparently unrelated factors to forty-nine! Clearly this number is unmanageable for use in future investigation.

If the strictly statistical techniques for reducing variables still leaves forty-nine, some other exploratory method must be employed or at least added. A developmental approach to isolating variables has several appealing features. It seems promising to attempt to trace the developing individual through his sequence of typical interpersonal dealings, as a method of identifying the most basic interpersonal areas from which others are derivable. A consideration of this developmental process (discussed in more detail below), and some formulations presented by certain investigators, notably Bion, led the author to the conclusion that three interpersonal areas seemed to cover most interpersonal behavior. Later analysis of certain relevant literature (see Chapter 3) lent weight to the proposition that three areas would prove adequate for fruitful investigation.

As the description of these three areas, here called inclusion, control, and affection, progressed the fable came to mind of the blind men who disagreed over the characteristics of an elephant because each was exploring a different sector. It seems that various investigators are describing different aspects of the elephant—the three need areas—but apparently they are describing the same elephant. Thus clinicians discuss unconscious forces, small-group investigators describe overt behavior, child psychologists report on early interpersonal relations, and sociologists are interested in roles and group structures. But there seems to be heartening convergence toward the same set of variables, even though the approaches differ. The problem, then, is to give a complete description of the "elephant" and point out

Reprinted by permission of the author and the publishers from William C. Schutz. *The Interpersonal Underworld*, Palo alto, Calif.: Science and Behavior Books, 1966., pp. 13–33.

[1] T. French, *Summary of Factor Analytic Studies of Personality* (Princeton, N.J.: Educational Testing Service, 1956)

which aspects are being described by each observer. This chapter attempts to provide a complete description of the three basic interpersonal areas as basic needs, by showing how they appear in personality structure, in overt behavior, and in pathological behavior: In Chapter 3 a brief summary is given of selected studies which seem to fit into various parts of this scale.

Interpersonal Need

The concept of interpersonal need, often called "social need," has been discussed by many authors[2] but because it forms the central part of this book it is important to describe in what sense the term will be used.

The term "interpersonal" refers to relations that occur between people as opposed to relations in which at least one participant is inanimate. It is assumed that, owing to the psychological presence of other people, interpersonal situations lead to behavior in an individual that differs from the behavior of the individual when he is not in the presence of other persons. An optimally useful definition of "interpersonal" is one such that all situations classified as interpersonal have important properties in common—properties that are in general different from those of noninterpersonal situations. With this criterion for a definition in mind, the following specifies the meaning of "interpersonal situation." (The term "interpersonal" shall be used as equivalent to the term "group.")

An interpersonal situation is one involving two or more persons, in which these individuals take account of each other for some purpose, or decision, D. It is described from a particular point of reference, usually either that of one of the participants or of an outside observer. It is also specified as existing during a stated time interval. Thus a complete statement of an interpersonal situation has the form:

"From the standpoint of O (or A, or B), A takes account of B for decision D during time interval t_1 to t_n."

"A takes account of B for decision D" means that when A considers what alternative to select for decision D one criterion for his choice is his expectation of B's response to his choice. This expectation does not require that A make a different decision because of the influence of B; it simply means that his criteria for making the decision are supplemented.

For example, if a man who is sitting on a bus trying to decide whether or not to give up his seat to an elderly lady considers the reaction of the attractive young woman across the aisle, he is taking account of the young woman whether or not he gives up his seat. From his point of view the relation is interpersonal, since he takes account of her. From the standpoint of the young woman the situation may not be interpersonal at all, since she may not even be aware of his presence. Further, A may take account of B for one decision, for example, giving up a bus seat, as in the previous example, but not for another, for example, deciding which cobbler to patronize a week later. In addition, the degree to which A takes account of varies

[2] N. B. Miller and J. Pollard, *Social Learning and Imitation*: (New Haven, Conn.: Yale University Press, 1941).

with time. Our bus rider may be taking account of the lady during the bus ride (i.e., t_1 to t_n) but not at all when watching television that evening (i.e., after t_n).

The type of investigation will determine which point of reference for defining the term "interpersonal" will be most useful. Sometimes it is useful to consider an interpersonal situation from the standpoint of an individual, as when we speak of an interpersonal need. Sometimes it is more advantageous to consider a situation interpersonal only if the "taking account of" relation is reciprocal, that is, perceived by both members of a dyadic (two-person) relation (see Chapter 7). Sometimes the point of view of observers will decide whether a situation is interpersonal, regardless of the reports of the individuals involved in the relation. For conceptual clarity the important requirement in describing an interpersonal relation is that the point of reference be specified.

The phrase "face-to-face" used frequently by other writers when defining "interpersonal" or "group" has been omitted from the present definition. As shall be elaborated below, the property of physical presence is an important variable within the scope of interpersonal behavior, closely related to the area of inclusion. Further, it is often useful to consider situations as interpersonal in which behavior is determined by expectations of the behavior of others, even if the others are not physically present. It therefore seems more useful to leave the term "interpersonal" free of the face-to-face condition and consider as a separate problem the effect of that condition on behavior.

The other term in the phrase under discussion is "need." A "need" is defined in terms of a situation or condition of an individual the nonrealization of which leads to undesirable consequences. An interpersonal need is one that may be satisfied only through the attainment of a satisfactory relation with other people. The satisfaction of a need is a necessary condition for the avoidance of the undesirable consequences. An interpersonal need is one that may be satisfied only through the attainment of a satisfactory relation with other people. The satisfaction of a need is a necessary condition for the avoidance of the undesirable consequences of illness and death. A discrepancy between the satisfaction of an interpersonal need and the present state of an organism engenders a feeling in the organism that shall be called anxiety.

There is a close parallel between biological needs and interpersonal needs, in the following respects:

1. A biological need is a requirement to establish and maintain a satisfactory relation between the organism and its physical environment. An interpersonal need is a requirement to establish a satisfactory relation between the individual and his human environment. A biological need is not satisfied by providing unlimited gratification. An organism may take in too much water and drown, as well as too little water and die of thirst. The need is satisfied by establishing an equilibrium between the amount of water inside and outside the organism. The same is true for the "commodities" exchanged between people. An individual's needs may be unfulfilled either by having, for example, too much control over his human environment and hence too much responsibility, or too little control, hence not enough security. He must establish a satisfactory relation with his human environment with respect to control.

2. Nonfulfillment of a biological need leads to physical illness and sometimes death. Nonfulfillment of an interpersonal need leads to mental (or interpersonal) illness and sometimes death. Unsatisfactory personal relations lead directly to difficulties associated with emotional illness. Death, either through suicide or resulting from the more general loss of motivation for life, results when interpersonal dissatisfaction is prolonged.

3. The organism has characteristic modes, which are temporarily successful, of adapting to lack of complete satisfaction of biological needs. The organism also has characteristic ways, which are temporarily successful, of adapting to nonsatisfaction of interpersonal needs. For the interpersonal situation the terms "conscious" and "unconscious" needs are sometimes used to describe the phenomena at issue.

The distinction between a conscious and an unconscious need finds a parallel in a biological condition such as drug addiction. In drug addiction the immediate (conscious) need is to satisfy the immediate craving and to adjust the body chemistry so that the pain is reduced. The more basic (unconscious) need is to adjust the body chemistry back to the state where the drug is no longer required. The pain or anxiety felt when the organism is in a situation which does not allow for the satisfaction of these two needs is different in each case. In the first there is the immediate deprivation, analogous to an interpersonal situation in which an individual's characteristic psychological adjustment mechanisms (for example, defenses) cannot operate. To illustrate, if denial were the defense used by an individual in the affection area and he were placed in a situation in which close personal relations were called for, he would feel an immediate anxiety caused by the discrepancy between the demands of the situation and his most comfortable behavior pattern. The more basic anxiety or interpersonal imbalance stemming from the general inadequacy of the defense to ward off the need for affection is analogous to the physical discomfort caused by the discrepancy between the chemical balance produced by the drug addition and the normal chemical balance.

This analogy assumes a particular interpersonal relation that optimally satisfies interpersonal needs, parallel to an optimal chemical balance. This assumption is made, although it is difficult to test. Perhaps it parallels the condition in which the psychoanalyst attempts to place his patient. The analyst has a conception of an optimal psychological condition for a given individual toward which the person strives. This condition goes deeper than the reinforcement of the patient's defense mechanisms, which protect him from undesirable impulses. The optimal state is one in which defenses are only minimally required. It is this psychological state that is analogous to the concept of an optimal interpersonal relation.

These parallels between the interpersonal and biological needs will be specified more precisely in the following discussion. Other aspects of this problem could be mentioned at this point, such as the phylogenetic continuity of interpersonal needs, their universality cross-culturally, and possible physiological correlations. However, this would take the discussion too far afield. The main point is that in many important ways interpersonal needs have properties closely parallel of biological needs.

Inclusion, Control, and Affection

Now comes the problem of describing the elephant, that is, providing a complete description of interpersonal variables sufficient to provide a framework for integration and future investigation in the field.

To construct such a schema it is necessary to determine the most relevant parameters for describing important aspects of the interpersonal variables. These parameters may then be used as the classification variables for generating a matrix to encompass the interpersonal behavior of interest. This process is called "substructing" by Lazarsfeld and Barton,[3] and "facet analysis" by Guttman.[4] It has the virtue of providing all possible combinations of parameter values so that omissions or duplications are easily recognized.

The parameters chosen should delineate salient differences worthy of preservation in personality description. Differences on these parameters represent important behavioral differences which are helpful, even necessary, when behavioral characteristics are related to external factors, for example, childhood experiences, productivity, compatibility, leadership. The matrix generated by the parameters represents the types of available data. The methods of obtaining the data (such as introspection, questionnaire, observation, projective test) are independent of the matrix. Any method of data collection is permissible for any type of data. The parameters:

1. *Observability*—the degree to which an action of an individual is observable by others. This parameter is dichotomized into action and feeling. An action is usually more observable to outsiders, a feeling usually more observable to the self.

2. *Directionality*—the direction of the interaction with respect to originator and target. This parameter is trichotomized into (a) self toward other, (b) other toward self, and (c) self toward self. The last category is interpersonal in the sense that it represents interaction between the self and others who have been interiorized early in life.

3. *Status of Action*—whether the behavior is in the inclusion, control, or affection area.

4. *State of Relation*—whether the relation is desired, ideal, anxious or pathological.

Table 1 summarizes the terms and concepts discussed in this chapter. This table, in a sense, is the "elephant."

---

[3] P. Lazarsfeld and A. Barton, "Qualitative Measurement in the Social Sciences," in D. Lerner and H. Lasswell, The Policy Sciences (Stanford, CA: Stanford University Press, 1951).

[4] L. Guttman, "Principal Components of Scalable Attitudes," in Mathematical Thinking in The Social Sciences, ed. by P. Lazarsfeld (Glencoe, IL: Free Press, 1954).

TABLE 1

Matrix of Relevant Interpersonal Data—"The Elephant"

<table>
<tr><td colspan="3"></td><td colspan="3">Inclusion</td></tr>
<tr><td colspan="3"></td><td>Self to Other (Actions)</td><td>Other to Self (Reactions)</td><td>Self to Self</td></tr>
<tr><td colspan="2" rowspan="2">Desired Interpersonal Relations (Needs)</td><td>Act</td><td colspan="2">Satisfactory relation re interaction and inclusion behavior 1</td><td rowspan="4">Feeling that I am siignificant 15</td></tr>
<tr><td>Feel</td><td colspan="2">Satisfactory relation re feelings of mutual interest 2</td></tr>
<tr><td colspan="2" rowspan="2">Ideal Interpersonal Relations</td><td>Act</td><td>Social 3</td><td>People include me 4</td></tr>
<tr><td>Feel</td><td>I am interested in people 5</td><td>People are interested in me 6</td></tr>
<tr><td rowspan="4">Anxious Interpersonal Relations (Anxieties)</td><td rowspan="2">Too much activity</td><td>Act</td><td>Oversocial 7</td><td>Social-compliant 8</td><td rowspan="4">I am insignificant (I don't know who I am; I am nobody) 16</td></tr>
<tr><td>Feel</td><td>I am not really interested in people 9</td><td>People aren't really interested in me 10</td></tr>
<tr><td rowspan="2">Too little activity</td><td>Act</td><td>Undersocial 11</td><td>Counter-Social 12</td></tr>
<tr><td>Feel</td><td>I am not interested in people 13</td><td>People are not interested in me 14</td></tr>
<tr><td rowspan="2">Pathological Interpersonal Relations</td><td colspan="5">Too much 17</td></tr>
<tr><td colspan="2">Too little</td><td colspan="3">Psychotic (Schizophrenia) 18</td></tr>
</table>

<table>
<tr><th colspan="3">Control</th><th colspan="3">Affection</th></tr>
<tr><td>Self to Other (Actions)</td><td>Other to Self (Reactions)</td><td>Self to Self</td><td>Self to Other (Actions)</td><td>Other to Self (Reactions)</td><td>Self to Self</td></tr>
<tr><td colspan="2">Satisfactory relation re power and control behavior 19</td><td rowspan="4">Feeling that I am responsible 33</td><td colspan="2">Satisfactory relation re love and affection behavior 37</td><td rowspan="4">Feeling that I am siignificant 51</td></tr>
<tr><td colspan="2">Satisfactory relation re feelings of mutual respect 20</td><td colspan="2">Satisfactory relation re feelings of mutual affection 38</td></tr>
<tr><td>Democrat 21</td><td>People respect me 22</td><td>Personal 39</td><td>People are friendly to me 40</td></tr>
<tr><td>I respect people 23</td><td>People respect me 24</td><td>I like people 41</td><td>People like me 42</td></tr>
<tr><td>Autocrat 25</td><td>Rebel 26</td><td rowspan="4">I am incompetant (I am studpid, irrespon-sible) 34</td><td>Over-personal 43</td><td>Personal-compliant 44</td><td rowspan="4">I am insignificant (I don't know who I am; I am nobody) 52</td></tr>
<tr><td>I don't trust people 27</td><td>People don't trust me 28</td><td>I don't really like people 45</td><td>People don't really like me 46</td></tr>
<tr><td>Abdicrat 29</td><td>Submissive 30</td><td>Under-personal 47</td><td>Counter-personal 48</td></tr>
<tr><td>I don't really respect people 31</td><td>People don't really respect me 32</td><td>I don't like people 49</td><td>People don't like me 50</td></tr>
<tr><td colspan="3">Obsessive-compulsive 35</td><td colspan="3">Neurotic 53</td></tr>
<tr><td colspan="3">Psychopath 36</td><td colspan="3">Neurotic 54</td></tr>
</table>

The Three Interpersonal Needs

The interpersonal need for inclusion is defined behaviorally as the need to establish and maintain a satisfactory relation with people with respect to interaction and association. "Satisfactory relation" includes (1) a psychologically comfortable relation with people somewhere on a dimension ranging from originating interaction with all people to not initiating interaction with anyone; (2) a psychologically comfortable relation with people with respect to eliciting behavior from them somewhere on a dimension ranging from always initiating interaction with the self to never initiating interaction with the self.

On the level of feelings the need for inclusion is defined as the need to establish and maintain a feeling of mutual interest with other people. This feeling includes (1) being able to take an interest in other people to a satisfactory degree and (2) having other people interested in the self to a satisfactory degree.

With regard to the self-concept, the need for inclusion is the need to feel that the self is significant and worthwhile.

The interpersonal need for control is defined behaviorally as the need to establish and maintain a satisfactory relation with people with respect to control and power. "Satisfactory relation" includes (1) a psychologically comfortable relation with people somewhere on a dimension ranging from controlling all the behavior of other people to not controlling any behavior of others and (2) a psychologically comfortable relation with people with respect to eliciting behavior from them somewhere on a dimension ranging from always being controlled by them to never being controlled by them.

With regard to feelings, the need for control is defined as the need to establish and maintain a feeling of mutual respect for the competence and responsibleness of others. This feeling includes (1) being able to respect others to a satisfactory degree and (2) having others respect the self to a satisfactory degree.

The need for control, defined at the level of perceiving the self, is the need to feel that one is a competent, responsible person.

The interpersonal need for affection is defined behaviorally as the need to establish and maintain a satisfactory relation with others with respect to love and affection. Affection always refers to a two-person (dyadic) relation, "Satisfactory relation" includes (1) a psychologically comfortable relation with others somewhere on a dimension ranging from initiating close, personal relations with everyone to originating close, personal relations with no one; (2) a psychologically comfortable relation with people with respect to eliciting behavior from them on a dimension ranging from always originating close, personal relations toward the self, to never originating close, personal relations toward the self.

At the feeling level the need for affection is defined as the need to establish and maintain a feeling of mutual affection with others. This feeling includes (1) being able to love other people to a satisfactory degree and (2) having others love the self to a satisfactory degree.

The need for affection, defined at the level of the self-concept, is the need to feel that the self is lovable.

This type of formulation stresses the interpersonal nature of these needs. They require that the organism establish a kind of equilibrium, in three different areas, between the self and other people. In order to be anxiety-free, a person must find a comfortable behavioral relation with others with regard to the exchange of interaction, power, and love. The need is not wholly satisfied by having others respond toward the self in a particular way; nor is it wholly satisfied by acting toward others in a particular fashion. A satisfactory balance must be established and maintained.

Inclusion, Control, and Affection Behavior

Thus far these key terms have been discussed only from the standpoint of their status as interpersonal needs. Since the value of the theory is dependent to a large extent on the cogency and clarity of these terms, it is important to describe them as fully as possible. In later chapters many different ways of describing these terms will be introduced, including

1. Examples;
2. Synonyms (Chapter 2);
3. A description of aspects of these behaviors at various levels of personality (Chapter 2);
4. A description of the interconnection between these terms and other terms in theory, such as "compatibility" (Chapter 6);
5. A description of the relations between these areas and factors found by other investigators (Chapter 3);
6. A description of these areas as applied to literary works (Chapter 9); and
7. A measuring instrument FIRO-B (Fundamental Interpersonal Relations Orientation-Behavior), which measures two aspects of each of the three areas (Chapter 4).

Inclusion behavior is defined as behavior directed toward the satisfaction of the interpersonal need for inclusion.

Control behavior is defined as behavior directed toward the satisfaction of the interpersonal need for control.

Affection behavior is defined as behavior directed toward the satisfaction of the interpersonal need for affection.

In general, *inclusion behavior* refers to association between people. Some terms that connote a relation that is primarily positive inclusion are "associate," "interact," "mingle," "communicate," "belong," "companion," "comrade," "attend to," "member," "together," "join," "extravert." Some terms that connote lack of, or negative, inclusion, are "exclusion," "isolate," "outsider," "outcast," "lonely," "detached," "withdrawn," "abandoned," "ignored."

The need to be included manifests itself as wanting to be attended to, to attract attention and interest. The classroom hellion who throws erasers is often objecting mostly to the lack of attention paid him. Even if he is given negative affection he is partially satisfied, because at least someone is paying attention to him.

In groups, people often make themselves prominent by talking a great deal. Frequently they are not interested in power or dominance but simply prominence. The "joker" is an example of a prominence seeker, very much as is the blond actress with the lavender convertible.

In the extreme, what is called "fame" is primarily inclusion. Acquisition of fame does not imply acquisition of power or influence: witness Marilyn Monroe's attempt to swing votes to Adlai Stevenson. Nor does fame imply affection: Al Capone could hardly be considered a widely loved figure. But fame does imply prominence, and signifies interest on the part of others.

From another standpoint, behavior related to belonging and "togetherness" is primarily inclusion. To desire to belong to a fraternal organization by no means necessarily indicates a liking for the members or even a desire for power. It is often sought for its "prestige value," for increase of "status." These terms are also primarily inclusion conceptions, because their primary implication is that people pay attention to the person, know who he is, and can distinguish him from others.

This last point leads to an essential aspect of inclusion, that of identity. An integral part of being recognized and paid attention to is that the individual be identifiable from other people. He must be known as a specific individual; he must have a particular identity. If he is not thus known, he cannot truly be attended to or have interest paid to him. The extreme of this identification is that he be understood. To be understood implies that someone is interested enough in him to find out his particular characteristics. Again, this interest need not mean that others have affection for him, or that they respect him. For example, the interested person may be a confidence man who is exploring his background to find a point of vulnerability.

At the outset of interpersonal relations a common issue is that of commitment, the decision to become involved in a given relation or activity. Usually, in the initial testing of the relation, individuals try to identify themselves to one another to find out which facet of themselves others will be interested in. Frequently a member is silent for a while because he is not sure that people are interested in him. These behaviors, too, are primarily in the inclusion area.

This, then, is the flavor of inclusion. It has to do with interacting with people, with attention, acknowledgement, being known, prominence, recognition, prestige, status, and fame; with identity, individuality, understanding, interest, commitment, and participation. It is unlike affection in that it does not involve strong emotional attachments to individual persons. It is unlike control in that the preoccupation is with prominence, not dominance.

Control behavior refers to the decision-making process between people. Some terms connoting a relation that is primarily positive control are "power," "authority," "dominance," "influence" "control," "ruler," "superior officer," "leader." Some terms trial connote primarily a lack of, or negative, control are "rebellion," "resistance," "follower," "anarchy," "submissive," "henpecked," "milquetoast."

The need for control manifests itself as the desire for power, authority, and control over others and therefore over one's future. At the other end is the need to be controlled, to have responsibility taken away. Manifestations of the power drive are very clear. A more subtle form is exemplified by the current magazine advertising campaign featuring the "influential." This is a person who controls others through the power he has to influence their behavior.

The acquisition of money or political power is a direct method of obtaining control over other persons. This type of control often involves coercion rather than more subtle methods of influence like persuasion and example. In group behavior, the struggles to achieve high office or to make suggestions that are adopted are manifestations of control behavior. In an argument in a group we may distinguish the inclusion seeker from the control seeker in this way: the one seeking inclusion or prominence wants very much to be one of the participants in the argument, while the control seeker wants to be the winner or, if not the winner, on the same side as the winner. The prominence seeker would prefer to be the losing participant; the dominance seeker would prefer to be a winning nonparticipant. Both these roles are separate from the affectional desires of the members.

Control behavior takes many subtle forms, especially among more intellectual and polite people. For example, in many discussion groups where blackboards are involved, the power struggle becomes displaced onto the chalk. Walking to the blackboard and taking the chalk from the one holding it, and retaining possession, becomes a mark of competitive success. Often a meeting is marked by a procession of men taking the chalk, writing something, and being supplanted by another man for a further message. In this way propriety is maintained, and still the power struggle may proceed.

In many gatherings, control behavior is exhibited through the group task. Intellectual superiority, for one thing, often leads to control over others so that strong motivation to achieve is often largely control behavior. Such superiority also demonstrates the real capacity of the individual to be relied on for responsible jobs, a central aspect of control. Further, to do one's job properly, or to rebel against the established authority structure by not doing it, is a splendid outlet for control feelings. Doing a poor job is a way of rebelling against the structure and showing that no one will control you, whereas acquiescence earns rewards from those in charge which satisfies the need to be respected for one's accomplishments.

Control is also manifested in behavior toward others controlling the self. Expressions of independence and rebellion exemplify lack of willingness to be controlled, while compliance, submission, and taking orders indicate various degrees of accepting the control of others. There is no necessary relation between an individual's behavior toward controlling others, and his behavior toward being controlled. The domineering sergeant may accept orders from the lieutenant with pleasure and gratefulness, while the neighborhood bully may also rebel against his parents; two persons who control others differ in the degree to which they allow others to control them.

Thus the flavor of control is transmitted by behavior involving influence, leadership, power, coercion, authority, accomplishment, intellectual superiority, high achievement, and independence, as well as dependency (for decision making), rebellion, resistance, and submission. It differs from inclusion behavior in that it does not require prominence. The concept of the "power behind the throne" is an excellent example of a role that would fill a high control need and a low need for inclusion. The "joker" exemplifies the opposite. Control behavior differs from affection behavior in that it has to do with power relations rather than emotional closeness. The frequent difficulties between those who want to "get down to business" and those who want to get to "know one another" illustrate a situation in which control behavior is more important for some and affection behavior for others.

In general, *affection behavior* refers to close personal emotional feelings between two people. Affection is a dyadic relation; it can occur only between pairs of people at any one time, whereas both inclusion and control relations may occur either in dyads or between one person and a group of persons. Some terms that connote an affection relation that is primarily positive are "love," "like," "emotionally close," "positive feelings," "personal," "friendship," "sweetheart." Some terms that connote primarily lack of, or negative, affection are "hate," "dislike," "cool," "emotionally distant."

The need for affection leads to behavior related to becoming emotionally close. An affection relation must be dyadic because it involves strong differentiation between people. Affectional relations can be toward parental figures, peers, or children figures. They are exemplified in friendship relations, dating, and marriage.

To become emotionally close to someone involves, in addition to an emotional attachment, an element of confiding innermost anxieties, wishes, and feelings. A strong positive affectional tie usually is accompanied by a unique relation regarding the degree of sharing of these feelings.

In groups, affection behavior is characterized by overtures of friendship and differentiation between members. One common method of avoiding a close tie with any one member is to be equally friendly to all members. Thus "popularity" may not involve affection at all; it may often be inclusion behavior, whereas "going steady" is usually primarily affection.

A difference between affection behavior, inclusion behavior, and control behavior is illustrated by the different feelings a man has in being turned down by a fraternity, failed in a course by a professor, and rejected by his girl. The fraternity excludes him and tells him, in effect, that they as a group don't have sufficient interest in him. The professor fails him and says, in effect, that he finds him incompetent in his field. His girl rejects him, and tells him, in effect, that she doesn't find him lovable.

Thus the flavor of affection is embodied in situations of love, emotional closeness, personal confidences, intimacy. Negative affection is characterized by hate, hostility, and emotional rejection.

In order to sharpen further the contrast between these three types of behavior, several differences may be mentioned.

With respect to an interpersonal relation, inclusion is concerned primarily with the formation of the relation, whereas control and affection are concerned with relations already formed. Basically, inclusion is always concerned with whether or not a relation exists. Within existent relations, control is the area concerned with who gives orders and make decisions for whom, whereas affection is concerned with how emotionally close or distant the relation becomes. Thus, generally speaking, inclusion is concerned with the problem of in or out, control is concerned with top or bottom, and affection with close or for.

A further differentiation occurs with regard to the number of people involved in the relation. Affection is *always* a one-to-one relation, inclusion is *usually* a one-to-many relation, and control may be either a one-one or a one-many relation. An affectional tie is necessarily between two persons, and involves varying degrees of intimacy, warmth, and emotional involvement which cannot be felt toward a unit greater than one person. Inclusion, on the other hand, typically concerns the behavior and feelings of one person toward a group of people. Problems of belonging and membership, so central to the inclusion area, usually refer to a relatively undifferentiated group with which an individual seeks association. His feelings of wanting to belong to the group are qualitatively different from his personal feelings of warmth toward an individual person. Control may refer to a power struggle between two individuals for control over each other, or it may refer to the struggle for domination over a group, as in political power. There is no particular number of interactional participants implied in the control area.

Control differs from the other two areas with respect to the differentiation between the persons involved in the control situation. For inclusion and affection there is a tendency for participants to act similarly in both the behavior they express and the behavior they want from others; for example, a close, personal individual usually likes others to be close and personal also. This similarity is not so marked in the control area. The person who likes to control may or may not want others to control him. This difference in differentiation among need areas is, however, only a matter of degree. There are many who like to include but do not want to be included, or who are not personal but want others to be that way toward them. But these types are not as frequent as the corresponding types in the control area.

Types of Interpersonal Behavior

For each area of interpersonal behavior three types of behavior will be described: (1) deficient—indicating that the individual is not trying directly to satisfy the need, (2) excessive—indicating that the individual is constantly trying to satisfy the need, (3) ideal—indicating satisfaction of the need, and (4) pathological.

In delineating these types it is assumed that anxiety engendered by early experiences leads to behavior of the first, second, and fourth types, while a successful working through of an interpersonal relation leads to an individual who can function without anxiety in the area. The development origins are dealt within Chapter 5. For simplicity of presentation the extremes will be presented without qualifications. Actually, of course, the behavior of any given individual could be best described as some combination of behavior incorporating elements of all three types at different times, for instance, the oversocial, undersocial, and social.

Inclusion Types

The Undersocial

The interpersonal behavior of the undersocial person tends to be introverted and withdrawn. Characteristically, he avoids associating with others and doesn't like or accept invitations to join others. Consciously he wants to maintain this distance between himself and others, and insists that he doesn't want to get enmeshed with people and lose his privacy. But unconsciously he definitely wants others to pay attention to him. His biggest fears are that people will ignore him, generally have no interest in him, and would just as soon leave him behind.

Unconsciously he feels that no one ever will pay attention to him. His attitude may be summarized by, "No one is interested in me. I'm not going to risk being ignored. I'll stay away from people and get along by myself." There is a strong drive toward self-sufficiency as a technique for existence without others. Since social abandonment is tantamount to death, he must compensate by directing his energies toward self-preservation; he therefore creates a world of his own in which his existence is more secure. Behind this withdrawal lie anxiety and hostility, and often a slight air of superiority and the private feeling that others don't understand him.

The direct expression of this withdrawal is nonassociation and noninteraction with people, lack of involvement and commitment. The more subtle form is exemplified by the person who for one reason or another is always late to meetings, or seems to have an inordinate number of conflicting engagements necessitating absence from people, or the type of person who precedes each visit with, "I'm sorry, but I can't stay very long."

His deepest anxiety, that referring to the self-concept, is that he is worthless. He thinks that if no one ever considered him important enough to receive attention, he must be of no value whatever.

Closely allied with this feeling is the lack of motivation to live. Association with people is a necessary condition for a desire to live. This factor may be of much greater importance in everyday interaction than is usually thought. The degree to which an individual is committed to living probably determines to a large extent his general level of enthusiasms, perserverance, involvement, and the like. Perhaps this lack of concern for life is the ultimate in regression: if life holds too few rewards, the prelife condition is preferable. It is likely that this basic fear of abandonment or isolation is the most potent of all interpersonal fears. The simple fear that people are not interested in the self is extremely widespread, but in scientific analyses it, too often, is included as a special type of affectional need. It is extremely useful, however, to make clear the distinction between inclusion and affection.

The Oversocial

The oversocial person tends toward extraversion in his later interpersonal behavior. Characteristically, he seeks people incessantly and wants them to seek him out. He is also afraid they will ignore him. His interpersonal dynamics are the same as those of the withdrawn person, but his overt behavior is the opposite.

His unconscious attitude is summarized by, "Although no one is interested in me, I'll make people pay attention to me in any way I can." His inclination is always to seek companionship. He is the type who "can't stand being alone." All of his activities will be designed to be done "together." An interesting illustration of this attitude occurs in the recent motion picture, "The Great Man." José Ferrer, as a newspaper man, is interviewing a woman about her reasons for attending the funeral of a television celebrity.

> "Because our club all came together," she replies.
> "But," Ferrer persists, "why did you come here?"
> "I came here because the rest came here."
> "Were you fond of the dead man?"
> "Not especially," she replies, "but we always do things together."

This scene (the dialogue is from memory) nicely illustrates the importance of being together presumably as an end in itself. The interpersonal behavior of the oversocial type of person will then be designed to focus attention on himself, to make people notice him, to be prominent, to be listened to. There are many techniques for doing this. The direct method is to be an intensive, exhibitionistic participator. By simply forcing himself on the group he forces the group to focus attention on him. The more subtle technique is to try to acquire status through such devices as name dropping, or by asking startling questions. He may also try to acquire power (control) or try to be well liked (affection), but for the primary purpose of gaining attention. Power or friendship, although both may be important (depending on his orientation in the other two interpersonal areas), is not the primary goal.

The Social

To the individual for whom the resolution of inclusion relations was successful in childhood, interaction with people presents no problem. He is comfortable with people and comfortable being alone. He can be a high or low participator in a group, or can equally well take a moderate role, without anxiety. He is capable of strong commitment and involvement to certain groups and also can withhold commitment if he feels it is appropriate.

Unconsciously, he feels that he is a worthwhile, significant person and that life is worth living. He is fully capable of being genuinely interested in others and feels that they will include him in their activities and that they are interested in him.

He also has an "identity" and an "individuality." Childhood feelings of abandonment lead to the absence of an identity; the person feels he is nobody. He has no stable figures with whom to identify. Childhood feelings of enmeshment lead to confusion of identity. When a child is nothing but parts of other people and has not had sufficient opportunity to evaluate the characteristics he observes in himself, he has difficulty knowing who he is. The social person has resolved these difficulties. He has integrated aspects of a large number of individuals into a new configuration which he can identify as himself.

Inclusion Pathology

Failure to be included means anxiety over having no contact with people. Unsuccessful resolution of inclusion relations leads to feelings of exclusion, of alienation from people, of being different and unacceptable, and usually the necessity of creating a phantasy world in which the nonincluded person is accepted. Inclusion, because it is posited to be the first of interpersonal relations to be dealt with by the infant, has strong narcissistic elements and other close similarities to the description by psychoanalysts of the interpersonal characteristics in the oral stage. Hence a pathological difficulty in the inclusion area leads to the most regressed kind of behavior, that concerned with belonging to people, being a significant individual. This syndrome is very much like the functional psychoses. In Ruth Munroe's description of the Freudian explanation of psychoses these points are made clear:

> The essential feature of Freud's explanation of psychotic conditions may be stated as the greater depth of regression. The adult never lapses back to infancy all of a piece of course. . . . Freud felt, however, that the truly psychotic manifestations belong to the pre-oedipal period—indeed to the stage of narcissism before the ego has property developed. The mechanisms of psychoses are the archaic mechanisms of the infant before secure object relations have been established.[5]

The last line of this quotation is especially pertinent to demonstrating the close relations between the Freudian discussion of psychosis and the area of inclusion. The phrase, "before secure object (interpersonal) relations have been established," certainly bears a close resemblance to the preceding discussion of the problems of becoming included in the social group.

It appears, then, that difficulty in establishing a satisfactory relation with other persons, with regard to inclusion or contact, when difficulty reaches a pathological state, leads to psychosis, especially schizophrenia. This statement does not mean that all conditions now called psychosis are caused by difficulties in the inclusion area, nor does it necessarily mean that all inclusion problems will, if pathological, become psychoses; nor does it even imply that there are "pure" inclusion problems uncontaminated with other areas. It implies only that there is a close relation between disturbance in the inclusion area and psychosis.

Psychosis, especially schizophrenia, appears to be related more to the undersocial pattern than the oversocial. The lack of identity and inability to be alone, if carried to the extreme, would correspond to the pathological extreme of the oversocial.

[5] Ruth Munroe, Schools of Psychoanalytic Thought (New York: Dryden, 1956), p. 288.

Control Types

The Abdicrat

The abdicrat is a person who tends toward submission and abdication of power and responsibility in his interpersonal behavior. Characteristically, he gravitates toward the subordinate position where he will not have to take responsibility for making decisions, and where someone else takes charge.

Consciously, he wants people to relieve him of his obligations. He does not control others even when he should; for example, he would not take charge even during a fire in a children's schoolhouse in which he is the only adult; and he never makes a decision that he can refer to someone else. He fears that others will not help him when he requires it, and that he will be given more responsibility than he can handle. This kind of person is usually a follower, or at most a loyal lieutenant, but rarely the person who takes the responsibility for making the final decision. Unconsciously, too, he has the feeling that he is incapable of responsible adult behavior and that others know it. He never was told what to do and therefore never learned. His most comfortable response is to avoid situations in which he will feel helpless. He feels that he is an incompetent and irresponsible, perhaps stupid, person who does not deserve respect for his abilities,

Behind this feeling are anxiety, hostility, and lack of trust toward those who might withhold assistance. The hostility is usually expressed as passive resistance. Hesitancy to "go along" is a usual technique of resistance, since actual overt rebellion is too threatening.

The Autocrat

The autocrat is a person whose interpersonal behavior often tends toward the dominating. Characteristically, he tries to dominate people and strongly desires a power hierarchy with himself at the top. He is the power seeker, the competer. He is afraid people will not be influenced or controlled by him—that they will, in fact, dominate him.

Commonly, this need to control people is displaced into other areas. Intellectual or athletic superiority allows for considerable control, as does the more direct method of attaining political power. The underlying dynamics are the same as for the abdicrat. Basically the person feels he is not responsible or capable of discharging obligation and that this fact is known to others. He attempts to use every opportunity to disprove this feeling to others and to himself. His unconscious attitude may be summarized as, "No one thinks I can make decisions for myself, but I'll show them. I'm going to make all the decisions for everyone, always." Behind this feeling is a strong distrust that others may make decisions for him and the feeling that they don't trust him. This latter becomes a very sensitive area.

The Democrat

For the individual who has successfully resolved his relations with others in the control area in childhood, power and control present no problem. He feels comfortable giving or not giving orders and taking or not taking orders, as is appropriate to the situation. Unconsciously, he feels that he is a capable, responsible person and therefore that he does not need to shrink from responsibility or to try constantly to prove how competent he really is. Unlike the abdicrat and autocrat, he is not preoccupied with fears of his own helplessness, stupidity, and incompetence. He feels that other people respect his competence and will be realistic with respect to trusting him with decision making.

Control Pathology

The individual who does not accept control of any kind develops pathologically into a psychopathic personality. He has not been adequately trained to learn the rules of behavior established for respecting the rights and privileges of others. Ruth Munroe says,

> The major Freudian explanation for this condition is that there has been a serious failure of superego development. The practical image has not been adequately internalized in the form of conscience but remains the policeman at the corner—an external force. Truly, the behavior of the psychopath is childish without the limited experience of the child. When the resources of adulthood are used without the inner controls of adulthood the resultant behavior is very likely to be deplorable. Object relations generally are poor of necessity since good early object relations would have led to more adequate superego development.[6]

Affection Types

The Underpersonal

The underpersonal type tends to avoid close personal ties with others. He characteristically maintains his dyadic relations on a superficial, distant level and is most comfortable when others do the same to him. Consciously, he wishes to maintain this emotional distance, and frequently expresses a desire not to get "emotionally involved"; unconsciously he seeks a satisfactory affectional relation. His fear is that no one loves him. In a group situation he is afraid he won't be liked. He has great difficulty genuinely liking people. He distrusts their feeling toward him.

His attitude could be summarized by the "formula," "I find the affection area very painful since I have been rejected; therefore I shall avoid close personal relations in the future." The direct technique for maintaining emotional distance is to reject and avoid people to prevent emotional closeness or involvement activity, even to the point of being antagonistic. The subtle technique is to appear superficially friendly to everyone. This behavior acts as a safeguard against having to get close to, or become personal with, any one person. ("Close" and "personal" refer to emotional

---

[6] Ibid., p. 292

closeness and willingness to confide one's most private concerns and feelings. It involves the expressions of positive affection and tender feelings.) Here the dyadic relation is a threatening one. To keep everyone at the same distance obviates the requirement for treating any one person with greater warmth and affection.

The deepest anxiety, that regarding the self, is that he is unlovable. He feels that people won't like him because, in fact, he doesn't "deserve" it. If people got to know him well, he believes, they would discover the traits that make him so unlovable. As opposed to the inclusion anxiety that the self is of no value, worthless, and empty, and the control anxiety that the self is stupid and irresponsible, the affection anxiety is that the self is nasty and bad.

The Overpersonal

The overpersonal type attempts to become extremely close to others. He definitely wants others to treat him in a very close, personal way. His response may be summarized by the formula, "My first experiences with affection were painful, but perhaps if I try again they will turn out to be better." He will be striving in his interpersonal relations primarily to be liked. Being liked is extremely important to him in his attempt to relieve his anxiety about being always rejected and unlovable. Again, there are two behavorial techniques, the direct and the subtle. The direct technique is an overt attempt to gain approval, be extremely personal, intimate, and confiding. The subtle technique is more manipulative, to devour friends and subtly punish any attempts by them to establish other friendships, to be possessive.

The underlying dynamics are the same as those for the underpersonal. Both the overpersonal and the underpersonal responses are extreme, both are motivated by a strong need for affection, both are accompanied by strong anxiety about ever being loved, and basically about being unlovable, and both have considerable hostility behind them stemming from the anticipation of rejection.

The Personal

For the individual who successfully resolved his affectional relations with others in childhood, close emotional relations with one other person present no problem. He is comfortable in such a personal relation, and he can also relate comfortably in a situation requiring emotional distance. It is important for him to be liked, but if he isn't liked he can accept the fact that the dislike is the result of the relation between himself and one other person—in other words, the dislike does not mean that he is an unlovable person. Unconsciously, he feels that he is a lovable person who is lovable even to people who know him well. He is capable of giving genuine affection.

Affection Pathology

Neuroses are commonly attributed to difficulties in the area of affection. Ruth Munroe says,

> The early bloom of sexuality, which cannot possibly come to fruition, is called the phallic stage to differentiate it from true

> genitality leading to mature mating and reproduction. At this period attitudes are formed which are crucial for later heterosexual fulfillment and good relations with people generally. For this reason it is the stage most fraught with potentialities for neurotic distortion .[7]

The discussion of pathology in this chapter should be supplemented with the discussion of the childhood origins of various adult behavior patterns presented in Chapter 5. Combining the early experience and present behavior with the pathological classification will provide a more complete picture of the process of personality development and disintegration.

Summary

To summarize, difficulties with initiating interaction range from being uncomfortable when not associating with people ("can't stand to be alone"—the oversocial) to not feeling comfortable initiating interaction ("can't stand being with people"—the undersocial). Difficulties with controlling others range from not feeling comfortable controlling the behavior of anyone ("can't tell anyone what to do"—the abdicrat) to not feeling comfortable when unable to control everyone ("always have to be in charge"—the autocrat). Difficulties with originating close, personal relations range from being uncomfortable when unable to establish a sufficiently close, personal relation ("can't get close enough"—the overpersonal) to being uncomfortable when getting too close and personal with someone ("don't like to get emotionally involved with people"—the underpersonal).

This description could be stated in psychoanalytic terms with little if any difference in meaning. In the struggle between the id and the superego to determine the individual's behavior the excessive response in each area represents the triumph of the id. The restrained response results from the triumph of the superego. The ideal response represents the successful resolution of the id impulses, the demands of the superego, and external reality; it therefore corresponds to the triumph of the ego.

In each of the nonideal (extreme) types described there are anxiety, hostility, and ambivalence. (One outcome of this analysis is to suggest that each of these widely used terms could be divided profitably into three types.) Anxiety arises from a person's (a) anticipation of a nonsatisfying event (for instance, being ignored, dominated, rejected) and (b) fear of exposure, both to self and others, of what kind of person he "really" is—his inadequate self-concept. The anxiety indicates that these behavior patterns are inflexible, since anxiety usually leads to rigid behavior. The threat involved in changing behavior is too great to allow for much flexibility. Hostility also follows from anxiety; so the hostility, too, may arise in three ways.

Finally, ambivalence is also present in the nonideal behaviors, since the behavior pattern being utilized is necessarily unsatisfactory. In many instances an

[7] Ibid., p. 199.

overpersonal individual, for example, will occasionally become underpersonal, and vice versa. Complete reversals are to be expected more than slight modifications, especially for the extreme behavior patterns. The characterization of a person's behavior can describe only his most usual behavior, not his invariable behavior.

Consider this . . .

- If you were to assess your own predisposition on Schutz's three interpersonal needs (inclusion, control, affection), how do you believe each of these needs has influenced your self-concept?
- As you consider your own predisposition on Schutz's three interpersonal needs, how do you believe each of these needs has influenced your feelings about personal relationships in your life?
- As you consider your own predisposition on Schutz's three interpersonal needs, how do you believe each of these needs has influenced your behavior as you developed personal relationships in your life?
- As you reflect on Schutz's theory of interpersonal needs, what piece of information did you find most valuable in helping you understand your own behavior or the behavior of others in personal relationships? Why?
- Schutz initially believed that these three dimensions are relatively stable within persons throughout the life span; however, his later work suggested that individuals may change on these dimensions throughout the life span. Which position would you support? Why?

CHAPTER 2

THEORETICAL INSIGHTS INTO PERSONAL RELATIONSHIPS

In Chapter 2 of her text, *Relational Communication*, Julia Wood introduces the concept of "theory" as a way to describe, explain, predict or control a communication phenomenon. Specifically, she introduces eight theories that will be revisited throughout this course to provide greater understanding of our personal relationships. These theories examine communication in personal relationships from four broad perspectives: 1) society, 2) social communities, 3) individual/intrapersonal, and 4) developmental (relationship processes).

Since Wood explores theories that have already been developed, I thought it would be helpful to read one scholar's quest to develop a communication theory. In this reading, Linda Acitelli, a psychology professor at the University of Houston, describes a journey prompted by a course assignment in graduate school. As she began to summarize and critically review literature on a topic of interest, marital intimacy, she noted that the literature seemed to stimulate more questions about intimacy than it answered. Once she considered these unanswered questions, she began to visualize a model to identify factors that influence relationship awareness – a starting point for understanding intimacy.

From the model she created, Acitelli then began to develop a theoretical framework for understanding relationship awareness. As she traces the development of her theory, she describes the questions that evolved along the way as well as the research she and colleagues conducted to answer those questions. It is particularly interesting to read Acitelli's discussion of individual factors and situational contexts that influence relationship awareness; through her research she continually attempts to apply her theory to specific relationships.

Acitelli's theory is an ongoing work in progress. She writes that her most recent work has focused on the influence sociocultural factors contribute to relationship awareness. Specifically, she hopes to explain, and eventually predict, the influence of such individual factors as personal identity and relationship beliefs found within the larger sociocultural context. She concludes by noting future lines of research that might be explored and useful applications of her theory for relationship therapy.

As you reflect on this reading, I hope you will draw three important conclusions about quality theories: 1) they are generated by simple, everyday questions; 2) they are a continual work in progress; and 3) they are grounded in practical application. Valuable theories are not just comprised of philosophical "gobbledygook" that carries no meaning for our everyday lives; instead, they are developed and refined to describe, explain, predict, and control phenomena found in our everyday lives.

Relationship Awareness: Crossing the Bridge Between Cognition and Communication

Linda K. Acitelli

Theories are often born out of puzzlement. Sometimes the puzzles are intellectual and sometimes they are practical juxtaposing the theoretical with the practical, the author describes the processes whereby the concept of relationship awareness was developed and expanded. Relationship awareness involves attending to relationships. Such attention can take the form of thinking or talking about relationships. The concept of relationship awareness began to form during the process of fulfilling an assignment in graduate school. The concept was later expanded to include the situational contexts and the individual factors that modify the association between relationship awareness and relationship satisfaction. The next phase of the theory broadened the contexts in which relationship awareness is examined. Theorizing on relationship awareness has begun to incorporate sociocultural contexts. By examining the role of cultural beliefs on thinking and talking about relationships, this new development also has the potential to extend our understanding of the underlying factors that determine whether the effects of relationship awareness are positive or negative. Applications of the theory to other domains are also discussed.

Relationship awareness involves attending to relationships. One can attend to relationships by thinking or by talking about them. Thus, the concept of relationship awareness bridges cognition and communication. The ideas in this paper will cross another bridge, the bridge between theory building as an intellectual, scholarly, systematic process and theory building as a result of chance encounters, everyday events, and circumstance. Like the article, "Sampling couples to understand them" (Acitelli, 1997), which mixed the theoretical with the practical, this paper will describe the formal observations and ordinary circumstances leading to the process of theory development. As Isaac Asimov is reported to have said, "The most exciting phrase to hear in science, the one that heralds new discoveries, is not 'Eureka' (I found it!), but 'Hmm . . . that's funny.'"

Often, theories are born out of puzzlement. The theorist sees puzzles in everyday things that most of us take for granted. Theory building is as much about how the theorist thinks as it is about what the theorist thinks. Therefore, the processes involved in developing a theory (the how) will be interspersed with a description of the theory (the what). Before elaborating the formal observations gained through the literature and research, I will discuss the ordinary circumstances that led to these observations.

In the Beginning: A Theory in the Making

As a graduate student, I had the assignment to do a literature review on marital intimacy. I was told to think critically about—not merely to summarize—the literature I was reviewing. I was not sure I completely understood what that meant. So I approached the task of reviewing the literature on intimacy with puzzlement of a practical kind. I asked myself, "How am I going to present a review of the literature that fairly represents it and is at the same time critical?" So, I immersed myself in the existing literature on intimacy. Much of it describes the components of intimacy and the ways in which it is expressed in behavior, such as self-disclosure, physical affection, and expressions of emotional closeness. Just when I was about to give up on the question of being critical, I started having Asimov's "That's funny" moments. There seemed to be a gap between what the literature described as intimate and my idea of intimacy. In the literature at the time, self-disclosure seemed to be the hallmark of intimacy, and several studies on the topic defined intimacy as reciprocal self-disclosure. That was puzzling. It assumed that relationships become more intimate merely because partners disclose to one another about themselves. All we really know is that they are disclosing to one another, and that the partners may or may not be learning more things about each other. What does it tell us about what is going on between them?

Surely becoming intimate involves, to some extent, all of the components mentioned in the literature. Nonetheless, I could not keep from asking the question, "If you and I are talking, which kind of talk will make us feel closer: me talking about myself and you talking about yourself, or us talking about how we relate to one another?" Although it seems commonplace now, at that time there was very little theorizing about people reflecting on their own relationships (Acitelli & Duck, 1987). That is, what happens when partners in a relationship think or talk about their relationship? Practically speaking, it solved the problem of fulfilling my assignment to be critical because I identified an important area that had received little attention. Theoretically, it gave me an idea, relationship awareness, that has kept me steeped in "that's funny" moments for many years.

Later, in 1989, I wrote a grant proposal for funding that would allow me to do the work I wanted to do in the place where I wanted to live. The feedback on the first submission of the proposal was an important turning point in developing the framework for the first phase of the theory. The reviewers consistently expressed a need for a theoretical framework and a need to know how the concept, relationship awareness, fits into the continuum of research. What I could explain was that there was no smooth continuum of research. What little research I could find came from disparate disciplines.

I needed a theoretical framework. After expressing my frustration to my former advisor, he said, "People like pictures. Why don't you try drawing a picture of what you mean?" I said, "You mean those little boxes and arrows that people use to represent concepts?" "Yes," he replied. About an hour later, I had drawn the model in Figure 1. My advisor said, "That will work," and I was surprised, thinking, "That's it? That's funny. That was too easy, too obvious." I did not trust the simple model. What I had not realized was that it was not easy at all. I had been thinking about these ideas for years. What seemed like an easy drawing exercise came from years of thinking about the process of thinking and talking about relationships and the various factors that might be involved. However, it was just the beginning. What began as an examination of a single variable (relationship awareness) eventually evolved into the process of developing a theory about cognition and communication in relationships. The following section describes the theory that has evolved from integrating and expanding on the literature.

A Theory in Progress: Phase 1

The enormous growth in relationship research has spawned a number of areas of interest. One area that has become fairly well established is an interest in individuals' perspectives of themselves, their partners, and their relationships. This area has emerged from a convergence of different perspectives (for example, social cognition, interpersonal perception, and interpersonal communication). Studies in the 1980s (e.g., Franzoi, Davis, & Young, 1985; Veroff, Douvan, & Kulka, 1981) showed how partners' increased awareness of themselves and their partners lead to increases in relationship satisfaction. This research suggested that the next logical step would be to test the hypothesis that an awareness of the relationship between oneself and one's partner, as well as a communication of that awareness, influences couple satisfaction.

My program of research is to address this hypothesis (e.g., Acitelli, 1993, 1997; Acitelli, Rogers, & Knee, 1999). The original aims were to explore the situational contexts and the individual factors that moderate the association between relationship awareness and relationship satisfaction (e.g., Acitelli & Antonucci, 1994; Acitelli, Douvan, & Veroff, 1993; Acitelli et al., 1999). Figure 1 provides a general model for organizing the literature relating to the idea that relationship awareness and satisfaction are linked. It also helps to identify what guides the current studies. Although the model is admittedly general, it will help to clarify ambiguous causal directions, to specify the domains in which the model proves to be useful and to identify areas in which there are unanswered questions.

FIGURE 1
General Framework for Studies on Relational Thinking and Talking

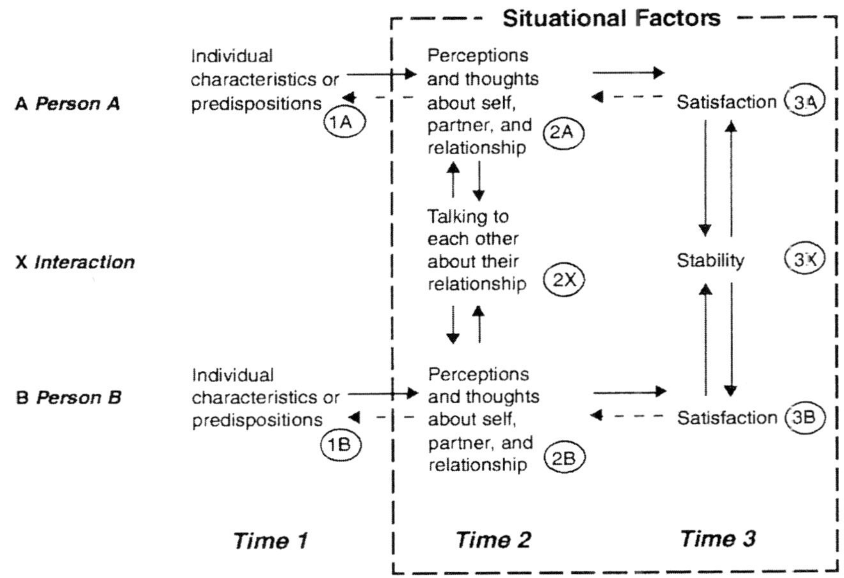

The boxes can be viewed in rows (A, B, or X) or in columns (1, 2, or 3). Rows A and B represent individual phenomena relating to persons A and B, whereas row X is interpersonal. The columns represent order in time: Column 1 represents phenomena that exist before persons A and B meet; column 2 depicts thoughts and behaviors that occur after persons A and B meet; and column 3 represents the outcomes of both thoughts and behaviors that occur in column 2. Phenomena in columns 2 and 3 occur within the context of the relationship, represented by the area surrounded by broken lines. The length of time represented in this model can vary widely. It is assumed that the causal directions implied by the solid arrows hold for relationships in their initial stages. Over time, it is possible that the phenomena occurring in columns 2 and 3 can affect the phenomena in columns 1 and 2, respectively; hence, the broken arrows go from columns 2 and 3 to columns 1 and 2.

Before discussing specific studies emerging from this model, an example will help to clarify its components. Say that persons A and B have just met and are about to form some kind of relationship with one another. They each have their own individual characteristics (lA, 1B) that can influence how they think about one another (2A, 2B). Perhaps person A is shy, and person B is outgoing. Over time (the length of time will vary between partners and relationships), partners become aware (2A, B) that they have a relationship and begin to talk to each other about it (2X). What they say may be concrete ("I'm glad we like the same kinds of movies.") or abstract ("Isn't it interesting how two people who seem so different like the same things?"). Such statements can, in turn, influence their thoughts about one another and the relationship (back to 2A and 2B). These cognitions can affect each partner's evaluation of and satisfaction with the relationship (3A, 3B). Partner satisfaction also influences how long they are likely to stay in the relationship (stability—3X).

The above example depicts a relationship in its beginning stages and in a relatively positive context. Length of relationship and the emotional tone of the situation are just two of the contextual factors expected to influence the frequency, content, and consequences of relational thinking and talking. The following review will demonstrate how previous work fits into and clarifies concepts in the general model depicted in Figure 1. Concepts will be followed by the label of the box (lA, 2A, etc.) into which they can be integrated.

Relationship Awareness

Relationship awareness has been introduced to provide a framework for studying the effects of thinking and talking about relationships (Acitelli, 1988, 1992, 1993; Acitellli & Duck, 1987; Burnett, 1987; Cate, Koval, Lloyd, & Wilson, 1995; Martin, 1991; Snell, 1988). Relationship awareness (2A, 2B) is defined as a person's focusing attention on interaction patterns—comparisons or contrasts between partners in the relationship. Included are thoughts about the couple or relationship as an entity. This awareness is not meant to imply how accurate an individual's portrayal of a relationship is, but rather the frequency of and orientation toward thinking in relational terms. Furthermore, talking in relational terms (2X) is considered a manifestation of relationship awareness because "the focus of awareness, the giving of attention, which accompanies both [thinking and talking], is what is at issue" (Burnett, 1984). Other theorists (Burnett, 1987; Cate et al., 1995) include thinking about partners in their conceptions of relationship thinking. However, relationship awareness focuses solely on the relationship and is important because the consequences of such thinking and talking are different from those when the focus is on the partners. For example, couples in conflict are less likely to remain in conflict if the focus of their conversations can shift from an individual partner (partner blame) to the relationship (Acitelli, 1988; 1993; Bernal & Baker, 1979). The links between cognition and communication in relationships and relationship satisfaction are complex and depend on a number of situational and individual factors (Acitelli, 1992, 1996; Acitelli et al., 1993; Acitelli et al., 1999).

Individual Factors and Situational Contexts

As Berger and Kellner (1964) posit that marriage is the construction of a social reality, others (particularly Laing, Phillipson, & Lee, 1966) have shown that perceptions of self and partner may be the threads from which the fabric of the social reality is crafted. This program has woven another important thread into this fabric: partners' perceptions of their relationships. What the research has shown is that people are aware of their relationships to varying degrees, and that their relationship awareness can be construed as both a dispositional and a situational factor that can be an important influence on the success of their relationships. A primary goal of this work has been to examine perceptions of self, partner, and relationship, and to see how these perceptions influence relationship and individual well-being.

Research has revealed the variables (e.g., gender, identity, length of relationship, and marital status) that condition the strength of the effects of the interaction illustrated in box 2X. In Figure 1, they make up the intrapersonal (lA, 1B) and interpersonal factors (2A, 2B) that affect the interaction (2X) located within the square area enclosed by broken lines labeled "Situational Factors.'

Gender and the Meaning of Relationship Awareness. Figure 1 depicts individual characteristics (lA, 1B). One such characteristic is gender. Based on the literature regarding gender differences in the value of intimacy and relationships, we (the research team) expected our studies of relationship awareness to reflect those differing values. Thus, we expected the arrow between columns 2 and 3 to be stronger for women than for men. In an earlier interview study (Acitelli, 1992), 42 married couples (84 individuals) were asked to talk about their lives, as opposed to their relationships, and open-ended responses were reliably coded for relationship awareness based on the definition previously provided. Results showed that, for wives, both marital and life satisfaction were related to the proportion of time spent talking about the marital relationship. Conversely, the husbands' marital and life satisfaction were not related to relationship talk. This study suggests that focusing attention on the marital relationship is important to wives' satisfaction. Similar analyses on data from 238 couples in the Detroit area have replicated and extended this work (Acitelli & Clair, unpublished raw data). Men's and women's relationship talk (based on the same open-ended questions) is negatively correlated with both partners' depression and positively correlated with a sense of equity in the relationship. However, for women, relationship talk was also associated with six additional outcome variables: greater satisfaction with the relationship, feeling competent as a relationship partner/wife, feeling cared for in the relationship, having less tension about the partner and their sexual relationship, and having less anxiety in general. Although there are some links between relationship awareness and men's outcomes, these data seem to indicate that there are more areas in women's relationships and lives where focusing on relationships has implications. Our data also indicate that the links between focusing on the relationship and relationship outcomes are different for men and women over time. Relationship talk at one time point predicted decreased positive relations for married men and increased positive relations for married women 2 years later.

Another study also demonstrates that talking about the relationship is perceived by spouses differently depending on the situation. In this experimental study, Acitelli (1988) examined the effects of talking about the relationship on perceptions of spouses' feelings of contentment. Married couples read stories about couples where spouses either talk or do not talk about the relationship in pleasant or unpleasant situations. In a short questionnaire following each story, individual spouses rated the fictional spouses' feelings of happiness in general and with regard to the specific conversation. Analyses revealed that the discrepancy between ratings of husbands' feelings for relational talk and nonrelational talk was greater in an unpleasant story than in a pleasant story. Hence, relationship talk was perceived as making more of a difference to husbands in unpleasant situations than in pleasant ones. This pattern was not found for ratings of wives' feelings. This gender difference may reflect the point that husbands view relationship talk as instrumental (used as a tool for fixing things, and so especially valuable in a conflict situation), whereas wives feel equally as good about relationship talk in either setting. Further corroboration of this point comes from the study (Acitelli, Veroff, & Hassan, 2000) from the project on the first years of marriage (Veroff, Douvan, & Hatchett, 1995). The findings indicated that men see relationship talk as a means to an end, whereas women may see it as an end in itself or as something to be valued for its own sake, yet with consequences for relationship satisfaction. This study supported the idea that relationship talk means different things to men and women.

Gender and Relationships In Context. Other studies consistently demonstrate that relational variables, those that emphasize the connection between partners, are more important to the well-being and relationship satisfaction of wives than that of husbands. These relational variables include wives' understanding of husbands in conflict situations, wives seeing their husbands as similar to themselves, and giving to and receiving social support from their husbands.

One study (Acitelli et al., 1993) focused on newlywed spouses' perceptions of each other's behaviors during conflict. In general, the findings indicated that, the more husbands report demonstrating constructive behaviors, the happier they are with their marriages, and that the less husbands and wives report using destructive tactics, the happier the husbands are with their marriages. For wives, how partners' perceptions are related to one another is more important than each single, separate report. For example, the degree to which wives understand their husbands and the degree to which they see their husbands as similar to themselves are related to their marital well-being. This study demonstrated that, compared to husbands, wives' marital well-being is more connected to how their perceptions relate to their husbands, whereas, compared to wives, husbands' marital well-being is more strongly related to what each spouse perceives he or she is doing individually. Thus, in the context of conflict where gender differences are likely to be exposed, husbands reveal their orientations to being separate and wives reveal their orientation to being connected.

Another study (Acitelli & Antonucci, 1994) revealed a gender difference in the importance of social support in older married couples. Results showed that perceptions of giving, and receiving and reciprocity were more consistently related to wives' well-being than to husbands'. These findings suggested that perceptions of social support within marriage are more important to the well-being and marital satisfaction of wives than to the well-being and marital satisfaction of husbands. This result can be interpreted both methodologically and theoretically. Perhaps the measures of social support assess behaviors that were perceived as supportive to women but not to men. Most of the social support items were indicative of partners talking intimately to each other, behavior that is often shown to vary by gender. Moreover, the support received from wives may match husbands' expectations of marriage so well that it had no effect on their marital satisfaction or well-being. Other scholars (Hochschild, 1983; Thompson, 1993) have suggested that when wives' actions confirm their husbands' sex-role expectations, there may be little recognition of those actions. Conversely, for women, reciprocity of emotional social support with husbands was more unusual (women were more likely to give and receive from children and friends; Depner & Ingersoll-Dayton, 1985). Hence, variations in perceived reciprocity of support had relatively strong relations with wives' well-being.

In sum, the evidence indicates that women's well-being is tied to relationally oriented variables, such as relationship talk, wives' understanding of husbands, wives' seeing their husbands as similar to themselves, and women's giving to and receiving social support from their partners. Such relationship variables are more complexly related or are not related at all to men's well-being. So far, then, the arrow leading from 2 to 3 in Figure 1 is more direct and perhaps stronger for women than for men. These gender differences lead to questions about other possible moderators and mediators of relationship awareness and satisfaction. Perhaps the different effects of relationship awareness on men and women depend on the way they see themselves. Some theorists (e.g., Jordan & Surrey, 1986; Markus & Oyserman, 1989) have proposed that a woman's self-concept is more relational than a man's self-concept. With these ideas in mind, we conducted a study to test the hypothesis that the link between thinking positively about the relationship and marital satisfaction is moderated by relational identity, and not by biological sex per se (Acitelli & Young, 1996; Acitelli et al., 1999). That is, the more a person's identity is connected to others, the more thinking positively about the relationship will be linked to his or her happiness.

Studies of Identity. We (Acitelli & Young, 1996; Acitelli, et al., 1999) argue that the degree to which one's self-concept is relational partially determines whether engaging in relational thinking benefits one's relationship. As noted previously, relationship thinking to some extent determines relationship satisfaction. If relationships are a central part of one's identity, then thinking about them may be tied to a person's values and associated with something very positive and important to the person. Such thinking should affect such people more, making them feel better about the relationship. For those low in relational self-concept, thinking about the relationship should have little effect on their satisfaction with it. We also hypothesized that, for a married individual, an identity more specific to his or her own relationship would perhaps be the more important moderator of the link between relationship thinking and relationship satisfaction. So we devised measures for a general relational identity and a specific couple identity by asking participants to rate themselves on various descriptors and to rate how important these descriptors were to the way they saw themselves.

Our findings supported our predictions, although the results for married couples went in the opposite direction of that expected. The link between positive relationship thinking and satisfaction was stronger for those who scored higher on relational identity for unmarried couples only. Thus, in order for unmarried partners with high relational identities to feel satisfied with the relationship, they needed to think positively about the relationship. However, for married couples, the lower a person's couple identity, the stronger the association between positive relationship thinking and satisfaction was. Perhaps unmarried partners do not consider their specific relationship to be central to their identity, whereas this may be a relatively automatic tendency among those who are married. If a distinct and more specific type of relational self-concept or couple identity exists for married couples, then positive relationship thinking would function differently for married people than for unmarried dating partners. For married people, having a strong couple identity may go hand in hand with thinking positively about the relationship, though it may not be a conscious process. Spouses with a couple identity are implicitly keeping their relationship in "tacit awareness"; that is, the couple becomes the lens through which they view the world (Wegner & Giuliano, 1982).

Whereas much of our research thus far concerns relationship awareness and satisfaction, further evidence adds a behavioral component. One study (Garrido & Acitelli, 1999) shows that, regardless of gender, the more relational one's identity, the more likely one is to report performing traditionally female household tasks and the less likely one is to perform traditionally male household tasks. Not only do we demonstrate how relational identity is linked to cognition and affect, we also show that it is linked to expected behaviors. This study also supports the idea that relational identity rather than biological sex is a key component in predicting gender-linked behaviors.

Similarity and Relationship Beliefs. A series of studies (beginning with Kenny & Acitelli, 1994) were designed to examine the importance of stereotyped responses in contributing to similarity. One study (Acitelli, Kenny, & Weiner, 2001) examined partner similarity in beliefs about what makes a good marriage. We found that stereotypical beliefs contribute more to similarity of beliefs than to unique similarity between partners. Furthermore, it was shown that the more one endorsed the stereotypical belief profile, the more satisfied one was with her or his relationship. However, the current work cannot inform us about other cultural beliefs that may exist within the U.S., as our sample was primarily White. Thus, we need to test the hypothesis that cultural beliefs in the form of familism, collectivism, and independence are associated with family values, different religious beliefs, sex-role ideology, and so forth, and can determine different beliefs about relationships. With an ethnically diverse sample, we could address these issues.

The above studies were important steps in discovering how perceptions of the self, partner; and relationship can affect partner well-being in the relationship. Several studies indicated that relationship awareness has different outcomes for men and women and that marital status and identity are moderators of these effects. Further, many findings are consistent across variables or contexts (e.g., situations of conflict and social support). We also found that endorsement of a stereotypical profile of beliefs about marriage leads to positive relationship outcomes, but reduces unique similarity between the partners. Each study made its own contribution and suggested new directions for further studies that would extend previous work in important ways.

Few attempts have been made by others to examine the intersection of sociocultural contexts with relationship processes (Allan, 1993; Duck, West, & Acitelli, 1997; Gaines, 1995; Veroff et al., 1995). Research on relationships often isolates the dyadic unit from the broader contexts in which it is imbedded (Allan, 1993; Milardo & Wellman, 1992). Although the U.S. is becoming more ethnically diverse, only 8% of the samples used in longitudinal relationship research are non-White samples, and the majority consists of samples with little variability in ethnic and demographic makeup (Karney & Bradbury, 1995). Much of the existing cross-sectional research on personal relationships (see Duck et al., 1997) has focused on White college students or clinical samples of married couples. Further, increasing numbers of health and well-being outcomes for non-White populations are hypothesized to be due, in part, to social structures oriented toward a White population (Fernando, 1984; Jackson et al., 1996; Kreiger, 1990; Williams & Collins, 1995). It is imperative to study relationships within a wider range of ethnic groups because effects previously assumed to be universal are likely to be moderated or modified by sociocultural practices and beliefs. As far as I know, this type of relationship research has not yet been done, but the ideas leading to the expansion of the theory from the situational to sociocultural are spelled out here. The primary focus of the revised theory is to examine the effects that thinking and talking about relationships within various sociocultural contexts have on the relationship and to investigate the underlying factors that determine whether the effects are positive or negative.

A Theory In the Making: Transitions

After working at the Institute for Social Research for several years on the grant that funded the research on Phase 1 of the theory, I took a position at the University of Houston. This change provided me with an opportunity to conduct cultural research and to investigate how relationship dynamics might be different in different cultures. Houston is quite diverse ethnically. Hispanics and Whites (or European Americans) make up the majority (about 70%) of the population and are almost equal in numbers. The 2000 census reveals that Hispanics now outnumber Whites in Houston proper. Blacks (or African Americans) make up about 25% of the population, and Asians about 5%. So, in consultation with a research firm that is known for its research in the Hispanic community, it was decided to focus on the three ethnic groups comprising the majority of the Houston population (Hispanics, European American, and African American). Unfortunately, the Asian population, though highly visible in terms of contributions to the community, was not included in the application of the theory. Although practical matters kept me from including the Asian group, the general theoretical framework of Figure 2 could apply to any ethnic group.

A Theory Still in Progress: Phase 2

Figure 2 provides a general framework for organizing the existing literature related to sociocultural factors and for thinking and talking about relationships. Like Figure 1, it is not intended as a causal model in the strict sense of the term. Similar to Figure 1, the model in Figure 2 can help to clarify ambiguous causal directions and to specify the domains in which there are unanswered questions. Note that Figures 1 and 2 are very much alike. Each framework, in terms of the meaning of rows and columns, is similar. However, there are important changes, represented in the new Column 1 (sociocultural factors). Now there are 4 columns (1, 2, 3, or 4). Although phenomena in columns 3 and 4 occur within the situational context of the relationship, represented by the area surrounded by broken lines, phenomena in columns 1, 2, 3, and 4 occur within the broader sociocultural context represented by the area surrounded by the solid line. Thus, one new component of this theory is an expansion of the model's boundaries by adding the sociocultural context. Another is the aim to extend our understanding of the underlying factors by examining the role of cultural beliefs on thinking and talking about relationships.

FIGURE 2

Relationship Awareness and Sociocultural Factors

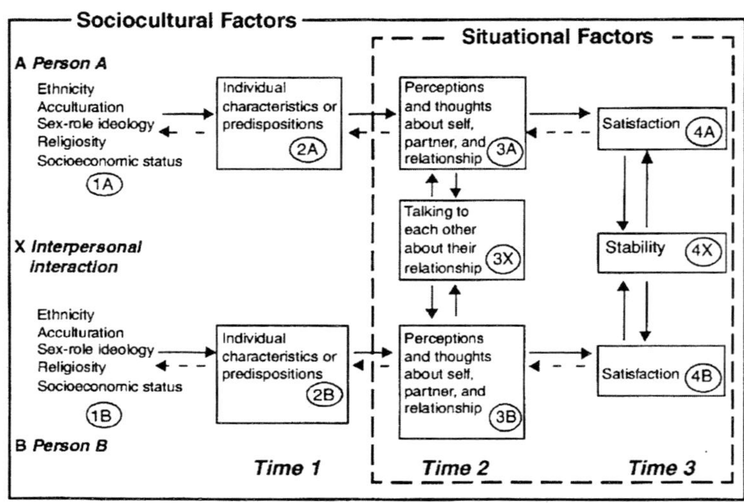

An example will help to clarify what the addition of the sociocultural factors means. Compare this example to the one used to clarify Figure 1. Suppose that persons A and B are each of Hispanic heritage (lA, 1B), have just met, and are about to form some kind of relationship with each other. Person A's grandparents are originally from Mexico and have lived in the U.S. for 50 years; thus, she and her parents were born in the U.S. Person B's family lived in Mexico until he was 18 years old, and he recently moved to the United States. Thus, person A is third generation and Person B is first generation. Persons A and B each have their own individual characteristics and beliefs (2A, 2B) that can influence how they think about each other (3A, 3B). Person B may believe more in a traditional sex-role orientation than Person A, who has lived in the the U.S. culture for a longer period of time. Over time (the length of time will vary between partners and relationships), partners become aware (3A, 3B) that they have a relationship and begin to talk to each other about it (3X). What they say may be concrete ("I'm glad we like the same kinds of movies") or abstract ("Isn't it nice how two people with different backgrounds get along so well?"). Such statements can, in turn, influence their thoughts about one another and the relationship (back to 3A and 3B). These cognitions can affect each partner's evaluation of and satisfaction with the relationship (4A, 4B). Partner satisfaction also influences how long they are likely to stay in the relationship (stability—4X).

The above example depicts a relationship in its beginning stages and in an apparently positive situation. As time goes on, persons A and B may become aware of their differences in their beliefs about how men and women are supposed to behave (i.e., sex-role ideology). Whether this awareness is good or bad for their relationship may depend on several factors. Factors that predict the well-being of relationships in one context may be detrimental in another. Ethnicity, religiosity, acculturation, and support networks are just a few of the sociocultural factors expected to interact with the link between a relationship focus and relationship happiness. Length of relationship and the emotional tone of the situation are just two of the situational factors influencing the frequency, content, and consequences of relational thinking and talking. Although a particular relationship may be seen as personally constructed by two individuals, the relationship is "sufficiently embedded in socioeconomic relations and sociocultural practices for their form to be taken for granted and accepted as 'obvious' and 'natural' [within that group]" (Allan, 1993). Presumably the more the form of the relationship is taken for granted within a particular sociocultural group, the less likely would be the need for partners to negotiate or define the relationship through talk, even though it may differ from what is obvious to another ethnic group. Therefore, the sociocultural context may influence the extent to which talking about the relationship is valued and practiced. For example, the extent to which partners are similar in cultural background may determine whether persons A and B talk about their similarities and differences and whether such talk will benefit their relationship. However, the arrows do not go from sociocultural factors (1A, B) directly to such talk (3A, B) because these behaviors are believed to be mediated by individual cognition, in the form of general relationship schemas (Baldwin, 1992; Planalp, 1987) specific to one's culture. These schemas contain cultural prescriptions concerning how one behaves in relationships and are more likely to be automatic than under conscious control. The following literature review will demonstrate how previous work fits into the general model depicted in Figure 2.

What follows are the factors that have not been explored directly or that need further examination with regard to partners focusing on their relationships (3A, 3B). To our knowledge, there is no literature making direct links between relationship awareness and sociocultural factors. Thus, hypotheses are based on what little we do know about relationship dynamics within different ethnic populations.

The Broader Sociocultural Context

Sociocultural context is a general, but complex concept. Although the reality cannot be dissected into discrete, unrelated components, for the sake of clarity and simplicity, sociocultural context is made up of five components: ethnicity, acculturation, sex-role ideology, religiosity, and socioeconomic status (SES). An individual's ethnicity is operationally defined as the group or descriptor with whom one identifies when asked, "What is your ethnic background or origins?" (Tucker & Mitchell-Kernan, 1995). For example, people could identify themselves as Black, African American, Hispanic, Mexican, Latina, Italian, German, or White. It is expected that the importance of ethnicity will vary from person to person. Thus, ethnicity alone is not predicted to directly account for differences in relationship dynamics, but rather other factors that vary, in part, as a result of a person's ethnicity. Whereas many ideological factors can be influenced by culture (e.g., religiosity, sex-role ideology), other factors relate more to social structure (acculturation, SES). As all of these factors are related to one another in varying degrees, a key issue is the degree to which each makes a unique contribution to relationship outcomes.

Acculturation is one such factor. It has been defined as the extent to which individuals who live in a normative context for an extended period of time gradually learn and adopt aspects of the new culture. More broadly, it is seen as a process by which individuals undergo change in response to contact with other cultures and can thus include changes by the majority culture as well (Berry, Poortinga, Segall, & Dasen, 1992). To incorporate the broader view, we operationalize acculturation as the extent to which one is immersed in the majority (White or European American) culture whether one is a recent immigrant or is native to this country.

As relationship talk has been identified as a way to define a relationship, especially in its early stages, it is expected that when culturally defined traditional sex-roles are adopted within a marriage or relationship, less relationship talk will be explicit or recognized as valuable and needed. It is also expected that, if a couple is immersed in any ethnic group's cultural traditions (i.e., the less acculturated they are), it is more likely they will have that culture's beliefs about the roles a man and woman should fulfill (sex-role ideology). Therefore, little or no association is expected between relationship talk and relationship satisfaction among couples when both partners have a strong identification with an ethnic group's traditions that strongly prescribe and support such roles.

However, if a particular cultural group values talking about the relationship, then such talking will benefit the relationship. Each individual is expected to vary on acculturation and/or ethnic identity. If partners differ in the extent to which they embrace a particular culture's view of heterosexual relationships, they may need to talk about their relationship to come to a consensus about specific roles.

Similar hypotheses could be tested with regard to religiosity, the extent to which religious or spiritual beliefs are important and central to one's life. Although religiosity could have an impact on sex-role ideology, which, in turn, could influence relationship dynamics as discussed above, religion can also affect other beliefs. For example, to many religions, the marital union is sacred and divorce is unthinkable. As there is very little research on the impact of religion on relationship dynamics among various ethnic groups, our hypotheses are extrapolations from studies that discuss religion and well-being. In general, people who are religious are happier than people who are not (Meyers & Deiner, 1995), and marital outcomes seem to be better in marriages where both partners are religious (Brody, Stoneman, & Flor, 1996). As second generation Hispanics are less religious than first generation Hispanics (Roof & Manning, 1994), religiosity and acculturation are negatively correlated. In this context, relationship talk might be associated with poorer relationship outcomes, such that talking about the relationship suggests a stepping out of traditional roles dictated by religion, and may be indicative of problems in the relationship.

Socioeconomic status (SES), often defined by level of education and income, has also been shown to be associated with relationship outcomes (Tucker & Mitchell-Kernan, 1995; Vinokur & van Ryn, 1993). From this literature, we may hypothesize that the more a couple worries about finances, the less likely their talk will be to focus on the relationship, regardless of ethnicity. Stressors related to low income, such as difficulties paying for housing and meals, often become a higher priority than how the relationship is functioning. We also need to be careful not to confuse SES with ethnicity, as they are often related.

Relationship Status and Sociocultural Context

An examination of how relationship status and broader social contexts interact with relationship awareness is needed. The meaning of marriage and commitment between White couples and Black couples has been hypothesized to be different (Gaines, 1995; Veroff et al, 1995). Furthermore, Nock's (1995) study from the National Survey of Families and Households compared married to cohabiting couples and found that the poorer outcomes associated with cohabiting in general are even greater within the Hispanic population (compared to African Americans and Whites). There is also research suggesting that the divorce rate among Hispanics is lower than that among Whites (Becerra, 1988). Religiosity may be a factor that precludes thoughts about divorce (making divorce unthinkable) and makes living together while unmarried unacceptable. However, the research also suggests that, the more Hispanics are acculturated into the mainstream U.S. society, the more their divorce rate increases and approaches that of Whites (Frisbie, Ortiz, & Kelly, 1985). These findings suggest that cultural changes are related to changes in relationships, and more specifically to how people define and think about relationships. Thus, the link between relationship status and relationship talk may be moderated by cultural values (e.g., religiosity, acculturation).

Individual Factors and Sociocultural Context

The following underlying factors are individual (as opposed to interpersonal) factors that can influence and be influenced by relationship awareness:

Identity. Research and theory have consistently shown that women's self-concepts (or identities) are more relational (interdependent, connected, communal), whereas men's self-concepts are more independent (autonomous, separate, agentic; Cross & Madson, 1997; Douvan & Adelson, 1966; Gilligan; 1982; Jordan & Surrey, 1986; Markus & Oyserman, 1989). However, these identities are not exclusively the domain of one sex or the other (e.g., there are men who think of themselves as relational and women who think of themselves as independent). Thus, many researchers have abandoned the terms feminine and masculine in favor of these nongendered terms (e.g., Acitelli & Young, 1996; Cross & Madson, 1997; Garrido & Acitelli, 1999).

Not surprisingly, the current program of research has supported the idea that a woman's sense of self is more relationally oriented as compared to heterosexual men. Our work has uncovered different aspects of the relational (or interdependent) identity, much as Markus (1977) and Linville (1985) distinguish different selves or aspects of the self. Not only is there evidence that a broader relational identity has links to thinking about the relationship, but also that a more specific couple identity moderates the link between such thinking and satisfaction (Acitelli et al., 1999).

Questions remain about yet another sense of identity, that is, ethnic or group identity. Are there parallels between individual (relational and autonomous) and group (collective and independent) identities? That is, if a society is considered collective, by extension, one might hypothesize that more collective cultures would imbue individuals with the value of thinking and talking about relationships, and thus that sex-roles would be less defined and differentiated. However, Baumeister & Sommer (1997) point out that being collective refers to one's relationship with a group rather than with one partner. If so, this idea could help explain why collective cultures also have traditional and defined sex-role orientations. Standing out is not approved in collective cultures (Markus & Kitayama, 1991; Triandis, Leung, Villareal, & Clack, 1985); therefore, if traditional male-female roles are part of the cultural norm, nontraditional relationships between men and women would be akin to standing out and less likely to occur in collective societies. What needs to be done is to extend the concept of individual identities to group identities, and to explore how such identities affect relationship dynamics. This extension may help explain how collective societies, which seem more communal, can have sharper divisions in sex-roles where men are more separate and women are more relational. An important question to be answered is: How might these different aspects of identity moderate the link between relationship awareness and relationship satisfaction?

For example, a study of mixed-ethnic relationships found that ethnic identity was more predictive of relationship quality than was a categorical measure of ethnicity (Gurung & Duong, 1999). This finding underscores the idea that factors other than ethnicity help explain ethnic differences in relationship dynamics. More specifically, we hypothesize that group or ethnic identities would increase the tacit (unspoken) form of relationship awareness but decrease the focal (explicit talk about the relationship) form. That is, individuals who identify with groups that are characterized as collective and/or more family-oriented (e.g., African Americans: Gaines, 1995; and Hispanics: Sabogal, Marin, Otero-Sabogal, Marin, & Perez-Stable, 1987) are expected to be more likely to see themselves as part of a couple and part of a family. Thus, their relationship happiness is expected to depend less on explicit talk about the relationship than on their "we" orientation, which precludes explicit talk about the relationship.

Relationship Beliefs. Individuals have different beliefs about what constitutes a good relationship (Eidelson & Epstein, 1982; Fletcher & Kininmonth, 1992; Knee, 1998). Such beliefs have been shown to play important roles in relationship outcomes (Crohan, 1992; Fletcher & Fitness, 1996; Knee, 1998). For example, one's belief that conflict is bad for a relationship helps to determine whether the frequency of conflict predicts negative relationship outcomes (Crohan, 1992). Similarly, individuals' implicit theories about relationships have been shown to influence relationship initiation, maintenance, and longevity (Knee, 1998). Further, beliefs about relationships may be part of a larger belief network that includes sociocultural values (e.g., religiosity and sex-role ideology). Thus, the moderating effect of relationship beliefs may elucidate potential ethnic group differences in relationship outcomes. If ethnic group differences are found in the frequency of thinking and talking about relationships as well as in their effects on relationship outcomes, these differences might be a function of cultural values and relationship beliefs. As far as we know, these issues have not been examined empirically. However, sociocultural factors are expected to interact with these associations such that links between relationship awareness and satisfaction among partners whose beliefs about relationships are similar are not as strong.

As many of our hypotheses are based on similarity of beliefs rather than on ethnicity per se, the hypotheses regarding similarity of perceptions and beliefs apply to all couples regardless of ethnic group. Depending upon the extent to which beliefs about relationships are similar between partners, relationship awareness may play less of a role in their understanding of the relationship because there may be implicit understandings between partners with similar beliefs about their relationship. Conversely, partners within dyads may differ with regard to such factors as acculturation, ethnic identity, or sex-role ideology. When they become aware of these differences, they may spend more time talking about their relationship because their partners' behaviors may not fit their expectations. Talking about such differences with a relationship perspective (rather than engaging in partner blame) is expected to benefit the relationship in the long run.

Often, thinking and talking about the relationships is a large part of couples' therapy. One clinical implication of Phase 2 of the theory is that it may help couple therapists to clarify the sociocultural factors that determine whether thinking and talking about the relationship is beneficial or harmful to couples' well-being. However, much work is needed to understand the extent to which sociocultural factors influence relationship functioning, particularly with regard to relationship awareness. So far, this theory has been applied only to heterosexual relationships. The potential extension and applications of this theory to other types of relationships (e.g., same-sex) and contexts are vast. The interplay between relationship awareness and social networks (e.g., family members and friends) is an area that needs to be investigated. One extension that has begun to bear fruit is the application of relationship awareness to couples in which one partner has a chronic illness (Acitelli & Badr, 2000). We argue that couples who see chronic illness as a relationship challenge will fare better than those who see it as an individual challenge. This application is likely to lead to Phase 3, which will be discussed in future papers, and shows that a theory is always a work in progress.

Consider this . . .

- It is human nature for inquisitive beings to observe the world around them and, based on these observations, create theories about how the world works. Given your inquisitive nature, provide an example of a "theory" you have developed to describe, explain, predict, or control some phenomenon you've observed in your everyday life. How have you tested your theory?
- As you reflect on Acitelli's description of her journey, what aspect of theory development do you find most interesting? Why?
- After reviewing Acitelli's theory of relationship awareness, what do you consider the greatest strengths of her theory? What do you consider the limitations of her theory?
- How might Acitelli's theory of relationship awareness be used to describe, explain, predict, or control a specific relationship in your life? Give a specific example to illustrate.

Author

Linda K. Acitelli is an associate professor in the Department of Psychology at the University of Houston. An earlier version of this paper was presented at the preconference, Building Theories of Communication, at the International Communication Association annual conference, Washington DC, May 23, 2001.The author wishes to thank Pamela Kalbfliesch, Ascan Koerner, Mary Anne Fitzpatrick, and other participants at the workshop for their helpful feedback on the article. Correspondence concerning this article should be addressed to Linda K. Acitelli, Department of Psychology, University of Houston, Houston, TX 77204; phone: (713) 743-8567; email: acitelli@uh.edu.

References

Acitelli, L. K. (1988). When spouses talk to each other about their relationship. *Journal of Social and Personal Relationships, 5,* 185-199.

Acitelli, L. K. (1992). Gender differences in relationship awareness and marital satisfaction among young married couples. *Personality and Social Psychology Bulletin, 18(l),* 102-110.

Acitelli, L. K. (1993). You, me, and us: Perspectives on relationship awareness. In S. W. Duck (Ed.), *Understanding relationship processes 1: Individuals and relationships* (pp. 144-174). London: Sage.

Acitelli, L. K. (1996). The neglected links between marital support and marital satisfaction. In G. R. Pierce, B. R. Sarason, & I. G. Sarason, *Handbook of social support and family relationships* (pp. 83-103). New York: Plenum.

Acitellli, L. K. (1997). Sampling couples to understand them: Mixing the theoretical with the practical. *Journal of Social and Personal Relationships, 14,* 243-261.

Acitelli, L. K., & Antonucci, T. C. (1994). Gender differences in the link between marital support and satisfaction in older couples. *Journal of Personality and Social Psychology, 67,* 688-698.

Acitelli, L. K., & Badr, H. (2000, September). *Perspectives on relationship awareness and satisfaction: Implications for couples and coping.* Presented to the International Workshop on Stress and Coping in Couples, University of Fribourg, Switzerland.

Acitelli, L. K., & Clair, S. (1996). [*Couples and well-being*]. Unpublished raw data.

Acitelli, L. K., Douvan, E., & Veroff, J. (1993). Perceptions of conflict in the first year of marriage: How important are similarity and understanding? *Journal of Social and Personal Relationships, 10,* 5-19.

Acitelli, L. K., & Duck, S. W. (1987). Intimacy as the proverbial elephant. In D. Perlman & S. W. Duck (Eds.), *Intimate relationships: Development, dynamics and deterioration* (pp. 297-308). Beverly Hills, CA: Sage.

Acitelli, L. K., Kenny, D. A., & Weiner, D. (2001). The importance of similarity and understanding of relationship partners' beliefs about the ideal marriage. *Personal Relationships, 8,* 167-185.

Acitelli, L. K., Rogers, S., & Knee, C. R. (1999). The role of relational identity in the link between relationship thinking and relationship satisfaction. *Journal of Social and Personal Relationships, 16,* 591-618.

Acitelli, L., Veroff, J., & Hassan, H. (2000). *Taking a relationship perspective increases marital well being: A path analysis.* Unpublished manuscript.

Acitelli, L. K., & Young, A. M. (1996). Gender and thought in relationships. In G. Fletcher & J. Fitness (Eds.), *Knowledge structures and interactions in close relationships: A social psychological approach* (pp. 147-168). Hillsdale, NJ: Eribaum.

Allan, G. A. (1993). Social structure and relationships. In S. W. Duck (Ed.), *Understanding relationship processes 3: Social context of relationships* (pp. 1-25). Newbury Park, CA: Sage.

Baldwin, M. W. (1992). Relational schemas and the processing of social information. *Psychological Bulletin, 112,* 461-484.

Baumeister, R. E, & Sommer, K. L. (1997). What do menwant? Gender differences and two spheres of belongingness: Comment on Cross and Madson. *Psychological Butietin, 122,* 38-44.

Becerra, R. M. (1988). The Mexican American family. In C. H. Mindel, R. W. Habenstein, & R. Wright, Jr. (Eds.), *Ethnic families in America* (3rd ed., pp. 141-159). New York: Elsevier.

Berger, P., & Kellner, H. (1964). Marriage and the construction of social reality. *Diogenes, 46,* 1-24.

Bernal, G., & Baker, J. (1979). Toward a metacommunicational framework of couple interaction. *Family Process, 18,* 293-302.

Berry, J. W., Poortinga, Y. H., Segall, M. H., & Dasen, R. R. (1992). *Cross-cultural psychology: Research and applications.* New York: Cambridge University Press.

Brody, G. H., Stoneman, Z., & Flor, D. (1996). Parental religiosity, family processes, and youth competence in rural, two-parent African American families. *Developmental Psychology, 32,* 696-706.

Burnett, R. (1984, July). *Thinking and communicating about personal relationships: Some sex differences.* Paper presented at the International Conference on Personal Relationships, Madison, WI.

Burnett, R. (1987). Reflection in personal relationships. In R. Burnett, P. McGhee, & D. C. Clarke (Eds.), *Accounting for relationships: Explanation, representation and knowledge* (pp. 74-93). London: Methuen.

Cate, R. M., Koval, J. E., Lloyd, S. A., & Wilson, G. (1995). The assessment of relationship thinking in dating relationships. *Personal Relationships, 2,* 77-95.

Crohan, S. E. (1992). Marital happiness and spousal consensus on beliefs about marital conflict. A longitudinal investigation. *Journal of Social and Personal Relationships, 9,* 89-102.

Cross, S. E., & Madson, L. (1997). Models of the self: Self-construals and gender. *Psychological Bulletin, 122,* 5-37.

Depner, C. E., & Ingersoll-Dayton, B. (1985). Conjugal social support: Patterns in later life. *Journal of Gerontology, 40,* 761-766.

Douvan, E., & Adelson, J. (1966). *The adolescent experience.* New York: Wiley.

Duck, S., West, L., & Acitelli, L. K. (1997). Sewing the field: The tapestry of relationships in life and research. In S. Duck (Ed.), *Handbook of personal relationships* (2nd ed., pp. 1-23). Wiley.

Eidelson, R. J., & Epstein, N. (1982). Cognition and relationship maladjustment: Development of a measure of dysfunctional relationship beliefs. *Journal of Consulting and Clinical Psychology, 50,* 715-720.

Fernando, S. (1984). Racism as a cause of depression. *International Journal of Social Psychology, 30,* 41-49.

Fletcher, G. J. O., & Fitness, J. (Eds.) (1996). *Knowledge structures and interactions in close relationships: A social psychological approach.* Hillsdale, NJ: Eribaum.

Fletcher, G. J. O., & Kininmonth, L. (1996). Measuring relationship beliefs: An individual difference measure. *Journal of Research in Personality, 26,* 371-397.

Franzoi, S., Davis, M. H., & Young, R. D. (1985). The effects of private self-consciousness and perspective taking on satisfaction in close relationships. *Journal of Personality and Social Psychology, 48,* 1594-1594.

Frisbie, W. P., Orriz, W., & Kelly, W. R. (1985). Marital instability trends among Mexican Americans as compared to Blacks and Anglos: New evidence. *Social Science Quarterly, 66,* 587-601.

Gaines, S. O. (1995). *Relationships between members of cultural minorities. Understanding relationship processes 6: Under-studied relationships* (pp. 51-88). London: Sage.

Garrido, E. E, & Acitelli, L. K. (1999). Relational identity and the division of household labor. *Journal of Social and Personal Relationships, 16,* 619-637.

Gilligan, C. (1982). In a different voice: *Psychological theory and women's development.* Cambridge, MA: Harvard University Press.

Glenn, N. D. (1990). Quantitative research on marital quality in the 1980's: A critical review. *Journal of Marriage and the Family, 53,* 818-831.

Gurung, R. A. R., & Duong, T. (1999). Mixing and matching: Assessing the concomitants of mixed ethnic relationships. *Journal of Social and Personal Relationships, 16,* 639-657.

Hochschild, A. (1983). The managed heart. Berkeley: University of California.

Jackson, J. S., Brown, T. N., Williams, D. R., Torres, M., Sellers, S. L., & Brown, K. (1996). Racism and the physical and mental health status of African Americans: A thirteen-year national panel study. *Ethnicity and Disease, 6,* 1 32-147.

Jordan, J. V., & Surrey, J. L. (1986). The self-in-relation: Empathy in the mother-daughter relationship. In T. Bernay & D. W. Cantor (Eds.), *The psychology of today's woman: New psychoanalytic visions* (pp. 88-104). Cambridge, MA: Harvard University Press.

Karney, B. R., & Bradbury, T. N. (1995). The longitudinal course of marital quality and stability: A review of theory, method, and research. *Psychological Bulletin, 18,* 3-34

Kenny, D. A., & Acitelli, L. K. (1994). Measuring similarity in couples. *Journal of Family Psychology, 8,* 417-431.

Knee, C. R. (1998). Implicit theories of relationships: Assessment and prediction of romantic relationship initiation, coping and longevity. *Journal of Personality and Social Psychology, 74,* 360-370.

Kreiger, N. (1990). Racial and gender discrimination: Risk factors for high blood pressure? *Social Science and Medicine, 30,* 1273-128 1.

Laing, R. D., Phillipson, H., & Lee, A. R. (1966). *Interpersonal perception: A theory and a method of research.* New York: Springer.

Linville, P. W. (1985). Self-complexity and affect extremity: Don't put all of your eggs in one cognitive basket. *Social Cognition, 3,* 94-120.

Markus, H. (1977). Self-schemata and processing information about the self. *Journal of Personality and Social Psychology, 35,* 63-78.

Markus, H., & Kitayama, S. (1991). Culture and the self: Implications for cognition, emotion, and motivation. *Psychological Review, 99,* 215-238.

Markus, H., & Oyserman, D. (1989). Gender and thought: The role of the self-concept. In M. Crawford & M. Hamilton (Eds.), *Gender and thought* (pp. 100-127). New York: Springer-Verlag.

Martin, R. W. (1991) Examining personal relationship thinking: The relational cognition complexity instrument. *Journal of Social and Personal Relationships, 8,* 467-480.

Meyers, D. G., & Diener, E. (1995). Who is happy? *Psychological Science, 6,* 10-19.

Milardo, R. M., & Wellman, B. (1992). The personal is social. *Journal of Social and Personal Relationships, 9,* 339-342.

Nock, S. L. (1995). A comparison of marriages and cohabiting relationships. *Journal of Family Issues, 16,* 53-76.

Planalp, S. (1987). Interplay between relational knowledge and events. In R. Burnett, P. McGhee, & D. C. Clarke (Eds.), *Accounting for relationships: Explanation, representation and knowledge* (pp. 175-191). London: Methuen.

Roof, W. C., & Manning, C. (1994). Cultural conflicts and identity: Second generation Hispanic Catholics in the United States. *Social Compass, 41,* 171-184.

Sabogal, F., Marin, G., Otero-Sabogal, R., Marin, B. V., & Perez-Stable, E. J. (1987). Hispanic familism and acculturation: What changes and what doesn't? *Hispanic journal of Behavioral Sciences, 9,* 397-412.

Snell, W. E. (1988). *The relationship awareness scale: Measuring relationship-consciousness, relationship monitoring, and relationship anxiety.* Unpublished manuscript, Southeast Missouri State University, Cape Girardeau, Missouri.

Thompson, L. (1993). Conceptualizing gender in marriage: The case of marital care. *Journal of Marriage and the Family, .55,* 557-569.

Triandis, H. C., Leung, K., Villareal, M. J., & Clack, F. L. (1985). Allocentric versus ideocentric tendencies: Convergent and discriminant validation. *Journal of Research in Personality, 19,* 395-415.

Tucker, M. B., & Mitchell-Kernan, C. (1995). Social structural and psychological correlates of interethnic dating. *Journal of Personality and Social Psychology, 67,* 341-361.

Veroff, J., Douvan, E., & Hatchett, S. J. (1995). *Marital instability: A social and behavioral study of the early years.* Greenwich, CT: Greenwood.

Veroff, J., Douvan, E., & Kulka, K. (1981). *The inner American.* New York: Basic Books.

Vinokur, A. D., & van Ryn, M. (1993). Social support and undermining in close relationships: Their independent effects on the mental health of unemployed persons. *Journal of Personality and Social Psycbology, 65,* 330-359.

Wegner, D. M., & Giuliano, T. (1982). The forms of social awareness. In W. J. Ickes (Ed.), *Personality, roles, and social behavior* (pp. 165-198). New York: Springer-Verlag.

Williams, D. R., & Collins, C. (1995). Socioeconomic and race differences in health. *Annual Review of Sociology, 21,* 349-386.

CHAPTER 3

COMMUNICATION: THE CENTRAL DYNAMIC IN PERSONAL RELATIONSHIPS

In Chapter 3 of her text, *Relational Communication*, Julia Wood explains that the study of symbols leads us to conclude that communication is not just a straightforward exchange of information between participants. Instead, communication in relationships reflects the mutual influence participants exert on one another within the relationship; simply put, I affect you and I am simultaneously affected by you as we create our relationship. The primary focus of this chapter, then, is to explore ten premises about communication in personal relationships that reflect this "relational perspective" on human communication.

In this reading, "Theoretical Foundations," L. Edna Rogers (Professor of Communication at the University of Utah) and Valentin Escudero (Professor of Psychology and Director of the Family Intervention Masters Program at the University of La Coruna in Spain) provide a valuable overview of the work that laid the foundation for the relational perspective of human communication. Both historically and conceptually, the authors explain how this perspective focuses primarily on the study of participant interaction and mutual influence; as such, this perspective frames the study of relationships in terms of such concepts as connection, negotiated identities, evolving patterns, and levels of meaning.

When you read the history of those who developed the relational perspective, please note that these scholars frequently reflect the disciplines of psychology, sociology, anthropology, philosophy, and linguistics. The communication discipline, relatively new among these disciplines, has drawn from the work of these scholars to develop relational communication only during the past thirty years. I would never devalue the work of communication scholars who have explored and developed relational communication over the past three decades; however, I do believe it is important for communication students to appreciate the many scholars from multiple disciplines who have contributed to this work.

While the extensive overview of scholarly work presented in this reading may seem overwhelming at times, don't lose sight of the "big picture" as you digest this material. My hope is that you will gain an appreciation for the breadth of disciplines that lead to the development of the relational perspective of human communication. As you read about the work of individual scholars, tie their terminology, concepts, and research to the ten premises Julia Wood discusses in Chapter 3. Since Wood draws from the work of these scholars, you will find a direct link to the premises she develops in her chapter. Finally, after you complete the reading, step back to reflect on how the relational perspective of human communication may provide valuable insight into the understanding of personal relationships in your life.

Theoretical Foundations

L. Edna Rogers and Valentin Escudero

L. Edna Rogers
University of Utah

Valentin Escudero
University of La Coruña

Social relationships lie at the heart of our humanness, and in turn, communication lies at the heart of our relationships. In constructing the social worlds we inhabit, there is an intimate tie between communication and relationship, with each interwoven in the other. This interconnection represents an underlying premise of the relational communication perspective. Thus, while it is assumed that our relationships contextualize and influence our lives, it is also assumed that our relationships are constituted and shaped through our communication processes.

Communication is seen as the life-giving, social-sustaining essence of relationships, the interactive process by which relationships come into being, take shape, are built up or torn down in the ongoing ebb and flow of their evolutionary course. Viewed from this perspective, communication is not of a singular nature, but a joint, social adventure, with relationships continually in process, malleable and changeable, tranquil at times, and at times, tenuous. Negotiating relationships, as McCall and Simmons (1966) suggested, is often a "hazardous gamble" (p. 201), with the making and unmaking of relationships in the hands—and hearts—of the makers. Relationships form the "bedrock" of our social existence, yet rest on the "shifting sands" of our communicative behaviors.

The basic, constitutive nature of communication was captured, some years ago, in a statement by Duncan (1967), "We do not relate and then talk, but we relate in talk" (p. 249). More recently, Shotter (1993) expanded the idea that "our ways of talking are formative of social relations" (p. 10) by noting the inherent contingencies of the communicative process when he stated, "to talk in new ways, is to 'construct' new forms of social relation, and, to construct new forms of social relation ... is to construct new ways of being" (p. 9). Not only do our relationships, but the very essence of our being, lie within our ways of talking. Among relational scholars, even though guided by different perspectives, there is a growing consensus on the constitutive quality of communication and the social implications of our talk.

The once, somewhat radical notion expressed by Berger and Kellner (1964) that "in a fundamental sense it can be said that one converses one's way through life" (p. 4) such that relationships can be viewed as "ongoing conversations" (p. 3), has increasingly gained acceptance in contemporary studies of relationships. From the beginning, this idea has been central in the formation of the relational communication perspective. Rooted within the influence of system and cybernetic principles, relational communication, both conceptually and empirically, has focused on the formative, consequential processes of communication. As the name implies, relational communication represents a communication-based, interactional approach to the study of personal and social relationships.

The relational perspective, also known as the pragmatic (Fisher, 1978) or interactional (Watzlawick & Weakland, 1977) perspective of human communication, is grounded within an epistemology that places primary importance on the study of interaction, or in the words of Bateson (1979), on "the pattern which connects" (p. 8). The relational approach represents a conceptual and analytical shift from the study of individual acts, per se, to the study of system-level qualities of interactions that evolve from ongoing combinations of communicative behaviors into transactional patterns that in turn, combine into larger, patterns of relational form.

With this perspective, relationships are viewed as the emergent social structurings that are created and defined by the relational members' communication patterns with one another. Through the process of message exchange, system members reciprocally define self in relation to other, and simultaneously, define the interactive nature of their relationship. In playing out these everyday social dramas of relationships, offered definitions can be resisted, modified, accepted, or ignored. Thus, each member is seen as a necessary part of the whole, actively influencing one another with their individual lines of action, yet the "socialness" of the drama resides in the mutually constructed patterns of relationship.

Elaborating on this view, relationships are visualized as unfolding, moving "art forms," analogous to a relational dance, creatively shaped by the temporal patterning of the participants as they flow in and around, toward and against and away from one another via their communicative behaviors. When we think of relationships, we think of a coming together, of interrelating, of acting in awareness of one another. We often speak of being involved, of connecting with others, developing common threads, forming social bonds, of being tied to one another—of being in a relationship, such that a social unity or wholeness is formed that lies beyond the individual members.

In line with these common ways of speaking, the language of relationships from an interactional perspective is a language of connectedness, temporalness, patternedness, and embeddedness. The inherent connective principle of relationships rests on the interdependency of the relational members and their behaviors, such that each simultaneously influences and is influenced by the other. Whether fleeting or long-term, the members' interrelatedness is instantiated in the temporal, unfolding flow of communication. The jointly produced and reproduced patterns formed in the ongoing interactional processes characterize and define the members' relationship. Enactments of the present merge into more encompassing, contextualizing patterns of relationship that influence future enactments, as well as, remembered pasts. Thus, relationships are continually contextualized by multiple levels of ecological embeddedness of patterns within patterns which are further embedded within and influenced by the sociocultural contexts in which they take place. Grounded within this language of relationships, the relational communication perspective gives primary attention to the connective principles of process, pattern, and form.

This introductory statement on relational communication gives an initial flavor of the perspective's epistemological stance and sets the scene for the extended discussions of the conceptual and methodological focus of the perspective in the chapters to come. In the present chapter, historical influences and conceptual underpinnings prominent in the development of the relational approach are considered, first, within the broad strokes of related social thought, and second, within the finer drawn lines of the founding legacy of relational communication.

Relational Thinking: A Broad View

The theoretical foundations of the relational communication perspective are most clearly linked to the writings of Bateson and those of the early members of the Mental Research Institute (MRI), Jackson, Watzlawick, Weakland, Bavelas, Sluzki, and others, comprising what became commonly known as the Palo Alto Group. However, before turning to these writings, a limited but illustrative selection of earlier work providing a general backdrop to relational thinking, is considered. Thus, this section presents a broad overview within which to situate more contemporary thinking about relationships.

In a recent essay reviewing historical frames of relational thought, Stewart (1998) suggested a philosophical foregrounding of relational thinking is evident in the (5th century B.C.) ontological claims of the sophists in contrast with those of the more established and long privileged, Aristotelean view. This contrast may have provided one of the earliest clashes between viewing "reality" as constructed, relative, and changeable versus objective, ordered, and absolute. These fundamental differences, as Stewart and others point out, are still evident in current communication research and continue to form the basis of contemporary metatheoretical and methodological debates.

However, in tracing a less distant past of socially oriented thought, we move much further up in history (and perhaps, more familiar territory) to Feuerbach's (1843) philosophical view of the essential socialness of human experience. In his critique of Hegelian idealism which held that the mind or spirit (Geist) was the only true reality, Feuerbach turned Hegel's ontology of ascending stages of self-consciousness on its head by arguing that the essence of our humanness lies not in the idealistic, higher realm of absolute reason, but in the lived, social relationships of "man-to-man." Although Feuerbach's argument was also subject to criticism (most notably by Marx, 1845, who argued that Feuerbach did not take the thrust of his critique far enough), Feuerbach's philosophical views represented a pivotal move toward a human experience-based, social ontology (Theunissen, 1984). In opposition to the prevailing one-sided orientation, Feuerbach argued the alienating nature and meaninglessness of the socially separated self, and in doing so, emphasized the fundamental emptiness of the concept of self without the complementary other.

The social, relationally bound orientation expressed by Feuerbach, implicating the necessary inclusion of "the other," has been elaborated and extended in a number of later writings, including Buber's philosophical development of the construct of "the between." Rejecting the traditional one-fold view, Buber (1958) saw the human world as twofold, of "being-in-relation" with other. He further saw the twofold, human interconnection being located in talk, in word pairs, and argued that language, conceived of as dialogue, is the locus of human reality. In his view, the inherent "one with the other" quality of dialogue, rests not in one, nor in the other, but in "the between" (Buber, 1965, p. 203). Buber's view is in close concert with the recently discovered translinguistic or dialogic ideas of Bakhtin (1986) and Volosinov (1973), in that words express "the one in relation to the other" much like a "bridge thrown between" oneself and the other (p. 86). Through dialogue, a one-with-other unity of differentiated self and other is simultaneously formed.

Both of these lines of thought place dialogue at the center of our "interhuman" relations with others. Each emphasizes the co-constructed, connective qualities of language. Similar to Buber, Volosinov (1973) clarified the significance of language by stating that it is not found in "the abstract system of linguistic forms, not the isolated monologic utterance, and not the psychophysiological act of its implementation, but the social event of verbal interaction implemented in an utterance or utterances" (p. 94), which form "the reciprocal relationship between speaker and listener' (p. 85). The turn toward viewing communication as dialogue is increasingly evident in contemporary work (e.g., Baxter & Montgomery, 1996; Cronen, 1995; Rawlins, 1992; Shotter, 1993).

The foregoing ideas flow easily into those of Simmel (1950) and his overriding focus on the communicative "forms of sociation" (p. 41). For Simmel, all social phenomena find their moorings in the emergent structuring of everyday social interaction, whether taking the form of social play, aesthetics, conflict, group cohesion, or institutional ritual. And at the most general level, Simmel (1950) likewise asserts, it is only through the interactions with others that society itself is possible. Based on this view, Simmel argued that "the description of the forms of interaction is the science of society in its strictest and most essential sense" (pp. 21-22); thus, interaction was seen as the basis of social order and the legitimate arena for the study of social relations.

Simmel's wide ranging analysis of social life was marked by a keen sensitivity of the less obvious, yet observable interaction forms which constituted principles of social unity. To capture these principles, Simmel analytically distinguished forms of sociation (interaction) from the content of the interaction. Their complementary nature was clear, but so too was the observation that interaction always presents itself in some form, whereas a particular form can be enacted in any number of ways of specific content. Thus, in order to develop conceptual level descriptions on which to construct theories of social relationships, Simmel argued the necessity of analytically focusing on the forms of sociation.

Not only did Simmel's distinction between content and form prefigure Bateson's duality of message level meaning, but importantly, Simmel (writing in the late 1800s, early 1900s) recognized the cybernetic principles of the recursive, multiple-leveled features of interaction. He spoke of the circularity of social life in his descriptions of the simultaneous interdependency of the visible and invisible threads that are woven between persons in the interaction process. In his words, relationships "develop upon the basis of reciprocal knowledge and this knowledge upon the basis of the actual relations [interactions]" (1950, p. 309). Simmel (1950) saw this "unity into which both elements fuse" as "one of the deep-lying circuits of intellectual life where an element presupposes a second element which yet, in turn, presupposes the first." In their alternation, interaction is revealed as "where being and conceiving make their mysterious unity empirically felt" (p. 309).

Simmel's approach is not centered on the individual, yet takes into account the invisible threads, "pictures of each in the other," that arise out of and influence the interaction, nor centered on the heavy hand of society, although its spatial-temporal influence is recognized, but rather on the socially formed qualities of the interactive processes. And for Simmel, these forms are mutually constructed in the most common manner of all social life, in conversation. Thus, similar to Buber (a student of Simmel's), the focal point of Simmel's work, forms of sociation, resides in the social unity of "the between."

Simmel's influence has been extensive, both in Europe and the early development of American sociology and the Chicago School. In particular, his ideas were evident in the work of the School's early founders, Park, Burgess, Thomas, and Mead, among others, and their theories of human conduct, urban ecology, family relations, and notably, symbolic interaction with the locus of the self rooted in interaction. As articulated by Mead (1934), "selves must be accounted for in terms of the social process, and in terms of communication" (p. 49). Further, Simmel's insights into the dynamics of relationships—dyadic, triadic, and larger group differences, the unique vulnerability of intimate relations, the strain toward totality, coalition formation, to name but a few—have also found a prominent place in later work, including Goffman's (1959, 1967) Interaction studies of social order, McCall and Simmons' (1966) role-identity model, Coser's (1956) theory of conflict, Caplow's (1968) coalition analysis, and as well, relational communication.

While recognizing the breadth of social thought that could be called upon to exemplify relational thinking, for this overview, a final consideration of earlier work is Weber's classic delineation of the basic elements of social relationships, stemming from his distinction between social action and social interaction. Weber (1947), a contemporary of Simmel, who at times, was both an advocate and critic of Simmel, but nevertheless influenced by him, defined the term social relationship as:

> the behavior of a plurality of actors in so far as ... the actions of each takes account of that of the others; the social relationship thus consists entirely and exclusively in the existence of a probability that there will be, in some meaningfully understandable sense, a course of social action. (p. 118)

In Weber's view, the defining criteria for speaking of a social relationship require "at least a minimum of mutual orientation" between the actors which "can and usually will have consequences for the course of action and the form of the relationship," and a probability of continuing social interaction, "which constitutes the 'existence' of the social relationship" (p. 119).

McCall (1970), in his work on relationships, drew specifically on Weber's definition in stating that "a relationship is at base, the existence of a substantial probability of interaction between two persons" (p. 4), with the type of social bonds uniting the members influencing the "form the interaction will likely assume" (p. 4).

McCall (1970, 1988) and McCall and Simmons (1991) viewed relationships as forms of social organization and argue the necessity (and difficulty) of taking into account the multiple levels of analysis in studying relationships. In their "role-identity" model (McCall & Simmons, 1966), they include both interpretive and behavioral dimensions in explicating the negotiated, interactional dynamics of relationships.

Although Weber is typically not cited, contemporary studies that provide a definition of relationship (which is somewhat rare) commonly include definitional features outlined by Weber. For instance, Hinde (1997) described a relationship as involving "a series of interactions between two people, involving interchanges over an extended period of time" which involve "some degree of mutuality, in the sense that the behaviour of each takes some account of the behaviour of the other" and there is "some degree of continuity between the successive interactions" (pp. 37-38). A relationship "is not a static entity but a process in continuous creation through time" (Hinde, 1987, p. 38). Hinde (1997) distinguished, as did Weber, a fleeting, singular encounter from a relationship which is based on a series of interactions. "A relationship exists only when the probable course of future interactions between the participants differs from that between strangers" (p. 38).

As additional definitional illustrations, Kelley et al. (1983) defined close relationships as the interconnections between two people's interactions that are based on "strong, frequent, and diverse interdependence that lasts over a considerable period of time" (p. 38). In contrast, weakly connected, infrequent, limited and fleeting interactions characterize distant relationships. Wilmot's (1995) description of a relationship builds on, at base, a mutual recognition of being perceived (Level 1) to the cumulative interactions of the participants (Level 11) which shape future interactions. In Wilmot's words, "A relationship emerges from its history and continually reemerges and transforms over time ..." (p. 3). Or more simply put, Gottman (1982) stated, "a relationship consists of the temporal forms that are created when two people are together" (p. 943). Although phrased differently, core definitional features identified by Weber are evident in these more contemporary, conceptual definitions of relationships.

By taking a broad view, we find, with even this brief excursion into past lines of social thought, a history of relational thinking that has been longer in the making than often realized, and one that richly contexualizes and in many ways complements, present relational views. Much of the work cited has had its particular influence felt in our thinking about how to study relationships relationally. Clearly, ideas rarely, if ever, stand alone, but are embedded within other ideas. With this thought, and a broader historical view as background, we now turn to a more closely tied set of influences on the development of the relational communication perspective.

Relational Communication: A Closer View

The legacy on which the relational communication perspective rests is the movement from an epistemology of objects to an epistemology of pattern, from a focus on "things," to a focus on relationships. This paradigmatic shift has been the result of multiple, evolving lines of influence. To borrow from the title of Bateson's 1972 volume, slightly rephrased, this movement represents steps to an ecology of form, with each of the steps representing a recalibration of thinking, based in large part on a stream of ideas brought into awareness with the advent of general systems theory, information theory, and cybernetics.

Traditionally, theoretical concerns and research practices in communication were firmly entrenched within the established epistemology of objects, a way of knowing which accords primary importance to the study of singular events or individual entities. In the interpersonal area of study this was notably the case with many of the early communication models borrowed from psychology. In contrast, the relational perspective is founded on an epistemology of form, an approach that gives prominence to interaction patterns over individual acts, and interrelationships over unilateral cause. In describing these differences, Dell (1983) noted that with a shift in attention to "shapes, forms and relations" (p. 251), objects become inseparable from the pattern within which they are embedded, and thus, of secondary interest while pattern becomes primary. Dell also points out that the word real, rooted in the Latin word res meaning thing, is commonly associated with an object-focused perspective, such as the idea of a "real" reality. Again in contrast, with a relational perspective realities are seen as punctuated and constructed, and when viewed within different frames, readily changeable. In title and text, Watzlawick's (1976) book, *How Real Is Real?*, underscored the idea of multiple realities, and cautions against the common delusion "that there is only one reality" (p. xi).

The development of a relational view necessitated not simply a modification of traditional modes of thought, but a fully reformulated line of thought. Bateson (1972), early on criticized the behavioral sciences for being tied far too long to the wrong half of the ancient substance—form dichotomy. In modeling classical physics, the central focus of study has been on substance, but in Bateson's view "mental process, ideas, communication, organization, differentiation, pattern and so on, are matters of form rather than substance" (p. xxv). Thus, Bateson (1951) argued that a reversal in thinking was necessary for a "new order of communication" to emerge (p. 209). With a focus on form, emphasis is placed on the centrality of communication behavior, interactive processes, emergent patterns and evolving, multileveled orders of pattern. An ecology of form based on patterns that connect was fundamental to what Bateson (1972) termed ecological wisdom, "knowledge of the larger interactive system" (p. 433).

Within this epistemological frame, a relationship is seen, in the most primary sense, as "a connective principle" (Ellis, 1981, p. 220), based on the interrelatedness of difference. Differences come into being by drawing distinctions (Spencer-Brown, 1973); relationships come into being by drawing distinctions together. Only in terms of how distinctions "stand in relation" to one another, can we speak of relationship. The relationship lies in the connection. Systemic thinking which underlies an epistemology of form, is "premised upon the differentiation and interaction of parts" (Bateson, 1979, p. 100). Thus, by drawing communicative enactments together in more encompassing patterns, more of the holistic quality of the relationship comes into being.

What Bateson (1979) labeled "double description," he saw as necessary for depicting relational pattern. In typical style (or perhaps this is a pattern), Bateson by analogy illustrates this process.

> It is correct (and a great improvement) to begin to think of the two parties to the interaction as two eyes, each giving a monocular view of what goes on and, together giving a binocular view in depth. This double description is the relationship. (p. 142)

As two eyes in combination generate a binocular view, combined actions generate pattern and relationship. Double description involves the combining of a unit of action or interaction with another unit to form a more encompassing unit of pattern description. With the interweaving of successive levels of double description, more global patterns evolve.

The formulation of the basic constructs of symmetry and complementarity by Bateson in the early 1930s, were based on double descriptions of interaction. Bateson's early career was spent doing anthropological field work among the Iatmul and Balinese on a research project investigating culture contact and change. From the beginning, Bateson resisted the accepted research strategy of the time of using a priori categories for describing culture in terms of basic social institutions. He sought a more grounded approach based on diachronic behavioral descriptions of cultural practices as an alternative to the procedures outlined by the research granting committee. His 1935 writing of "Culture Contact and Schismogenesis" represents an interesting mix of a younger scholar's deference and yet fully articulated resistance to the sponsoring Social Science Research Council's approach. Bateson's suggestion was to study the problem (of acculturation) first, since "the problem itself remains vague" (p. 178), and then attempt a reasoned answer based on the conceptual schemes that emerge from detailed behavioral observations, rather than apply a predetermined framework onto behaviors. Bateson (1935) pointed out that a priori strategies overlook the holistic, overlapping nature of cultural systems; he argued the questionable, If not fallacious, assumption that cultural traits can be classified under a single social institutional category, as indicated in the following quote:

> our categories "religious, economic," etc, are not real subdivisions which are present in the cultures which we study, but are merely abstractions which we make for our own convenience when we set out to describe cultures.... In handling such abstractions we must be careful to avoid Whitehead's 'fallacy of misplaced concreteness' ... (p. 179)

It was in this 1935 article that Bateson first described the process of schismogenesis and the concepts of symmetry and complementarity as a way of differentiating behavior patterns within and between culture groups. With the publication of Naven (1936), Bateson's analytical attention moved away from group-based differentiation of cultural configurations toward a more dyadic application of these concepts focused on the "reactions of individuals to the reactions of other individuals," with schismogenesis referring to the potential process of increased differentiation "resulting from cumulative interaction between individuals" (1936, p. 175). (See Rogers, 1981, for details on the evolution of these concepts.) Bateson (1979) identified symmetry as "those forms of interaction that could be described in terms of competition, rivalry, mutual emulation, and so on," and complementarity as "interactional sequences in which the actions of A and B were different but mutually fitted each other (e.g. dominance-submission, exhibition-spectatorship, dependence-nurturance)" (p. 208). In depicting symmetrical patterns the participants' communicative behaviors mirror one another, such as in exchanges of boasting/boasting, opposing/opposing, agreeing/agreeing. With complementary patterns, the participants' behaviors are maximally different, for example, assertion/submission, question/answer, giving/ receiving, and so on.

In these early writings, Bateson also introduced the initial idea of "higher" orders of pattern by combining patterns with patterns, as illustrated with his application of the concept of reciprocity. One form of reciprocity, termed reciprocal complementarity, refers to the sequential reversal of the participants' position in a complementary pattern; another form described by Bateson, refers to the pattern combination of symmetry and complementarity which Lederer and Jackson (1968) later termed a "parallel" pattern of relationship. In either case, Bateson (1935) indicated that a pattern of reciprocity checks the progressive tendency toward schismogenesis by being "compensated and balanced within itself" (p. 182). Keeney (1983) cited an analogy given by Bateson using the marital system as an example of this self-regulating process in which Bateson suggested:

> If the marriage becomes too complementary, you can put them on a tennis court and they'll feel better. Or if it becomes too symmetrical or rivalrous, you just wait for one of them to sprain an ankle and then they'll both feel better. (p. 40)

Although Bateson's original formulation of these interaction concepts was at a time prior to the onset of the cybernetic "revolution," his process-based analysis of pattern was in that direction; as Bateson (1972) reflected, "The writing of Naven had brought me to the very edge of what later became cybernetics" (p. x). Bateson credited the series of Macy Conferences held during the 1940s and early 1950s on cybernetics as being highly influential on his subsequent thinking (Bateson & Mead, 1976).

The period following World War II was a time when the influx of ideas from cybernetics, along with information theory and general systems theory, was being felt across the sciences, from biology to mathematics, and as well, in communication. The confluence of these related perspectives ushered in a heightened period of paradigmatic rethinking of prior modes of thought. The fundamental reordering of conceptual and analytical concern was the movement from substance to organization, from energy to information. Systems theory (von Bertalanffy, 1968) provided a general set of organizing principles which could be applied to any system including social systems. These principles centered on the integration of interdependent component parts into patterns of multileveled, unified wholes, which cannot be reduced to, nor explained by the separate, individual parts. Systemic thinking views "the world in terms of relationship and integration" (Capra,

1982, p. 266), where "form becomes associated with process, interrelation with interaction, and opposites are unified through oscillation" (p. 267).

From cybernetics (Wiener, 1948) and information theory (Shannon & Weaver, 1949) came new insights into how information processing occurs within systems, and importantly, their implications for human communication systems. The cybernetic principle of self-organizing processes immanent in maintaining system wholeness rests on the ongoing oscillations of stability and change, a dialectic of oppositions in which each promotes the other, creating a potential state of system flux. The interplay of these system dynamics are governed through the flow of feedback information occurring within the system. Thus, in terms of the cybernetic processes of self-regulation, a system is continually informing itself about itself through recursively ordered, feedback loops of "messages-in-circuit" between and among the system components. As with systems theory, the generalized nature of cybernetic principles allows their application across systems.

For instance, in the study of family systems, Jackson (1965) saw the value of a cybernetic approach and proposed that the family be viewed as a "self-regulating system" guided by family rules. Kantor and Lehr (1975) in their conceptual model of the family, described the family as "primarily an information processing system" with "distance regulation" being the basic information processed. In their view, families, as all social systems, are continually informing their members through the communicative process of interaction as to "what constitutes a proper and optimal distance" (p. 222) both within and outside the family boundaries, along a multiple of relational dimensions, emotional, ideological, spatial, temporal, power, etc. The application of a systemic-cybernetic approach significantly alters the modeling of communication processes, with unidirectional cause-effect models replaced by cyclic models of patterned interaction. With this refraining, different types of questions arise, such as those suggested by Bavelas and Segal (1982) which ask: "What circles are happening in this family? Are there behaviors that lead to other behaviors that lead back to themselves?" (pp. 103-104).

The contributions of information theory are readily apparent in the development of communication technology (Rogers, 1994) and early message models (Berlo, 1960), but as well in other developments in communication. Building off the concept of entropy (uncertainty), information theory (Shannon & Weaver, 1949) is noted for the mathematically derived method of measuring the amount of information of a given message in relation to the level of redundancy within the communication system. Redundancy is equated with the degree of organization (i.e., predictability) exhibited in the system. By considering the level of redundancy of a system over time, information theory provided a basic approach for analyzing communication systems as stochastic processes in terms of the probability of a system moving to a given state (pattern) from a prior state (Parks, Farace, Rogers, Albrecht, & Abbot, 1976). The utility of the Markov chain model of analysis is demonstrated in the research chapters in Part II. The sequential analysis of interaction, critical for describing relational patterning, was a formidable challenge in the 1970s when few options existed. Fortunately, a number of techniques for analyzing sequentially ordered data have since been developed (see chap. 3).

An additional aspect of the work on information theory, although perhaps less well recognized, is that it provided the context for Bateson's formulation of levels of message meaning. Based on the type of information (data) utilized by different computer systems, communication engineers distinguished three types of information transformation, identified as digital, analogic, and formal relation codifications. The levels of abstraction inherent in these distinctions promoted a clearer recognition of the different forms and functions of message behavior, and importantly, that messages simultaneously "give off" meaning at multiple levels.

In terms of these codified differences, Bateson (1951) shaped his conceptual distinctions of message meaning levels. In Bateson's words, "Whatever communication we consider, be it the transmission of impulses in a neural system or the transmission of words in a conversation, it is evident that every message in transit has two sorts of meaning" (p. 179). He also introduced the more general, global term of metacommunication, defined as "communication about communication," which he further described as "all the exchanged cues and propositions about (a) codification and (b) relationship between the communicators" (p. 209). Using the language of information theory and cybernetics, Bateson referred to the informational or content meaning of a message as "report," and the contexualizing instructional or relational meaning of a message as "command." Thus, the report (content) level of meaning provides representational, digital information which is simultaneously contextualized by the presentational, analogic form of information provided by the command (relational) level of meaning. It is at the higher, meta levels of relational meaning that participants in a communication system present and negotiate definitions of one another and their relationship, and where, in interpersonal and intimate relationships, these co-defined patterns matter the most. As Bateson (1972) later emphasized, what we humans care most about are our patterns of relationship, "where we stand in love, hate, dependency, trust, and similar abstractions vis à vis somebody else. This is where it hurts us to be put in the wrong" (p. 470).

The concept of relationship implies a meta distinction. Bateson (1972) drew on Russell's theory of logical types to further frame the meaning of meta level distinctions, which he described as "the relation between classes of different logical type" (p. 307). However, rather than viewing logical types as a discrete hierarchy of classes, Bateson (1979) later and more appropriately referred to logical typing as "orders of recursiveness" (p. 218). This view, in line with cybernetic thinking, led to his description of the ecological patterning of communication as a dialectic of process and form, with encompassing levels of pattern emerging from the cyclic movement from process to form and back to process, creating circling spirals of meta level patterns. (It should be noted that Bateson did not use the theory of logical types as an injunction against paradox, as did Russell, but rather built on the paradoxical nature of communication for developing theories, for example, of play, learning, and double bind.)

Reflecting on his work, Bateson (1979) indicated that "my procedures of inquiry were punctuated by an alternation between classification and the description of process. I had proceeded, without conscious planning, up an alternating ladder from description to the vocabulary of typology" (p. 209). He refers to this "back and forth" movement, from descriptions of process to classifications of form, as a recursively ordered "zigzag ladder," with each diagonal step embedded, within the ascending levels of description and classification of process and form. Thus, in the process of communication, descriptions of actions form categories of action, actions combine into interactions which form patterns (classifications) of interaction, and so on, with patterns combining into broader descriptions of relational form. Simultaneously, process shapes form and form shapes process. In this manner, the participants' interactions create the defining qualities of their relationship, and these qualities influence the ongoing defining interactional processes in a continuous dialectic of process and form.

From the breadth of ideas put forward by Bateson, the most fundamental in the development of the relational perspective were: the primary focus placed on communication, the meta level conceptual distinctions of content and relational message meaning, the dialectic of process and form, double description and the formulation of symmetrical and complementary patterns of interaction. Yet, for communication and relational scholars, Bateson's ideas remained out of view, and in a sense, lay dormant for many years. For example, the time lapse between Bateson's original formulation of symmetry and complementarity (which are now common fare in communication texts) and any reference to these constructs by communication researchers was approximately 35 years.

It wasn't until Bateson's association with members of the Palo Alto-based Mental Research Institute (MRI) during the 1950s, when working on a research project in Menlo Park, that his ideas began to receive wider attention among family researchers and therapists, and this awareness came largely through the writings of members of MRI. (See Wilder-Mott and Weakland, 1981, for a history of this period.) And it wasn't until the writing of The Pragmatics of Human Communication by Watzlawick, Beavin, and Jackson (1967) that communication scholars became more aware of these ideas.

The Pragmatics volume has had a pronounced influence not only on interpersonal communication, but on the discipline of communication as a whole. Since its publication, it has been one of the most widely cited texts in the field of communication. From the beginning, it served as a catalyst for a qualitative shift in thinking about communication and relationships. Drawing on a wide range of resources and illustrations in expanding Bateson's work, the authors of Pragmatics provided an accessible, integrated communication perspective for studying human relationships. This text became and remains the best know [sic] treatise on the conceptual foundations of the relational communication perspective.

The pragmatic perspective offered an alternative view of communication to the one traditionally taken, and that was to focus on communication itself, in other words, to focus on the observable behavioral processes of interaction, rather than on the cognitive, intrapsychic aspects of the individuals involved. The goal was not to supplant the value of individual-based theories, but to treat the interactors' behaviors as primary data and the locus of communication-based theories. In actuality, behavior is the basic source of data. As Sigman (1998) noted, "All there really is (for us as humans to experience and for us as researchers to study) is communication behavior" (p. 66). In taking an interactional stance, the perspective proffered a fundamental change in the unit of analysis and thus, the basis of explanation, from the inferred attributes of the individuals to the observable properties of their interaction. This seemingly simple idea, analogous to a figure-ground reversal (Bavelas & Segal, 1982) of bringing the relationship up-front as figure with the individuals receding into the background, was nevertheless profound in its implications.

The crux of these implications are presented in Watzlawick et al.'s (1967) axiomatic propositions, which form the central core of the pragmatic perspective. Although these were put forward as tentative propositions, in large part these well-known and oft-cited axioms have stood the test of time. Perhaps one reading of this is the fact that the axioms continue to spark debate on fundamental issues, such as the question of communication intentionality (Bavelas, 1990; Motley, 1990), but more solid evidence is provided by the programs of research described in the second part of the present volume.

Each of the five axioms involves a contextual frame, and each is interrelated with the others. To review briefly, the first underscores the social context of communication in that not all behavior is communicative in nature, but behavior "in an interactional situation has message value, i.e., is communication," that is, reciprocally influence others (Watzlawick et al., 1967, pp. 48-49). The second axiom refers to the "report/command" levels of message meaning, in which the meta level of relational meaning contextualizes the content meaning. In a related manner, the "digital/analogical" axiom refers to the duality of message codes, such that the digital is always contextualized by the analogical mode. Yet, the complexity is double-fold, in that the digital mode, while always analogically contextualized, can also "comment on" and thus, serve as a meta level contextualization of both the digital and analogical aspects of messages. The proposition that the nature of the relationship is contingent on "punctuation" takes into account that how an ongoing sequence of communicative behavior is framed or organized influences the message meaning. And the final axiom, proposes that symmetry and complementarity, based on the similarity or difference of the communicational interchanges, represent two general patterns of relationship. Through the extended explication and illustration of these basic axioms, the Pragmatics volume provided a window into how one might, research-wise, put a pragmatic, relational perspective into effect.

Based on these conceptual premises, a major part of the early work in relational communication was the development of a transactional language of relationship and a methodology for indexing communication processes at this level. For, as Jackson (1965) stated, "It is only when we attend to transactions between individuals as primary data that a qualitative shift in conceptual framework can be achieved" (p. 4). The constructs of symmetry and complementarity, in particular, served as prototypes of the necessary paradigmatic shift from single message variables to transactional level measures. A full explication of these methodological procedures is taken up in the following chapter.

The main theoretical guide for relational communication research has been the general principles of systems theory and cybernetics which emphasize the interdependency of relational members and the cyclic informative processes by which members establish, maintain, modify or redefine their relationship. A major theoretical supposition is the relational functionality of relatively flexible patterns of interaction which simultaneously rest on and encourage a dialectic interplay along the various dimensions of interrelating. Applied to interpersonal relationships, this proposition holds that viable relations will manifest patterns of communication that offer sufficient confirmation and acceptance of the members' reciprocal relational definitions for producing relatively predictable pattern configurations, yet at the same time allow sufficient pattern modification and alternation to fit fluctuating relational dynamics and changing contexts and circumstances. In contrast, it is predicted that overly redundant patterns of interaction will contain less potential for negotiating accommodation and change and will be associated with negative relational evaluations and outcomes. It is also assumed that insufficient patternedness (i.e., chaos) will likewise be related to negative relationship consequences. As Bateson suggests, patterns of extremes are always toxic. Thus, it is proposed that optimal or adequately functioning systems develop and maintain patterns of connectedness, but not over amounts of chaotic processes nor interactional redundancy.

Yet there is always present the potential movement toward what Bateson called the "tyranny of pattern," as illustrated by patterns of escalating symmetry and rigid complementarity. Escalating symmetry results in unsettled relational definitions and instability whereas rigid complementarity leads to oversettled, stifling stability. Relational processes contain within themselves the potential seeds of their own demise, what builds them up may come like a cancer to tear them down (Simmel, 1950). Recurring patterns and the resulting cumulative differentiation, as described earlier, have schismogenetic tendencies (Bateson, 1936). Over time, there is a progressive potential to move toward "more of the same" (Watzlawick, Weakland, & Fisch, 1974). This tendency toward more of the same and the difficulty in counterbalancing this process are further projected to be more likely the more intimate the relationship. Workable relationships are theorized to evidence the dialectic fluidity of self-correcting cybernetic processes that counter the tendencies toward schismogenesis and overly redundant patterns of interaction.

Conclusion

The goal of this chapter was to provide an historical and conceptual context within which to place the development of the relational communication perspective. In tracing the movement of relational thinking, we find in both earlier and more contemporary thought a decided turn toward a social, communication-centered approach to the study of human relationships. The unfolding of the ideas put forward in this review, which form the foundational roots of relational communication, each in their own way say something about the social, systemic, temporal, circular, reflexive, multileveled complexities of communication. The general confluence, or coming together of these conceptual influences converge on the central ideas of process and form.

The relational communication perspective offers an interactional approach for studying these constitutive and formative aspects of relationships. Although it is one thing to argue the importance of studying interaction, it is quite another to put the argument into action. The next two chapters address the methodological and analytic procedures involved in putting into action the research application of the relational communication approach.

Consider this . . .

- As a paradigm for viewing relationships, how does the relational perspective of human communication differ from the linear perspective of human communication?
- Given what you learned about Systems Theory in Chapter 2 of Julia Wood's text, how is the relational perspective of human communication similar to that theory as a framework for studying personal relationships? What concepts are relevant for the study of both systems and relationships?
- Briefly describe what you consider to be three key concepts that provide valuable insight into understanding personal relationships from the relational perspective.
- Using a significant personal relationship in your life as the basis for your analysis, explain how those three key concepts provide you valuable insight into understanding the nature of your relationship.

References

Bakhtin, M. (1986). *Speech genres and other late essays* (V. W. McGee, Trans.). Austin: University of Texas Press.

Bateson, G. (1935). Culture, contact and schismogenesis. *Man, 35,* 178-183.

Bateson, G. (1936). *Naven.* Cambridge, England: Cambridge University Press.

Bateson, G. (1951). Information and codification: A philosophical approach. In J. Ruesch & G. Bateson (Eds.), *Communication: The social matrix of psychiatry* (pp. 168-211). New York: Norton.

Bateson, G. (1972). *Steps to an ecology of mind.* New York: Ballantine Books.

Bateson, G. (1979). *Mind and nature: A necessary unity.* New York: Bantam, Books.

Bateson, G., & Mead, M. (1976). For god's sake, Margaret. *Coevolution Quarterly, 10,* 32-44.

Bavelas, J. B. (1990). Behaving and communicating: A reply to Motley. *Western Journal of Speech Communication, 54,* 593-602.

Bavelas, J. B., & Segal, L. (1982). Family systems theory: Background and implications. *Journal of Communication, 32,* 99-107.

Baxter, L., & Montgomery, B. (1996). *Relating: Dialogues and dialectics.* New York: Guilford Press.

Berger, P., & Kellner, H. (1964). Marriage and the construction of reality: An exercise in the microsociology of knowledge. *Diogenes, 46,* 1-25.

Berlo, D. (1960). *The process of communication.* New York: Holt, Rinehart & Winston.

Buber, M. (1958). *I and thou* (R. G. Smith, Trans.). New York: Scribner's & Sons.

Buber, M. (1965). *Between man and man* (R. G. Smith, Trans.). New York: Macmillan.

Caplow, T. (1968). *Two against one.* Englewood Cliffs, NJ: Prentice-Hall.

Capra, F. (1982). *The turning point: Science, society and the rising culture.* New York: Simon & Schuster.

Coser, L. (1956). *The functions of social conflict.* New York: Free Press.

Cronen, V. E. (1995). *Coordinated management of meaning: The consequentiality of communication and the recapturing of experience.* In S. J. Sigman (Ed.), The consequentiality of communication. Hillsdale, NJ: Lawrence Erlbaum Associates.

Dell, P. (1983). Researching the family theories of schizophrenia: An exercise in epistemological confusion. In D. Bagarozzi, A. Jurich, & R. Jackson (Eds.), *Marital and family therapy: New perspectives in theory, research and practice* (pp. 236-261). New York: Human Sciences Press.

Duncan, H. D. (1967). The search for a social theory of communication in American sociology. In F. Dance (Ed.), *Human communication theory* (pp. 236-263). New York: Holt, Rinehart & Winston.

Ellis, D. (1981). The epistemology of form. In C. Wilder-Mott & J. Weakland (Eds.), *Rigor and imagination: Essays from the legacy of Gregory Bateson* (pp. 215-230). New York: Praeger.

Feuerbach, L. (1843). *Grundsätze der philosophie der zukunft* [Principles of the philosophy of the future]. Zurich: Zurich & Winterthru.

Fisher, B. A. (1978). *Perspectives on human communication.* New York: Macmillan.

Goffman, E. (1959). *The presentation of self in everyday life.* Garden City, NY: Doubleday.

Goffman, E. (1967). *Interaction ritual: Essays on face-to-face behavior.* New York: Anchor Books.

Gottman, J. (1982). Temporal form: Towards a new language for describing relationships. *Journal of Marriage and the Family, 44,* 943-962.

Hinde, R. (1987). *Individuals, relationships and culture.* Cambridge, England: Cambridge University Press.

Hinde, R. (1997). Relationships: A dialectical perspective. East Sussex, UK: Psychology Press.

Jackson, D. D. (1965). The study of the family. *Family Process, 4,* 1-20.

Kantor, D., & Lehr, W. (1975). *Inside the family.* New York: Harper & Row.

Keeney, B. (1983). *Aesthetics of change.* New York: Guilford Press.

Kelley, H., Berscheid, E., Christensen, A., Harvey, J., Huston, T., Levinger, G., McClintock, E., Peplau, L., & Peterson, D. (1983). *Close relationships.* New York: Freeman.

Lederer, W. J., & Jackson, D. D. (1968). *The mirages of marriage.* New York: Norton.

Marx, K. (1956). Theses on Feuerbach. In T. Bottomore & M. Rubel (Trans.), *Karl Marx: Selected writings in sociology and social philosophy* (pp. 67-70). London: Watts & Co. (Original work published in 1845)

McCall, G. (1970). The social organization of relationships. In G. McCall (Ed.), *Social relationships* (pp. 3-34). Chicago: Aldine.

McCall, G. (1988). The organizational life cycle of relationships. In S. Duck (Ed.), *Handbook of personal relationships* (pp. 467-484). New York: Wiley.

McCall, G., & Simmons, J. (1966). *Identities and interaction.* New York: Free Press.

McCall, G., &Simmons, J. (1991). Levels of analysis: The individual, the dyad and the larger social group. In B. Montgomery & S. Duck (Eds.), *Studying interpersonal interaction* (pp. 56-81). New York: Guilford Press.

Mead, G. H. (1934). *Mind, self and society.* Chicago: University of Chicago Press.

Motley, M. (1990). On whether one can(not) not communicate: An examination via traditional communication postulates. *Western Journal of Speech Communication, 54,* 1-20.

Parks, M., Farace, R., Rogers, L. E., Albrecht, T., & Abbot, R. (1976, April). Stochastic process analysis of relational communication in marital dyads, Paper presented at the International Communication Association meetings, Portland, Oregon.

Rawlins, W. K. (1992). *Friendship matters: Communication, dialectics, and the life course.* Hawthorne, NY: Aldine de Gruyter.

Rogers, E. M. (1994). *A history of communication study.* New York: Free Press.

Rogers, L. E. (1981). Symmetry and complementarity: Evolution and evaluation of an idea. In C. Wilder-Mott & J. Weakland (Eds.), *Rigor and imagination: Essays from the legacy of Gregory Bateson* (pp. 231-251). New York: Praeger.

Shannon, C., & Weaver, W. (1949). *The mathematical theory of communication.* Urbana: University of Illinois Press.

Shotter, J. (1993). *Conversational realities.* Thousand Oaks, CA: Sage.

Sigman, S. J. (1998). Relationships and communication: A social communication and strongly consequential view. In R. L. Conville & L. E. Rogers (Eds.), *The meaning of "relationship" in interpersonal communication* (pp. 47-67). Westport, CT: Praeger.

Simmel, G. (1950). *The sociology of Georg Simmel* (V- Wolff, Trans.). New York: Free Press.

Spencer-Brown, G. (1973). *Laws of form.* New York: Bantam Books.

Stewart, J. (1998). Historical frames of relational perspectives. In R. L. Conville & L. E. Rogers (Eds.), *The meaning of "relationship" in interpersonal communication* (pp. 23-46). Westport, CT: Praeger.

Theunissen, M. (1984). *The other: Studies in the social ontology of Husserl, Heidegger, Sartre and Buber* (C. Macann, Trans.). Cambridge, MA: MIT Press.

Volosinov, V. (1973). *Marxism and the philosophy of language* (L. Matejka & I. R. Titunik, Trans.). Cambridge, MA: Harvard University Press.

von Bertalanffy, L. (1968). *General systems theory: Foundations, development, applications.* New York: Braziller.

Watzlawick, P. (1976). *How real is real?* New York: Random House.

Watzlawick, P., Beavin, J., & Jackson, D. (1967). *Pragmatics of human communication.* New York: Norton.

Watzlawick, P., & Weakland, J. (Eds.). (1977). *The interactional view.* New York: Norton.

Watzlawick P., Weakland, J., & Fisch, R. (1974). *Change: Principles of problem formation and problem resolution.* New York: Norton.

Weber, M. (1947). *The theory of social and economic organization* (A. Henderson & T. Parsons, Trans.). Glencoe, IL: Free Press.

Wiener, N. (1948) *Cybernetics.* Cambridge, MA: MIT Press.

Wilder-Mott, C., & Weakland, J. (Eds.). (1981). *Rigor and imagination: Essays from the legacy of Gregory Bateson.* New York: Praeger.

Wilmot, W. (1995). *Relational communication.* New York: McGraw-Hill.

CHAPTER 4

RELATIONAL CULTURE: THE NUCLEUS OF INTIMACY

In Chapter 4 of her text, *Relational Communication*, Julia Wood begins to explore the unique "culture" participants create in their personal relationships. She discusses the processes, the structures, and the practices that she believes coordinates meaning for individuals who create a relational culture. Before discussing these central dynamics as a way to understand relational culture, Wood identifies five features of relational cultural that serve as her framework for study: 1) relational cultures reflect unique content; 2) relational cultures are systems; 3) relational cultures are created through process; 4) relational cultures are the product of reciprocal, mutual influence; and 5) relational cultures may be healthy or unhealthy. It is this final feature, the unhealthy nature of relational cultures that we will explore in greater depth.

In this reading, "The Dark Side of Jealousy and Envy: Desire, Delusion, Desperation, and Destructive Communication," Guerrero and Andersen explore the impact of unhealthy communication in relationships – often termed the "dark side" of relational communication. Specifically, the authors begin by making distinctions between the emotions of jealousy and envy as they are reflected in relationships. From there, Guerrero and Andersen use examples found in both literature and popular culture to describe the "paradox" society has created in addressing both of these powerful emotions; in many ways, society is both intrigued and fascinated by these emotions while simultaneously repulsed and reviled by them. As you read these familiar examples, reflect on how these images have shaped your views of these two emotions.

While there are both positive and negative aspects of jealousy and envy, Guerrero and Andersen then begin to focus on the "dark side" of these two powerful emotions. First, they explore the intrapersonal effects related to fear, anger, and sadness within our own sense of personal identity. Second, the authors explore the interpersonal effects of jealousy and envy related to uncertainty, suspicion, distrust, competitiveness, retaliation, conflict, and even violence found in personal relationships. They discuss specific communication behaviors often manifested in our personal relationships when the "dark side" of these emotions creates relational dissatisfaction. Finally, note the tables included in the article that identify and describe specific behaviors indicative of destructive communication; these tables offer powerful examples of behavior typically found in unhealthy personal relationships.

Although this reading focuses primarily on the "dark side" of jealousy and envy often found in unhealthy relationships, the authors certainly conclude that only by acknowledging and understanding these behaviors can we begin to address them in relationships. Though not extensive, they offer some discussion of communication strategies that may be used to address these emotions with the goal to create healthier, more satisfying personal relationships in our everyday lives.

Dark Side of Jealousy and Envy: Desire, Delusion, Desperation, and Destructive Communication

Laura K. Guerro
Arizona State University

Peter A. Anderson
Son Diego State University

"Where there's no emotion, there's no motive for violence."

-Spock to Kirk on an episode of Star Trek (Wincelberg, 1966)

A New York Times headline screams: "Texas Executes Man who Killed his Ex-Girlfriend out of Jealousy" (August 15, 1995). For months, television news covered the O. J. Simpson trial, with all its implications for jealousy and domestic violence. Television docudramas have been made about a teenager (Amy Fischer) who maims her alleged lover's wife, a high school student who stabs and kills a popular girl that she idolizes (in *A Friend to Die For*), and a high society La Jolla, CA, wife (Betty Broderick) who kills her husband and his secretary/lover. Movies such as *Fatal Attraction*, which portrays a jealous, obsessive ex-lover's acts of violence, and *The Lion King*, which features Scar's envy of his brother, King Mufasa, and his nephew, Simba, earn millions of box office dollars. Indeed, if Spock had lived on earth in the 20th century, the media accounts of emotion-laden crimes would have provided ample anecdotal evidence for the validity of his statement on the human condition. Moreover, Spock would likely have concluded that jealousy, and to a lesser extent its sister construct, envy, are prime elicitors of violence.

Fortunately, emotions such as jealousy and envy do not always cumulate in violence, and they do not always have negative consequences for individuals and relationships. In fact, these emotions sometimes have positive effects. Jealousy can show love and affection. It can also help a person realize the extent to which he or she cares about another. As Salovey and Roein (1985) stated, "jealousy can be a reasonable and healthy emotion. Sometimes the irrational feelings of jealousy can be taken as signs of caring and devotion, rather than as possessiveness and insecurity" (p. 29). Pines (1992) argued that jealousy can lead people to re-examine their relationships, to stop taking their partners for granted, to feel more passionate toward their partners, and to become more committed to their relationships. In addition, Pines noted that jealousy can function as a sign of commitment, an emotion intensifier, and a relationship protection device.

Like jealousy, envy has positive consequences, such as when it leads to self-improvement and accomplishment. Parrott (1991) distinguished between malicious and nonmalicious jealousy. He noted that Aristotle made a similar distinction between envy that motivates "people to take good things away from others" and envy that motivates "people to improve themselves" (p. 9). As Smith (1991) argued,

"Understanding why some individuals can use unflattering social comparisons as a basis for more constructive, emulative impulses, whereas other[s] seem overcome by destructive, hateful feelings, is an important social-psychological problem" (p. 96).

Despite potential benefits of jealousy and envy, in most situations, these emotions have negative consequences for individuals and their relationships. Jealous or envious individuals typically feel negative emotions, such as fear and/or anger, and worry about the state of their relationships or accomplishments. In more rare cases, physical violence occurs. White and Mullen (1989) summarized the potential negative consequences of romantic jealousy: "Jealousy involves the outrage of an act of infidelity, of disloyalty; it threatens loss of the central relationship; it involves humiliation; it raises an intensely ambivalent eroticism; it escalates interpersonal conflict within the relationship; and it is accompanied by uncertainty, frustration, and helplessness" (p. 233).

In this chapter, we concentrate on the dark side of jealousy and envy by focusing on the negative impact that the experience and expression of these emotions can have on individuals and relationships. The chapter begins by distinguishing jealousy from envy and placing these two emotions in a historical and social context. Then we focus on some of the darker consequences of jealousy and envy. These include intrapersonal reactions, such as feeling anger, fear, or sadness; evaluating oneself as inferior to others; and experiencing lowered self-esteem, as well as interpersonal outcomes, such as loss of trust, competitiveness, aggressive communication, and violence. We also briefly discuss how communication is used to cope more effectively with jealousy and envy.

Distinctions Between Jealousy And Envy

Although jealousy and envy are generally considered to be related, they are distinctly different constructs. Research shows that people tend to view jealousy as the broader construct (see Smith, Kim, & Parrott, 1988) and readily use it to describe feelings that are truly jealous (e.g., feeling hurt that your current dating partner talks on the phone a lot with his ex-girlfriend or boyfriend) as well as those that are envious (e.g., feeling upset because someone at work always upstages you). People who feel jealous tend to experience a variety of emotions, including envy. In fact, Pines and Aronson (1983) asked people to rate how jealous they would feel in situations involving 9 potential rivals (e.g., a family member, someone they knew and found similar to them, or someone they disliked and knew little about). They found that people reported the most intense jealousy when the rival was someone they knew and envied.

Research also suggests that jealousy is a more prototypic emotion than is envy (Shaver, Schwartz, Kirson, & O'Connor, 1987). The words jealousy and zeal share a common etymology, suggesting that fervor and intensity are part of jealous emotion. Jealousy almost always involves emotional experiences such as anger, fear, and sadness. In contrast, envy is less passionate and more cognitive, such as when a person wishes he or he [sic] was as attractive as someone else, but does not feel resentment toward the beautiful person or sadness about one's own shortcomings. Given that jealousy is the broader term, it is not surprising that social scientists have focused more attention on jealousy than envy, especially in the last few decades (Parrott, 1991).

There are several other important distinctions between the sister constructs of jealousy and envy. The two emotions differ in terms of who possesses the desired person or trait, what other emotions and perceptions accompany them, and how society views their experience and expression.

Possession of the Desired Person or Trait

The concept of relationship possession helps distinguish jealousy and envy (Bryson, 1977; Salovey & Rodin, 1989). Generally, jealousy occurs when people feel they are in danger of losing a valued relationship that they already possess. In the case of romantic jealousy, lovers fear losing the love and/or exclusivity they share with their partners. Yet, jealousy is not limited to romantic relationships. Jealousy can occur between friends, coworkers, or family members (Parrott, 1991). Consider the following examples:

> Sarah and Teresa are best friends. They usually spend part of their weekend together going to the movies, to nightclubs, or just talking. Then Teresa meets Ron, falls head over heals in love with him, and starts spending more time with him and less time with Sarah, who fears that she is losing her relationship with Teresa.
>
> Steve is an associate producer at a large television station. He enjoys his work and is extremely proud of his position, especially because he is highly regarded by the executive producer who gives him full autonomy to make programming decisions. Then Rita comes along and impresses the executive producer with her programming expertise.
>
> Bob and Samantha have been married for 5 years when they have their first child. With the birth of their son, Bob begins to feel neglected because Samantha is so busy caring for their new son. It seems to him that all of Samantha's affections are now directed at the newborn.

All of these examples represent ordinary, potential jealousy situations. In each case, Sarah, Steve, and Bob are likely to feel threatened; something they value—whether it be the time they spend with their friend, the work they enjoy doing, or the attention they receive from their spouse—is in jeopardy of being taken away or changed. Notice that in each of these cases, the potentially jealous person perceives that he or she possesses a valued relationship, but is in danger of losing it or at least of having it altered in an undesirable manner. Thus, jealousy involves a threat to a desired, pre-existing relational state.

Envy, in contrast, occurs when a person does not possess a valued commodity, but wishes to possess it. The commodity could be a relationship with someone, a material possession, a position of power or status, or a personal characteristic such as intelligence, humor, or beauty. Parrott (1991) conceptualized envy as occurring "when a person lacks what another has and either desires it or wishes the other did not have it" (p. 4). Envy is strongest when it leads to a negative comparison between oneself and others in an area highly relevant to one's self-concept (Salovey & Rodin, 1989; Salovey & Rothman, 1991). Because envy is derived from the Latin inuidre, which translates as "to see intensively," envy always involves comparing one's own situation to that of a scrutinized other.

In many situations, our self-comparisons to others are negative, but we do not feel envy. For example, when we watch the Olympic games we admire the speed of the sprinters and the grace of the gymnasts, but we do not necessarily envy them. This is especially true if the skills they possess are not in an area that is personally relevant to us. In other words, most of us do not expect to be able to compete with world-class athletes, and we do not long to do so. Instead, we expect to enjoy their performances, to feel happiness at their successes, and disappointment at their defeats. If envy is felt, it is likely to be of the admiring or nonmalicious variety. In contrast, if you were a moderately successful professional golfer in your late 40s, you might be quite envious of younger players, such as Tiger Woods, who have already achieved high levels of success and international recognition. In this case, a comparison is likely to be drawn in a highly relevant area of self-identity.

The following examples further illustrate scenarios that are likely to produce negative self-to-other comparisons and envious feelings:

> Jim studies hard for all his classes. It is important for him to do well because he hopes to get into medical school. His roommate, Mark, however, rarely studies and gets better grades than he does.
>
> Christie is in love with Ryan, yet Ryan does not even notice her. He is too infatuated with Victoria, a beautiful, outgoing woman whom he recently started dating.
>
> Randy works extremely hard to keep a roof over his family and to provide them with life's necessities. He feels resentment toward John, who inherited money from his wealthy family and only has to work part-time.

Notice that in all these cases someone else possesses the commodity (whether it be intelligence, affection from a loved one, or a life of wealth and leisure) that the envious person wishes to possess. Such situations call forth an implicit negative comparison between the envious person and the rival.

Notice also that only two relations are necessary for envy to occur: An envious person who desires something and a rival who possesses the desired commodity. In the case of jealousy, however, there is always a "triangle of relations" (Parrott, 1991, p. 16; see also Farrell, 1980). This is not to say that envy cannot co-occur with jealousy within a triangle of relationships. Indeed, the previous example of Christie, Ryan, and Victoria illustrates that envy can occur within love triangles. In this case, however, Christie does not possess Ryan's affections and she is likely to envy Victoria's ability to attract him to her. In other words, Christie wishes she could trade places with Victoria—a common wish when one is envious. Similarly, people are likely to feel envious if their romantic partner mentions how good looking someone is, although there is no possibility for the partner to become involved with the third party. For instance, a wife may comment that a movie star is gorgeous. Her husband knows that she will almost certainly never meet the handsome actor, so he has no reason to fear losing the relationship to him. He is likely, however, to envy the actor's good looks. Thus, although jealousy and envy are separate phenomena, they can co-occur.

Related Emotions and Perceptions

Research demonstrates that jealousy and envy are qualitatively different emotional experiences. Most definitions of jealousy center on feelings of fear that result from threat. For example, White and Mullen (1989) conceptualized romantic jealousy as "A complex of thoughts, emotions, and actions that follows loss of or threat to self-esteem and/or the existence or quality of the romantic relationship" due to the actual or potential interference of a rival (p. 9). In contrast, most definitions of envy focus on feelings of longing and resentment. Smith, Parrott, and Diener (1990), for instance, demonstrated that feelings of inferiority and resentment are at the heart of the envious experience. Parrott (1991) argued that envy is typically composed of feelings of longing, inferiority, resentment, guilt, and admiration. Berke (1988) stated that "envy is a state of exquisite tension, torment, and ill will provoked by an overwhelming sense of inferiority, impotence, and worthlessness" (p. 19).

Two studies shed further light on these distinctions. Smith et al. (1988) examined people's everyday conceptions of both jealousy and envy. Their research illustrated that people associated jealousy with suspiciousness, rejection, hostility, fear of loss, and hurt. These jealous feelings and reactions involve a triangle of relations. The jealous person may be suspicious that a rival relationship exists, feel rejected in favor of the rival, and fear losing the partner to the rival. In contrast, Smith et al. found envy to associate more strongly with feelings of inferiority, dissatisfaction, self-criticism, and motivation to improve. Only a dyadic comparison is necessary for these reactions to occur.

Parrott and Smith (1993) further demonstrated the qualitative distinctions between jealousy and envy. In this study, self-reported responses (to recalled and hypothetical situations) were adjusted for intensity level because jealousy is typically experienced as a stronger emotion than is envy. When intensity level was controlled, several substantial differences between jealousy and envy emerged. Jealousy was distinguished from envy by higher scores in four areas: (a) distrust, including feeling betrayed, rejected, and suspicious; (b) fear, including feeling worried, anxious, and threatened; (c) uncertainty, including feeling confused about the state of the relationship; and (d) loneliness, including feeling left out and abandoned. Four reactions also differentiated envy from jealousy. Specifically, envious individuals experienced more: (a) disapproval of their own feelings; (b) longing for what another person possesses; (c) motivation to improve oneself; and (d) degradation, which included feeling humiliated and inferior. Insecurity appears to be related to both jealousy and envy. However, the insecurity stemming from jealousy is more strongly focused on uncertainty about the status of one's relationship or position, whereas insecurity associated with envy centers more squarely on one's perceived inferiority to others.

Jealousy and envy may not only produce different emotional reactions and perceptions, but they may also originate in different emotions. Ciabattari (1988) proposed the interesting hypothesis that jealousy and envy originate in love and hate, respectively. According to this view, jealousy (though it may ultimately lead to hate) can only exist when a person loves someone and wants to protect the relationship. In contrast, envy stems from resenting or hating someone for having something you do not possess. If this is true, then the functions that jealousy and envy serve are very different. On the positive side, jealous individuals should strive to protect and maintain their relationships, whereas envious individuals should strive to improve themselves so they are competitive with the rival. On the negative side, jealous individuals may become overly possessive and demanding, whereas envious individuals may strike out against those people who make them feel inferior. Ciabattari's predictions, however, await scientific testing.

Historical Context and Social Significance

Jealousy and envy have different societal meanings, partially because of the historical contexts surrounding them as their meanings evolved. In the following section, we show that both jealousy and envy have social significance and can lead to aggression and violence. We also show that although jealousy and envy are both frequently condemned in our society, envy is generally seen as the more evil culprit, despite being felt with less intensity and leading less often to grave consequences. As Parrott (1991) stated:

> "The hostility that accompanies envy is not socially sanctioned, whereas that accompanying jealousy often is" (p. 79).

The Paradoxical Societal View of Jealousy. Jealousy and its paradoxes have intrigued writers for centuries, as plays such as Shakespeare's *Othello*, operas such as Bizet's Carmen, and novels such as Zola's *The Beast in Man* attest. These historic works, along with the media reports on violence resulting from jealousy, send our society a message that jealousy is a highly dangerous and uncontrollable emotion. Jealousy itself is personified as a "green-eyed monster." The perception that jealousy is an uncontrollable emotion is so powerful that in American courts people who kill their spouses out of jealousy can sometimes claim temporary insanity. In other cases, individuals who kill someone in the heat of jealous passion are convicted of manslaughter rather than second-degree murder (Delgado & Bond, 1993). Salovey and Rodin (1989) noted that the legal definition of manslaughter is as "any intentional killing committed under the influence of extreme mental or emotional disturbance for which there is a reasonable explanation or excuse" (pp. 239-240). Such is one paradox of jealousy: Jealousy-induced violence is reprehensible, but sometimes perceived as justifiable.

Jealousy has always been a two-edged sword—an expression of love on the one hand, of perceived paranoia on the other; positively valued in some relationships, but distressing in others. In *The Immortals*, Korda's (1992) fictional account about John Kennedy's (JFK) alleged affair with Marilyn Monroe, both JFK and Marilyn are portrayed as dealing with the jealousy and suspicion of their respective spouses, Jackie Kennedy and Joe Dimaggio. In one scene, JFK acts jealous when Marilyn mentions other men:

> "You're jealous!" She cried.
>
> "The hell I am."
>
> "You are ... Oh, sweetheart, don't worry. I like a man to be jealous."
>
> "You do? What about Joe? You're always complaining about the fact that he's jealous."
>
> "Oh honey, he's my husband! A jealous husband is no fun at all. A jealous lover is a whole different story." (p. 65)

Like Marilyn, many people have ambivalent attitudes stemming from a paradox between autonomy and commitment (see Baxter, 1988). Jealousy in a committed relationship may be perceived as an unjustified and unnecessary constraint on individual autonomy. Jealousy in an uncommitted relationship may symbolize love and connection.

Societal attitudes about jealousy have been characterized by paradox, ambivalence, and dynamism. Clanton (1989) conducted an intriguing analysis of all magazine articles on jealousy indexed in *The Reader's Guide to Periodical Literature* from 1945 to 1985. He found two very different trends. From 1945 to 1965, jealousy was treated as "proof of love." As Clanton summarized, "virtually all of the articles in popular magazines said that a certain amount of jealousy was natural, proof of love, and good for marriage" (p. 182). Readers were cautioned, however, to avoid irrational displays of emotion. Women, in particular, were told to curb their own emotional expressions of jealousy but to interpret their husband's expression of jealousy as a sign of love and affection. This view is consistent with the idea that jealousy serves as a device to help people retain their mates and protect the relationship (see Buss, 1988). As Delgado and Bond (1993) claimed, historically jealousy has been positively valued" (p. 1337).

From 1970 to 1980, jealousy was depicted in the popular press as a "personality defect" (Clanton, 1989). At this time, people began feeling guilty about being jealous. Jealousy was viewed as evidence that a person was distrustful, suspicious, and/or insecure, as well as unable to properly manage emotion (Stearns, 1989). Moreover, some articles "suggested that jealousy was becoming outdated as society moved into an era of 'liberated' relationships between men and women" (Clanton, 1989, p. 183). Within such a liberated society, jealousy was seen as abnormal, paranoid, and irrational and as having only negative effects on relationships. Stearns (1989) summarized the sentiments of this era by stating, "Though a few magazine articles found tiny windows of merit in jealousy, as against the unadulterated blasts, they were at best silver specks in a very dark cloud" (p. 121).

So where are we today? Contemporary attitudes remain ambivalent and paradoxical. We are repulsed and fascinated by jealousy. Jealousy is a more frequent topic of magazine articles today than ever before. Moreover, the 1990s explosion of television talk shows and docudramas revolving around jealousy has increased public awareness of this sometimes destructive emotion. Jealousy is still portrayed as a personality defect on many of these shows, possibly because this depiction highlights the dramatic, negative consequences of jealousy and makes a better story. Yet, in the 1990s age of AIDS awareness, monogamy is valued more than it was in the 1970s and 1980s (Brehm, 1992). The renewed emphasis on affectionate, committed relationships and safe sex suggests that jealousy is justified in many situations. Indeed, unsafe sex during an extradyadic affair can affect both the emotional and physical well-being of all three members of the romantic triangle.

Taken together, a sociological and historical perspective on jealousy suggests that paradox is operating. Jealousy is seen as a stronger, more potentially violent emotion than is envy, it is often seen as a personality defect, and yet there are still times when it is socially sanctioned. Aune and Comstock (1996; Comstock & Aune, 1995), for example, found that romantic partners saw jealousy experience and expression as unpleasant, but fairly acceptable in their relationships. Similarly, Fitness and Fletcher (1993) reported that most people generally "understand and forgive each other's occasional insecurity and jealousy, despite the widespread belief that jealousy is a destructive, unacceptable emotion in close relationships" (p. 957).

Jealousy is also paradoxical in that it creates a dilemma. As Stearns (1989) contended, people may "scorn jealousy, regarding it as an emotion at once juvenile and outdated," yet they may still feel "susceptible and even on occasion justify their [jealous] feeling" (p. 129). The experience and expression of jealousy by relational partners is quite natural. One of the reasons people tolerate jealous partners is that they have experienced jealous thoughts and feelings themselves. Indeed, jealousy of all types, particularly emotional and behavioral jealousy, is correlated within dyads, indicating that jealous people are attracted to one another or that jealousy is reciprocated by one's relational partner (Guerrero, Eloy, Jorgensen, & Andersen, 1993).

Perhaps unjustifiably, jealous individuals need reassurance and understanding from their partners rather than judgment. However, when jealousy becomes violent and/or obsessive, most people find it unacceptable. Indeed, Delgado and Bond (1993) found that most people do not view jealousy as a better justification for homicide than financial issues. Yet, our court system, as well as our conventional wisdom, provides some level of social acceptance and personal sympathy for the jealous lover who engages in destructive, seemingly uncontrollable behavior. Delgado and Bond labeled jealousy as the "oldest excuse for wrong doing" (p. 1338). White and Mullen (1989) noted that, "The so-called 'crime of passion' has always aroused both fascination and considerable sympathy for the offender" (p. 231). Whether it is a friend telling another friend, "I understand why you hit her; she really hurt you badly when she slept with him" or a jury acquitting an individual who injured another because she was "temporarily insane with jealousy," our society sends a dual message: Highly jealous individuals are insecure and volatile, but we should understand and sympathize with their pain. Such a message has dangerous implications for our personal relationships because we expect others to forgive our aggressive actions when we are jealous.

The Paradoxical Societal View of Envy. Like jealousy, envy has fascinated writers for centuries. Aristotle (1886) stated:

> Envy (is) defined as a species of pain felt at conspicuous prosperity on the part of persons like ourselves ... not with any view to our personal advantage but solely because they are prosperous. As regards the occasions of envy, the goods which provoke it have already been stated; for all achievements or possessions of which we covet the reputation or are ambitious, all things which arouse in us a longing for reputation, as well as all the various gifts of fortune are practically without exception natural objects of envy. (pp. 158-159)

In Shakespeare's *Julius Caesar*, envy permeates Roman politics. In the Bible, the book of Genesis contains several accounts of envy. For example, one passage describes how Jacob made one of his son's, Joseph, a long tunic. Joseph's brothers see the tunic, realize that their father loves Joseph best, and "hate him so much that they would not even greet him." (Gen. 37: 3, *New American Bible*). Later, the brothers' envious hatred leads them to sell Joseph to Midianite traders, who take him to Egypt to be sold as a slave.

The Bible also provides a foundation for the contemporary view of envy as morally wrong. Specifically, the 10th commandment dictates that a person shall not covet someone else's spouse or property. Envy is also considered one of the seven deadly sins. Parrott (1991) reported that envious individuals, as opposed to jealous individuals, are more likely to feel shame, embarrassment, guilt, "sinfulness , and worry about disapproval (see also Parrott & Smith, 1993). This modern day evidence suggests that envy is still viewed as a socially condemned, morally reprehensible emotion. This is at least partially due to the perception that envy stems from a deficit within oneself, whereas jealousy can stem from one's righteous indignation over another's indiscretions.

In individualistic, capitalistic countries like the United States or Great Britain, envy is particularly likely to flourish. Individualism naturally leads people to compare themselves to others. As Salovey and Rodin (1989) stated, "In a competitive culture, individualistic concerns for material possessions, status, and affection are often manifested as envy" (p. 241). Scholars (e.g., Burke, Genn-Bash, & Haines, 1988; Tracy, 1991) also argued that competitiveness is an integral part of North America's economy, politics, and social policies. Furthermore, capitalism allows people from widely different social stations to interact within the same society, making comparisons inevitable. Competition and envy then become mechanisms by which to better oneself and to try to move up the "social ladder" (Tracy, 1991). Indeed, during the 1980s era of the me generation, Ciabattari (1988) asked: "Will the '90s be the age of envy?" (p. 47)

The U.S. Declaration of Independence declares that all people are created equal, yet we know from experience that this is not the case. People inherit, acquire, and possess unique combinations of traits and talents. As Parrott (1991) stated:

> It is a fact of life that people are unequal. Certainly some inequalities stem from injustice, but even in a just world some people would be born with more beauty than others, some would receive more of a given talent than others, some would fairly

> come to acquire more possessions than others, and so forth. It is difficult to imagine that these differences among peers could be made not to matter. When one contemplates how common the situations promoting envy are, one appreciates envy's potential ubiquity and influence. (p. 8)

In most societies, laws and policies are erected to protect people from envy and to try to maintain some level of equality (see Schoeck, 1969). Of course, whether these laws and policies are fair depends on your perspective. Affirmative action is a case in point. Proponents of affirmative action claim that such a policy is necessary to ensure a fair system of equal access for all Americans, for without affirmative action, underrepresented groups would not be operating on a level playing field. Opponents of affirmative action contend that the policy is unjust because it gives some unqualified applicants an unfair advantage and causes reverse discrimination. Clearly, the issue at stake is how to provide people with equal, yet fair opportunity.

In interpersonal relationships, envy is often seen as selfish and petty. Our friends and loved ones expect us to be happy for them when they accomplish something. If we are envious, our negative emotion violates their expectations. Instead of being able to validate their happiness by sharing it with us, envy disconfirms their accomplishment and dampens their mood. Interestingly, envy and pride (two of the seven deadly sins) are probably associated with one another in some cases. Salovey and Rothman (1991) noted that often people have a hard time accepting compliments and become embarrassed when they receive excessive praise. Demure acceptance of compliments and embarrassed responses to praise may function to decrease the likelihood of envy. As noted previously, some scholars differentiated between malicious and admiring envy. A boastful individual is more likely to elicit malicious envy and hostility, whereas a modest individual is more likely to elicit admiring envy and liking.

Taken together, this evidence suggests that most people regard envy as a socially inappropriate emotion. Yet, modern society is likely to foster comparisons between people, making envy unavoidable. As with jealousy, envy can lead to violence, hostility, and political intrigue (Schoeck, 1969). Like jealousy, envy also presents people with a paradoxical situation: In many societies, people strive to be praiseworthy and to be compared favorably with their peers, yet when people appear too praiseworthy, they are likely to engender envy from others and to be resented and disliked.

Summary

Although jealousy and envy can be distinguished by who possesses the desired commodity, what the predominant accompanying emotions and perceptions are, and how society views them, they both have a similar quality at their core: Both revolve around desire. With jealousy, the desire focuses on preserving an existing relationship in the face of threats. With envy, the desire focuses on wanting something one does not have. In both cases, negative consequences can result.

The Dark Side of Jealousy and Envy

Jealousy and envy can result in numerous negative consequences for individuals and their relationships, notwithstanding the positive consequences mentioned earlier. In this section, we examine some of the most common negative consequences. These include the experience of a cluster of negative emotions and accompanying negative self-perceptions, negative relational outcomes, and destructive communicative behavior.

Intrapersonal Consequences: Negative Emotional Reactions and Self-Perceptions

Jealousy and envy are usually considered to be blended emotions because they are comprised of a number of distinct emotional experiences, such as anger and sadness. When these emotions are highly intense and negative, they may entrap jealous or envious individuals by making them increasingly fearful, suspicious, and insecure. Bryson (1991) discussed one common response to jealousy—emotional devastation, which includes feeling helpless, insecure, confused, inadequate, fearful, anxious, depressed, and exploited. Those experiencing emotional devastation report being unable to cope with other aspects of their lives and crying when they are alone. Thus, jealous emotional devastation encompasses the cognitive, emotional, and behavioral reactions that associate with "the serious negative emotional consequences of jealousy" (p. 180). When jealous individuals are so emotionally devastated that they doubt themselves and are unable to cope with other aspects of their lives, they are likely to dwell on their jealousy and to remain uncertain, suspicious, and irrational.

Envy can also be associated with emotional devastation, especially when envious individuals dwell on their shortcomings and their unfulfilled desires. Parrott's (1991) work shows that at least five different kinds of emotion may be a part of what we are terming envious emotional devastation: (a) frustrated desire; (b) sadness and distress over feelings of inferiority; (c) agent-focused resentment, which involves feeling anger and hatred toward "superior" others; (d) global resentment, which involves feeling a general resentment toward the injustice of circumstances or fate; and (e) guilt over wishing rivals ill will.

Blame is also an essential characteristic of envious emotional devastation, with the most emotionally devastated people blaming everyone, including themselves, for their problems. Statements such as "Nothing ever goes my way," "I can't do anything right," and "Everyone seems out to get me" are symptoms of envy proneness. Furthermore, both agent-focused and global resentment add to the perception that the envious person cannot achieve success in comparison to others. After all, if an envious person believes that others are naturally superior, that fate and circumstances are unjust, and that they just fail to measure up to other people, they are likely to see attempts at improving themselves as pointless. For these individuals, it is easier to give up and harbor resentment toward more fortunate others than to face more rejection and more negative self-to-other comparisons by trying to improve oneself.

Emotions associated with jealousy and envy are summarized in Table 2.1. Because the majority of these emotions are negatively valenced, the experience of jealousy and envy can be emotionally devastating. Although passion, love, pride, and appreciation are positive emotions that can accompany jealousy and admiration and liking can accompany envy, the emotions most central to both jealousy and envy are fear, anger, and sadness.

Fear. Both jealousy and envy are typically associated with feelings of fear, but the type of fear that accompanies these emotions is different. Jealous fear, which is more common than envious fear, stems from two interrelated sources—fear of abandonment and relational loss (White & Mullen, 1989) and uncertainty about the state of the relationship (Bringle, 1991). Envious fear, on the other hand, stems from fear of failure and/or rejection, and anxiety over "the prospect of undesirable future outcomes, and uncertainty about one's self" (Parrott, 1991, p. 13).

Fear emanates from humans' self-protection needs. The potential loss of a mate deprives an individual of biological resources (i.e., the ability to reproduce offspring), relational resources (i.e., a loving, nurturing companion), and personal resources (i.e., less self-esteem or social status).

TABLE 2.1

Emotional Reactions Most Commonly Associated With Jealousy and Envy

JEALOUSY	ENVY
1. Anger, rage, or hatred toward partner or rival (A, ASI, B2, KR, PI, P2, S2, SSK, TM, WM)	1. Anger, hatred, or resentment towards the rival (BS, CBL, P2, S1).
2. Fear, anxiety, or panic over possible abandonment or relationship change (A, ASI, B2, CS, P1, P3 SSK, TM, WM)	2. Distress and anxiety stemming from one's feelings of inferiority (CBL, P2, S1, SKP, SR2
3. Sadness or grief over actual or potential relationship loss (WM)	3. Sadness, discontent, and hopelessness stemming from one's own shortcomings (BS, CBL, P2, S1, SKP, SR1, SR2).
4. Hurt over being betrayed (B1, B3, SKP)	4. Guilt over harboring ill will toward others (BS, P2, PS, SR1)
5. Envy of the rival's relationship with the partner and/or the rival's positive characteristics (CS, WM).	5. Despair that you will never posses the valued commodity that the rival possesses.
6. Heightened sexual arousal or passion (B2, PA, WFR, WM)	6. Longing and/or frustrated desire (BS, P2)
7. Positive affect, including love, appreciation, and pride toward the partner (A, B1, GA).	7. Admiration and liking for the rival (P2).

Note: A = Arnold (1960); ASI = Ausubel, Sullivan & Ives (I 980); B1 = Baumgart 1990; B2 = Bohm (1961); B3 = Bryson (1991); BS= Bers & Rodin (1984); CBL= Campos, Barrett, Lamb, Goldsmith, & Stenberg (1983); CS = Clanton & Smith (1977); GA = Guerrero &Andersen (in press); KR= Klein & Riviere (1964); P1 = Panskeep (1982); P2 = Parrott (1991); P3 = Plutchik (1980); PS = Parrott & Smith (1993); PA = Pines & Aronson (1983); S1 = Smith (1991); S2 = Solomon (1976); SSK = Shaver, Schwartz, Kirson, & O'Connor (1987); SKP = Smith, Kim, & Parrott (1988); SRI = Salovey & Rodin (1984); SR2 = Salovey & Rothman (1991); TM = Teismann & Mosher (1978); WFR = White, Fishbein, & Rutstein (1981); WM = White & Mullen (1989).

Fear is typically communicated both verbally (Rimé, Mesquita, Philippot, & Boca, 1991) and nonverbally (Ekman, Friesen, & Ellsworth, 1972), probably to elicit comforting or sympathy. In the case of jealousy-induced fear, its experience and subsequent expression may elicit sympathy and relational repair, particularly if it accompanies integrative communication (Andersen, Eloy, Guerrero, & Spitzberg, 1995).

Of course, fear is often based on unrealistic or imagined threats that become phobic responses. White and Mullen (1989) provided recommendations for the treatment of infidelity delusions, a major and dark source of jealousy reactions. Their reviews of treatments include antipsychotic medication, electroconvulsive therapy, psychoanalytic approaches, and cognitive-behavior therapies. Of course, different remedies are necessary for treatment of jealousy stemming from actual jealousy, as opposed to delusional jealousy.

A prototype perspective also helps explain why jealousy and envy are associated with fear. Sharpsteen (1991) argued that many of the events that are seen as prototypical antecedents of fear are also likely to produce jealousy and envy. For example, Shaver et al. (1987) reported that the threat of social rejection, the possibility of loss or failure, and loss of control or competence are all situations that generally elicit fear. Perceived threats to self-esteem are at the heart of experiences of both jealousy and envy. Perceived threats to the relationship uniquely accompany the experience of jealousy. Thus, generalized threats produce fearful reactions, with more specialized forms of threats (i.e., those that focus on threatening one's relationship or one's self-esteem) producing not only fear, but also jealousy or envy.

Anger. Anger is such a powerful part of the jealousy experience that Bryson (1991) included it as a factor separate from emotional devastation. Jealous anger includes feeling angry at the partner and rival, feeling betrayed and disappointed in the partner, and feeling a need to get revenge.

Jealousy-related anger is highly associated with feelings of betrayal. For example, when romantic relationships end, people are particularly likely to be angry when they are replaced by a rival. Mathes, Adams, and Davies (1985) examined emotional reactions to four possible scenarios—losing a romantic relationship because of fate, destiny, rejection, or the inference of a romantic relationship. Anger was relatively high for both the rejection and interference situations, but particularly high for the latter. A cross-cultural study conducted by Bryson (1991) suggests that individuals who feel betrayed also tend to doubt their partners, feel angry toward their partners, give their partners the cold shoulder, end the relationship, or spy on their partners.

Research also indicates that jealous individuals are more likely to be angry at the partner than the rival (Mathes & Verstraete, 1993; Mullen & Maack, 1985; Paul, Foss, & Cglloway, 1993), especially when the anger is intensely hostile or violent (White & Mullen, 1989). Daly and Wilson (1983), for example, found that jealous individuals are more likely to direct anger and violence toward spouses than rivals. Paul et al. (1993) explained that the partner is the more likely target of anger and aggression for at least four reasons:

1. The jealous individual typically has greater access to the partner.
2. It is the partner, not the rival, who is perceived as breaking a commitment and engaging in an act of betrayal.
3. The rival may not know the extent to which the partner is already committed, and, thus, the rival may be unknowingly engaging in a hurtful act.
4. It may be difficult for the jealous person to blame the rival for being attracted to the partner when he or she feels the same attraction.

Nonetheless, anger toward the rival appears to be likely if the rival is a close friend of the jealous person. Parker (1994) suggested that when the rival is someone who is not well-known to the jealous person, stress is generally confined to the romantic relationship. When the rival is a friend of the jealous person, stress pervades the entire social network. Indeed, Parker found that if the rival was a close friend, jealous individuals were unlikely to seek support from their social networks, perhaps because they felt betrayed and humiliated. As Parker summarized, feelings of betrayal and anger are likely "magnified when a close friend becomes a rival in a romantic relationship" (p. 26).

Taken together, these findings suggest that jealous individuals are most likely to experience anger when they feel betrayed by close relational partners. When the rival is unknown to them, anger is most likely directed at the partner. When the rival is a friend, anger is likely to be directed at both the partner and the rival and perhaps at the social network in general. Of course, some jealous individuals are also angry at themselves for acting in a way that they perceive pushed the partner away.

When envious individuals experience anger, it is usually rooted in resentment, hatred, and frustration rather than in betrayal. As Parrott and Smith (1993) noted, jealousy and envy can both produce hostility, but the type of hostility they produce is different: Jealous individuals tend to feel "anger over betrayal," whereas envious individuals tend to feel "resentment and rancor" (p. 907). Parrott (1991) also argued that, "It should be apparent that there are strong similarities between malicious envy and anger. In fact, the distinction between the two rests primarily on whether the hostility is justified" (p. 10).

Envious anger and resentment can be directed at a person, a group of people, or at the general state of affairs, but envy can also be experienced apart from any feelings of anger and hostility. As Parrott (1991) stated, "One may feel angry at the fates for making some people beautiful without feeling angry at beautiful people for being beautiful" (p. 11). In our close relationships with others, we expect some admiration, awe, or nonmalicious envy to exist, but not anger and resentment. For example, if we are bowling or playing tennis with friends, we label them as "bad sports" if they grow angry because they are losing.

Envious anger also stems from frustration. As Smith (1991) contended, envy can lead to anger because the envious person feels he or she cannot reach a goal or desired state that someone else has achieved. This frustration is often directed at the rival, who is seen as achieving success much too easily. As cognitive dissonance theory predicts, people find it difficult to reconcile the fact that they may work hard for something but not achieve it, whereas someone else appears to effortlessly obtain the same goal. To decrease dissonance (and the attendant frustration), envious individuals search for shortcomings in rivals. They also find reasons to dislike the rival in an effort to bolster their liking for themselves (e.g., "She might be a great tennis player, but she's not as smart or pretty as I am"). For example, Salovey and Rodin (1984) found that envious individuals reportedly felt anxious about interacting with rivals, did not want to pursue friendships with them, and disparaged them on various personal traits.

Sadness. Similar to fear, sadness is a common affective response when people experience jealousy and envy, yet the type of sadness differs depending on whether the individual is jealous or envious. Jealous sadness stems from the potential loss of a valued relationship and the loneliness that accompanies such loss. Envious sadness stems from one's feelings of inferiority, hopelessness, and helplessness.

Some research suggests that sadness is more central to envy than jealousy. The logic behind this argument is that sadness follows, rather than accompanies, the jealousy experience. White and Mullen (1989) put it this way:

> Sadness is present in most experiences of jealousy. The fear of a future that is depleted and empty usually leads to sadness. Sadness may well be muted, because jealousy is a state in which loss is feared rather than accepted, and sadness is likely to predominate in jealousy only when hope is abandoned. Jealousy is primarily a state of excitement and activation that is directed at the future and at changing that future, rather than a state of passive and sad acceptance. (p. 180)

White and Mullen also noted that jealousy-related depression is associated with feelings of guilt and worthlessness, as well as anger and suspicion. These feelings of worthlessness can lead jealous individuals to believe they deserve betrayal.

Work by Sharpsteen (1991) also supports the argument that intense sadness is most likely to follow rather than accompany jealousy. Arguing from a prototype perspective, Sharpsteen asserted that although jealousy is "a singular blend of anger, sadness, and fear," sadness is probably the least central of these emotions to the jealousy experience (p. 36). According to Shaver et al.'s (1987) prototype analysis, common antecedents of sadness include the loss of a valued relationship and separation from a loved one, which supports the contention that sadness is most likely to occur after relationship loss.

Some measure of sadness still commonly accompanies jealousy. Bringle (1991), for example, argued that in jealousy situations, "sadness results from the combination of high levels of commitment and relational losses that are irretrievable or the *possibility* of relationship termination" (p. 111, emphasis added). Mathes et al. (1985) argued that the loss of relationship rewards is responsible for the feelings of sadness elicited in jealousy situations. Certainly, jealous individuals often feel that they have lost trust in their partners and that "things will never be the same" even if the relationship continues. Thus, some level of sadness is expected to accompany jealousy because of the potential for relationship loss and the diminished reward value of the relationship.

Sadness appears to be a central, vital part of the experience of envy. Shaver et al. (1987) found that the prototypical antecedents of sadness included undesirable outcomes; rejection or exclusion; not getting what one wants, wishes for, or strives for; and having reality fall short of expectations. Thus, situations such as failing at a particular task, being rejected in favor of another, and receiving less praise than expected would all be likely candidates to produce sadness. When a rival is also involved (i.e., as the person who succeeds, is accepted, or receives the praise), envy is also likely to surface. It appears, then, that there are many situations that call forth both sadness and envy. This is not surprising given that negative comparisons to others and the resultant focus on one's own shortcomings are at the heart of the envious experience. Moreover, the desperate desire to possess something, followed by the disappointment of not achieving one's goal, appears to be a ready-made recipe for promoting sadness and despair. In short, the self-reflective process that produces feelings of envy is also likely to elicit feelings of sadness and discontent.

Both jealousy and envy are most likely to be accompanied by feelings of sadness when the jealous or envious person engages in brooding behavior and harbors deep feelings of low self-worth. In his study on reactions to jealousy, Bryson (1976, 1991) found a jealousy factor labeled *intropunitiveness*. Individuals scoring highly on this factor tended to internalize their jealous feelings and blame themselves for potential relationship termination or de-escalation. These individuals reported punishing themselves for being jealous rather than directing any negative affect toward the partner or the rival. Such self-directed blame is likely to lead to brooding and intense feelings of sadness. In Fitness and Fletcher's (1993) study of prototypical responses to emotion, jealousy was associated with brooding and negative feelings toward the self.

Lowered self-esteem is also likely to contribute to the sadness experienced with jealousy and envy. According to a survey conducted by Salovey and Rodin (1985), jealous and envious individuals tend to have low opinions of themselves, to see their "actual" selves as inferior to their "ideal" selves, and to value visible accomplishments and status symbols such as popularity, fame, wealth, positions of authority, and beauty. Parrott and Smith (1993) noted that jealousy and envy are both associated with lowered self-esteem and feelings of sadness, hopelessness, and despair. However, the explanatory mechanism is different for the two emotions. For jealousy, lowered self-esteem is likely due to feelings of projected rejection and loss. For envy, lowered self-esteem is likely a function of feelings of inferiority and longing.

Summary. The experiences of jealousy and envy often produce negative emotional reactions and self-perceptions. In the case of jealousy, individuals are likely to feel fear due to possible abandonment and relational loss, anxiety related to relational uncertainty, anger in response to perceived betrayal, and sadness at the prospect of potentially losing a valued relationship. In the case of envy, individuals are likely to fear rejection, experience anxiety or despair due to their perceived inferiority, and feel sad and hopeless if they do not see a way of improving their situation. In both cases, lowered self-esteem is a likely outcome because a negative self-to-other comparison has been made. Jealous individuals generally believe that their partners compared them unfavorably to a rival. Envious individuals make the unfavorable self-to-other comparison themselves.

Despite the considerable inner turmoil that jealousy and envy often produce, these emotions are more than purely intrapersonal phenomena. Both emotions originate in social interaction and/or social comparison, both usually have consequences for relationships, and both are expressed in interpersonal communication. In the following section, we outline some negative interpersonal consequences of these emotions, including the destructive forms of communication that are used to express jealousy and envy. We begin by examining the relational outcomes and communicative behaviors that are associatedwith jealousy (see Table 2.2 for a listing of relevant communication strategies).

Interpersonal Consequences and Communication Related to Jealousy

Uncertainty, Suspicion, and Distrust. Romantic jealousy is associated with three interrelated intrapersonal experiences—uncertainty, suspicion, and distrust. When individuals suspect that their partners are involved with rivals or distrust their partners, they are likely to experience high levels of relational uncertainty Likewise, when people are uncertain about the state of their relationships, they may feel there is greater potential for their partner to become involved with a rival. Suspicion and distrust are also likely to co-exist, although distrust is likely to be the most pervasive when uncertainty is reduced so that suspicions are confirmed.

TABLE 2.2

Negatively Valenced Communicative Behaviors Associated With Uncertainty, Distrust, and Suspicion

Behaviors and Definition/Examples
Surveillance and Guarding
1. Surveillance/vigilance. Behaviors that function to verify the partner's actions and reduce uncertainty about the nature of the rival relationship, for example, spying on the partner or looking through the partner's personal belongings and calling the partner unexpectedly to verify her/his whereabouts.
2. Concealment/restriction. Behaviors that function to conceal the partner and/or to restrict the partner's access to potential rivals, for example, refusing to introduce the partner to potential rivals and refusing to take the partner to a party where rivals would be present.
3. Monopolizing the partner's time. Behaviors that function to maximize the time the partner spends with the jealous person and minimize the time the partner spends with potential rivals, for example, planning joint activities that take up all of the partner's time and insisting that the partner spends all her/his free time with you.
(continued)

Communication With the Rival

1. Information seeking. Communicating with the rival in order to find out more about the rival and the rival relationship, for example, talking with the rival to determine what kind of a person he or she is and asking the rival questions about the relationship with the partner.
2. Derogation of the mate to rivals. Disclosing negative information (whether true or untrue) about the partner in an effort to discourage the rival from pursuing the partner, for example, telling the rival that the partner is not very bright and is irritable and telling the rival that having a relationship with her/him is a bad experience.
3. Rival threats. Threatening the rival through the use of aggressive communication, hostility, and warnings, for example, staring coldly at the rival, trying to intimidate the rival, or threatening to hit the rival.
4. Violence Toward rivals. Actually causing physical harm to the rival or the rival's property, for example, pushing the rival out of the way and vandalizing the rival's car.

Signs of Possession

1. Verbal signs of possession. Verbal communication that asserts the relationship between the jealous person and the partner, for example, introducing the partner as one's "husband, " "wife," "girlfriend," and so forth and bragging to rivals about how much she or he and the partner love one another.
2. Physical signs of possession. Nonverbal communication that functions as relationship displays, for example, holding the partner's hand when others are around and kissing the partner in front of potential rivals.
3. Possessive ornamentation. Utilizing objects to display the relationship, for example, asking the partner to wear a ring or letterman's jacket and hanging the partner's picture in prominent places.

Avoidance

1. Physical and emotional withdrawal. Withdrawing from the partner, for example, spending less time with the partner and withdrawing affection from the partner.
2. Situation avoidance. Avoiding jealousy-provoking situations, for example, refusing to go places where jealousy could surface and avoiding situations where the rival might be present.
3. Unwillingness to communicate. Refusing to communicate with the partner, for example, becoming quiet around the partner and failing to call the partner on the telephone.

Note: Category labels and examples are adapted from Buss (1988) and Guerrero et al. (1995).

As White and Mullen (1989) stated, "Sadly, trust is often abandoned when jealousy takes root. The past actions and future intentions of the partner are exactly what jealousy puts in question; the fidelity of the partner is at issue, and therefore he or she cannot be trusted" (p. 233). Similarly, Buunk (1991) noted that when jealousy is a reactive emotional response to a partner's infidelity, many people label their emotion as anger rather than jealous per se. This is because infidelity is usually perceived as a disloyal act of betrayal that diminishes relational trust.

Relational uncertainty, suspicion, and distrust prompt a number of communicative responses to jealousy that have the potential to be valenced negatively. Four such responses are surveillance and guarding, communication with the rival, possessiveness, and avoidance (see Table 2.2).

Surveillance behavior is typically used to reduce uncertainty and guard the relationship. Guerrero and Afifi (1997), for example, found that individuals who wanted to reduce uncertainty about the rival relationship reported engaging in surveillance behaviors and restricting the partner's access to potential rivals. Pfieffer and Wong (1989) described cognitive jealousy as a composite of suspicious thoughts and worries and behavioral jealousy as a group of surveillance behaviors, including actions such as questioning the partner about her or his whereabouts, paying a surprise visit to the partner to see who is with her or him, and looking through the partner's belongings for evidence of an affair. In this and many other conceptualizations of jealousy, cognitive suspicion and behavioral jealousy are inextricably linked. Buss (1988) discussed several guarding or mate retention behaviors, including vigilance, mate concealments and monopolization of the mate's time. These guarding behaviors are most likely to be used when the jealous individual is suspicious or worried about the partner's potential involvement with others.

Communication with the rival is also associated with uncertainty reduction and mate guarding. Guerrero and Afifi (1997) found that jealous individuals who wanted to reduce uncertainty about the rival relationship were likely to communicate with the rival directly (e.g., ask them how long they have known their partner or tell them to keep away from the partner). Bryson (1976, 1991) reported that jealous individuals sometimes seek information by confronting the rival. Jealous individuals also denigrate their partners in front of others as a method of discouraging rivals from pursuing their partners. For instance, a male might tell a rival that his girlfriend is demanding, lazy, or even that she has a social disease (Buss, 1988). In more rare circumstances, jealous individuals threaten rivals through verbal aggression, intimidation, or physical violence.

Signs of possession are also used to ward off potential rivals. Interestingly, signs of possession also function to show how devoted and close a couple is. For example, tie signs (e.g., holding hands, or wearing a wedding ring) reflect affection and caring between relational partners. However, these signs also function as a public signal that the partner is "taken." Jealous individuals may publicly flaunt their relationship with the partner when they are suspicious and/or distrustful. In this case, signs of possession are designed to reduce the rival's uncertainty about the unavailability of the partner. Buss (1988) described three types of possessiveness cues—verbal, physical, and ornamentation (see Table 2.2). Pinto and Hollandsworth (1984) discussed several ways that people display possessiveness, including discouraging the partner from making new friends and spending excessive amounts of time with the partner. Possessive individuals feel lonely and worry when they are separated (even briefly) from their partners. Due to high levels of suspicion and distrust, possessive individuals also feel an insatiable need to keep the partner to themselves by isolating the partner from a broader social circle (Pinto & Hollandsworth, 1984).

Finally, uncertainty and suspicion sometimes lead individuals to avoid active communication with their partners. Schaap, Buunk, and Kerkstra (1988) found a small but significant association between jealousy and an avoidant conflict style. Specifically, jealous individuals became unwilling to discuss relational problems and retreated (both physically and emotionally) from conflict situations. Afifi and Reichert (1996) used an uncertainty reduction theory framework to explain the association between jealousy and avoidance. According to these authors, jealousy is a highly uncertainty-proking situation. Indeed, their research shows that jealousy increases motivation to decrease uncertainty. Afifi and Reichert also found a tendency for uncertain, jealous individuals to avoid communicating with their partners, presumably because they felt uncertain regarding the partner's reaction.

Retaliation, Conflict, and Violence. Because jealousy is such an intense emotion and because it can engender feelings of deep hurt and betrayal, jealous individuals sometimes engage in aggressive, manipulative, and/or violent behavior (see Table 2.3). Buunk (1991) discussed the link between intense jealous feelings and aggressive behavior. Specifically, he argued that:

> In a normal, satisfying relationship there will usually be a preference for problem solving and compromise, and for taking into account the interests of the other person. However, when the other shows a clear interest in someone else, the tendency to be cooperative will diminish ... and the [jealous] individual's attitude seems to become ... more competitive and aggressive. (p. 165)

Schaap, Buunk, and Kerkstra (1988) examined associations between five conflict styles and jealousy. They found that jealousy was most strongly associated with an aggressive conflict style (r = .78), although it also [sic] associated with compromise (r = .42), soothing (r = .40) and avoidance (r = .27). Jealousy was inversely related to problem solving (r = -.21), as Buunk (1991) argued.

Sometimes jealous individuals feel a strong desire to enact revenge against their partners. Bryson (1976, 1991) discussed the concept of reactive retribution, which involves active attempts to get back at the partner who provoked jealous feelings. Reactive retribution includes behavior such as counterjealousy inductions, becoming sexually aggressive with others, criticizing the partner in front of others, and dating others to get back at the partner. Guerrero and Afifi (1997) discussed retaliation as a potential goal in jealousy situations. According to these authors, retaliation functions to vent frustration, anger, and hurt, and also serves to restore equity by "evening the score" (p. 8).

TABLE 2.3

Negatively Valenced Communicative Behaviors Associated With Retaliation and Conflict

Behaviors and Definitions/Examples
Aggressive Communication
1. Distributive communication. Direct and aggressive communication with the partner, for example, yelling at and arguing with the partner and making accusations and criticizing the partner's actions.
2. Active distancing. Indirect modes of communicating aggression to the partner, for example, pointedly ignoring the partner and acting cold and distant; withdrawing affection.
Manipulation Attempts
1. Counterjealousy inductions. Attempts to make the offending partner feel jealous too, for example, threatening to date and/or have sex with other people and flirting with a third party to make the partner jealous.
2. Guilt inductions. Attempts to make the offending partner feel guilty about her/his actions, for example, crying and telling the partner how hurt you are and threatening to harm oneself if the partner leaves.
Violent Behaviors
1. Violence toward the partner. Actions that physically harm the partner in some way, for example, slapping the partner and cutting off the partner's hair so he or she looks "ugly "
2. Violence Toward Objects. Directing aggression toward physical objects, for example, slamming doors or throwing dishes and throwing the partner's possessions out of the house.

Note. Category labels and examples are adapted from Buss (1988) and Guerrero et al. (1995).

Common retaliation strategies include aggressive communication and manipulation. Guerrero and Afifi (1997) found that individuals who wanted to get even with their partners engaged in behaviors such as arguing with the partner, making accusations, giving the partner "the silent treatment, trying to make the partner feel guilty, and trying to induce counterjealousy." Similarly, Buss (1988) forwarded a punishment strategy, which comprises tactics such as becoming angry, ignoring the partner, threatening to terminate the relationship, yelling at the partner, and breaking off communication.

Unfortunately, jealous individuals sometimes go beyond verbal aggression and manipulation and resort to violence. In the midst of an epidemic of interpersonal violence and the current publicity of sensational court cases, jealousy has been shown to be a major contributor to violence. Hansen's (1991) comprehensive review of literature concluded "that male sexual jealousy may be the major source of conflict in an overwhelming majority of spousal homicides in North America. Similarly, numerous studies have noted the prevalence of jealousy as a motive in non-fatal wife abuse" (p. 225). Considerable research has also shown that jealousy, money, and alcohol are the three key antecedents of violence in the United States and Great Britain (see Delgado & Bond, 1993, for a review). Stets and Pirog-Good (1987) found the jealousy variable to increase females' use of violence in dating relationships by 240%. Sugarman and Hotaling (1989), in their review of the literature on dating violence, came to the startling conclusion that "in every study in which a respondent had a chance to list jealousy as a cause, it was the most frequently mentioned reason" for violence in dating relationships (p. 12). Similarly, Laner (1990) found that jealousy was one of the top precipitators of violence among high school- and college-age dating couples. She further argued that couples often see jealousy "as the 'real' problem, and violence as merely an 'ordinary' or predictable response to the problem" (p. 320).

As discussed previously, violence has historically been a socially sanctioned course of action in jealousy situations, which makes it more difficult to stop and easier to excuse. This unfortunate state of affairs may explain why some people tolerate violent jealousy. Fortunately, however, there is reason to believe that the link between jealousy and violence is weakening. The percentage of jealousy-related murders in the United States has declined since the mid-1970s, dropping from 10.7% of all murders in 1964 to only 2% of all murders in 1987 (Delgado & Bond, 1993; Stearns, 1989). The largest drop occurred from 1975 to 1976, when the percentage decreased from 7.3% to 2.8%. From 1975 to 1987, the rate stayed under 3%, suggesting that jealousy is regarded as a less justifiable motivation for violence now than it was previously (Stearns, 1989).

Jealous violence stems from imagined, as well as real, extradyadic interaction. In his book on morbid jealousy that results from delusions of infidelity, Mowat (1966) described the history of murder at the British "lunatic asylum," Broadmoor: "Possessed of these delusions, the jealous man persistently accuses his wife or mistress of infidelity. Thirty of the male murderers and all six of the female murderers accused their partners of infidelity" (p. 92). White and Mullen (1989), who reviewed numerous studies on the association between jealousy and violence, concluded that pathologically jealous individuals are sensitive to "every nuance in [their] environment that may hint at unfaithfulness" (p. 226). They also describe how jealous violence is triggered by symbolic association. For example, in their case studies, White and Mullen reported that one woman attacked her husband when he asked for a beer because she believed that he had an affair with a bar maid. Another woman gripped hold of a rival's clothing and told her to stay away from her husband. The rival's throat constricted and she began making choking noises and trying to breathe. At this point, the jealous woman associated the heavy breathing with the sound the rival would make when having sex with her husband. The jealous woman then became even more violent.

Given these vivid examples, it might seem that jealousy biologically leads to inevitable violence (see Guerrero & Andersen, 1998 for a discussion of sociobiological forces contributing to jealousy). Such is not the case. Among the thousands of jealous episodes that occur each day, few result in violence. However, whereas violence is not a common consequence of jealousy, jealousy is a common antecedent of violence. As Hupka (1991) pointed out, 37% to 50% of the U.S. population has extramarital affairs, but less than .01% of the U.S. male population commits murder in response to jealousy. Guerrero, Andersen, Jorgensen, Spitzberg, and Eloy (1995) found violence to be a relatively infrequent response to jealousy. Nonetheless, a significant percentage of murders are jealousy induced. This is another paradox of jealousy. Few emotions create such a unique combination of fear, anger, and sadness. For a small percentage of the population, this emotional devastation leads to extreme violence.

In some cases, violence and/or verbal aggression is used as a form of guarding and protecting the relationship or manipulating the relational partner. Paul et al. (1993) argued that whether we like it or not, aggressive action can sometimes be functional. They contended that jealousy-induced aggression can lead people to feel guilty and rethink their actions. Moreover, if the offending partner does not show any regret, the jealous individual probably extrapolates that there is a high likelihood of similar transgressions occurring in the future and may thereby terminate the relationship. Despite the potential functions that aggression might serve, Paul et al. cautioned that "physical aggression is unlikely to strengthen the relationship. Emotional hurt is more likely to do the job" (p. 403). In the long run, we believe that emotional hurt is damaging to the relationship as well.

Relational (Dis)Satisfaction. All of the communicative behaviors just discussed—ranging from active distancing, to distributive communication, manipulation and threats, avoidance, and violence-have been found to have some negative impact on relational satisfaction. Jealousy, in general, associates with relational dissatisfaction. For example, two recent studies (Andersen et al., 1995; Guerrero & Eloy, 1991) found that cognitive jealousy shares a robust negative association with relational satisfaction. The causal nature of this relationship has yet to be determined, but it is likely that individuals who are dissatisfied with their relationships are likely to think that their partners are also, dissatisfied, and therefore, their partners may be involved with or interested in others. It is also likely that the jealousy experience itself can lead to relational dissatisfaction, particularly when negative emotional reactions and aggressive, manipulative behaviors occur. It is likely, then, that the association between jealousy and relational satisfaction operates as a bidirectional process.

However, jealousy is not always destructive. Research suggests that couples who use integrative communication methods often emerge from the jealousy situation feeling secure and gaining new insight into their relationships. Integrative communication, such as disclosing jealous feelings, questioning the partner in a nonaccusatory fashion, and discussing the future of the relationship often leads to open discussion and promotes relational satisfaction (Andersen et al., 1995). Expressing negative emotion also promotes relational happiness under certain circumstances. Andersen et al. found that when jealousy-related emotions such as anger, frustration, and sadness were communicated alone or alongside distributive communication, active distancing, and/or avoidance, the result was decreased relational satisfaction. However, when negative emotions were expressed in the midst of discussing the problem via integrative communication, satisfaction levels were at their peak. It may be that the expression of negative emotion, within the context of integrative communication, leads the partner to see the jealous person as open, sincere, and caring.

Other communicative responses to jealousy, collectively labeled *compensatory restoration behaviors* (see Guerrero, Andersen, Jorgensen, Spitzberg, & Eloy, 1995), may also be associated with relational satisfaction. Compensatory restoration behaviors encompass strategies designed to improve the self or the relationship in an effort to retain the partner. Guerrero et al. listed tactics such as trying to improve one's appearance and trying to be the best partner possible as compensatory restoration behaviors. Buss (1988) discussed similar tactics, including resource display (e.g., spending money on or buying gifts for the partner), sexual inducements (e.g., giving in to the partner's sexual requests), enhancing physical appearance (e.g., using make-up and/or wearing the latest fashions), and emphasizing love and caring (e.g., being especially complimentary, affectionate, and helpful). Because these behaviors demonstrate love, caring, and a concern for the relationship, they sometimes promote relational satisfaction. However, if these behaviors are seen as desperate attempts to win back the partner, they are actually counterproductive (Guerrero et al., 1995).

Another tactic listed by Buss (1988), labeled *submission and debasement*, is especially likely to be viewed as such a desperate ingratiation attempt. Submission and debasement involves engaging in behaviors such as promising to change in order to please the partner, going along with everything the partner says, giving in to the partner's wishes, and becoming the partner's "slave" (p. 299). Even if these behaviors are successful in preserving the relationship, they are likely to promote low self-esteem.

Interpersonal Consequences and Communication Related to Envy

Coping With Negative Self-Evaluation. Because envy is precipitated by some type of negative self-to-other comparison, our close relationships with friends, family, and romantic partners form fertile ground for promoting envy, rivalry, and competition. Two theoretical frameworks help explain this phenomenon—Social comparison theory and the self-evaluation maintenance view (Messman, 1995; Salovey & Rodin, 1989).

Festinger's (1954) social comparison theory is predicated on the principles that people are driven to evaluate themselves and people make self-evaluations by comparing themselves to others. Research and theory indicates that these self-to-other comparisons are most likely to be made in the context of our interpersonal networks. Festinger, for example, argued that people tend to compare themselves with similar others. A study by Dakin and Arrowood (1981) provides support for this principle by demonstrating that people were most likely to compare themselves to others who were relatively close to them in terms of ability. Because similarity is a cornerstone in many friendships, it is logical that self-to-other comparisons tend to occur within the confines of such relationships. In addition, people spend time with their friends making them proximal targets for competitive comparisons.

The self-evaluation maintenance view (Tesser & Campbell, 1982), which was built on some of the premises of social comparison theory, is grounded in the notion that positive self-evaluation is a primary motive behind the actions of most individuals, particularly in Western cultures. Accoridng to this theory, positive self-evaluation occurs through the process of self-reflection and comparison to others. Reflection is likely to occur under several conditions, such as when people fall short or exceed their own expectations for achieving goals. In addition to having an internal yardstick for evaluating ourselves, Tesser and Campbell (1982; Tesser, 1986) argue that we use other people's successes and failures as points of reference for reflection and comparison, especially when those people are close to us. For example, if a good friend suddenly achieves a high degree of financial success, you may question whether your own financial situation is acceptable.

In a test of the self-evaluation maintenance view, Salovey and Rodin (1984) tested and found support for the contention that envy is strongest under three eliciting conditions.

1. There must be a negative self-to-other comparison.
2. This comparison must be in an area that is highly self-relevant to the potentially envious person.
3. The envious person and the rival should be similar in abilities and/or share a close relationship.

When these conditions are present, envy is likely to be experienced and the envious person should engage in coping behaviors to help alleviate negative affect. Salovey and Rodin (1988, 1989) forwarded three such coping strategies: (a) self-reliance, which includes avoiding outward emotional expression, keeping busy, and refusing to ask others for help; (b) self-bolstering, which includes concentrating on one's positive qualities and doing nice things for oneself; and (c) selective ignoring, which includes re-evaluating the importance of a goal so that it is no longer highly self-relevant. Communicative behaviors associated with these coping strategies might include the following: avoiding communication with the rival, spending time with people who are positively reinforcing, engaging in activities in which one has exceptional ability, and talking about one's achievements in which one has exceptional ability, and talking about one's achievements with others.

Intense feelings of envy may also lead a person to behave negatively toward the rival. Based on Salovey and Rodin's (1984) findings, it appears that envious individuals not only avoid communicating with the rival, but also bad mouth them. For example, an envious person may point out a rival's negative characteristics to others. If others agree with these negative assessments and show liking for the envious person, the sting of the initial self-to-other comparison is diminished. Obviously, communicative behaviors such as these can have negative effects on the relationship between the envious person and the rival.

Competitive Behaviors. New research on the link between competitiveness and communication suggests that avoidance and bad mouthing the rival are only two of several strategies that envious individuals use to cope with their feelings (see Messman, 1995, 1996; Messman & Cupach, 1996). Messman (1995) argued that competitiveness occurs when people make social comparisons for purposes of self-evaluation. When the self-to-other comparison is negative, people are likely to experience envy. To examine the link between competitiveness and communication, Messman asked students to describe the types of behaviors that they typically view as competitive. Using a thematic content analysis to sort these behaviors, Messman found five overarching categories of themes—antagonistic behaviors, success-oriented behaviors, comparative behaviors, antisocial behaviors, and context-bound behaviors. Of these, antagonistic and antisocial behaviors appear to be particularly likely to produce negative relational consequences. Therefore, we discuss these two strategies in more detail (see Table 2.4).

Antagonistic behaviors promote self-to-other comparisons. Individuals who express superiority and/or brag are particularly likely to become targets of malicious envy. These individuals may possess low self-esteem and feel a strong need to present themselves as superior. As Salovey and Rodin (1988) found, individuals sometimes cope with envy by engaging in self-bolstering. Certainly, communicative behaviors, such as expressed superiority and bragging, are part of the self-bolstering process.

Envious individuals also make themselves feel better by belittling others. Rather than casting themselves as superior, individuals who belittle cast others as inferior. The result, however, is the same. The envious individual has bolstered her or his own self-image at the expense of another. Belittling may also accompany the cognitive strategy of selective ignoring, which involves reducing the importance of certain skills and abilities. As a case in point, imagine finding out that one of your close friends and colleagues received a prestigious award that you coveted. Rather than facing the idea that your friend is more worthy than you are, you might convince yourself that the award was not that important. Salovey and Rodin (1984) also provided a nice example of this. They described a situation in which a colleague informs them that his article on jealousy will be published as the lead article in a prestigious journal. Because the authors also publish research on jealousy, they speculate that this news would be likely to elicit envy. To maintain their positive definitions of self and reduce the threat that their colleague poses, Salovey and Rodin (1989) speculated that they might cognitively downgrade the journal or write the journal editor a letter describing the study's flaws. If the envious person went a step further and verbalized these thoughts to the colleague (e.g., "That journal's not that great anyway" and "Did you consider correcting these flaws ...?), belittling would occur.

TABLE 2.4

Competitive Behavior Likely to Be Associated with Negative Relational Outcomes

Behaviors and Definition/Example

Antagonistic Behaviors

Behaviors That Encourage Negative Self-to-Other Comparisons

1. Expressed superiority. Actions that cast oneself as superior to others, for example, correcting other people in front of others
2. Belittling. Actions that cast others as inferior to oneself, for example, downplaying, dismissing, or laughing at another person's ideas, telling the partner that s/he got "lucky" when he or she accomplished something, and saying that the partner's accomplishment is "not such a big deal."
3. Bragging. Actions that call undue attention to one's achievements, for example, telling others about one's achievements or showing people a big paycheck.
4. Aggressiveness. Verbal or nonverbal behaviors that challenge or intimidate others, for example, frequently disagreeing with someone and becoming argumentative, and giving people the "evil eye."
5. Insincerity/manipulation. Using manipulation to force a negative self-to-other comparison, for example, acting phony or condescending or forcing a compliment.
6. Subterfuge. Purposeful actions that are designed to diminish the rival's positive image, for example, making negative, untrue remarks about the rival to others, trying to make the rival lose concentration so he or she will perform poorly, and making it seem as though the rival cheated.

Antisocial Behaviors

Behaviors That Reflect Competitiveness and/or Envy-Proneness

1. Social distance. Behaviors directed at the rival that show disinterest and avoidance, for example, avoiding direct eye contact with the rival, not paying attention to what the rival is saying, and staying away from the rival in social situations.
2. General anxiety/defensiveness. Behaviors that show anxiety and/or defensiveness, for example, acting nervous when it is time to perform a task, becoming especially serious when engaging in a competitive task, and acting defensive when one does poorly.
3. Noncooperative efforts. Behaviors that indicate unwillingness to work with a group, for example, suddenly working harder when someone else in the group starts doing well, refusing to help others in the group do better, and working alone instead of with others.
4. Self-focus. Behaviors that demonstrate self-absorption, for example, using "I" rather than "we" when speaking about a joint project, insisting on doing things a certain way, and dominating discussions.

Note. This table is adapted from Messman's (1996) work on competitiveness.

Another form of behavior that is often perceived as competitive is subterfuge (Messman, 1996). When people use this strategy, they are intentionally trying to prevent the rival from excelling or from maintaining a positive self-image within the social network. For example, an envious person might try to harm the rival's reputation. Strategies such as this are probably most likely to be used when individuals experience intense envy or rivalry. Rivalry is somewhat different from envy in that neither person possesses the valued commodity and both are actively seeking it (Bryson, 1977; Salovey & Rodin, 1989). Whether the situation involves envy or rivalry, subterfuge is likely to be used when people want others to evaluate them more positively than a rival and/or when people want to get revenge at the rival.

The final two forms of antagonistic behaviors—aggressiveness and insecurity or manipulation—involve communication styles that reflect a competitive orientation (Messman, 1996). Aggressive behaviors are viewed as personally challenging and often intimidating, and therefore, they likely lead to competition and self-to-other evaluations. Insecurity or manipulation behaviors appear to force others to either make a positive evaluation of the communicator or a negative evaluation of themselves. For example, people who fish for compliments are trying to bolster their positive images of themselves, whereas people who act condescending or stand offish imply that the sender's message is not worthwhile.

Messman (1996) also described four types of antisocial behaviors. The first of these—social distance—involves showing disinterest and avoiding interaction with the rival. This strategy corresponds with Salovey and Rodin's (1984) research, that found people want to avoid future interaction with rivals. When individuals are faced with a person who engenders a negative self-to-other comparison, a natural reaction is to avoid them and thus, to avoid feeling badly about themselves. The second antisocial behavior, general anxiety or defensiveness, is likely a symptom of envy proneness and competitiveness. Individuals who take competitive situations to heart are most likely to be nervous when performing important tasks and become defensive if the task is not performed well. The final two antisocial behaviors—noncooperative efforts and self-focus—represent an unwillingness to work with others and a need to be the best or the leader when conversing with others. These two objectives may appear contradictory on the surface, however, when you consider that competitive people want to stand apart from others (but also want to be recognized for their accomplishments), such actions make sense.

All of the antagonistic and antisocial behaviors just described lead to negative interpersonal consequences. Some behaviors falling under Messmans (1996) success-oriented theme also promote negative consequences. For example, Messman discussed behaviors such as making a bet with someone, openly challenging someone's position, and telling a group that the most important thing is to win. These behaviors increase the self-relevance of a skill or topic area, which can lead to envy. In addition, some people reported that they or their partners got upset when they lost. These types of success-oriented behaviors appear likely to promote conflict and separation rather than harmony and solidarity.

Relational (Dis)Satisfaction. Because envy and competitiveness are often found within the context of close relationships, it is natural to wonder how envious thoughts, emotions, and behaviors affect relational satisfaction. It appears obvious that many of the behaviors discussed are detrimental to relationships. Behaviors such as expressed superiority and bragging are likely to make others uncomfortable. Moreover, because envy and pride are popularly perceived as two of the seven deadly sins, individuals who verbally express their superiority are viewed as arrogant rather than self-confident. Behaviors such as belittling, aggressiveness, and insincerity or manipulation are also likely to promote relational dissatisfaction because they force others to take a defensive stance. Put simply, most people do not want to be around someone who is constantly disagreeing with or belittling them; although such a process may help one person bolster positive self-to-other evaluations, it causes the other person to see herself or himself more negatively.

Messman and Cupach (1996) confirmed the contention that many antagonistic and antisocial behaviors negatively affect relationships. In their study, friends completed questions regarding competitive communication, facework (i.e., how they present themselves to one another), and interpersonal solidarity. Results showed that across same-sex and cross-sex friendships, malevolent competitive behaviors were negatively associated with interpersonal solidarity. Malevolent competition was measured with items such as: "My friend tries to 'one-up' me," "My friend responds unhappily to something I did well," "My friend might make it seem like I am cheating when we play a game," and "My friend acts stand-offish when wishing me well."

Certain competitive behaviors, however, were positively related to interpersonal solidarity. Specifically, behaviors that reflected achievement competition appear to associate with positive relational outcomes (Messman & Cupach, 1996). These behaviors include saying that one wants to work hard and excel, sharing one's achievements with others without bragging, and asking about the friend's accomplishments. Interestingly, these behaviors are competitive in that they could call forth a self-to-other comparison; however, they are framed in a way that emphasizes accomplishments over defeats and solidarity over conflict.

Finally, it is noteworthy that nonmalicious or admiring envy leads to liking and relational satisfaction. Such envy is likely to occur when the ability, talent, or personal characteristic in question is only self-relevant for one of the relational partners. For example, a husband might be immensely proud of his wife's ability to understand finances and build them a sound investment portfolio because he is not good with numbers. Two friends may brag about one another's successes in two different areas such as academics and athletics. In these cases, people are likely to admire their partners for possessing desirable traits. In addition, they might bask in the reflected glory of their partner's accomplishments (see Salovey & Rodin, 1989). In such cases, the idea that your relational partner is a good, talented, and worthwhile person, coupled with the knowledge that your partner has chosen you as a companion, is likely to lead you to evaluate yourself positively. Similarly, to the extent that relational partners possess positive personal characteristics and abilities, they have the power to deposit rewards into the relationship, which ultimately makes the relationship more satisfying.

Conclusion

Although we primarily focused on the dark side of jealousy and envy, it should be evident that these emotions have a bright side as well. Jealousy and envy are related yet distinct constructs. Both experiences are accompanied by a similar constellation of emotion that includes anger, fear, and sadness. The cause of the emotions, however, differs. Jealousy, which is the broader of the two constructs is associated with fear over the prospect of losing a valued relationship, anger over betrayal, and sadness over potential relationship loss. Envy, on the other hand, is rooted in anger at oneself and resentment toward others, fear stemming from perceptions of inferiority, and sadness regarding one's failures and shortcomings. Both jealousy and envy are associated with more negative than positive emotions, but the positive emotions should not be overlooked. Jealousy can show love and appreciation, add romance to a dull relationship, or help one realize the extent of care and commitment he or she feels for another. Envy can lead to admiration and self-improvement.

Similarly, although jealousy and envy sometimes lead to destructive forms of interpersonal communication and, ultimately, to relational dissatisfaction, at other times, these emotions lead to understanding and solidarity. Thus, it appears that the way jealousy and envy are expressed is a key determinant of relational satisfaction. Jealous individuals who show distrust by monitoring their partners' actions and becoming possessive, as well as those who show their anger through verbal or physical aggression, are likely to push their partners further away. Similarly, those who handle envy by engaging in negatively valenced, competitive behaviors, such as belittling, bragging, manipulation, and subterfuge, are likely to alienate others, which in turn, leads to even stronger feelings of resentment and inferiority. However, the picture is not as dark as it might at first seem. When jealous individuals approach the situation by discussing the problem with their partner in a calm and constructive manner, a new relational understanding may emerge. Jealousy sometimes serves a protective function by prompting the jealous individual to express love and affection when the relationship is in danger of going astray. Envy can also be functional, especially when it is used as a motivational tool to improve oneself. Thus, as with many human emotions, jealousy and envy have both a dark, dysfunctional side and a bright, functional side. Understanding both sides of these complex emotions is an important enterprise for scholars, clinicians, and all who value their relationships with others.

Acknowledgment

We thank Susan Messman for sharing her work on competitiveness with us and for her valuable comments on the competitiveness section of this chapter.

Consider this . . .

- As the authors discuss differences between the emotions of jealousy and envy, what additional factors might you suggest be used to distinguish the two emotions?
- As you reflect on the many examples from literature and popular culture that depict society's view of these two emotions (jealousy and envy), how have such portrayals influenced your personal view of these two emotions?
- How has your view of these emotions affected your personal relationships? Does your view change given the nature of the relationship? If so, give a specific example to illustrate.
- How has the "dark side" of jealousy and envy affected your own sense of personal identity? Give an example to illustrate.
- How has the "dark side" of jealousy and envy created dissatisfaction in a personal relationship? What specific behaviors reflected unhealthy communication in this relationship? Give an example to illustrate.
- Now that you have a better understanding of the "dark side" of jealousy and envy, how might you use different communication tools to address these issues in your personal relationships?

References

Afifi, W. A., & Reichert, T (1996). Understanding the role of uncertainty in jealousy experience and expression. *Communication Reports, 9,* 93-103.

Andersen, P. A., Eloy, S. V., Guerrero, L. K., & Spitzberg, B. H. (1995). Romantic jealousy and relational satisfaction: A look at the impact of jealousy experience and expression. *Communication Reports, 8,* 77-85.

Aristotle. (1886). *The Rhetoric* (J. E. C. Welldon, Trans.). London: Metheun (Original work published in 344 B.C.)

Arnold, M. B. (1960). *Emotion and personality.* New York: Columbia University Press.

Aune, K. S., & Comstock, J. (1996, May). *The effect of relationship length on the experience, expression, and perceived appropriateness of jealousy.* Paper presented at the annual meeting of the International Communication Association, Chicago.

Ausubel, D. P., Sullivan, E. V., & Ives, S. W. (1980). *Theory and problems of child development.* New York: Grune & Stratton.

Baumgart, H. (1990). *Jealousy.* Chicago: University of Chicago Press.

Baxter, L. A. (1988). A dialectical perspective on communication strategies in relational development. In S. W. Duck (Ed.), *Handbook of personal relationships: Theory, research, and interventions* (pp. 257-273). New York: Wiley

Berke, J. H. (1988). *The tyranny of malice: Exploring the dark side of culture and character.* New York: Summit Books.

Bers, S. A., & Rodin, J. (1984). Social comparison jealousy. A developmental and motivational study. *Journal of Personality and Social Psychology, 47,* 766-769.

Bohm, E. (1961). Jealousy. In A. Ellis & A. Abarbanel (Eds.), *The encyclopedia of sexual behavior* (vol. 1, pp. 567-574). New York: Hawthorn Books.

Brehm, S. S. (1992). *Intimate relationships* (2nd ed.). New York: McGraw-Hill.

Bringle, R. G. (1991). Psychosocial aspects of jealousy: A transactional model. In P Salovey (Ed.), *The psychology of jealousy and envy* (pp. 103-131). New York: Guilford.

Bryson, J. B. (1976, September). *The nature of sexual jealousy: An exploratory paper.* Paper presented at the annual meeting of the American Psychological Association, Washington, DC.

Bryson, J. B. (1977, September). *Situational determinants of the expression of jealousy.* Paper presented at the annual meeting of the American Psychological Association, San Francisco, CA.

Bryson, J. B. (1991). Modes of responses to jealousy-evoking situations. In P Salovey (Ed.). *The psychology of envy and jealousy* (pp. 1-45). New York: Guilford.

Burke, T, Genn-Bash, A., & Haines, B. (1988). *Competition in theory and practice.* London: Croom Helm.

Buss, D. M. (1988). From vigilance to violence: Tactics of mate retention in American undergraduates. *Ethology and Sociobiology, 9,* 291-317.

Buunk, B. P (1991). Jealousy in close relationships: An exchange-theoretical perspective. In P. Salovey (Ed.), *The psychology of jealousy and envy* (pp. 148-177). New York: Guilford.

Campos, J. J., Barrett, K. C., Lamb, M. E., Goldsmith, H. H., & Stenberg, C. (1983). Socioemotional development. In M. M. Haith & J. J. Campos (Eds.), *Handbook of Child Psychology: Vol. 2. Infancy and developmental psychobiology* (4th ed., pp. 783-915). New York: Wiley.

Ciabattari, J. (1988, December). Will the '90s be the age of envy? *Psychology Today, 47-50.*

Clanton, G. (1989). Jealousy in American culture 1945-1985: Reflections from popular literature. In D. D. Franks & E. D. McCarthy (Eds.), *The sociology of emotions: Original essays and research papers* (pp. 179-193). Greenwich, CT: JAI.

Clanton, G., & Smith, L. G. (1977). *Jealousy.* Englewood Cliffs, NJ: Prentice-Hall.

Comstock, J., & Aune, K. S. (1995, May) *Is jealousy prescribed or against the rules: Comparisons among same-sex friends, cross-sex friends, and romantic partners.* Paper presented at the annual meeting of the International Communication Association, Albuquerque, NM.

Dakin, S., & Arrowood, A. J. (1981). The social comparison of ability. *Human Relations, 34,* 80-109.

Daly, M., &Wilson, M. (I 983). *Sex, evolution, and behavior.* Boston, MA: Willard Grant Press.

Delgado, A. R., & Bond, R. A. (1993). Attenuating the attribution of responsibility: The lay perception of jealousy as a motive for wife battery. *Journal of Applied Social Psychology, 23,* 1337-1356.

Ekman, P, Friesen, W V, & Ellsworth, P. (1972). *Emotions in the human face: Guidelines for research and integration of findings.* New York: Pergamon.

Farrell, D. M. (1980). Jealousy. *The Philosophical Review, 89,* 527-529.

Festinger, L. (1954). A theory of social comparison processes. *Human Relations, 7,* 11-140.

Fitness, J., & Fletcher, G. J. O. (1993). Love, hate, anger, and jealousy in close relationships: A prototype and cognitive appraisal analysis. *Journal of Personality and Social Psychology, 65,* 942-958.

Guerrero, L. K., & Afifi, W. A. (1997, June). *Toward a functional approach to studying strategic communicative responses to jealousy.* Paper presented at the annual meeting of the International Network on Personal Relationships, Oxford, OH.

Guerrero, L. K., & Andersen, P. A. (1998). The experience and expression of romantic jealousy. In P A. Andersen & L. K. Guerrero (Eds.), *The handbook of communication and emotion: Research, theory, applications, and contexts* (pp. 155-188). San Diego, CA: Academic Press.

Guerrero, L. K., Andersen, P. A., Jorgensen, P. F., Spitzberg, B. H., & Eloy, S. V. (1995). Coping with the green-eyed monster: Conceptualizing and measuring communicative responses to romantic jealousy. *Western Journal of Communication, 59,* 270-304.

Guerrero, L. K., & Eloy, S. V. (1991). Relational satisfaction and jealousy across marital types. *Communication Reports, 5,* 23-31.

Guerrero, L. K., Eloy, S. V., Jorgensen, P. F., & Andersen, P A. (1993). Hers or his? Sex differences in the communication of jealousy in close relationships. In P. Kalbfleisch (Ed.), *Interpersonal communication: Evolving interpersonal relationships* (pp. 109-131). Hillsdale, NJ: Lawrence Erlbaum Associates.

Hansen, G. L. (1991). Jealousy: Its conceptualization, measurement, and integration with family stress theory. In P. Salovey (Ed.), *The Psychology of jealousy and envy* (pp. 211-230). New York: Guilford.

Hupka, R. B. (1991). The motive for the arousal of romantic jealousy. In P Salovey (Ed.), *The psychology of jealousy and envy* (pp. 252-270). New York: Guilford.

Klein, M., & Riviere, J. (1964). *Love, hate, and reparation.* New York: Norton.

Korda, M. (1992). *The immortals.* New York: Poseidon Press.

Laner, M. R. (1990). Violence or its precipitators: Which is more likely to be identified as a dating problems? *Deviant Behavior, 11,* 319-329.

Mathes, E. W., Adams, H. E., & Davies, R. M. (1985). Jealousy: Loss of relationship rewards, loss of self-esteem, depression, anxiety, and anger. *Journal of Personality and Social Psychology, 48,* 1552-1561.

Mathes, E. W., & Verstraete, C. (1993). Jealous aggression: Who is the target, the beloved or the rival? *Psychological Reports, 72,* 1071-1074.

Messman, S. J. (1995). *Competitiveness in close relationships: The role of communication competence.* Unpublished doctoral dissertation, Ohio University, Athens, OH.

Messman, S. J. (1996, February). *Competitiveness and communication: Conceptualization and operationalization.* Paper presented at the annual meeting of the Western States Communication Association, Pasadena, CA.

Messman, S. J., & Cupach, W. R. (1996, November). *Perceptions of competitive communication behavior in friendship: Associations with face predilections and solidarity.* Paper presented at the annual meeting of the Speech Communication Association, San Diego, CA.

Mowat, R. R. (1966). *Morbid jealousy and murder.* London: Tavistock.

Mullen, P E., & Maack, L. H. (1985). Jealousy, pathological jealousy, and aggression. In D. P. Farrington & J. Gunn (Eds.), *Aggression and dangerousness* (pp. 103-126). New York: Wiley

Panskeep, J. (1982). Towards a general psychobiological theory of emotions. *Behavioral and Brain Sciences, 5,* 407-467.

Parker, R. G. (1994, November). *An examination of the influence of situational determinants upon strategies for coping with romantic jealousy.* Paper presented at the annual meeting of the Speech Communication Association, New Orleans, LA.

Parrott, W. G. (1991). The emotional experiences of envy and jealousy. In P Salovey (Ed.), *The Psychology of jealousy and envy* (pp. 3-30). New York: Guilford.

Parrott, W. G., & Smith, R. H. (1993). Distinguishing the experiences of envy and jealousy. *Journal of Personality and Social Psychology, 64,* 906-920.

Paul, L., Foss, M. A., & Galloway, J. (1993). Sexual jealousy in young women and men: Aggressive responsiveness to partner and rival. *Aggressive Behavior, 19,* 401-420.

Pfeiffer, S. M., & Wong, P. T. (1989). Multidimensional jealousy. *Journal of Social and Personal Relationships, 6,* 181-196.

Pines, A. (1992). *Romantic jealousy: Understanding and conquering the shadow of love.* New York: St. Martin's Press.

Pines, A., & Aronson, E. (1983). Antecedents, correlates, and consequences of sexual jealousy. *Journal of Personality, 51,* 108-136.

Pinto, R. P., & Hollandsworth, J. G., Jr. (1984). A measure of possessiveness in intimate relationships. *Journal of Social and Clinical Psychology, 6,* 505-510.

Plutchik, R. (1980). *Emotion: A psychoevolutionary theory of emotion.* New York: Harper & Row.

Rimé, B., Mesquita, B., Philippot, P., & Boca, S. (1991). Beyond the emotional event: Six studies of the social sharing of emotion. *Cognition and Emotion, 5,* 435-465.

Salovey, P., & Rodin, J. (1984). Some antecedents and consequences of social-comparison jealousy. *Journal of Personality and Social Psychology, 47,* 780-792.

Salovey, P., & Rodin, J. (1985, September) The heart of jealousy. *Psychology Today, 22-25,* 28-29.

Salovey, P., & Rodin, J. (1988). Coping with envy and jealousy. *Journal of Social and Clinical Psychology, 7,* 15-33.

Salovey, P, & Rodin, J. (1989). Envy and jealousy in close relationships. In C. Hendrick (Ed.), *Close relationships* (pp. 221-246). Newbury Park: Sage.

Salovey, P., & Rothman, A. J. (1991). Envy and jealousy. Self and society. In P Salovey (Ed.), *The psychology of jealousy and envy* (pp. 271-286). New York: Guilford.

Schaap, C., Buunk, B., & Kerkstra, A. (1988). Martial conflict resolution. In P. Noller & M. A. Fitzpatrick (Eds.), *Perspectives on marital interaction* (pp. 203-244). Philadelphia: Multilingual Matters.

Schoeck, H. (1969). *Envy: A theory of social behavior.* New York: Harcourt Brace.

Sharpsteen, D. J. (1991). The organization of jealousy knowledge: Romantic jealousy as a blended emotion. In P Salovey (Ed.), *The psychology of jealousy and envy* (pp. 31-51). New York: Guilford.

Shaver, P. R., Schwartz, J., Kirson, D., & O'Connor, C. (1987). Emotion knowledge: Further explorations of a prototype approach. *Journal of Personality and Social Psychology, 52,* 1061-1086.

Sharpsteen, D. J. (1991). The organization of jealousy knowledge: Romantic jealousy as a blended emotion. In P Salovey (Ed.), *The psychology of jealousy and envy* (pp. 31-51). New York: Guilford.

Smith, R. H. (1991). Envy and the sense of injustice. In P Salovey (Ed.), *The psychology of jealousy and envy* (pp. 79-99). New York: Guilford.

Smith, R. H., Kim, S. H., & Parrott, W. G. (1988). Envy and jealousy. Semantic problems and experiential distinctions. *Personality and Social Psychology Bulletin, 14,* 401-409.

Smith, R. H., Parrott, W G., & Diener, E. (1990). *The development and validation of a scale for measuring enviousness.* Unpublished manuscript.

Solomon, R. C. (1976). *The passions.* Garden City, NY: Doubleday.

Stearns, P. N. (1989). Jealousy: *The evolution of an emotion in American history.* New York: New York University Press.

Stets, J. E., & Pirog-Good, M. A. (1987). Violence in dating relationships. *Social Psychology Quarterly, 50,* 237-246.

Sugarman, D. B., & Hotaling, G. T. (1989). Dating violence: Prevalence, context, and risk markers. In M. A. Pirog-Good & J. E. Stets (Eds.), *Violence in dating relationships: Emerging social issues* (pp. 3-32). New York: Praeger.

Teismann, M. W, & Mosher, D. L. (1978). Jealous conflict in dating couples. *Psychological Reports, 42,* 1211-1216.

Tesser, A. (1986). Some effects of self-evaluation maintenance on cognition and action. In R. M. Sorrentino & E. T Higgins (Eds.), *Handbook of motivation and cognition* (pp. 435-464). New York: Guilford.

Tesser, A., & Campbell, J. (1982). Self-evaluation maintenance and the perception of friends and strangers. *Journal of Personality, 50,* 261-279.

Texas executes man who killed his ex-girlfriend out of jealousy (1995, August 15). The New York Times, p. Al.

Tracy, L. (1991). *The secret between us: Competition among women.* Boston, MA: Little, Brown.

White, G. L., Fishbein, S., & Rutstein, J. (1981). Passionate love and the misattribution of arousal. *Journal of Personality and Social Psychology, 41,* 56-62.

White, G. L., & Mullen, P. E. (1989). *Jealousy: Theory, research, and clinical strategies.* New York: Guilford.

In Chapter 4 of her text, *Relational Communication*, Julia Wood begins to explore the central dynamics of relational culture by discussing the dialectical processes we experience in our personal relationships. As she notes, dialectics are contradictory dynamics inherently bound in relationships as we strive to meet personal needs of the participants. The tensions created by these dialectics are not something we resolve; instead, they are a process through which we continually navigate and manage our personal relationships. As such, these dialectical tensions inevitably influence the relational culture we create.

In her article entitled, "Communication in Intercultural Relationships," Ling Chen (Associate Professor of Communication Studies at Hong Kong Baptist University) examines the influence of dialectical tensions in the intercultural relationship. Specifically, she begins with a discussion of how any cultural difference, broadly defined to include such characteristics as national origin, ethnic background, religious affiliation, gender, sexual orientation, or age, will influence the unique relational culture created in a personal relationship. Through her extensive literature review, Chen discusses the influence of cultural differences on various stages of relationship development including initial interaction and relationship formation as well as various aspects of relationship sustenance and progression. From there, she explores how stereotypes and cultural identity influence the dynamic process of creating a unique relational culture within intercultural relationships.

Once Chen discusses the influence of these interpersonal dynamics on intercultural relationships, she then uses a dialectical approach to explore both the internal and external contradictions experienced in intercultural relationships. These contradictions focus primarily on three basic interpersonal processes: 1) information sharing (i.e., openness-closedness); 2) interdependence (i.e., autonomy-connection); and 3) relationship variability (i.e., predictability-novelty). As you read Chen's dialectical approach to her broad perspective on intercultural relationships, continue to use Julia Wood's discussion of dialectics in Chapter 4 as a reference point for understanding this theory and its general applications.

Finally, as Chen draws her discussion of intercultural relationships to a close, she makes a valuable observation about the study of intercultural relationships. She notes that such relationships are, by nature, both interpersonal and intercultural; to provide valuable insight about these relationships, we must study the constant interface between the individual and the relationship as well as the constant interface between the relationship and culture. Chen believes that the complex interfaces which serve to serve link the individual, relationship, and culture are best studied from a dialectical approach because this approach allows us to understand the ever-present tension among these forces and their subsequent impact on the relationship.

Communication in Intercultural Relationships

Ling Chen
Hong Kong Baptist University

Research on intercultural relationship communication is still in its infancy, with limited studies on intercultural communication in interpersonal relationships such as intercultural marriage, dating, and friendship. Interest in intercultural marriages arises mainly from a practical need to understand marriages between partners of different cultural backgrounds as a social phenomenon. Research on other intercultural relationships including friendship grows out of interests in intercultural communication as a whole: Relationships are a context in which intercultural communication occurs. Despite an absence of systematic inquiry, issues have emerged that are essential to communication in intercultural relationships. Whereas many issues are the same as those in relationships in general, such as intimacy and privacy, some have greater salience or impact, such as dealing with differences and social perception of the intercultural relationship.

In this chapter, I discuss communication in intercultural relationships in two parts. In the first, I review the literature on relational processes in intercultural relationships. In the second section, I propose a dialectical approach to the study of intercultural relationships. Informed by the dialectical perspective to relational communication (Baxter & Montgomery, 1997), I discuss the peculiarity of dialects in intercultural relationships and explore directions for communication studies. As cultural difference between relationship partners necessarily sets intercultural relationships apart from intracultural ones, the discussion starts with a brief review of underlying cultural influences on relational communication.

Relational Processes In Intercultural Communication

Cross-Cultural Variability

Culture here refers to cultures or cultural groups of all levels (national, ethnic, gender, age, etc.). Views on and the practice of interpersonal relationships vary across cultures, often along conceptual dimensions such as individualism and collectivism (see Gudykunst & Lee, Chapter 2 in this volume). Cross-cultural studies have identified cultural influence on several aspects of communication in intercultural relationships.

Social penetration. Social penetration occurs with increase of self-disclosure, in topic variety and intimacy of information, and thus, the development of relationship intimacy. Culture's influence on relational communication is most evident in self-disclosure. Scholars (G. Chen, 1995; Ting-Toomey, 1991) have reported that, in a same relationship type, members of cultures or cultural groups high in individualism (e.g., United States, France, Anglo-Americans) tend to self-disclose more than those from low individualistic cultures (e.g., Japan, China, Asian Americans). This difference may reflect culturally stipulated intimacy of relationships by type; for example, Japanese perceive romantic relationships as less intimate than Americans (Gudykunst & Nishida, 1986). Also, because self-disclosure is a form of direct communication preferred by individualistic cultures, members of individualistic cultures would self-disclose more.

Uncertainty management. The work of Gudykunst and associates has informed us much about cultural differences in this area. Members of collectivistic cultures reportedly feel more uncertain interacting with outgroups than with ingroups, whereas members of individualistic cultures reported no distinction. In managing uncertainty, for example, Japanese have more attribution confidence interacting with ingroup friends than do Americans. Consistent to their orientation toward group or individual, cultures differ in the type of information sought in initial interactions (i.e., group- vs. personal-based backgrounds, respectively) and in the effect of communication frequency on uncertainty reduction, found for individualistic cultures only (see Gudykunst, 1989, for an overview).

Ingroup versus outgroup communication. Cultures higher in collectivism are found to make greater ingroup-outgroup distinctions, as is consistent with the concept of collectivism. In a cross-cultural study of perceptions of interaction, Gudykunst, Yoon, and Nishida (1987) found that members of cultures higher in collectivism differentiated ingroups and outgroups more in their perceptions of the synchronization, personalization, and difficulties of interaction with others. American respondents made the least distinction, followed by Japanese and Korean respondents, respectively. Similarly, Gudykunst et al. (1992) reported that Chinese samples differentiated between ingroup and outgroup members in self-disclosure, whereas no ingroup-outgroup differentiation was found for the Australian and U.S. samples.

Relationship Development

Cultural differences assert influences on intercultural communicators from the very start and throughout the process of relationship development.

Initial interaction. Initial interaction is often crucial if a relationship is to continue and even more so for intercultural relationships, for the initial social penetration proves more difficult in these relationships (Lee & Boster, 1991). Studies (e.g., L. Chen, 1995, 1997) have suggested that intercultural communicators in initial interaction are less perceptive and less responsive than intracultural communicators, and they may need explicit message input and adaptive verbal strategies to increase interaction involvement and facilitate interaction. Similarly, topic sharing is positively associated with the perception of intercultural accommodation and interaction involvement (Chen & Celaga, 1994). Appropriate communicative strategies leading to perceived accommodation and proper involvement may facilitate intercultural interaction beyond the initial encounter.

Relationship formation. What starts an intercultural relationship represents an old scholarly interest that relates indirectly to communication. Studies have examined dating, or romantic, relationships for reasons, attributes of individuals, and contextual circumstances for entering a personal relationship across cultural boundaries. There is much similarity regarding reasons of relationship formation in intercultural and intracultural relationships. Studies (e.g., Gurung & Duong, 1999; Kouri & Lasswell, 1993; Lampe, 1982; Shibazaki & Brennan, 1998) have found that same- and interethnic dating couple members entered relationships for similar reasons. They formed a dating relationship because of personal liking for each other or perceived common interests and goals, and they also reported similar levels of relationship intimacy, commitment, and relationship satisfaction. With respect to reasons for relationship formation, therefore, intercultural relationships appear to be more similar to intracultural relationships than different.

As for personal attributes of individuals likely to be involved in intercultural romantic relationships, both individual and social characteristics of groups that influence individuals on an aggregate level have been investigated. Greater strength of ethnic identity and personal preference for intercultural contact are found to facilitate formation of intercultural romantic relationships (e.g., Nguyen, 1998; Parsonson, 1987; Shibazaki & Brennan, 1998). Educational level and socioeconomic status of individuals also predict likelihood of such a relationship (e.g., Mills, Daly, Longmore, & Kilbride, 1995; Sung, 1990; Tucker & Mitchell-Kernan, 1995). Sex and ethnicity (e.g., Clark-Ibanez, 1999; Fujino, 1997), on the other hand, seem to interact with the factor of social dominance and status: Members of the dominant group, compared with nondominant group members, are less likely to enter intercultural relationships. (See the section on status.) In the case of immigrants, the higher their degree of acculturation, the more likely they are to form intercultural relationships (Hanassab & Tidwell, 1998; Hwang, Saenz, & Aguirre, 1997; Nguyen, 1998). In addition, diversity of friendship circles, individual comfort level, and social stereotypes of the opposite sex in various cultural groups are found to have influences on the initiation of intercultural dating or romantic relationships (Chan, 1990; Clark-Ibanez, 1999). Contextual factors such as propinquity, group size, and sex ratio have been found to exert strong structural constraints on marriage partner choices (Anderson & Saenz, 1994; Fujino, 1997; Hwang et al., 1997). The same is true for the social status of the group (Back, 1993; Blau, 1994; Collier & Bornman, 1999; Hoffman & Schwarzwald, 1987). Diversity of parents' friends and family attitudes toward intercultural dating or marriage facilitate or discourage these relationships (Clark-Ibanez, 1999; Mills et al., 1995).

Perceived similarity. An important factor in intercultural relationship formation, romantic or nonromantic, is perceived similarity, based on the perspective of similarity-attraction. Studies typically report perceived similarity associating with the likelihood of intercultural interaction (Grant, 1993; Osbeck, Moghaddam, & Perreault, 1997; cf. McDermott, 1991). Many studies also focus on specific aspects of similarity. Obot (1988) shows that African Americans perceive persons with similar values as more attractive and rated them more positively on nonaffective traits than they did targets with dissimilar values. Simard (1981) reports language and attitude similarity as important for French- and English-speaking ethnic groups in Canada in their interethnic interactions, more so than factors such as comparability in occupation or social class. Collier and Bornman (1999) note that for interethnic friendship in South Africa, perceived group dissimilarity in what is considered acceptable, appropriate behaviors toward a friend greatly discourages formation of intercultural friendship. Lee and Gudykunst (in press) report that perceived similarity in communication styles predicted attraction between European and non-European Americans. This suggests that similarities in cultural and sociological backgrounds play a role mainly during the orientation and exploratory affective stage of relationship formation (Gareis, 1995, 1999; Kouri & Lasswell, 1993). A few studies further suggest perceived similarity between intercultural partners as a function of communication that takes place (e.g., Horenczyk & Bekerman, 1997; Hubbert, Gudykunst, & Guerrero, 1999). From a communication perspective, it seems that the relationship between similarity and intercultural relationship formation is an interactive one: Greater perceived similarity facilitates a communicative relationship; interactions, once started, may lead to perception of greater similarity or convergence of partners' behavior, or both.

Relationship sustenance and progression. Once a relationship is formed, how partners manage to develop and maintain the relationship is the focus of interest. Investigating North American-Japanese relationships, Gudykunst and associates have examined personal accounts of individuals on their relationships. For opposite-sex romantic relationships (Gudykunst, Gao, Sudweeks, Ting-Toomey, & Nishida, 1991), they generalized themes of typicality, communication competence, similarity, and involvement and reported that the presence, form, and interconnections among themes and subthemes varied by the type of relationship. For example, cultural dissimilarities were not mentioned frequently as affecting the relationship in acquaintance relationships but were noted as important in the romantic relationships. Personal accounts of female intercultural relationships (Sudweeks, Gudykunst, Ting-Toomey, & Nishida, 1990) revealed four similar themes: communication competence, similarity, involvement, and turning points. The presence, form, and interconnections among the relational themes varied across intimacy levels. For example, in low-intimacy relationships, cultural differences were used to explain lack of intimacy, whereas when intimacy of relationship is high, cultural differences are mentioned without judgment or as a positive factor. The study also found that the subthemes of cultural similarity, language/cultural knowledge, and accommodation emerged more frequently in these relationships than in those between same-culture members. Overall, both studies found that intimacy of relationship is associated with empathy expressed and mutual accommodation between the partners.

Of mixed marriages, Rohrlich (1988) notes the visible movement from problem-oriented studies to adjustment analysis. The problem of intercultural marriage typically was identified as arising from social prejudice and an inability to deal with cultural and gender role expectation differences or demands for rapid acculturation (Breger & Hill, 1998; Crohn, 1998). Alternatively, personal narratives of intercultural couples are studied for a view from inside the mixed marriage. Johnson and Warren (1994) reported that in sharp contrast to many outsiders who understand mixed marriages solely in the large sociocultural context, to couples in the mixed marriage the relationship is primarily personal affairs between individuals. The couples' accounts of development, sustenance, and maintenance of their long-term relationships revealed it as a process of mutual adjustment and learning where its "mixed" character matters more to others around them. They pointed out that "relationships within all marriages are at times difficult and trying. But not always more so because they are 'mixed.' Happiness, loving and sharing are equally attributes of marriage. No less so because they are 'mixed' " (Johnson & Warren, 1994, p. 12). On the other hand, relationship matters for intercultural couples tend to become more complicated as a result of their being mixed and, thus, different. For this reason, commitment, tolerance of differences, and the ability to go against family and/or society are more critical for success of the relationship (e.g., Chan & Wethington, 1998; McGuire, 1992).

Uncertainty management. Cognitive uncertainty that individuals experience directly inputs into their relationship development. Communication is the only means of uncertainty management, which, in turn, is necessary for communication to proceed. Intercultural communicators reportedly perceive their partners to be less similar to themselves as compared with intracultural partners (Gudykunst, 1983; Lee & Boster, 1991). They also report less confidence in making attributions about their interaction partner and less interpersonal attraction. More directly, intercultural communicators report greater uncertainty and less positive expectations than those in intracultural interactions (Gudykunst & Shapiro, 1996). Greater anxiety is related with greater uncertainty. The more communicators are uncertain, the more they feel apprehensive about communicating in intercultural encounters (Neuliep & Ryan, 1998). The uncertainty and anxiety, however, decrease as interaction continues over time (Hubbert et al., 1999). In established intercultural relationships, uncertainty is reduced with the increase of intimacy level in the relationship as well as across relationship types (Gudykunst, 1985; Gudykunst, Nishida, & Chua, 1986).

Self-disclosure. Little has been done regarding this important topic in intercultural relationship. A few intercultural studies have reported findings in support of social penetration theory. Generally, communicators in initial intercultural encounters are likely to have higher levels of self-disclosure than in first meetings with a stranger from the same culture (e.g., Gudykunst & Nishida, 1984). The greater amount of self-disclosure, however, is simply due to greater unfamiliarity between communicating partners and, thus, remains superficial, for participants in initial intercultural interaction rarely request intimate information (Lee & Boster, 1991). In existing intercultural relationships, social penetration corresponds with the intimacy level of the relationship type and is comparable to similar intracultural relationships (Gudykunst, 1985; Gudvkunst et al., 1986). Social penetration deepens as an intercultural relationship progresses from the initial encounter to acquaintance and to friendship. Frequency and intimacy of self-disclosure increase after the initial foundation for the relationship has been established (Gudykunst, Nishida, & Chua, 1987; Hubbert et al., 1999). This positive relationship between self-disclosure and relationship intimacy has prompted Rohrlich (1988) to suggest a creative use of self-disclosure: Intercultural couples consciously self-disclose perceived aspects of differences in each other to increase understanding and preempt possible problems related to the difference. Where expectations and role perceptions are immediately different, awareness and discussion of how spouses see themselves would enable partners to match impression with perceived self-image of their spouse.

Communication Processes

Intercultural relationship communication by default involves intercultural issues such as stereotypes and cultural identity.

Differences and stereotypes. Individuals in intercultural relationships encounter differences at two levels. They face cultural differences between them and learn to interact in spite of the difference. They also face the fact that their relationships are different from what is common in society and, thus, tend to be stereotyped. Relationship partners deal with the first type of difference through communication of mutual respect and acceptance. There must be perceived respect for or willingness to accept differences and overcome stereotypes (e.g., Collier, 1996; Collier & Bornman, 1999; Hecht, Ribeau, & Sedano, 1990). Respect and acceptance are expressed in everyday mundane exchanges, such as requests for more information or expressed curiosity to learn about the other, and contribute positively to establishment of an intercultural friendship (e.g., Chen, Isa, & Sakai, 1996; Collier & Bowker, 1994; Hecht, Larkey, & Johnson, 1992). Social stereotypes about intercultural romantic relationships are dealt with by seeking or building social networks for support (e.g., Johnson & Warren, 1994; Spickard, 1989).

Cultural identity. Cultural or ethnic identity has a dynamic role in intercultural relationships. Individuals with strong and insecure cultural identification tend not to interact cross-culturally and, consequently, have no or few intercultural relationships of any type. Individuals with strong and secure or those with weak cultural identification are more likely to enter an intercultural relationship. This applies to sojourners, immigrants, and ethnic groups alike (e.g., Hanassab & Tidwell, 1998; Nguyen, 1998; Strom, 1988). This pattern is shown in intercultural dating of individuals at different stages of ethnic identity transformation. Those at stages characterized by security in or rejection of ethnic identity are more likely to date outside of their ethnic group than those at stages with insecure or strong ethnic identity (Chung, 1990). An explanation is that individuals with strong ethnic identity tend to perceive potential outgroup dating partners with greater social distance and less trust and receptivity (Chung & Ting-Toomey, 1999).

As communicators, members of major ethnic groups in the United States and South Africa have described rules for ethnic identity enactment as important for intercultural friendship (Collier, 1996; Collier & Bornman, 1999). Ethnic identity enactment rules vary between groups. Latino and Asian Americans abide by respect, exchanging ideas, and learning more about the other's cultural background; expressing understanding and appreciating culture are rules for African Americans; showing respect for other cultures, for Anglo Americans. For all South African ethnic groups, identity rules include explaining differences and learning from one another. In spite of the variety in identity rules, violation of these rules is perceived by all to be inappropriate to the intercultural friendship.

Cultural identity is dynamic in many other ways. Communicators report awareness of a gradual shift from cultural identity to individual identity as an intercultural relationship develops. This is reflected in topics of conversation, perceptions of closeness, and reported conscious observations of this movement of identity (Hubbert et al., 1999). From a different perspective, Larkey and Hecht (1995) examined African American and European American interethnic interactions and found ethnic identity to be negatively related to interethnic communication satisfaction in less intimate relationships and no significant relationship to interethnic communication with friends. Cultural identity is present but not salient in a closer relationship or in a more intimate stage of a relationship. It is also argued that in actual interactions, different facets or levels of the cultural identity (national, ethnic, gender, age, etc.) may alternately emerge into salience depending on the circumstances and nature of the interaction, which must be negotiated and managed in communication (Collier, 1996).

Social power and status. Dominance defined as social power and status is often communicated unequivocally in intercultural relationships. Status-based differentiation in psychological aspects is observable and expressed in communication. In intergroup interactions, members of nondominant groups, blacks and females, were reportedly perceived as more homogenized with less individuality than members of dominant groups, whites and males (Cabecinhas & Amancio, 1999). The perception of similarity-attraction is reportedly stronger when the target is a member of a nondominant group than when it is a dominant group member (Osbeck et al., 1997), reflecting a stereotypical belief that members of minority groups "keep to themselves" and "won't mix" (Back, 1993). Studies have also shown that members of the dominant group are more likely to assume their cultural rules to be the norms and standard, expecting everyone to conform to these rules (Collier & Bornman, 1999; Collier & Bowker, 1994)

Research has indicated social status equality to be a positive predictor of interethnic marriages between Mexican Americans and white Americans (Anderson & Saenz, 1994). Nondominant groups/cultures are relatively more receptive to this unconventional marital form, especially when the outgroup partner is from a dominant cultural group (Sung, 1990; Tuch, Sigelman, & MacDonald, 1999), a fact that members of nondominant groups/cultures are also more aware of. Overall, social perceptions of an intercultural relationship vary in degrees of disapproval based on the ethnicity, gender, and status combination of partners involved (Mills et al., 1995). Social judgment and attribution of intercultural relationships are more negative when directed at partners from nondominant groups (Breger & Hill, 1998).

Social perceptions and social support. By and large, intercultural relationships or marriages are perceived negatively across cultural and ethnic groups (e.g., Agranat & Titov, 1994; Bizman, 1987; Levkovitch, 1990), although there is evidence of increased tolerance among the U.S. population ("Race Relations," 1991; Tuch et al., 1999). The more intimate relationships are perceived more negatively than are the less intimate ones (Garcia & Rivera, 1999). People consider love as significantly more important in ethnically heterogeneous marriages than in homogeneous ones, but rate homogeneous couples as more compatible (Bizman, 1987). As a result, intercultural couples have reported significantly more external problems with parents, extended family members, relatives, friends, and the community (e.g., Graham, Moeai, & Shizuru, 1985; Nguyen, 1998; Rosenblatt, Karis, & Powell, 1995). There are usually greater assimilation pressures on a spouse, usually the wife, toward accepting the culture of the other spouse (Breger & Hill, 1998; Graham et at., 1985). These findings indicate that for an intercultural marriage to succeed it demands considerably more sacrifice, patience, and commitment.

Social perceptions of intercultural relationships are directly reflected in the social support to partners in such relationships that may "make or break the relationship" (Spickard, 1989). Social support operates at every stage of relational development contributing substantially to the growth, maintenance, or dissolution of a relationship. The support or lack of it is communicated in various messages that comment or give advice on some general or specific aspects of the relationship or on its development, often by explicitly or implicitly comparing the relationship with community expectations or other relationships in the community (Payne, 1998). A salient perception of individuals in interethnic relationships is reportedly a lack of support from the general public (Chan & Wethington, 1998; Rosenblatt et al., 1995), so much so that Shibazaki and Brennan (1998) in discussing their study on interethnic dating offer the suggestion that "the trouble with inter-racial relationships is not race, it's racism" (p. 254). Social support in intercultural relationships is so important that intercultural couples often seek communities or form their own social networks where they may find support (Gaines & Ickes, 1997; Johnson & Warren, 1994).

Commitment and attachment. Of special importance to the sustenance of intercultural relationships is commitment to the relationship, when relationship partners talk about their differences, share experiences, and express mutual support in the face of adversity (Johnson & Warren, 1994; McGuire, 1992; Rosenblatt et al., 1995). Haas and Stafford (1998) in their study on gay men and lesbians in committed relationships note that being "out" as a couple to one's social networks is a means of strengthening the relationship against social stigma. The practice may well apply to other intercultural relationships encountering social disapproval. Presentation of themselves in public as a unit communicates the relationship partners' commitment to the relationship, not only to the community but also to each other, hence the positive effect on the relationship.

On the other hand, commitment also affects communication in the relationship. Gaines and colleagues (Gaines et al., 1999; Gaines et al., 1997) investigated interethnic couples for the association between relationship attachment and response to marital conflict situations. Securely attached relationship partners reportedly displayed greater accommodative tendencies. Securely, compared to insecurely, attached individuals consistently produced lower level of destructive or relationship-threatening responses (e.g., exit and neglect), whereas insecure attachment was a positive correlate of destructive responses.

A Dialectical Approach

A dialectical approach explicates social phenomena with a small set of conceptual assumptions about contradiction (Baxter & Montgomery, 1997). It holds that contradictions, known as dialectics, are inherent to social life and change is the norm (Mao, 1965): Amid dialectics people constantly act and are acted upon to manage the tension. This perspective provides a meta-theoretical framework for a systematic understanding of communication in intercultural relationships. Integrating the literature reviewed above, this section discusses the dialectics in intercultural communication most relevant to personal relationships and examines the interplay of intercultural and relationship dialectics. The discussion serves to organize the scattered research on intercultural relationships and explores directions for future research.

Interpersonal Relationship Dialectics

Relationship partners experience from the very start various internal and external contradictions (Werner & Baxter, 1994). Interpersonal communication scholars have identified six dialectics that are internal or external to the relationship surrounding the interrelated matters of information sharing, interdependence, and variability (Baxter, 1988, 1993; Baxter & Montgomery, 1997; Rawlins, 1992). Information sharing bears on the contradictions of openness-closeness within and revelation-nonrevelation outside the relationship, about how much relationship partners share information about each other, and about how much they share relationship information with others in their social networks and with the society at large. Autonomy-connection and separation-integration are internal and external contradictions relating to interdependence. These dialectics involve the extent to which relationship partners give up individuality to bond into an entity and participate in interaction with others in the community or focus on the relationship interaction. Relationship variability underlies the internal predictability-novelty and external conventionality-uniqueness contradictions. The dialectics are about how partners interact with and relate to each other in predictable ways without losing interest and contribute to stability as well as change of their culture and society.

Intercultural Communication Dialectics

Among the contradictions salient in intercultural communication (Martin & Nakayama, 1999), the dialectics of difference-similarity, individual-culture, and personal-social are particularly relevant to intercultural relationships, which represent the fundamental contradictions in communication between individuals (internal), between individuals and the culture of their partners (external), and between individuals and their respective cultures (external). The dialectic of difference-similarity essentially defines intercultural interaction. Although communication is impossible without a minimal common ground, the need to communicate often results from differences in the first place. The contrast between communicators in their cultural upbringings is such that they often find it hard to keep a balance between meaning assignment attributed to the individual or to the culture, hence the individual-culture dialectic. Attention solely on the cultural risks stereotyping and losing sight of the person, whereas an emphasis on the individual overlooks cultural influences and cultural identification. The pull between the personal and the social arises out of the relationship between individuals and society. It is individuals who communicate, but the capacity in which individuals communicate always represents a social role. Even the private communication between two individuals occurs between two individual social members and with social impact.

Dialectics in Intercultural Relationships

In intercultural relationships, intercultural dialectics juxtapose relational dialectics. Arising from the fundamental human needs of information sharing, interdependence, and variability (Bochner, 1984), the latter contradictions underlie every facet of a relationship. Manifestation of dialectics takes on myriad forms in concrete conditions and matters, which may be internal or external to a relationship. Regardless, both are important to the survival of the relationship as an entity with a social standing.

Openness-closeness: Internal information sharing. Internally, due to the dialectic of difference-similarity, intercultural relationship partners' self-disclosure or routine communication may look rather different from that in similar intracultural relationships regarding the kind of information exchanged. Although self-disclosure varies with the relationship type, information on many taken-for-granted aspects of life, redundant in intracultural relationships, may take on considerable importance for partners in any intercultural relationships (Rohrlich, 1988). On the other hand, disclosure may affect partners' mutual perceptions where it matters, in cultural identity and stereotypes (Braithwaite, 1991). To communicate with consideration of both idiosyncratic wants of the partners and the cultural identification each wishes acknowledged is evident of the individual-culture dialectic at work.

The interplay of openness-closeness and difference-similarity dialectics underlies the management of uncertainty/anxiety and perceived similarity, which decreases or increases over time in a relationship (Hubbert et al., 1999). We may learn how it occurs by identifying the kind of information exchanged and the pace of exchange in various relationship contexts. Similarly, the two dialectics may play out in partners' efforts to deal with differences and stereotypes. When intercultural friends express respect for or acceptance of differences between them and willingness to learn more about each other (Chen et al., 1996), what they want to learn about the other and how they communicate respect and acceptance will inform us of their experience of the dialectics.

Revelation-nonrevelation: External information sharing. Externally, there may be pressure for relationship partners to make known the nature of their intercultural relationship. Here the contradiction of personal-social also bears on the situation. The social dimension of a relationship is highlighted when others in the community and social networks want to know how to react to the relationship or interact with relationship partners. In contrast, possible consequences of the revelation, such as negative social perception and social sanction (Bizman, 1987), may give rise to greater desires on the part of the partners to have control of the information about their relationship as a personal affair. On the other hand, revelation is necessary to gain needed social support. To explore the interplay of revelation-nonrevelation and personal-social, selection of information to reveal by relationship partners and selection of certain others as receivers of the information are worthy topics. As outsiders tend to make attributions about motivations of individuals in intercultural relationships (Shibata, 1998) and predictions about the future of such relationships (Payne, 1998), also relevant is the information that others are interested in about a relationship and the partners involved.

Autonomy-connection: Internal management of interdependence. This dialectic operates in relationship partners' attempts to connect with each other. The simultaneous presence of the similarity-difference contradiction may necessitate particular efforts and greater connection desires on the part of intercultural partners for the relationship to form and be sustained (Shibazaki & Brennan, 1998). By the same token, commitment of partners to their relationships may take on greater importance in maintenance and development of a relationship. Connection desires and commitment enable partners to redefine what is similar and what is different between them on the basis of the relevance of their cultures to their personal lives to mitigate the dialectical tensions (Aguilera, 1992).

The intersection of individual-culture and autonomy-connection contradictions in intercultural relationships underlies the issue of cultural identity. Partners relate to each other as individuals who are at the same time cultural members. Whether the pull is toward or away from the end of cultures of those involved decides whether relationship partners move toward or against autonomy. The individual-culture tension is found in daily communication between relationship partners in, for example, their negotiation on acceptable behaviors between them. The outcome depends on whether each attributes certain behaviors to culture or to a personality trait. Greater tolerance is exercised when the other's behavior is perceived as culture specific; the same perception of self-behavior is a ground for its legitimacy (Romano, 1997). For an intercultural relationship to form and be sustained, a baseline is mutual respect of cultural identity (Gudykunst et al., 1991; Sudweeks et al., 1990).

A three-way interplay of similarity-difference, individual-culture, and autonomy-connection dialectics in a relationship conceivably also influences the strength of cultural identities of individual partners and, thus, the relationship. Attention on a specific aspect of cultural difference between the partners, for example, may bring new appreciation of their own cultures and a reinforced, more secure cultural identity. Specific outcome always depends on actual substantiation of the dialectics involved.

Separation-Integration: External management of interdependence. Externally, intercultural relationship partners face a double bind created by the interaction of separation-integration and similarity-difference dialectics. Relationships of any type, just as individuals in a relationship, are by default part of a culture (Baxter & Montgomery, 1996). Conventional forces in the culture require a relationship to be included to receive support and protection. At the same time, the same forces tend to become barriers to easily integrating an intercultural relationship, because of its differences from other relationships. To mediate between the opposing ends of the contradiction, relationship partners often take the initiative to select or even establish their own community and social networks. They may move to another location—even another country—or consciously socialize with others of similar experience or similar views on the relationship (Johnson & Warren, 1994). Studies on these networking activities would inform us of the manner in which the above dialectics transpire in intercultural relationships. On the other hand, albeit a much harder and slower process, relationship partners' political and social interactions with the society at large may facilitate redefinition of similarity and difference in terms of race, class, and culture. Aguilera (1992) has contended that the extent to which interracial marriage is practiced in a society is a good indicator of harmonious racial relations. Social acceptance and endorsement of intercultural relationships are a sign of social change. Change in a society's view on similarity and difference will affect the way in which intercultural relationships are positioned in the integration-separation dialectic.

Managing interdependence also involves the personal-social dialectic, as relationship partners may have very different views than the society at large regarding the nature of their relationship. That social perceptions of intercultural relationships tend to be negative is manifestation of forces pushing for separation and for a social view of personal relationships (Rosenblatt et al., 1995). Countermoves on the part of the relationship partners include public expression and proclamation of commitment to the relationship. In this sense, formation of alternative social networks, as does disassociation from unsympathetic families or intimacy display in public, functions to reclaim the private and independent dimension of a relationship. Relationship partners are holding onto their right to personal decisions without separating from society, thus unfolding the dynamics of interdependence.

Predictability-novelty: Internal variability. Internally, disparity in partners' cultural backgrounds brings to an intercultural relationship more novelty and less predictability. Novelty, therefore, is a marked characteristic of this type of relationship, a conventional wisdom substantiated by extensive support from the research. However, the dialectic of predictability-novelty may play out rather differently with the contradictions of individual-culture and similarity-difference also in the game. On one hand, as a relationship progresses, each developmental stage, with different priorities and foci of attention, brings anew issues thought to have been long resolved (Romano, 1997). Often it involves matters that the partners experience together for the first time and that have to do with cultural value orientations such as collectivism-individualism. Value orientations are internalized early in life in enculturation and hard to change, and they may surface as newly discovered differences that must now be renegotiated for a mutually agreeable solution. In the process, the partners may take another look at each other and at themselves. As they decide what is negotiable and what is not negotiable for the relationship, they also reevaluate what is cultural and what is individual about each other.

On the other hand, partners of a long-term intercultural relationship, such as marriage, have grown accustomed to each other and their cultural differences. At later stages of social penetration, they may be desensitized to the cultural side of each other and thus behave more like their counterparts in an intracultural relationship (Gaines & Ickes, 1997). In this case, partners may be less likely to detect certain belatedly surfaced cultural differences. Some may attribute these differences as being personal and respond with less tolerance, leading to severe marital difficulties. The scenario provides another explanation for the higher divorce rate among intercultural couples reported in some studies (Ho & Johnson, 1990). Cultural difference, however, is a never-exhausted resource. Conscious efforts to explore the resource may help keep relationships exciting and rewarding. Unfortunately, we currently know very little about this aspect of intercultural relationships.

Conventionality-uniqueness External variability. In any given community, desire for stability and convention tend to outweigh desire for change in normal circumstances. Social perceptions, as a reflection of the conventionality-uniqueness mechanism, are generally negative toward intercultural relationships (Breger & Hill, 1998). The very form of intercultural relationship presents a deviation, a challenge to the convention. For intercultural relationship partners choosing to remain integrated despite social bias, several options are available in the pull between conventionality and uniqueness. With simultaneous presence of the dialectic of similarity-difference, the partners may deny their uniqueness and prove that their relationship lies within the parameter of and is not a deviation from social norms. Or they may own up to their unconventionality and persuade others that variety in the social fabrics is beneficial and valuable. A more difficult alternative is to evoke the personal-social dialectic and convince others that the relationship is private in nature with no impact on society.

The above options are conceptualizations of a new direction for research. We may examine the verbal and nonverbal communication strategies and practices people employ for external persuasion to manage the tension of each or a combination of the three dialectics. We may investigate how the relationship partners experience each or a combination of these dialectics (Haas & Stafford, 1998). Also, we may study how intercultural relationships are conceptualized in the minds of those who are involved in one, and how they perceive these contradictions. A better understanding of intercultural relationship and social change can be gained by looking at how relationship partners relate to society under different social conditions.

The manifestation of the conventionality-uniqueness dialectic is also seen in the role of social power and status in intercultural relationships. Whereas some scholars consider the states of privilege and disadvantage as a separate dialectical force (Martin & Nakayama, 1999), it can be subsumed under that of conventionality-uniqueness. Given the prevalence of hierarchical structure in most societies today, inequality of social status represents a specific aspect of conventions. There is a general acceptance of social hierarchy and a general bias for social power; cultural differences in this respect are a matter of degree, not of kind. The conventional force in this sense is one against the lower status and against the different. Thus, juxtaposition of conventionality-uniqueness and similar-difference contradictions, along with the working of personal-social contradiction, transpires in social perceptions and attitudes related to group status of individuals in the relationship.

Conclusion

An intercultural relationship is by nature both interpersonal and intercultural. The interface between the individual and the relationship, on one hand, and the relationship and the culture, on the other, has brought great complexity to communication in intercultural relationships. A dialectical approach offers a coherent understanding of the intricacies in such relationships. In this light, perceived similarity, uncertainty, cultural identity, social support, social status, and so on are all manifestations of dialectical forces. The corollary of dialectics is change, the inevitable and the constant in each and every aspect of social life (Mao, 1965). Every shift of a particular dialectic in the relationship will trigger other shifts, thereby developing the relationship. It is clear, then, that the dialectical perspective is compatible with the developmental perspective of intercultural relationships, albeit with different emphasis: The former focuses on the dialectical operations underlying relationship development, whereas the latter focuses on the relationship progression as a result or condition of dialectics (Gudykunst, Ting-Toomey, Sudweeks, & Steward, 1995). Last, a distinction in research is needed between insider and outsider perspectives (Gaines & Ickes, 1997), as two parties may not perceive or understand a relationship in similar ways. Although both are valid and informative, a tension exists between the two. Therein lies the essence of the dialectical approach, the ever-present struggle between polar forces and never a definite win one way or another: Neither diversity nor separation nor any one side of a contradiction can be the ultimate end state (Blau, 1994). All must be considered for a systematic understanding of the phenomena of intercultural relationships.

Consider this . . .

- As you consider the range of characteristics that fit into Chen's broad definition of "culture", what cultural characteristics do you believe create the greatest challenges to the development of personal relationships? Why?
- As Chen discusses the influence of cultural differences on the process of relationship development, what research findings do you believe are most valuable? Why?
- How do such issues as stereotypes or cultural identity influence the development of personal relationships? Give an example to illustrate.
- How do such issues as social power and status, perceived social support, and relationship commitment influence the development of personal relationships? Give an example to illustrate.

- Using Dialectical Theory as the basis of your discussion, describe how a cultural difference may create a dialectical tension within a personal relationship. Give an example to illustrate.

References

Agranat, A. B., & Titov, V N. (1994). Osobennosti demograficheskikh ustanovok moskovskikh assiriytsev: Traditsiya i sovremennaya situatsiya [Demographic features of Moscow's Assyrians: Tradition and the current situation]. Sotsiologicheskie Issledovaniya, 21, 59-63.

Aguilera, R. V (1992). Marriage between black and white people. Revista Espanola de Investigaciones Sociologicas, 60, 47-61.

Anderson, R. N., & Saenz, R. (1994). Structural determinants of Mexican American intermarriage, 1975-1980. Social Science Quarterly, 75, 414-430.

Back, L. (1993). Race, identity and nation within an adolescent community in south London. New Community, 19, 217-233.

Baxter, L. A. (1988). A dialectical perspective of communication strategies in relationship development. In S. Duck (Ed.), Handbook of personal relationships (pp. 257-273). New York: John Wiley.

Baxter, L. A. (1993). The social side of personal relationships: A dialectical perspective. In S. Duck (Ed.), Social context and relationships: Understanding relationship processes (Vol. 3, pp. 139-169). Newbury Park, CA: Sage.

Baxter, L. A., & Montgomery, B. M. (1996). Relating: Dialogues & dialectics. New York: Guilford.

Baxter, L. A., & Montgomery, B. M. (1997). Rethinking communication in personal relationships from a dialectical perspective. In S. Duck (Ed.), Handbook of personal relationships (pp. 325-349). New York: John Wiley.

Bizman, A. (1987). Perceived causes and compatibility of interethnic marriage: An attributional analysis. International Journal of Intercultural Relations, 11, 387-399.

Blau, P M. (1994). The paradox of multiculturalism. Unpublished manuscript, University of North Carolina at Chapel Hill, Department of Sociology.

Bochner, A. P (1984). The functions of communication in interpersonal bonding. In C. Arnold & J. Bowers (Eds.), Handbook of rhetorical and communication theory (pp. 544-621). Boston: Allyn & Bacon.

Braithwaite, D. O. (1991). Just how much did that wheelchair cost? Management of privacy boundaries by persons with disabilities. Western Journal of Speech Communication, 55, 254-274.

Breger, R., &, Hill, R. (Eds.). (1998). Cross-cultural marriage: Identity and choice. New York: Berg.

Cabecinhas, R., & Amancio, L. (1999). Asymmetries in the perception of other as a function of social position and context. Schweizerische Zeitschrift fuer Psychologie Revue Suisse de Psychologie [Swiss Journal of Psychology], 58, 40-50.

Chan, A. Y, & Wethington, E. (1998). Factors promoting marital resilience among interracial couples. In H. I. McCubbin, E. A Thompson, A. I. Thompson, & J. E. Fromer (Eds.), Resiliency in Native American and immigrant families (pp. 71-87). Thousand Oaks, CA: Sage.

Chan, M. (1990, December 19). Gentlemen prefer Asians: Why some Anglos are only attracted to Asian women. The Rafu Shimpo, 1, 4.

Chen, G. (1995). Differences in self-disclosure patterns among Americans versus Chinese. Journal of Cross-Cultural Psychology, 26, 84-91.

Chen, L. (1995). Interaction involvement and patterns of topical talk: A comparison of intercultural and intracultural dyads. International Journal of Intercultural Relations, 19, 463-482.

Chen, L. (1997). Verbal adaptive strategies in U.S. American dyadic conversations with U.S. American or East-Asian partners. Communication Monographs, 64, 1-22.

Chen, L., & Cegala, D. J. (1994). Topic management, shared knowledge and accommodation: A study of communication adaptability. Research on Language and Social Interaction, 27, 389-417.

Chen, L., Isa, M., & Sakai, J. (1996, November). Our communication with North Americans: A study of intercultural experience of Japanese visiting students. Paper presented at the annual conference of the Speech Communication Association, San Diego, CA.

Chung, L. (1990). Analysis of cultural identity and stereotypes as factors influencing interethnic dating. Unpublished manuscript, California State University, Fullerton, Department of Speech Communication.

Chung, L. C., & Ting-Toomey, S. (1999). Ethnic identity and relational expectations among Asian Americans. Communication Research Reports, 16, 157-166.

Clark-Ibanez, M. K. (1999). Gender, race and friendships: Structural and social factors leading to the likelihood of inter-ethnic dating. Unpublished manuscript, American Sociological Association.

Collier, M. J. (1996). Communication competence problematics in ethnic friendships. Communication Monographs, 63, 314-336.

Collier, M. J., & Bornman, E. (1999). Core symbols in South African intercultural friendships. International Journal of Intercultural Relations, 23, 133-156.

Collier, M. J., & Bowker, J. (1994, November). U.S. American women in intercultural friendships. Paper presented at the annual conference of the Speech Communication Association, New Orleans, LA.

Crohn, J. (1998). Intercultural couples. In M. McGoldrick (Ed.), Re-visionizing family therapy: Race, culture, and gender in clinical practice (pp. 295-308). New York: Guilford.

Fujino, D. C. (1997). The rates, patterns and reasons for forming heterosexual interracial dating relationships among Asian Americans. Journal of Social and Personal Relationships, 14, 809-828.

Gaines, S. O., Jr., Granrose, C. S., Rios, D. I., Garcia, B. F., Youn, M. S. P., Farris, K. R., & Bledsoe, K. L. (1999). Patterns of attachment and responses to accommodative dilemmas among interethnic/interracial couples. Journal of Social and Personal Relationships, 16, 275-285.

Gaines, S. O., Jr., & Ickes, W. (1997). Perspectives on interracial relationships. In S. Duck (Ed.), Handbook of personal relationships (pp. 121-145). Chichester, UK: Wiley.

Gaines, S. O., Jr., Reis, H. T., Summers, S., Rusbult, C. E., Cox, C. L., Wexler, M. O., Marelich, W.D., & Kurland, G. J.(1997).Impact of attachment style on reactions to accommodative dilemmas in close relationships. Personal Relationships, 4, 93-113.

Garcia, S. D., & Rivera, S. M. (1999). Perceptions of Hispanic and African-American couples at the friendship or engagement stage of a relationship. Journal of Social and Personal Relationships, 16, 65-86.

Gareis, E. (1995). Intercultural friendship: A qualitative study. Lanham, MD: University Press of America.

Gareis, E. (1999). Adult friendship: Examples of intercultural patterns. In M. E. Roloff (Ed.), Communication yearbook 22 (pp. 431-468). Thousand Oaks, CA: Sage.

Graham, M. A., Moeai, J., & Shizuru, L. S. (1985). Intercultural marriages: An intrareligious perspective. International Journal of Intercultural Relations, 9, 427-434.

Grant, P R. (1993). Reactions to intergroup similarity: Examination of the similarity differentiation and the similarity-attraction hypotheses. Canadian Journal of Behavioral Science, 25, 28-44.

Gudykunst, W. B. (1983). Similarities and differences in perceptions of initial intracultural and intercultural encounters. Southern Speech Communication Journal, 49, 49-65.

Gudykunst, W. B. (1985). A model of uncertainty reduction in intercultural encounters. Journal of Language and Social Psychology, 4, 79-98.

Gudykunst, W. B. (1989). Culture and development of interpersonal relationships. In J. Anderson (Ed.), Communication yearbook 12 (pp. 315-354). Newbury Park, CA: Sage.

Gudykunst, W. B., Gao, G., Schmidt, K. L., Nishida, T., Bond, M. H., Leung, K., Wang, G., & Barraclough, R. A. (1992). The influence of individualism-collectivism, self-monitoring, and predicted outcome value on communication in ingroup and outgroup relationships. Journal of Cross-Cultural Psychology, 23, 196-213.

Gudykunst, W. B., Gao, G., Sudweeks, S., Ting-Toomey, S., & Nishida, T. (1991). Themes in opposite sex, Japanese-North American relationships. In S. Ting-Toomey & F. Korzenny (Eds.), Cross-cultural interpersonal communication (pp. 230-258). Newbury Park, CA: Sage.

Gudykunst, W. B., &Nishida, T. (1984). Individual and cultural influences on uncertainty reduction. Communication Monographs, 51, 23-36.

Gudykunst, W. B., &, Nishida, T. (1986). The influence of cultural variability on perceptions of communication behavior associated with relationship terms. Human Communication Research, 13, 147-166.

Gudykunst, W. B., Nishida, T., & Chua, E. (1986). Uncertainty reduction in Japanese-North American dyads. Communication Research Reports, 3, 39-46.

Gudykunst, W. B., Nishida, T, & Chua, E. (1987). Perceptions of social penetration in Japanese-North American dyads. International Journal of Intercultural Relations, 11, 171-191.

Gudykunst, W. B., & Shapiro, R. B. (1996). Communication in everyday interpersonal and intergroup encounters. International Journal of Intercultural Relations, 20, 19-45.

Gudykunst, W. B., Ting-Toomey, S., Sudweeks, S., &, Stewart, L. (1995). Building bridges: Skills for a changing world. Boston: Houghton Mifflin.

Gudykunst, W. B., Yoon, Y. C., & Nishida, T. (1987). The influence of individualism-collectivism on perceptions of communication in ingroup and outgroup relationships. Communication Monographs, 54, 295-306.

Gurung, R. A. R., & Duong, T. (1999). Mixing and matching: Assessing the concomitants of mixed-ethnic relationships. Journal of Social and Personal Relationships, 16, 639-657.

Haas, S. M., & Stafford, L. (1998). An initial examination of maintenance behaviors in gay and lesbian relationships. Journal of Social and Personal Relationships, 15, 846-855.

Hanassab, S., & Tidwell, R. (1998). Intramarriage and intermarriage: Young Iranians in Los Angeles. International Journal of Intercultural Relations, 22, 395-408.

Hecht, M. L., Larkey, L. K., & Johnson, J. N. (1992). African American and European American perceptions of problematic issues in interethnic communication effectiveness. Human Communication Research, 19, 209-236.

Hecht, M. L., Ribeau, S., & Sedano, N. V. (1990).A Mexican American perspective on interethnic communication. International Journal of Intercultural Relations, 14, 31-55.

Ho, F. C., & Johnson, R. C. (1990). Intra-ethnic and inter-ethnic marriage and divorce in Hawaii. Social Biology, 37, 44-51.

Hoffman, M., & Schwarzwald, J. (1987). Moderating effects of educational standing on interethnic relations in the classroom. International Journal of Intercultural Relations, 11, 357-367.

Horenczyk, G., & Bekerman, Z. (1997). The effects of intercultural acquaintance and structured intergroup interaction on ingroup, outgroup, and reflected ingroup stereotypes. International Journal of Intercultural Relations, 21, 71-83.

Hubbert, K. N., Gudykunst, W. B., & Guerrero, S. L. (1999). Intergroup communication over time. International Journal of Intercultural Relations, 23, 13-46.

Hwang, S. S., Saenz, R., & Aguirre, B. E. (1997). Structural and assimilationist explanations of Asian American intermarriage. Journal of Marriage and the Family, 59, 758-772.

Johnson, W. R., & Warren, D. M. (Eds.). (1994). Inside the mixed marriage: Accounts of changing attitudes, patterns, and perceptions of cross-cultural and interracial marriages. Lanham, MD: University Press of America.

Kouri, K., & Lasswell, M. (1993). Black-white marriage. Marriage and Family Review, 19, 241-255.

Lampe, P (1982). Interethnic dating: Reasons for and against. International Journal of Intercultural Relations, 6, 115-126.

Larkey, L. K., & Hecht, M. L. (1995). A comparative study of African American and European American ethnic identity. International Journal of Intercultural Relations, 19, 483-504.

Lee, H., & Boster, F. (1991). Social information for uncertainty reduction during initial interactions. In S. Ting-Toomey & F. Korzenny (Eds.), Cross-cultural interpersonal communication (pp. 189-112). Newbury Park, CA: Sage.

Lee, C. M., & Gudykunst, W. B. (in press). Attraction in initial interethnic interactions. International Journal of Intercultural Relations.

Levkovitch, V. P. (1990). Marital relationships in binational families. Soviet Journal of Psychology, 11, 26-37.

Mao, T. (1965). On contradiction. Beijing: Foreign Languages Press.

Martin, J. N., & Nakayama, T. K. (1999). Thinking dialectically about culture and communication. Communication Theory, 9, 1-25.

McDermott, S. T. (1991). The generalizability of the communication to attraction relationship to intercultural communication: Repulsion or attraction? In J. A. Anderson (Ed.), Communication yearbook 14 (pp. 492-497). Newbury Park, CA: Sage.

McGuire, W. M. (1992). Key influences in interracial mate selection. Dissertation Abstracts International, 53, DA 9300188.

Mills, J. K., Daly, J., Longmore, A., & Kilbride, G. (1995). A note on family acceptance involving interracial friendships and romantic relationships. Journal of Psychology, 129, 349-351.

Neuliep, J. W., & Ryan, D. J. (1998). The influence of intercultural communication apprehension and sociocommunicative orientation during initial cross-cultural interaction. Communication Quarterly, 46, 88-99.

Nguyen, L. T. (1998). To date or not to date a Vietnamese: Perceptions and expectations of Vietnamese American college students. Amerasia Journal, 24(1), 143-169.

Obot, I. S. (1988). Value systems and cross-cultural contact: The effect of perceived similarity and stability on social evaluations. International Journal of Intercultural Relations, 12, 363-379.

Osbeck, L. M., Moghaddam, F. M., & Perreault, S. (1997). Similarity and attraction among majority and minority groups in a multicultural context. International Journal of Intercultural Relations, 21, 113-123.

Parsonson, K. (1987). Intermarriage. Journal of Cross-Cultural Psychology, 18, 363-371.

Payne, M. (1998). Waiting for lightning to strike: Social support of interracial couples. In J. N. Martin, T. K. Nakayama, & L. A. Flores (Eds.), Readings in cultural contexts (pp. 379-387). Mountain View, CA: Mayfield.

Race relations responses to General Social Survey. (1991, January 9). National Opinion Research Center. Los Angeles Times, p. A15.

Rawlins, W K. (1992). Friendship matters. New York: Aldine de Gruyter.

Rohrlich, B. F. (1988). Dual-culture marriage and communication. International Journal of Intercultural Relations, 12, 35-44.

Romano, D. (1997). Intercultural marriage: Promises and pitfalls (2nd ed.). Yarmouth, ME: Intercultural Press.

Rosenblatt, P C., Karis, T. A., & Powell, R. D. (1995). Multiracial couples: Black and white voices. Thousand Oaks, CA: Sage.

Shibata, Y (1998). Crossing racialized boundaries: Intermarriage between "Africans" and "Indians" in contemporary Guyana. In R. Breger &, R. Hill (Eds.), Cross-cultural marriage: Identity and choice (pp. 83-100). New York: Berg.

Shibazaki, K., & Brennan, K. A. (1998). When birds of different feathers flock together: A preliminary comparison of intra-ethnic and inter-ethnic dating relationships. Journal of Social and Personal Relationships, 15, 248-256.

Simard, L. M. (1981). Cross-cultural interaction: Potential invisible barriers. Journal of Social Psychology, 113, 171-192.

Spickard, P (1989). Mixed blood: Intermarriage and ethnic identity in twentieth-century America. Madison: University of Wisconsin Press.

Strom, W O. (1988). Cross-cultural friendships on the university campus: Testing the functional and identity validation models. Dissertation Abstracts International, 49, 3204A.

Sudweeks, S., Gudykunst, W B., Ting-Toomey, S., & Nishida, T. (1990). Developmental themes in Japanese-North American interpersonal relationships. International Journal of Intercultural Relations, 14, 207-233.

Sung, B. L. (1990). Chinese American intermarriage. Journal of Comparative Family Studies, 21, 337-352.

Ting-Toomey, S. (1991). Intimacy expression in three cultures. International Journal of Intercultural Relations, 15, 29-46.

Tuch, S. A., Sigelman, L., & MacDonald, J. A. (1999). Race relations and American youth, 1976-1995. Public Opinion Quarterly, 63, 109-148.

Tucker, M., & Mitchell-Kernan, C. (1995). Social structure and psychological correlates of interethnic dating. Journal of Social and Personal Relationships, 12, 341-361.

Werner, C. M., & Baxter, L. (1994). Temporal qualities of relationships: Organismic, transactional and dialectical view. In M. L. Knappy &, G. R. Miller (Eds.), Handbook of interpersonal communication (2nd ed., pp. 323-379). Thousand Oaks, CA: Sage.

CHAPTER 5

THE SOCIAL CONTEXT OF PERSONAL RELATIONSHIPS

In Chapter 5 of her text, *Relational Communication*, Julia Wood notes that relationships don't exist in isolation – as an island unto themselves. Instead, personal relationships must always be explored in the context of the larger culture that shapes and defines the individual identities of participants as well as the relationship itself. In her discussion, she describes how culture becomes a context of intimacy; cultures legitimate some personal relationships and do not legitimate others. She discusses two important social trends, technology and diversity, that have restructured and transformed our personal relationships in everyday life. Finally, she explores how these two social trends have influenced our personal identities within relationships.

As an extension of Wood's discussion, Ronald L. Jackson II in his article, "Cultural Contracts Theory: Toward an Understanding of Identity Negotiation," focuses primarily on the influence of diversity as we negotiate our cultural identity in personal relationships. Specifically, Jackson addresses the work of several noted intercultural communication scholars who have explored how cultural identity is developed and how it may be negotiated as a strategy for reducing intercultural conflict. He strongly believes that such work should be revisited as we explore the impact of diversity in our personal relationships.

Jackson begins his discussion by presenting an overview of Cultural Contracts Theory as it relates to identity negotiation. This theory examines the cultural value system (patterns of interaction, rules, and norms) that guides our everyday behavior, and thus, creates our cultural identity. Once Jackson lays out the broad perspective of this theory as it relates to identity negotiation, he then discusses eleven assumptions that serve to explain the basis of this theory as well as seven propositions that serve to predict behavior using this theory. Finally, he notes that this theory provides an interdisciplinary lens through which the impact of diversity can be explored in a variety of settings—rhetorical (grounded is the study of discourse/language), interpersonal, organizational, or mass mediated communication.

Perhaps the final lines written by Jackson in his article best reflect my reason to include it as an extension of Julia Wood's discussion in Chapter 5. As Jackson himself writes, "Often times, diversity experts seek to examine the possibilities in a world where differences are ignored and not valued. Truly, the most important challenge is not to determine what we can do without differences; it is to imagine what we can accomplish with them!" Keep this challenge in mind as you read about this theory and its impact on the many personal relationships in your life.

Cultural Contracts Theory: Toward an Understanding of Identity Negotiation

Ronald L. Jackson II

This essay introduces a nascent paradigm for exploring identity shifting and identity negotiation. Cultural Contracts Theory metaphorically explains the attitudinal and social predispositions interactants have when relating to others within and without one's own culture

In 1903, W.E.B. Dubois accurately predicted in his now-famous thinkpiece Souls of Black Folks that the principal conundrum of the twentieth century would be that of the color line. Now, one-hundred years later, I can assert without the slightest reservation that the primary crucible of the twenty-first century will be that of identities. It would be nice to think that as we speak we are simply exchanging information, but even in casual contact with others, we are constantly exchanging codes of personhood, worldview, indeed our identities.

The challenge is that multiple, changing, and confounded identities reflect difference. With this variegated difference comes conflict. It is what we do with that difference and incumbent conflict that is most critical to the development and sustenance of identities. Do institutions or individual interactants seek to manage, contain and control the difference and/or conflict? If so, does this activity constrict or crystallize identities? Furthermore, for what purposes or to what end do we seek to manage identities? These are all social, political and ontological questions that represent some of the intricacies of identity negotiation in everyday interaction with others.

The "negotiation of identity" is a general concept that has been in existence for as long as there have been intergroup and interpersonal differences; however, the terminology as we know it today first emerged in the field of communication via the work of Stella Ting-Toomey (1986). In 1986, Ting-Toomey created the identity validation model (IVM), which consists of three dimensions, one of which is communication. Communication is described as a critical dimension, which is the actual "identity-negotiation process between the self and relevant others" (p. 123). This identity negotiation paradigm refers to the careful selection of one among several role identities to engage within a particular communication context. Ting-Toomey (1999) continues and expounds on this line of thinking in her subsequent book-length explication of identity negotiation as a theory In this remarkable monograph, she asserts that identity negotiation is about the choices cultural interactants make in securing their self image or saving face.

Ting-Toomey's identity validation model and the subsequent identity negotiation theory are among the first interpretive frameworks found in the literature which not only indicate that identity is relational but also explicitly note that identity is constructed via a negotiation process. Uncertainty reduction theory (Berger & Calabrese, 1975) is the basis upon which Ting-Toomey's research on initial interaction is founded. However, negotiation was only considered a general phenomenon and not an actual construct in Berger and Calabrese's formula. Ting-Toomey (1986) proposed that future research examine the relational dilemmas and paradoxes that arise from members of two cultures "as they attempt to reach out and hold back at the same time, to seek for mutual validation, and yet at the same time to protect their own vulnerability" (p. 126). Ting-Toomey's work provides the primary impetus for cultural contracts theory. Like Ting-Toomey's identity negotiation paradigm, cultural contracts theory derives from personal experiences in the U. S. and dealing with almost-everyday episodes that represent a racial chasm between Whites and non-Whites,

Previous studies support the idea that human beings carry their undetachable identities into every cultural and conversational encounter (Giles & Johnson, 1987; Hecht, Jackson & Ribeau, 2003). Some of these parts of our cultural identities, usually the core, are highly secured and virtually immovable, while others may shift during a persuasive dialogue or sustained relationship. One of my concerns is how we select who is worthy of a sustained relationship in the first place. So, in part, cultural contracts theory also is inspired by uncertainty reduction theory, which concerns itself with initial interaction and beyond. From the time we are born and given a name by our parents, we are inextricably dependent on others to play a part in how we define ourselves and why we define ourselves as we do. Consequently, our identities are shaped and molded during interactions with others. We use others as guideposts for normative behavior and we also set up implicit and sometimes explicit "contracts" with others (individuals and groups), which indicate how we will progress with our relationships. Fisher (1998) posits that because every human being is different, humans are naturally incompatible. So, every relationship is met with conflict at some point; again, it is how the interactants manage that conflict that becomes key. Keep in mind that conflict does not have to be negative and neither does difference; it just means that two ideas or components are not parallel or the same. Valuation of difference begins with this premise.

Many studies recognize that conflict emanating from difference is the centerpiece of intercultural and interpersonal communication research. From Hofstede's (1980) dimensions of cultural variability, Brislin's (1983) "managing" and Cronen, Chen and Pearce's (1988) "coordinating" to Collier and Thomas' (1988) “coherent managing”, Gudykunst and Ting-Toomey's (1988) "bridging" and Jackson's (1999) "negotiating" of cultural difference, it has become clear that difference is not okay as is, but that something must be done with it. As both studies by Berger and Calabrese (1976) and Giles & Johnson (1987) point out, most human beings prefer to reduce uncertainty within social contexts.

Negotiation of cultural identity is just one strategy for reducing conflict. Ting-Toomey (1999) further developed her earlier use of the term cultural identity negotiation in order to coherently explain how public self-images are affected within human interactions via giving or losing face and by being mindful communicators. Ting-Toomey's concern for face in cross-cultural encounters makes sense given her interest in interpersonal communication and Korean-United States interactions. My early (1999) use of the term evolved from studying Black-White interactions in the United States; hence, it is much more directly aligned with the current study. The negotiation of cultural identity is defined as

> A bargaining process in which two or more individuals consider the exchange of ideas, values, and beliefs.... Negotiation of cultural identity is a process in which one considers the gain, loss, or exchange of his or her ability to interpret their own reality or worldview. (p. 10)

The present explication of cultural contracts theory sees that earlier work as a variation of "negotiating cultural identity" and as a metatheory that explores the exchange of cultural values and commitments; hence, "cultural contracts" theory is a rubric of this. Cultural Contracts paradigm is based on the idea that intercultural relationships may or may not be coordinated, depending upon the dynamics involved (such as power, boundaries, cultural loyalty, group identification, maturity, etc.). This coordination is initiated after an initial negotiation with the self. That is, identities, whether social, cultural or otherwise, have meaning for the individual when they are first negotiated personally. Although an individual may be aware of an ascribed racial identity that defines her as Black, that identification referent takes on significance when its meaning is negotiated within the self. That process is sometimes subconscious and/or happens quickly. After intrapersonal adjustments are made to accept, reject or compromise one's worldview or portions of it, then this ontological orientation is carried into relationships with others, where difference becomes paramount. Difference in an intercultural relationship does not have to be conflictual, but often times, just as in a new marriage, interactants must come to terms with value distinctions if the relationship is to be successful.

The proliferation of cultural identity studies in recent years has produced a peculiar inclination to see contact between cultures as conflictual (Fisher, 1997; Hecht, 1998; Singer, 1998; Ting-Toomey, 1999). Difference is perceived as interaction between divergent, disengaged, or unique positionalities anchored in a set of norms or standards that humans identify as culture. Consequently, efforts to define and discuss intercultural communication have often begun by exploring difference, while accenting competent understandings and appreciation of diverse perspectives.

This study accepts the challenge advanced by Ting-Toomey (1999). I strongly believe that identities are both highly complex and naturally occurring. One way to explicate how identities shift is by utilizing the "cultural contract" and "identity negotiation" metaphors. My goal here is quite simple. Within this essay, I will simply reintroduce the cultural contracts theory with its assumptions and propositions. It was created in 2001, and has since appeared in several manuscripts

(Hecht, Jackson & Ribeau, 2003; Jackson, 2002, in press; Jackson & Crawley, in press; Jackson, Morrison & Dangerfield, 2002; Jackson & Simpson, in press; Onwumechili et al., in press; Tierney & Jackson, 2002). Its core structure re-appears here with altered examples.

Cultural Contracts Paradigm and Identity Negotiation

The I-other dialectic that is implicit in the exploration of racially and socially asymmetrical identities can best be accounted for by examining the notion of cultural contracts as manifested products of identity negotiation during communication with others. As previously explained, with all identity negotiation, the assumption is that cultural difference translates into cultural conflict and therefore, something must be done with conflict. As a result, identity negotiation is about coordinating one's identity to match, compliment or not resist the presence of other cultural identities. As with any relationship, if others do not coordinate relationships with us in a fair, equitable manner, relational possibilities may dissolve. However, if one feels coerced and his/her life possibilities, financial means of survival or some other major factor is at stake, certain cultural contracts may be more appealing despite coercion.

Although seemingly simple in explanation, the cultural contracts paradigm was established to make sense of identity effects or outcomes as necessary end products of identity negotiation. This is accomplished by describing three contract typologies: ready to sign contract (assimilation), quasi-completed contract (adaptation), or co-created contract (mutual valuation). The tragic reality is that most people neither understand all of the contracts they have signed nor all of the implications of having signed them.

Generally, identity negotiation refers to a conscious and mindful process of shifting one's worldview and/or cultural behaviors, so it is possible to be cognizant of a choice to assimilate without understanding that assimilation might have a direct effect on future choice-making, such as in the case of a personnel manager who decides to hire someone based on a subconscious preference for the applicant who behaves similar to the manager.

Identity negotiation is about alterations in worldview. A shift in any one or any part of one of the cultural aspects of rural African American cultural identities constitutes the "signing" of a cultural contract. Everyone has "signed" at least one cultural contract in his/her life, and with every significant encounter, one or more of those cultural contracts is negotiated. As with the nigrescence model (Cross, 1971;1978; 1991), it is possible that a Black person matriculates through a process at the end of which s/he becomes culturally Black. Although this idea of becoming "culturally Black" seems essentialist, what it suggests is that a person who has assimilated or adapted his/her cultural identity can, over time, become divorced from his/her indigenous cultural ways of knowing. Eventually, this would disable him/her from ever signing what you will come to know as a co-created contract, because mutual validation only occurs among relational interactants who value themselves first.

It is important to note that the word "cultural" in cultural contracts is deliberate. It is impossible to exist without culture. Even if one is unable to articulate the particularities of the cultural value system to which he or she subscribes, there are still cultural patterns of interaction, rules, and norms that guide everyday behavior. So, with this cultural contracts paradigm, there is no such thing as a non-cultural or culturally generic contract and everyone has at least one cultural contract.

Everyone has identified or aligned him or herself with others throughout his/her life. This alignment is usually behavioral and cognitive. The Cultural Contracts paradigm is most concerned with sustained alignments, whether short or long-term. As with any negotiation, one can either choose to abide by an existing contractual arrangement or sign another contract. Although the concept of identity negotiation is simple, it is not always clear what is being negotiated, especially since identities are non-material. The cultural contracts paradigm has been introduced to make sense of what is actually being negotiated. The fundamental principles of cultural identity negotiation are summarized in the following list of theoretic assumptions and propositions of cultural contracts.

Core Theoretical Assumptions and Propositions

Assumptions 1-5

In assumptions 1-5, the rudiments of initiating a cultural contract are outlined. Think of negotiating a material item such as a house or an automobile. The first exposure one has to the item up for negotiation is usually via a one-way communicative venue such as advertising. So, if you are a prospective buyer, you contact the person with the product you want and begin to talk about points of sale. In human interaction processes, and particularly as it relates to cultural communication, the process is holistically the same, but differs in form. Instead of seeing an advertisement, the body, voice or written message becomes the mediated stimulus. Our bodies signify racial meaning and our minds comply with social meaning that is culturally constructed. So, in a rural community, an African American cultural identity is signified via the body as a visual cue and secondarily by the values, norms, behaviors and practices that constitute cultural understanding. As human beings, we ritualistically enact these cultural practices and our social perceptions facilitate everyday living. They give us a sense of belonging and attachment. This is especially important among minorities who are marginalized and treated as abnormal because of their difference. Their attachment to culture is a matter of survival and yet there is always a need for marginalized persons to seek centrality and to associate with members of the dominant and mainstream culture. Doing so is healthy, but frequently deleterious, because it reproduces the same anxieties and reinforcement of social positioning when their cultural identities are not treated as normal, legitimate, or okay. In the latter case where they are not dialectically approved by the dominant other, marginalized group members must make a choice to resist assimilation and maybe a certain measure of life satisfaction or to sign that ready-to-sign-contract in the absence of mutual validation. The assumptions are as follows:

Assumption 1: Human beings cannot exist without culture; culture is the basic organizing unit of social processes (Ting-Toomey, 1999).

Assumption 2: Cultural contracts are necessary for the sake of preserving, protecting, and defining the self, hence everyone has at least one. (There is no such thing as not having one, although you may not be aware of what your contract requires you to do. All contracts have fine print that may be overlooked without careful reading).

Assumption 3: Cultural contracts can be either temporary/episodic or long-term/enduring.

Assumption 4: Cultural difference among human interactants presupposes a need for coordination, which is manifested in cultural contracts (Cronen, Chen, & Pearce, 1988).

Assumption 5: Although important, there is not necessarily a mutual interest in relational coordination, identity negotiation or intercultural competence among all human interactants (Jackson, 1999). With these persons, "signing" is not the goal.

Assumptions 6-11

Assumptions 6-11 are designed to address the means, modes and functioning of cultural contracts as a communication product. Identities are communicated everyday in multiple ways. It would be nice to presume that we are simply exchanging ideas or just living without any need to deal with culture, but the reality is that we are all cultural beings and this gets accented every time we come in contact with cultural others. Their identities help them to make sense of the world. This is not new; Edward Sapir and Benjamin Whorf talked about this almost fifty years ago. They suggested that language determines thought. That is, the words, sounds and structure of language in a given culture help a person to articulate what they are experiencing. The typical example is that there are cultures where there are over one hundred words describing snow. That culture sees and understands snow much differently than North Americans who might have about ten words for snow. The language is not the only feature of culture that helps form identities. History is another. Personal and cultural histories offer a baseline for social cognition. Without history, one becomes confused about what to do in a given situation. They seek to reduce uncertainty and gain some control over how they will proceed. Rural African American identities are in a state of flux, as stated earlier in this essay. The duality is embedded in the Africanity of African American culture and the effect of being an African ancestor forcibly brought to the American context. So, there is both an African American resistance to and move toward being White, which means being a normal U. S. citizen. The resistance is due to a perceived need to maintain some attachment to the cultural community that supports African Americans and other minority rural inhabitants when dominant cultural others will not. The assumptions 6-11 are listed below.

Assumption 6: Identities are dynamic, not static; and they are influenced during interaction with others (Hecht, Jackson, & Ribeau, 2003).

Assumption 7: Every time people communicate, they are communicating their identities by expressing how they see the world (Hecht, Jackson, & Ribeau, 2003; Ting-Toomey, 1999).

Assumption 8: Communicators' personal histories and antecedent interactions influence the degree to which they are open to entering into identity negotiations with others (Jackson, 1999; Jackson & Crawley, in press).

Assumption 9: Because multiple identities are functioning simultaneously within communicative contexts, they may also be negotiated simultaneously (Collier & Thomas, 1988).

Assumption 10: The attempt to function as a "free agent" and "join" another culture is not always as profitable as it sounds; it is often stressful, shocking and isolating (Ting-Toomey, 1999).

Assumption 11: A contract will only be completed or "tendered" if there is a strong desire or perceived need for it, even if it is forcibly signed for the sake of survival (Jackson et al, in press).

Propositions 1-3

During the civil rights movement of the 1950s and 1960s, the rural south was in an uproar due to rural African Americans who could tolerate their secondary social positions no longer. The movement ended with some who forfeited their lives for the cause and others who lived to continue the legacy. Nonetheless, the movement was a lesson in the politics of identity and cultural contract negotiation. Asymmetrical power does not always translate into inferiority. Civil rights protestors proved that if principled protest is sustained, organized and lawful, results will be obtained. However, those who placed their locus of control externally never saw liberatory change. Returning to the negotiation of a material item such as a car, if you are emotionally invested or tied to a certain price for the car, it is highly unlikely you will sell it at a discount price. This example is not to illustrate that identities have price tags, but that if one is strongly committed to and strongly values one's own culture, there will likely be a greater sense of self-efficacy and a reduced desire to assimilate or adapt. Propositons 1-3 are below.

Proposition 1: When there is unequal power among interactants, strategic communication will take place (Giles & Johnson, 1987).

Proposition 2: There is a direct and proportionate relationship between power and self-efficacy (Orbe, 1998; Ting-Toomey, 1999).

Proposition 3: ff there is no perceived need to relationally coordinate, then there will also be a greater resistance to co-creating cultural contracts (Orbe, 1998). (These persons will either expect you to sign their contract or have none at all.)

Propositions 4-7

Propositions 4-7 are the final statements related to the cultural contracts typology. Given that we have already discussed power as a variable that contributes to signing a cultural contract, with all other things being equal, one's cultural loyalty or ethnolinguistic vitality, especially in a rural community will be high if living in close contact with members of the same culture. For example, no matter whether it is Creoles and Cajuns of New Orleans and its rural communities, Geechi and Gullah speaking communities in Georgia or South Carolina or Black Appalachians in Pennsylvania, linguistic communities are perpetually faced with the survival of language. As a result, their use of non-mainstream English, as African American rural inhabitants, represents a contract breach. Their lives, in part, depend on adaptation, but assimilation is heavily resisted and co-creation is not a first option, because it implies that their cultural identity is being called into question and may be eventually dissolved. The propositions 4-7 are below.

Proposition 4: As cultural loyalty and power increases, so does the likelihood that "ready-to-sign" cultural contracts will be prepared for other cultural relationships in advance (See Giles, et al. discussion of ethnic vitality).

Proposition 5: There are at least three types of cultural contracts: "ready-to-sign," (i.e. not budging; closest to win-lose) co-created (i.e. win-win and interdependent self-construal), and quasi-completed.

Proposition 6: If contracts are breached, there are penalties associated with this "rule" violation, one of which may be the cost of community ostracism. (Of course, there are "escape clauses" in fine print).

Proposition 7: When a breach or violation occurs, one of three actions will take place in varying degrees: termination or rupture of the relationship, tendering of a new or revised contract, or settling without penalty due to perceived high value of the relationship and low assessment of damage.

Cultural Contracts Theory is an innovative, interdisciplinary paradigm that can be used to assess identity issues that are rhetorical/discursive, organizational, interpersonal, or mass mediated. It is one lens through which we are able to examine how identities take shape and are retained on a daily basis. Often times, diversity experts seek to examine the possibilities in a world where differences are ignored and not valued. Truly, the most important challenge is not to determine what we can do without differences; it is to imagine what we can accomplish with them!

Consider this . . .

- In Chapter 5 of her text, *Relational Communication*, Wood explains that as the diversity of perspectives we encounter expands our sense of identity, our identities become saturated. How does Wood's discussion of "saturated selves" relate to Jackson's discussion of identity negotiation?
- Of the eleven assumptions that serve as the basis for Cultural Contracts Theory, which ones do you find most useful to explain the development of the cultural identities we bring to personal relationships?
- Of the seven propositions that serve as the basis for Cultural Contracts Theory, which ones do you find most useful to predict the impact of cultural identities as we create personal relationships? Why?
- How might an understanding of how Cultural Contracts Theory relates to identity negotiation provide new insight into the study of intercultural conflict? Why?
- As you consider the challenge Jackson offers in the closing lines of his article, what suggestions might you offer to address his challenge?

References

Berger, C. R., & Calabrese, R. J. (1975). Some explorations in initial interactions and beyond. *Human Communication Research*, 1, 99-112.

Brislin, R. (1983). Cross-cultural research in psychology. *Annual Review of Psychology, 34*, 363400.

Collier, M. J. & Thomas, M. (1988). Identity in intercultural communication: An interpretive perspective. In Y. Y. Kim & W. Gudykunst (Eds.), *Theories of intercultural communication.* Newbury Park, CA: Sage.

Cronen, V. E., Chen, V. & Pearce, W. B. (1988). Coordinated management of meaning. In Y. Y. Kim & W. B. Gudykunst (Eds.), *Theories of intercultural communication* (pp. 66-98). Newbury Park, CA: Sage.

Cross, W. (1971). The Negro-to-Black conversion experience. *Black World,* 13-27.

Cross, W. (1978). The Thomas and Cross Models on psychological nigrescence: A literature review, *Journal of Black Psychology 4,* 13-31.

Cross, W. (1991). *Shades of black, diversity in African American identity.* Philadelphia: Temple University Press.

Fisher, G. (1997). *Mindsets: The role of culture and perception in international relations.* Yarmouth, ME: Intercultural Press.

Giles, H., & Johnson, P. (1987). Ethnolinguistic identity theory: A social psychological approach to language maintenance. *International Journal of The Sociology of Language, 68*, 69-99.

Gudykunst, W. B. & Ting-Toomey, S. with Chua, E. (1988). *Culture and interpersonal communication.* Newbury Park, CA: Sage.

Hecht, M. L. (1998). *Communicating prejudice.* Thousand Oaks, CA: Sage.

Hecht, M. L., Jackson, R. L. & Ribeau, S. A. (2003). *African American communication: Exploring identity and culture.* Mahwah, NJ: Erlbaum.

Hofstede, G. (1980). *Culture consequences.* Beverly Hills, CA.: Sage.

Jackson, R. L. (1999). *The negotiation of cultural identity.* Westport, CT: Praeger.

Jackson, R. L. (2002). Exploring African American identity negotiation in the academy: Toward a transformative vision of African American communication scholarship. *Howard Journal of Communication, 12(4),* 43-57.

Jackson, R. L. (in press). Cultural contracts theory: Toward a critical rhetorical identity negotiation paradigm. In P. Sullivan & D. Goldzwig (Eds.), *Communities, creations, and contradictions: New approaches to rhetoric for the Twenty-first century.* Thousand Oaks, CA: Sage.

Jackson, R. L. & Crawley, R. (in press). White student confessions about an African American male professor: A cultural contracts theory approach to intimate conversations about race and worldview. *Journal of Men's Studies.*

Jackson, R. L. & Dangerfield, C. (2002). Defining Black masculinity as cultural property: An identity negotiation paradigm In L. Samovar & R. Porter (Eds.), *Intercultural communication: A reader.* (pp. 120-130). Belmont, CA: Wadsworth.

Jackson, R. L., Morrison, C. D., & Dangerfield, C. (2002). Exploring cultural contracts in the classroom and curriculum: Implications of identity negotiation and effects in communication curricula. In J. Trent (Ed.), *Included in communication: learning climates that cultivate racial and ethnic diversity.* (123-136). Washington, D.C.: National Communication Association & American Association of Higher Education.

Jackson, R. L. & Simpson, K. (in press). White positionalities and cultural contracts: Critiquing entitlement, theorizing and exploring the negotiation of white identities. *International and Intercultural Communication Annual, 26.*

Onwumechili, C., Nwosu, P., Jackson, R. L. & James-Hughes, J. (in press). In the deep valley with mountains to climb: Exploring multiple reacculturation. *International Journal of Intercultural Relations.*

Orbe, M. (1998). *Constructing co-cultural theory.* Newbury Park, CA: Sage.

Singer, M. (1998). *Perception and identity in intercultural communication.* Yarmouth, ME: Intercultural Press.

Tierney, S., & Jackson, R. L. (2002). Deconstructing whiteness ideology as a set of rhetorical fantasy themes: implications for intercultural alliance building in the United States. In M. J. Collier (Ed.), *Intercultural Alliances* (International and Intercultural Communication Annual, vol. 25), (pp. 81-106). Thousand Oaks, CA: Sage.

Ting-Toomey, S. (1986). Interpersonal ties in intergroup communication. In W.B. Gudykunst (Ed.), *Intergroup communication,* (pp. 114-126). Baltimore, MD.: Edward Arnold.

Ting-Toomey, S. (1999). *Communicating across cultures.* New York: Guilford Press.

In Chapter 5 of her text, *Relational Communication*, Julia Wood expands her discussion of "saturated selves" by noting that the myriad of perspectives we use to create our personal identity comes from situated knowledge; there is no such thing as absolute or universal knowledge since all knowledge is contextually bound. It is this perspective on situated knowledge that serves as the basis for Standpoint Theory, one of the eight theories explored by Wood throughout her text. In general, Standpoint Theory explores the way culture shapes what people experience -- how we interpret our own experiences, the experiences of others, and the nature of our personal relationships.

Communication scholars Mark P. Orbe and Kiesha T. Warren use Standpoint Theory as the basis of a study reported in their article entitled, "Different Standpoints, Different Realities: Race, Gender, and Perceptions of Intercultural Conflict." Specifically, these researchers analyzed facilitated focus group discussions of a 15-minute video clip from MTV's *The Real World* – an episode that captured a conflict between an 18-year old European American woman from a small town in Alabama and a 24-year old African American man from New Jersey. This phenomenological approach to the study of "situated knowledge" asks those who experience the event (viewing the video clip) to describe their experience of the event – to describe their standpoint of the event. Given the diverse nature of these focus groups (age, sex, and racial/ethnic identity), the researchers expected to find a variety of perspectives (standpoints) described by the participants who observed this video clip.

Using thematic analysis as their research tool, Orbe and Warren report their findings based on the diversity variables they explored. As you read the article, note the interesting excerpts taken directly from focus group transcripts as individuals describe their "situated knowledge"; these excerpts provide fascinating insight into the various standpoints of the participants. Furthermore, the researchers explore the impact of personal differences separate from cultural differences; they conclude that sometimes these personal differences are far more powerful than the cultural differences we often emphasize in the study of intercultural communication.

In discussing their findings, Orbe and Warren note the value of their research as well as the limitations of their study. Research that uses a phenomenological approach often reflects a limited sample size since extensive, in-depth transcripts of interviews or group discussions provide the data for analysis. Because the sample studied by Orbe and Warren consisted of just 44 subjects, they acknowledge concerns about the generalizeability of their research findings; however, such research provides a valuable foundation for future studies. Perhaps more important, this study confirms the value of Standpoint Theory as we explore both the similarities and differences in situated knowledge.

Different Standpoints, Different Realities: Race, Gender, and Perceptions of Intercultural Conflict

Mark P. Orbe and Kiesha T. Warren

Mark P. Orbe (Ph.D., Ohio University, 1993) is an associate professor in the Department of Communication and Center for Women's Studies at Western Michigan University. Kiesha T. Warren (M.A., Indiana State University, 1997) is a doctoral candidate in the Department of Sociology at Western Michigan University.

Considerable research exists on the general differences between African American and European American communication (Gresson, 1995; Hecht, Ribeau, & Alberts, 1989; Houston, 1997; Jackson, 1999; Martin, Hecht, & Larkey, 1994; McPhail, 1994; Orbe, 1994), however fewer studies have looked at conflict styles of these two groups (Kochman, 1981; Ting-Toomey, 1986). In a similar vein, scholars have given significant attention to the differences in how women and men engage in conflict (Markman, Silvera, Clements, & Kraft-Hanak, 1993; Putnam, 1983; Turner & Henzel, 1987). A more limited amount of research exists that specifically focuses on female and male perceptions of conflict (e.g., Lloyd, 1987). More recent research has begun to explore both the similarities and differences between men's and women's communication practices, including conflict styles (Canary & Dindia, 1998). Like Shuter and Turner (1997), we combine gender and race to explore the differences in how groups perceive communication episodes. In this regard, we suggest that by looking at intersections of both gender and race scholars are better apt to discover communication patterns that are not detectable when simply focusing on gender or race.

Our research is grounded in the assumption that perceptions of conflict are situated within a particular standpoint (Collins, 1986; Wood, 1992). As a means to explore how these standpoints inform one's perception(s) of communication, we utilized phenomenological inquiry to research the following question: How do different racialized/gendered groups perceive intercultural conflict?

Methodological Framework

Since our study used a videoclip excerpt from a television program to facilitate discussion, we looked to existing studies that examined the perceptions that diverse groups of people had in terms of specific mass media images (Cooks & Orbe, 1993; Orbe, Seymour, & Kang 1998). These studies provided clear direction for the ways that we organized the recruitment and organization of participants, implementation of focus group discussions, and subsequent analysis of transcripts.

Participants for this study were recruited primarily from undergraduate classes and community-based organizations in two different cities in the Midwest These persons (44 in total) represented a set of diverse standpoints in terms of age (18-51 years), sex (29 women and 15 men), and racial/ethnic identity (22 European Americans, 17 African Americans, 3 Asians, 1 Latino, and 1 Native American).

Following the strategies of earlier studies, these participants were organized by their sex and/or racial identity into eight focus groups: (a) one European American male group; (b) one African American male group; (c) two African American female groups; (d) two European American female groups; (d) one racially diverse female group; and (e) one racially diverse male and female group. To facilitate in-group discussions, researchers' identities were designed to match (at least to some extent) those of whom were in. the particular focus group (e.g., African American researcher for African American focus groups).

Focus groups ranged in size from three to ten participants and met for 40 to 75 minutes. A 15-minute video clip of MTVs *The Real World* (Season #1; New York cast) was shown to the group. This clip featured a "real-life" conflict situation captured on film in 1991 between an 18-year old European American woman from a small town in Alabama (Julie) and an 24-year old African American man from Jersey City, New Jersey (Kevin). Once the group had finished viewing the clip, the researcher facilitated a discussion by using several open-ended questions, including: "Can you describe what you saw taking place in the clip?," What did you think the conflict was about?" Can you describe your perceptions of each person's conflict style?," and "What are your thoughts about the appropriateness of how each person handled the conflict?". These questions served as an effective means to prompt discussion in terms of how participants perceived the conflict displayed in the videoclip; specific follow-up questions were also posed when participants' comments explored additional issues not explicitly identified in the initial set of questions. Each focus group discussion was audiotaped and subsequently transcribed by the facilitator/researcher that led the particular group.

Thematic Analysis

The eight focus group discussions, when transcribed verbatim, resulted in 58 pages of single-spaced text Consistent with the steps inherent to phenomenological inquiry (van Manen, 1990), our analysis process began with each researcher conducting her/his own preliminary review of each transcript. Once initial themes were identified, both researchers met face-to-face to share their insights. Over time, both sets of preliminary themes — which had a great deal of overlap in their initial form — were reexamined and ultimately merged into a collaborative analysis of the diverse perceptions of the conflict on MTV's *The Real World* (See Orbe, 1994, for a more complete description of phenomenological analysis).

Different Standpoints, Different Realities

As expected the different focus group compositions seemed to foster different types of discussions in terms of the conflict between Kevin and Julie. Within each of the homogeneous group discussions, for instance, certain perceptions of the conflict emerged as the dominant pattern. These will be explicated in the section below. Before we do so, however, it is important to recognize that while these ingroup patterns were consistent, some variations within groups were present. This point (and specifically how it relates to standpoint theory) will be explored within our discussion section.

Gender and/or race. Most focus groups were organized so that homogeneous groups could discuss perceptions of intercultural conflict. While discussions were multifaceted, clear patterns emerged. The two European American female groups, for instance, concluded that gender differences were most salient. The two African American female groups, however, defined the conflict primarily in terms of racial differences. Within the homogeneous focus groups, these primary perceptions guided other comments. European American women identified Kevin as the aggressor in the conflict and pointed to numerous examples of his intimidating behavior (e.g., his use of space and height to threaten Julie). In contrast African American women largely saw both individuals as "mutually aggressive." This point of disagreement was played out in a multiracial women's focus group discussion. Two African American women voiced anger because they perceived that Julie had "played up" the role of victim by crying and "acting as if she needed protection." Additionally, they pointed to how existing stereotypes concerning Black men also contributed to her success in bringing others to her defense. This perceptual difference is best captured in a series of comments from one exchange:

> *Aftican American woman #1:* People think stuff [have stereotypes] about Black people in general. Look at the police "he looked like," or "it appeared to me," or "he reached. . . " There is a general stereotype of the Black man or Black woman. That they are going to get in your face and they are going to hit you...I think that it might have played a factor in her saying "What are you going to do, hit me?" Because if it was a white guy in her face, I can't see her saying [it].
> *European American woman #1*: I can.
> *European American woman #2:* I can.
> *European American woman #3:* I can, too. Just because... the thing is when we feel intimidated it is because the other person is bigger, stronger, or coming at you. I think that its more of a gender issue.
>
> *African American woman #2:* I think that the "big Black guy" perception did play a part And he wasn't even physically big, so the stereotype was there ...

Immediately following this exchange, both of the African American women shared experiences where they had witnessed first-hand how stereotypes affect the ways that European Americans generally, and European American women specifically, interact with African American men. After a pause, the discussion continued:

> *European American woman:* I have a question [to an African American woman]. Would you be afraid if there was a taller, white male confronting you? If he was in your face like that—what we saw in the video—would you be afraid?
> *African American woman# 1:* Yes.
> *European American woman:* You see! I don't think it's that much of a racial issue. I think that it is more of a gender issue,

> *African American woman #2:* I think that, especially for black males, race plays a big part. I don't care what anyone says! I don't think that people like to admit it all of the time...But I think it does play a part. People don't like to admit that they think that or feel that way, but its a reality.

A few European American women admitted that such perceptions exist. However, they saw them as the "exception, not the rule." African American women disagreed, asserting that "Race is always an issue—whether you want to acknowledge it or not."

Personal differences. Within the European American male focus group, the conflict between Julie and Kevin was not about race or gender; it was about personal differences. Their discussion focused more on trying to understand the causes of their behaviors, and subsequently analyzing what should have been done by both participants in order to resolve their conflict. Attempts to see how gender and/or race played a part in the conflict appeared to be of little significance. Only one European American man commented on how Kevin had been stereotyped by others in the house: "I think that Kevin was being stereotyped by everyone in the house, just because of the way he acted in the past." However, as illustrated in his brief comments, this stereotype was based not on Kevin's race and/or gender, but on his past actions.

Another European American man acknowledged his perception that others would probably want to address the issue of race but denied its relevance: "Well, the whole issue of race, I knew that it was going to get brought up ... But it really had nothing to do with the issue of race at all. I mean there was zero race relevance to that." The comments of European American men highlighted thus far reflect an unwillingness to see the conflict between Julie and Kevin from alternative perspectives. However, one (and only one) European American man did share his attempt to see the conflict from a "minority" viewpoint: "I tried to hone in on the anger that was being placed there, and not on the race issue. But it is really hard not to do that." His comments suggest that the perceptions of European American males might be filtered by a standpoint that disallows them to see their own privilege positioning based on gender and race. In other words, they see race and gender, but find it difficult to understand how these markers are as important as personal (individual) differences.

More than just race. For the African American men involved in this study, the conflict was defined as an "interracial disagreement." In this regard, they — like African American women — recognized that "race is always in effect." Race clearly played a role, however, other factors were given equal attention in terms of how they affected Julie and Kevin. Interestingly though, gender was not mentioned among the African American male focus group. Their discussions, like those of the European American male group, did not touch on how gender differences impacted the conflict. Whereas European American men focused exclusively on personal differences, African American men identified personal and cultural differences that might have played a central role in the conflict.

"I think that it is a socioeconomic status issue," concluded one African American man. Others, in the same focus group, agreed but also identified how differences in age, geographical differences, and family upbringing were possible factors in Kevin and Julie's conflict. Additionally, African American men also shared how personal differences (e.g., "strong personalities") were intertwined with cultural differences. In short, African American men generally acknowledged race as one marker for the conflict, but explored how other factors pointed to a more complex understanding of their interaction.

Discussion

As expected, the different compositions of the focus groups seemed to foster different perspectives in discussing the conflict between Kevin and Julie. However, at this juncture, it is important to recognize that our interpretations of these discussions represent a fusion of the researcher expectations and the participants' actual meaning (Cooks & Orbe, 1993). Given the relatively small number of participants, additional research steps are needed to gain feedback for our interpretations from those that they seek to represent [Leslie & Orbe (in press) describe this element of phenomenological inquiry as a "post-syntagmatic spiral"]. Still, our analysis provides a preliminary interpretation of the issues discussed. With these limitations in mind, we offer the following brief discussion.

Standpoint epistemology (e.g., Harding, 1987, 1991; Hartsock, 1983) provides a productive lens to view our findings. According to standpoint theorists (Collins, 1986; Harding, 1987, 1991), life is not experienced the same for all members of any given culture. In explicit and implicit ways, our standpoints affect how we communicate as well as how we perceive the communication of others. Part of acknowledging diverse standpoints involves recognizing that different persons will perceive the world differently based on their experiences living in a racialized and gendered society. For African Americans, racial issues are interwoven into the past, present, and future of the United States. For European Americans, "it isn't always necessarily about race." In this regard, standpoint epistemology helps to explain our findings both in terms of how racialized and gendered standpoints prompted different interpretations of the same conflict.

Standpoint theories, however, are most productive when they are utilized to reveal both the similarities and differences within and among cultural groups (Wood, 1992). While persons share a core of experiences based on group membership (e.g., by race and/or gender), this does not negate the presence of differences within any singular group or the possibilities of similarities across groups. This is an important point given the findings of our study. Clear patterns of how different groups perceived conflict emerged, however, these patterns were not universal. For instance, a small (but distinct) number of European American women did speak to the role that race played in the conflict between Kevin and Julie. Within their comments, these persons related experiences (e.g., living in a diverse neighborhood or taking a Black Studies class) that encouraged an understanding if not an identification, with an alternative standpoint.

In conclusion, our study revealed how differences in perceptions of conflict can be understood within the different standpoints of racialized/gendered groups. It is, however, not without certain limitations. First, some of participants had previously seen the videoclip and therefore had a larger context from which to understand Kevin and Julie's conflict. Second, the relatively small number of research participants, especially those of Native, Latino, or Asian descent, limits the value of our analysis. Additional research has already begun to extend our comparisons beyond those of African American/European American women and men (Warren, Orbe, & Greer-Williams, forthcoming). Moreover, a greater commitment to honoring the voices of participants is needed to strengthen this research (Orbe, in press). Within this line of inquiry, qualitative researchers can use phenomenology to gain additional insight into the role that standpoint plays in various aspects of human communication processes.

Consider this . . .

- As you consider the research findings reported in this study, briefly describe some of the different standpoints you found most interesting. Why do these findings capture your interest?
- Based on the research findings reported in this study, how do personal differences (rather than cultural differences) sometimes account for our differences in "situated knowledge" or standpoints? Give an example to illustrate.
- Given the limitations of the study discussed by the researchers themselves, what suggestions would you offer to strengthen future research in this area?
- Using Standpoint Theory as the basis for your discussion, what other types of "situated knowledge" might we explore in our research? How might such "situated knowledge" provide valuable insight into our study of personal relationships?

Ronald L. Jackson II (Ph.D., Howard University, 1996), Associate Professor of Culture and Communication Theory, Department of Communication Arts & Sciences, Pennsylvania State University. Correspondence concerning this article should be addressed to Ronald L. Jackson II, Department of Speech Communication, Pennsylvania State University, 234 Sparks Building, University Park, PA 16802. Electronic mail may be sent via Internet to rlj6@psu.edu.

References

Canary, D. J., & Dindia, K. (Eds.). (1998). *Sex differences and similarities in communication: Critical essays and empirical investigations of sex and gender in interaction.* Mahwah, NJ: Lawrence Erlbaum Associates.

Collins, P. H. (1986). Learning from the outsider within: The sociological significance of black feminist thought. *Social Problems, 33(6)*, S14-S23.

Cooks, L. M., & Orbe, M. (1993). Beyond the satire: Selective exposure and selective perception in "In Living Color." *Howard Journal of Communications, 4(3)*, 217-233.

Gresson, A. D. (1995). *The recovery of race in America.* Minneapolis: University of Minnesota Press.

Harding, S. (Ed.). (1987). *Feminism & methodology.* Bloomington: Indiana University Press.

Harding, S. (1991). *Whose science? Whose knowledge? Thinking from women's lives.* Ithaca, NY: Cornell University Press.

Hartsock, N. C. M. (1983). The feminist standpoint: Developing the ground for a specifically feminist historical materialism. In S. Harding & M. D. Hintikka (Eds.), *Discovering reality: Feminist perspectives on epistemology, metaphysics, methodology, and philosophy of science* (pp. 283 -310). Boston: D. Reidel.

Hecht, M. L., Ribeau, S., & Alberts, J. K. (1989). An Afro-American perspective on interethnic communication. *Communication Monographs, 56*, 385-408.

Houston, M. (1997). When Black women talk with White women: Why dialogues are difficult. In A. Gonzalez, M. Houston, & V Chen (Eds.), *Our voices: Essays in culture, ethnicity, and communication* (pp. 187-195). Los Angeles, CA: Roxbury.

Jackson, R. L. (1999). *The negotiation of cultural identity: Perceptions of European Americans and African Americans.* Westport, CT: Praeger.

Kochman, T. (1981). *Black and white styles in conflict.* Chicago, IL: University of Chicago Press.

Leslie, K. B., & Orbe, M. (in press). "Medical crisis or miracle": A phenomenological inquiry of transplant recipient communication. *Health Communication.*

Lloyd, S. A. (1987). Conflict in premarital relationships: Differential perceptions of males and females. *Family Relations, 36*, 290-294.

Markman, H. J., Silvera, L., Clements, M., & Kraft-Hanak, S. (1993). Men and women dealing with conflicts in heterosexual relationships. *Journal of Social Issues, 49,* 107-125.

Martin, J. N., Hecht, M. L., & Larkey, L. K., (1994). Conversation improvement strategies for interethnic communication: African American and European American perspective. *Communication Monograph 61*, 236-255.

McPhaiL M. L. (1994). The rhetoric of racism. Latham, NM: University Press of America.

Orbe, M. (1994). "Remember, it's always whites' ball": Descriptions of African American male communication. *Communication Quarterly, 42(3)*, 287-300.

Orbe, M., Seymour, K., & Kang M. E. (1998). "Ethnic humor" and ingroup/outgroup positioning: Explicating perceptions of "All-American Girl." In Y. R. Kamalipour & T. Carilli (Eds.), *Cultural diversity and the U.S. media* (pp. 125-136). Albany: State University of New York Press.

Putnam, L. L. (1983). Lady you're trapped: Breaking out of conflict cycles. In J. J. Pilotta (Ed.), *Women in organizations: Barriers and breakthroughs* (pp. 39-53). Prospect Heights, IL: Waveland.

Shuter, R. & Turner, L. (1997). African American and European American women in workplace: Perceptions of conflict communication. *Management Communication Quarterly, 11,* 74-96.

Ting-Toomey, S. (1986). Conflict communication styles in black and white subjective cultures. In Y. Y. Kim (Ed.), *Interethnic communication* (pp. 75-88). Newbury Park: Sage.

Turner, L. H., & Henzel, S. (1987). Influence attempts in organization conflict: The effects of biological sex, psychological gender, and power position. *Management Communication Quarterly, 32-57.*

van Manen, M. (1990). *Researching lived experience: Humans science for action sensitive pedagogy.* Ontario, Canada: State University of New York Press.

Warren, K. T., Orbe, M., & Greer-Williams, N. (forthcoming). Perceptions of interpersonal/intercultural conflict: Recognizing cultural differences and similarities between and among Latino/as, African Americans, and European Americans. In D. Rios & A. Mohamed (Eds.), *Communication in brown & black: Latino and African American conflict and convergence in mass media and cross-cultural contexts.* Westport, CT. Greenwood Press.

Wood, J. T. (1992). Gender and moral voice: Moving from woman's nature to standpoint epistemology. *Women's Studies in Communication, 15(l)*, 1-24.

PART 2

The Evolution of Personal Relationships

CHAPTER 6

LAUNCHING PERSONAL RELATIONSHIPS

Part II of the course, Foundations in Interpersonal Communication, explores personal relationships from a developmental perspective – how we move into personal relationships, how we sustain and repair these relationships, and how we redefine or terminate these relationships. In Chapter 6 of her text, *Relational Communication*, Julia Wood discusses the communication tools we use to 'launch" or initiate personal relationships; she discusses elements of attraction, tools for reducing uncertainty, and characteristics of early interaction.

In his article entitled, "Communicating Under Uncertainty," communication scholar Charles Berger addresses the role of uncertainty in our everyday lives. He begins with a discussion of the vast sums of money both governments and corporations spend to uncover valuable information about friends as well as foes. Though the article was written in 1987 and the data reported would pale in comparison to today's budgetary expenditures, Berger's claim is perhaps even more valid in the context of our current political and economic climate. Simply put, reducing uncertainty about friends and foes continues to be "big business" for corporations and governments alike.

While Berger notes that uncertainty is the bane of economic and political decision-makers, he further notes that uncertainty is one of the greatest challenges we face as we initiate, maintain, sustain, redefine, or terminate our interpersonal relationships. Uncertainty reduction not only relates to our understanding of the other person in our interactions, but it also relates to our understanding of "self" as well. In his article, Berger provides an interesting discussion concerning the nature of uncertainty, as well as its inherent tie to communication, in a variety of social contexts. Through this discussion, Berger offers a brief overview of the theoretical construct we know as Uncertainty Reduction Theory (URT).

As we discussed in Chapter 2, a theory is valuable to the extent that it can help us describe, explain, predict, or control a phenomenon. Perhaps most interesting is Berger's discussion of three types of strategies we use to reduce uncertainty around us: 1) passive strategies, 2) active strategies, and 3) interactive strategies. Read carefully his discussion of the three-strategy typology as well as the tools and tactics used to employ each strategy. Following this discussion, Berger provides an extensive literature review concerning the impact of uncertainty on relationship development, intercultural encounters, and social support. He concludes by noting that Uncertainty Reduction Theory can provide a valuable framework for understanding the growth and/or decline (relational trajectories) of our personal relationships.

Communicating Under Uncertainty

Charles R. Berger

Uncertainty plays an enormously important role in many spheres of social life. Galbraith (1977) has argued we live in an "age of uncertainty" that is unlike previous historical epochs. Past political and economic life, according to Galbraith, was considerably more predictable than it is today. In addition, the advent of the nuclear age has raised current international stakes to such a degree that governments spend huge sums each year to uncover the future actions of both friends and foes. Consider the following statistics. During fiscal 1985, it is estimated that the Central Intelligence Agency will spend $99,300,000 on its operations, while the National Security Council will spend $4,605,000. In addition, the National Security Agency, with its classified budget, will spend millions more dollars on intelligence-gathering efforts. Most likely, the U.S.S.R. spends approximately equal numbers of rubles to support its intelligence community.

Not only does the U.S. government spend large amounts of tax money to try to reduce its international uncertainties, individual citizens are willing to pay dearly to reduce their uncertainties about the future course of stocks and other investment vehicles. It is estimated that Americans spend some $100,000,000 a year to obtain investment information (*Wall Street Week*, 1985). In addition, consider the substantial sums paid by businesses to economic forecasters and it becomes apparent that uncertainty reduction itself is a major business.

When individuals and corporations cannot reduce business and personal uncertainties, they spend large amounts of money to hedge against negative outcomes that may loom over the horizon. In 1983, $109 billion in net property and casualty insurance premiums were paid by individuals and corporations (A. M. Best, 1984a). During the same period, $119 billion in net premiums were paid for life and health insurance policies, excluding premiums paid to Blue Cross-Blue Shield (A. M. Best, 1984b). These figures demonstrate that the importance of the outcomes increases in a situation, persons and institutions are willing to invest considerable resources to try to predict and hedge against future events that may affect their outcomes. So pervasive are these uncertainty-reduction activities that decision making under uncertainty is a growing area of research in such academic disciplines as business (Hogarth, 1980) and cognitive psychology (Kahneman, Slovic, & Tversky, 1982). These investigators, as well as others, have sought to understand the strategies individuals employ to make judgments and decisions when complete information is unavailable to them.

Although economists, political scientists, sociologists, and psychologists have recognized the centrality of uncertainty in human affairs, communication researchers in general and interpersonal communication researchers in particular have only recently begun to acknowledge the importance of uncertainty in human communication. Early communication researchers (e.g., Berlo, 1960) did discuss Shannon and Weaver's (1949) mathematical theory of information, which deals with uncertainty in communication systems, however, such discussions did little to motivate either theory building or empirical research aimed at exploring the role played by uncertainty in human communication. Several psychologists (Heider, 1958; Kelly, 1955; Thibaut & Kelley, 1959) discussed the role played by uncertainty in interpersonal relationships, but these discussions had little impact upon communication researchers interested in the study of interpersonal processes. Thus, the main impact of Thibaut and Kelley's (1959) analysis of interpersonal relationships was their explication of the roles played by exchanges of rewards and costs in relationship development (e.g., Roloff, 1981). Their discussion of uncertainty was virtually ignored by communication researchers.

This state of affairs changed in 1975 when Calabrese and I (Berger & Calabrese, 1975) advanced an axiomatic theory designed to explain certain communication phenomena that we observed during initial interactions. We felt then, as we feel today, that a number of events occurring in such initial encounters can be explained in terms of uncertainty and uncertainty reduction. Although the theory was originally developed to explain certain initial interaction phenomena, it has recently been expanded to explain aspects of established romantic relationships (Parks & Adelman, 1983) and intercultural encounters (Gudykunst, Yang, & Nishida, 1985). These studies, as well as several others, have demonstrated three important points: First, uncertainty levels are important in relationships beyond the initial stages of their formation. Second, uncertainty is also important in communication contexts other than interpersonal ones. Third, and not surprisingly, the theory, as proposed by Berger and Calabrese (1975), contains some propositions of dubious validity.

A decade has elapsed since publication of the original theory, and it seems appropriate to see what directions it has taken and to sketch how it might be developed in the future. Thus the two primary goals of the present chapter are to assess the evolution of the theory since its inception and to plot some potential courses of future development. When the theory was first discussed (Berger & Calabrese, 1975), there was no official name given to it. Some dubbed it "initial interaction theory" while others called it "uncertainty theory." More recent discussions have used the term "uncertainty reduction theory" (URT). This more inclusive label seems to capture best the evolutionary direction of the theory.

Theoretical Evolution

The Nature of Uncertainty

Just as it is the bane of political and economic decision-makers, uncertainty is also a potential hobgoblin of interpersonal relationships. The task of interacting with a stranger, who in theory can behave and believe in a very large number of alternative ways and whose actions and beliefs remain to be explained, presents interactants with complex predictive and explanatory problems. These problems pertain both to understanding the other person in an interaction and understanding oneself. To interact in a relatively smooth, coordinated, and understandable manner, one must be able both to predict how one's interaction partner is likely to behave, and, based on these predictions, to select from one's own repertoire those responses that will optimize outcomes in the encounter. Uncertainty is not reduced for its own sake. Political and economic planners as well as communicators seek to reduce their uncertainties about their environments so that they can respond to these environments in ways that will assure goal achievement (e.g., Miller & Steinberg, 1975).

The idea that uncertainty is a function of the number of alternatives present in a situation and their relative likelihood of occurrence is, of course, taken directly from information theory (Shannon & Weaver, 1949). However, Berger and Calabrese (1975) extended this notion of uncertainty to include explanation. Thus uncertainty is a function of both the ability to predict and the ability to explain actions of other and of self. This explanatory component was added because of the importance accorded causal explanation by various attribution theorists (Heider, 1958; Jones & Davis, 1965; Kelley, 1967, 1971). This broader conceptualization of uncertainty holds that persons obtain information that allows them to increase their predictive certainty before they become concerned with the problem of why certain behaviors have or have not occurred. Berger, Gardner, Parks, Schulman, and Miller (1976) pointed out that obtaining the knowledge necessary for reducing explanatory uncertainty might be both more difficult and time consuming than acquiring information necessary for the reduction of predictive uncertainty. A similar discussion of levels of knowing was presented by Miller and Steinberg (1975) at about the same time.

This basic conceptualization of the uncertainty construct remains intact. Furthermore, Berger (1975) was able to demonstrate how information exchanged early in interactions can foster predictions about unknown attributes of the other (proactive attributions) and explanations of subsequent conduct during ongoing interactions (retroactive attributions). This distinction between proactive and retroactive attributional activity was incorporated into Clatterbuck's (1979) CLUES scale, which has been employed in a number of studies examining the relationships between uncertainty and other variables. Recently, Gudykunst and Nishida (1986) have modified the CLUES scale to increase its cross-cultural generalizability. Both the original and modified versions of the scale are displayed in the Appendix.

Communication and Uncertainty

Given the many combinations of verbal and nonverbal behaviors and the ranges of subtle modulations of these behaviors available to most normal interactants, it is amazing persons are able to carry out as many meaningful interactions with others as they apparently do. Of course, psychotherapists, organizational and media consultants, and others whose job it is to improve communication skills are quick to point out that persons playing a variety of roles fail to discharge their duties as they should because of "communication breakdowns" or "failures to communicate." Though such breakdowns and failures are certainly real and should be expected given the complex nature of communicative transactions, more often than not persons are able to achieve their interaction goals successfully. If the reader doubts the veracity of this assertion, consider all of the mundane interactions that most of us have during the course of an average day. Encounters with shopkeepers, ticket agents, waiters, coworkers, and a host of others usually go off without a hitch.

Communication and uncertainty are inextricably intertwined. Communicative actions are those things interactants frequently wish to predict and less frequently seek to explain, and it is through observations of communicative conduct that predictions and explanations are derived. This reciprocal relationship is central to URT. Axioms of the original theory posited reciprocal causal relationships between amount of communication and uncertainty and between nonverbal affiliative expressiveness and uncertainty; specifically, uncertainty is reduced as these variables increase, and decreases in uncertainty are responsible for increases in both verbal and nonverbal communication.

Although these relationships still seem somewhat plausible, Berger and Bradac (1982) recognized that there are circumstances under which communicative action might actually increase uncertainty. Persons are perfectly capable of acting in ways calculated to cloud their intentions in the eyes of others. Goffman (1969) presents an insightful analysis of how persons employ covering moves to mask their true intent and how observers employ uncovering moves to ascertain actual intentions. However, persons can deploy counter-uncovering moves to foil the uncovering moves made by observers. This process of increasing uncertainty through communicative action may not be intentional. Given certain combinations of alternative choices and specific contexts, some communicative choices might actually increase uncertainty because of the number of alternative interpretations available to observers. As Jones and Davis (1965) have argued, since positive actions can be motivated by either sincere or ulterior motives, they are not as reliable for making inferences about underlying dispositions as are negative behaviors that we assume are not motivated by ulterior motives.

In addition to the above possibilities, Planalp and Honeycutt (1985) have studied events that increase uncertainty in ongoing relationships. In their survey, respondents had little difficulty thinking of events that increased their uncertainty about persons whom they thought they knew well. These events—namely, competing relationships, unexplained loss of close contact, sexual behavior, deception, change in personality and values, and betraying confidence—exerted strong impacts upon cognitive, affective, and communication variables. In addition, a majority of the relationships studied became more distant or were terminated as a result of the events. Unfortunately, the way in which participants were asked to report on uncertainty-increasing events in their relationships may have biased them toward thinking about negative rather than positive events, although a few respondents did report positive events. This is an important point since persons can be pleasantly surprised by certain events in such relationships. Nevertheless, this study is significant because it supports the notion that communication does not always act to reduce uncertainty in relationships.

It is probably safe to assume that reduced communication between persons can impair their ability to predict and explain each other well. This prediction challenges the well-known aphorism, absence makes the heart grow fonder. Under the present view, absence and reduced interaction between persons are likely to lead to increased relational difficulties, especially when the individuals involved in the relationship are experiencing considerable change in their individual lives. There is some evidence to support this line of reasoning. Ayres (1979) found that both stranger and friend dyads asked each other about an equal number of questions during the initial few minutes of their interactions; however, friends asked significantly more evaluative questions of each other when compared with strangers. Thus sheer volume of information seeking in the two types of dyads was the same, but the kinds of information sought differed. Ayers's findings suggest that even friends may have reduced their uncertainties about each other each time they interact. Unfortunately, Ayres (1979) did not measure the length of time since the last interaction between the friends he studied. Had he done so, we would have expected question frequency to increase with time elapsed since the last interaction.

The relationship between uncertainty and communication is not simple. Lack of opportunity to communicate most certainly has the effect of raising uncertainty levels; however, the opportunity to interact may or may not produce reductions in uncertainty. Although it is safe to assume that communication is necessary for the reduction of uncertainty—unless, of course, one believes uncertainty can be reduced through ESP—the relationships between uncertainty and communication posited here differ from those advanced by Berger and Calabrese (1975). Moreover, the present discussion suggests that sheer volume of communication is probably not a good predictor of uncertainty reduction. Indeed, the quality rather than the quantity of information exchanged between interactants should have a greater impact upon the reduction of mutual uncertainties.

Social Context and Uncertainty Reduction

Berger and Calabrese (1975) suggested that the social context of interactions might provide uncertainty-reducing information. For example, persons first meeting at a political rally might begin their conversation by talking about the candidate rather than exchanging the usual biographic and demographic information; however, exchanges of such information might occur later in the same interaction. In this situation uncertainty is reduced by both parties making inferences about the reasons for the other' s presence at the rally. Most likely, persons would assume that others present at such a rally support the candidate, thus making the candidate a safe topic for a conversational opening.

Rubin (1977) varied the interaction context to see how it would affect the number and types of questions asked by interactants. In the ambiguous condition, persons were asked to form a general impression of others by asking them questions. In the specific condition, persons were asked to form impressions of their partners in terms of how they thought the partners would perform on a library job. Persons in the latter condition also were told to form their impressions by asking questions. This study revealed two findings relevant to the present issue: First, more questions were asked in the ambiguous context; second, more demographic questions were asked in the ambiguous context. In addition to these findings, Rubin (1979) reported that interactions in the ambiguous context lasted significantly longer than those in the specific context, and postinteraction ratings revealed that persons in the ambiguous context felt they had greater insight into their partners' personalities.

These findings support the notion that uncertainty can be reduced by the context of the interaction. Interactants in the ambiguous context faced the problem of reducing their uncertainties about their partners along many more dimensions than those in the specific context. To accomplish this task, they had to spend more time interacting with their partners and they had to ask them more questions. In addition, the questions they asked were primarily biographic and demographic. Answers to these broad background questions can be used to make inferences about attitudes and opinions not yet revealed in the conversation (Berger, 1975). Interestingly, the increased interaction time in the ambiguous context led interactants to feel they had a better grasp of their partners' personalities than did interactants in the specific context. This finding is not too surprising given the conversational task in the specific condition—that is, to form an impression of a person as a potential library assistant.

Although Rubin's findings clearly show the uncertainty-reducing properties of interaction contexts, the social context may increase interactants' uncertainty levels under certain conditions. One can imagine circumstances in which persons might structure interaction situations to maximize the uncertainty levels of the persons involved. Individuals may be intentionally misled so they do not discover a hidden agenda, or so many potential agendas are rendered possible that persons have a difficult time understanding exactly which one is operating at a given time. Thus the social context, like communicative action, can sometimes be used to raise uncertainty levels.

Uncertainty Reduction Strategies

Thus far we have examined the roles played by both communication and the interaction context in the uncertainty reduction process. There are, however, additional routes to uncertainty reduction. First, persons bring considerable knowledge with them to any interaction situation: information about persons in the form of person prototypes (Cantor & Mischel, 1977), role schemas, and typical event sequences or scripts (Abelson, 1981; Schank & Abelson, 1977). This knowledge enables the individuals to begin to understand others involved in the social situation and provides the procedural knowledge necessary to conduct the interaction. Such knowledge is vital for the conduct of most interactions (Abelson, 1981; Schank, 1982; Schank & Abelson, 1977; Winograd, 1980). Also in this long-term memory are schemes for the acquisition of new knowledge (i.e., procedural routines for acquiring new information). Obviously, such new information must be acquired if a relationship is to develop. This kind of procedural knowledge is extremely powerful because it enables us to acquire new knowledge. It is to these knowledge acquisition routines that I now turn.

In the original version of URT, Berger and Calabrese (1975) were not concerned with strategies for reducing uncertainty. Subsequently, attention was directed toward these knowledge acquisition strategies (Berger, 1979; Berger &

Bradac, 1982; Berger et al., 1976). These presentations advanced a typology of information-gaining strategies consisting of three broad strategy classes: passive, active, and interactive. Passive strategies are those in which the uncertainty reducer gathers information about a target through unobtrusive observation. Active strategies involve the observation of targets' responses to manipulations of the interaction environment but no direct interaction between observers and targets. Also included in this category is the acquisition of information about a target from third-party sources. Finally, interactive strategies involve direct, face-to-face contact between the information seeker and the target.

It is tempting to speculate which of these three classes of strategies is most effective in acquiring information. One might argue, for example, that interactive strategies are superior because the uncertainty reducer can control the target and can ask probing questions. However, it could also be argued that passive approaches are more effective because the observer can attend more closely to the target. In the passive mode, observers do not have to be concerned about their conduct during the inter-action. No research energy has been expended on this issue, but it is an important one to study from both theoretical and methodological points of view. Since researchers frequently make judgments of research participants after observing their interactions on videotape (passive mode), we might ask: Would these judgments correspond to those that would have been made had the observer actually interacted with the person (interactive mode)? My suspicion is that there would be significant changes in judgments as a function of shifts in observational context.

Research conducted to investigate knowledge acquisition strategies has revealed several important findings. Studies aimed at illuminating the passive strategies (Berger & Douglas, 1981; Berger & Perkins, 1978, 1979) suggest that when persons wish to acquire information about a target person using unobtrusive observation, they prefer to observe the target in social rather than solitary situations. In addition, social situations in which the target is highly involved in interaction with others are judged to be more informationally rich than social situations in which the target is relatively uninvolved with the others present. Finally, persons anticipating interaction with the target person consider informal social contexts to be potentially more informative than formal contexts. These findings suggest that informal, active social contexts are perceived to place fewer situational constraints on target persons and thus to be more informative about the target persons; in short, one can find out more about individuals conversing with others at a party than by observing them at a funeral or sitting in a room alone.

To date, little work has been done on active strategies of information acquisition. Obviously, this paradigm of information acquisition is widely employed in behavioral science research (i.e., the investigator manipulates a set of conditions and then observes participant responses to these manipulations). Whether persons perform such "experiments" in their everyday lives is an issue worthy of research. While little research has been done in the area of "naive social experimentation," some work has been reported that is germane to the question of how persons evaluate information about target persons that they receive from third parties. Hewes, Graham, Doelger, and Pavitt (1985) found that both college students and non-college students obtain about 65% of their information about others in their social networks from direct contact, with about 30% of their information being obtained from third-party sources. Though directly acquired information was rated significantly more useful than indirectly obtained information, the latter was judged to be "somewhat useful." This study also revealed that persons are quite aware of the possibility that information obtained from third-party sources is biased, and about 71% of the respondents claimed they were able to take these biases into account in interpreting these messages. Thus naive social actors and actresses may be somewhat more sophisticated at debiasing information they receive than the work of some psychologists suggests (Kahneman et al., 1982; Nisbett & Ross, 1980).

The Hewes et al. (1985) study represents an important step in the investigation of active strategies of information acquisition. Persons who study interpersonal communication tend to focus on exchanges occurring within dyads or groups that they observe. Obviously, face-to-face encounters are ideal for studying many communication phenomena. Nevertheless, it is naive to assume that persons gather all their information about each other in such contexts. In the early stages of dating relationships, for example, indirect modes of information acquisition may be more prevalent than direct ones and more significant types of information may be exchanged through indirect channels (e.g., "Do you think she really likes me?" or "Could you find out from him whether he really enjoyed our date last weekend?"). Certainly, when there is considerable self-presentational activity in a relationship, more accurate information may be available through third-party channels. Thus in organizational settings, a boss may give an unrealistically positive evaluation to a subordinate, but disclose his or her true evaluation of the subordinate to a confidant. The confidant, in turn, may disclose the boss's true evaluation to the subordinate. Such "informational triangles" are probably quite common in both formal organizations and relatively informal social networks. Obviously, these triangles are critical for uncertainty reduction and the evaluation of social information.

Interactive strategies for knowledge acquisition have received the bulk of our recent research attention. In a series of studies (Berger & Kellermann, 1983, 1985; Kellermann & Berger, 1994) we have sought to discover the information-seeking devices used during face-to-face interactions. Berger and Kellermann (1983) found three principal strategies: question asking, disclosure, and relaxation of the target. Interestingly, persons attempting to acquire large amounts of information do not necessarily ask any more questions than persons seeking to have a "normal conversation." Instead, persons in the high information-seeking mode ask their targets more questions concerned with explanations for their behavior and their future goals and plans. Moreover, persons interested in knowledge acquisition take advantage of floor possession to ask questions of their targets.

Kellermann and Berger (1984) found that persons seeking information tended to employ more positive nonverbal behaviors during their interactions than did persons unconcerned with information acquisition. These findings led to the hypothesis that strategy selection is governed by two main considerations: the efficiency of the strategy and its social appropriateness. Question asking, disclosure, and relaxing the target are ordered with respect to both dimensions; question asking is most efficient but potentially most intrusive, and relaxing the target least efficient but also least threatening. This line of reasoning suggests that there may be a tradeoff between these two dimensions when selecting information-gaining strategies. Furthermore, the significance of these dimensions extends beyond the selection of information-gaining strategies. For example, Rosenfeld (1966) and Mehrabian and Williams (1969) found that approval-seekers and persons attempting social influence displayed more positive nonverbal behaviors than persons not attempting to achieve these social goals. Their findings are quite similar to those obtained for our high information seekers (Kellermann & Berger, 1984). In general, these studies suggest that when persons attempt to achieve social goals, people try to induce their targets to like them in order to facilitate goal achievement.

Berger and Kellermann (1985) have discovered a series of offensive and defensive tactics that persons use to foil information-seeking attempts of others during the parry and thrust of conversations. Offensive tactics include focusing the conversation on the information seeker and asking the information seeker as many questions as possible. Such tactics prevent the seeker from querying the target. Defensive tactics include giving minimal and ambiguous responses to questions and giving off unaffiliative nonverbal behaviors. We are currently in the process of examining how information seekers respond to the communicative parries employed by their conversational partners. We suspect that patterns of strategy and countermeasure deployment emerge over time. One critical focus of this research is upon the *iterative mechanisms* underlying these exchanges through time.

For persons to conduct relatively coordinated interactions with others, they need person, role, and procedural knowledge. If the relationship is to progress beyond an initial interaction, interactants must acquire more specific information about each others' personalities, attitudes and preferences, and values. Persons can employ perceptual, cognitive, and communicative routines to acquire the needed information for understanding both their relational partners and themselves. Since the acquisition of such information is vital for continuance of the relationship, researchers need to gain an understanding of the strategies persons use to acquire it. Studies of these strategies will both add to our fund of knowledge about uncertainty reduction and enable us to aid those who have difficulty gaining understanding of others and themselves.

Uncertainty and Relationship Developement

Our discussion of uncertainty reduction strategies quite naturally leads to consideration of the role uncertainty plays in the development, maintenance, and dissolution of personal relationships. In the original statement of URT, Berger and Calabrese (1975) argued that uncertainty reduction leads to increases in attractiveness and that continued high levels of uncertainty in a relationship should produce lowered levels of attraction. Clatterbuck (1979) reported the findings of numerous investigations examining the relationship between uncertainty as measured by his CLUES scale and attraction. He found consistent correlations between CLUES and various attraction measures; in general, persons who felt they knew more about their relational partners were more attracted to them. The correlations across these studies were in the .20 to .35 range. Gudykunst et al. (1985) found consistent positive relationships between the CLUES attributional confidence measure and interpersonal attraction across acquaintance, friend, and dating relationships in a multicultural study involving persons from Japan, Korea, and the United States. Clatterbuck (1979) also reported consistently positive correlations between CLUES and the length of time persons had known each other. Similarly, using the Gudykunst et al. (1985) data, I found that across all three cultures levels of uncertainty were twice as high in acquaintance as in friend relationships.

The data collected by Clatterbuck (1979) as well as by Gudykunst et al. (1985) involved the use of self-report questionnaires. Laboratory investigations have revealed that uncertainty as manifested in speech behavior declines as interactions progress. For example, Lalljee and Cook (1973) reported that filled pause rate decreased and speech rate increased as interactions between strangers progressed. Sherblom and Van Rheenen (1984) found that mean word length, type-token ratio, and linguistic diversity all increased as interviews between strangers progressed. Conversely, several indices of immediacy (Mehrabian & Wiener, 1966) did not show expected changes. These findings, coupled with those cited above, provide some support for the notion that as relationships progress, uncertainty tends to be reduced; however, in light of the earlier discussion concerning the relationships between communication and uncertainty, it is possible that uncertainty levels can escalate at later stages of relationships (Planalp & Honeycutt, 1985).

While the notion that uncertainty is reduced over time seems reasonable, as long as persons involved in the relationships remain in contact with each other, the claim that the reduction of uncertainty leads to increased attraction is considerably more controversial. Scheidel (1977) has pointed out that persons can come to know things about others that trigger dislike. Furthermore, the uncertainty involved in romantic relationships might actually be a source of excitement and attraction (Livingston, 1980). Once it is reduced, the relationship might move to a less exciting, mundane level. These arguments cast doubt on one proposition advanced in the original version of URT. Thus some alternative possibilities will be considered here. In discussing them, it should be remembered that in its original form, URT was solely concerned with explaining events occurring during initial interactions. However, since some researchers have found that uncertainty plays an important role in more developed relationships (Gudykunst et al., 1985; Parks & Adelman, 1983; Parks, Stan, & Eggert, 1983; Sunnafrank, 1986), it seems worthwhile to extend URT in this direction.

Persistently high uncertainty levels should put considerable strain on relationships. Under conditions of high uncertainty, interaction is effortful and difficult; thus over a protracted time period, persons should develop negative affect toward the relationship. Even so, uncertainty with respect to various actions and beliefs may not always have a profound negative impact upon relationships; indeed, uncertainty in areas of peripheral concern enhance novelty and may actually be experienced as pleasant (Berlyne, 1960). Thus if a relational partner dresses unpredictably, and manner of dress is not important in the relationship, uncertainty in this domain should have little impact upon relational outcomes. If, however, a relational partner is subject to unpredictable mood changes, uncertainty in this domain might eventually undermine the relationship.

Uncertainty about another can also be reduced in such a way as to become certain that the other possesses numerous unattractive attributes. Obviously, such knowledge strains the relationship and increases pressures for its dissolution. Furthermore, uncertainty can be reduced in such a way that positive outcomes are predicted, thus fueling relational growth. Once these affective responses are formed, they will influence further efforts to reduce uncertainty. Persons will continue to reduce uncertainty about liked others and cease to reduce uncertainty about disliked others. This reasoning suggests a reciprocal relationship between uncertainty and attraction, with continued uncertainty reduction a function of the valence of affect toward one's partner.

Though correlational data (Clatterbuck, 1979; Gudykunst et al., 1985) support such a relationship between uncertainty and attraction, they cannot address the issue of the sequence of events involved in the relationship—that is, which of the two variables starts the process. On the one hand, initial affective responses to another that are related to judgments of physical attractiveness or other "surface features" may be responsible for driving the desire to reduce or not to reduce uncertainty. Zajonc (1980) opts for the primacy of affect over cognition in many judgment and decision-making situations. By contrast, it is possible that one must find out what another believes and how another behaves over time before affective judgments can be made. Most likely, initial global affective responses based upon readily observable attributes of the other are responsible for the presence or absence of initial uncertainty reduction attempts; however, if the interaction progresses beyond beginning stages, knowledge acquired through uncertainty reduction will very likely alter these initial global affective responses.

In support of the above reasoning, Parks and Adelman (1983) found that persons in romantic relationships who communicated more frequently with and received more support from members of their romantic partners' social networks demonstrated lower levels of uncertainty about their partners and were less likely to experience breakups of their relationships. It is important to reemphasize that in long-term relationships lack of interaction will probably have deleterious effects on the relationship because of rising uncertainty levels, but heightened levels of communication may or may not have positive effects on relational outcomes depending upon the nature of such interactions. Communication may act to reduce or increase uncertainty, as we noted earlier, and even when communication reduces uncertainty the nature of the interaction will determine affective outcomes.

Baxter and Wilmot (1984) investigated the strategies persons use to find out how their relational partners view the relationship. These "secret tests" are uncertainty reduction strategies designed to reveal how committed one's relational partner is to the relationship. Baxter and Wilmot (1984) focused upon opposite-sex relationships, although such "tests" are also used in same-sex relationships. For opposite-sex relationships, Baxter and Wilmot (1984) identified seven distinct types of strategies: asking third parties, triangles, directness tests (asking direct questions), separation tests (not interacting), endurance tests (testing limits, self-putdown), public presentation (presenting partner to others), and indirect suggestion (joking, hinting). These seven strategies can be classified in terms of the passive, active, and interactive strategy types of information acquisition strategies discussed earlier.

Baxter and Wilmot (1984) also reported that use of the seven "secret tests" varied in platonic, potentially romantic, and romantic relationships. Furthermore, females report using more "secret test" strategies than did males.

Although Baxter and Wilmot (1984) dealt with relationships in their relatively early stages, persons in established relationships are also likely to use some of these strategies to reduce uncertainties about their relational partners. The concept "established relationship" is something of a misnomer, since any relationship, no matter how long-lived or stable, is subject to the vagaries of uncertainty-producing events. When uncertainties surface in long-term relationships, such strategies as triangles, directness tests, and indirect suggestion might be used to reduce them, although some of the other strategies discussed above might not see extensive use in long-term relationships. The important point to recognize is that even long-term relationships are subject to potential undermining by uncertainty, and when uncertainty levels rise, persons in these relationships will generally take steps to reduce uncertainties about their relational partners.

Uncertainty in Intercultural Encounters

Some intercultural communication researchers have found uncertainty to be a fruitful starting point for their research. Gudykunst and Kim (1984) note the likelihood of elevated uncertainty when persons interact interculturally. This fact has been frequently invoked to explain the dismal history of U.S.-U.S.S.R. relations since World War II. This line of reasoning implies that relationships between the two superpowers would be considerably more amiable if persons on both sides gained greater understanding of the history and culture of the other nation. Such an understanding would presumably facilitate communication between the two nations and lower the probability of aggression.

Intuition suggests that uncertainty should be more pervasive in intercultural interactions; however, uncertainty and the strategies for its reduction probably vary across cultures. Some research has addressed this particular issue. Gudykunst (1983) employed Hall's (1976) notions of high- and low-context communications to examine cultural differences in the way uncertainty is handled in relationships. In distinguishing between high- and low-context communications, Hall (1976) asserts,

> A high-context (HC) communication or message is one in which most of the information is either in the physical context or internalized in the person, while very little is in the coded, explicit part of the message. A low-context (LC) communication is just the opposite, i.e., the mass of information is vested in the explicit code. (p. 79)

In Hall's system, such Asian cultures as those of China, Korea, and Japan are high-context cultures while those of the United States, Germany, Switzerland, and Scandinavia tend to be low context.

Gudykunst (1983) compared the responses of members of HC and LC cultures to a hypothetical situation which asked them to indicate what they would do upon meeting a stranger from their own culture at a party. Results revealed that members of HC cultures (1) are more cautious in initial interactions with strangers, (2) make more assumptions about strangers, and (3) ask more questions of strangers than do their LC culture counterparts. These findings led Gudykunst (1983) to conclude that while there are differences in uncertainty reduction strategies between HC and LC cultures, members of both types of cultures reduce their uncertainties by seeking background information from their interactive partners.

Gudykunst and Nishida (1984) reported that Japanese and American students asked to imagine themselves interacting with a stranger from a different culture indicated they would be more likely to ask questions of their partner and disclose more information about themselves than did persons asked to imagine themselves interacting with a stranger from their own culture. These findings support the idea that intercultural interactions are more uncertainty prone than intracultural interactions. Gudykunst and Nishida (1984) found no support for the proposition that cultural similarity by itself is related to interpersonal attraction. Instead, they found that the combination of cultural and attitudinal dissimilarity tends to lower estimates of interpersonal attraction, suggesting that in the intercultural context, similarities and attraction are not related in simple ways.

In a study already cited, Gudykunst et al. (1985) found consistent relationships between uncertainty and attraction across three kinds of relationships within three cultures. Attraction was positively associated with reduced uncertainty. We have noted, however, that under some conditions, reduced uncertainty might not lead to increased attraction; in fact, Gudykunst et al.'s (1985) version of URT suggests that attraction determines uncertainty reduction (i.e., we find out more about persons whom we like and less about persons whom we dislike). While this relationship is quite plausible, there is most likely some kind of complex, reciprocal relationship between these two variables. Nevertheless, the evidence adduced in this study, as well as that reported by Clatterbuck (1979), is impressive in its consistency across relationship types and cultures.

In addition to the relationship between uncertainty and attraction, Gudykunst et al. (1985) found no support for the propositions that (1) amount of communication reduces uncertainty, and (2) perceived similarities between persons reduce uncertainty. We have already considered why amount of communication may not be a good predictor of uncertainty reduction. Why perceived similarity fails to predict uncertainty reduction is not clear, although Clatterbuck (1979) noted that the similarity variable did not perform well as a predictor of CLUES scores. Perhaps similarity has a direct impact upon attraction which, in turn, affects uncertainty reduction with similarity exerting no direct effect on uncertainty. Further research is needed to resolve this particular problem. Finally, Gudykunst et al. (1985) report that the use of interactive strategies of uncertainty reduction is associated with increased attributional confidence. This finding coincides with Gudykunst and Nishida's (1984) finding that persons experiencing uncertainty in a culturally dissimilar interaction employ interactive strategies to a greater extent than do persons interacting with others from similar cultures.

Anyone who has traveled in another culture knows the havoc that uncertainty creates in daily living. Action sequences that are routine in one's own culture become obsolete. Driving, riding buses, making telephone calls, and ordering food may require learning new routines. Such learning requires considerable energy; thus, the fatigue that frequently plagues foreign travelers, usually attributed to "jet lag," may also result from the increased cognitive effort required to cope with new uncertainties. Moreover, even interethnic interactions within one's own country may be rendered effortful by uncertainty. As Simard (1981) pointed out in her study of Canadian Francophones and Anglophones, both groups "perceive it as more difficult to know how to initiate a conversation, to know what to talk about during the interaction, to be interested in the other person, and to guess in which language they should talk" (p. 179) when they interact with each other. The potential stress engendered by uncertainty in such encounters is worthy of research attention in its own right.

Uncertainty and Social Support

As just suggested, uncertainty can breed both stress and anxiety. It is also the case that uncertainty reduction can alleviate these aversive states. When persons are unsure of what is likely to occur, they are unable to respond adaptively so as to control their outcomes in the situation. Consider the individual who has been biopsied for a suspicious lump. The critical question is whether the growth is malignant; however, given no knowledge of the biopsy results, the individual can do little but worry about them. Once the individual knows the test findings, he or she can take action. Obviously, if the lump is benign, no action is necessary; however, even if it is malignant the individual can act to deal with the situation. Persons apparently find waiting for such results more stress provoking than receiving bad news. URT would predict that knowing is preferable to not knowing since persons can try to control outcomes when they are certain of their options. It is also obvious, however, that in the biopsy example, learning that one has cancer would probably increase stress and anxiety. What is being argued here, however, is that stress and anxiety will be greater when the results are unknown because of inability to respond adaptively to the situation.

Albrecht and Adelman (1984) have suggested that the positive role played by social networks in reducing stress and anxiety can be explained by uncertainty reduction. They propose that when persons communicate with others who share their plight, stress is alleviated because uncertainty is reduced by such interactions. Support networks provide the distressed individual with information that makes the environment more stable and predictable. When persons share their problems, they can assist each other in developing cognitive and action strategies; for example, persons may literally learn how to be parents of terminally ill children or how to deal with a terminal illness of their own. The acquisition and internalization of such information enable persons to respond to their environments more adoptively, and hence to gain more control over their outcomes.

The Uncertainty Heuristic

It seems appropriate to conclude this tenth anniversary presentation of URT by discussing some directions the approach might take researchers in the future. A number of potentially fruitful areas of inquiry are suggested by URT. Several of these have already been reviewed in this chapter; however, some additional areas of study are vet to be explored.

Relational Insurance

At the outset of this chapter, I pointed out that governments, businesses, and individuals are not only willing to spend large sums of money to try to reduce their uncertainties, but also to hedge against potential negative outcomes. The insurance industry rests on the notion that one should be willing to spend money to avoid financial jeopardy when disasters occur. It is interesting to consider whether persons employ similar hedges in their personal relationships. After all, one can never be absolutely sure that one's current relational partner will forever remain true, whether that partner be a friend or a lover.

Thibaut and Kelley (1959) invoked the concept of comparison level for alternatives (or CL_{alt}) as one hedge against potentially negative relational outcomes. Persons with numerous attractive alternative relationships are less likely to be dependent upon any particular relationship than are persons who have few available alternative relationships. Another hedge closely related to CL_{alt} is one's level of involvement in the relationship. Persons who are highly involved in a relationship are more vulnerable to the negative consequences of its demise than are less involved persons. This notion has been labeled by Walter and Hill (1951) as the "principle of least interest."

There appear to be other ways beside CL_{alt} and the principle of least interest for persons to insure themselves against the negative consequences of relational demises. For example, married persons with sufficient incomes to sustain themselves have a form of relational insurance. Other resources such as status and education also serve as forms of social insurance. Persons may employ still other means to minimize the likelihood of relational termination. For example, people sometimes require long periods of acquaintanceship before they are willing to commit themselves to a friendship. In the domain of romantic relationships, it is possible to opt for a long courtship before making a marriage commitment. Such strategies aim at reducing uncertainty about one's relational partner as much as possible before making serious commitments. This strategy appears effective in view of the apparently robust inverse relationship between amount of time known and uncertainty mentioned earlier in this chapter (Clatterbuck, 1979; Gudykunst et al., 1985). Finally, in recent years, some married couples have explicitly faced the possibility of divorce at the time of their marriage by entering into contracts that if violated become grounds for divorce. Moreover, these contracts may specify how property is to be divided between the ex-spouses in case of divorce. While this approach to marital relationships may strike some romantics as overly pessimistic and mechanical, the relatively high divorce rate suggests its potential adaptiveness.

Uncertainty and Relational Trajectories

Earlier it was pointed out that most communication researchers studying relationship development have employed some variant of social exchange theory (see Roloff, 1981) to explain why relationships develop and decline over time. In general, these theories explain relational growth by arguing that when rewards exceed costs for relational partners, relationships tend to escalate. Conversely, relational de-escalation results from unfavorable reward/cost ratios. These explanations are both parsimonious and intuitively appealing; moreover, they can be facilely invoked post hoc to explain why particular relationships have grown or declined.

From the perspective of the communication researcher, one difficulty with such explanations is that they bypass the communication process and focus attention on outcomes; in other words, interest is directed not at communicative conduct per se but rather at the net result of interactions. Communication as a process is assumed to be influential but is not studied. This chapter has stressed the importance of considering the interactions between cognitive activity and affect to understand relational growth and decline. Exclusive concern with affect or rewards and costs tells us little about how persons in relationships think about these exchanges or how they actually communicate about them to each other.

The position taken here is that URT is a more useful approach to the study of personal relationships for communication researchers than are the social exchange approaches. The URT perspective on personal relationships fosters questions about relationship development that center more directly on communicative action than do the research questions suggested by exchange theories. To determine what one's relational partner finds rewarding or costly, it is necessary to gather information using passive, active, or interactive strategies. Since any stimulus can constitute a reward or a cost depending upon individual interpretation, it is necessary to determine a person's meaning for a stimulus. For example, while most people find verbal praise rewarding, some low self-esteem individuals may interpret such praise as punishing or costly; they may interpret compliments directed at them as aversive. Only through uncertainty reduction can interactants determine which stimuli are rewarding and which are costly to their partners. When persons make such statements as "I like X" or "I dislike Y," they are indicating what is potentially rewarding or costly to them. Hence. uncertainty reduction is a necessary condition for the definition of the currency of social exchange, and it is through communicative activity that uncertainty is reduced.

The above argument does not imply that communication researchers should avoid studying interaction outcomes and focus their research efforts solely on communication process. What it does suggest, however, is that URT is more likely to encourage the study of communicative processes that produce outcomes, rather than simply explaining outcomes by recourse to reward/cost ratios without investigating communication. Moreover, URT recognizes the futility of studying reward and costs defined in some "objective," outside-observer sense. It is implausible to assume that persons have highly uniform definitions of the behaviors that are rewarding and costly in relationships: One person's meat may indeed be another person's poison. Thus subjective definitions of rewards and costs are essential to the workings of social exchange machinery. Subjective definitions become known through uncertainty reduction processes. What gives individuals the ability to exert control in relationships is the knowledge of what is rewarding and costly to their interaction partners and to themselves.

Finally, we pointed out earlier that uncertainty can be both a symptom and a cause of relationship decline. Communicative awkwardness may be symptomatic of underlying relational difficulties, and people involved in awkward relationships may find their partners increasingly unattractive precisely because it is so difficult to interact with them. Uncertainty increases communicative work to the point that persons retire from the relationship, either temporarily or permanently. Of course, after relationships have terminated, persons may expend considerable effort trying to reduce their uncertainty about the causes of the relationship demise. Considerable evidence indicates that persons engage in these uncertainty reduction activities after divorces and other relational endings (Harvey, Wells, & Alvarez, 1978; Orvis, Kelley, & Butler, 1976). Interestingly, though social exchange theories may have something to say about why relationships terminate, they appear to have little to say about post-termination behaviors.

Uncertainy Beyond Interpersonal Relationships

Even though discussions of URT have generally focused on interpersonal and intercultural communication, URT is also relevant to such areas as organizational and mass communication. New employees face prediction and explanation problems similar to those faced by strangers in informal relationships, and the stakes may be considerably higher in the organizational context. As a result, new employees might be expected to take out larger relational insurance policies than strangers meeting in a more informal context. New employees should be particularly careful in revealing information about themselves when compared to strangers at a party. Moreover, new employees may be more reticent to befriend fellow employees for fear of affiliating with the "wrong" persons. As pointed out earlier, when the stakes are high persons will spend resources to hedge against negative outcomes. Jablin and Krone (in press) have presented a very lucid account of the processes by which new employees reduce their uncertainties in organizational contexts. Lester (1987) has developed an axiomatic theory designed to explain how new employees reduce their uncertainties in organizational cultures. This model serves to organize findings in the organizational socialization area in a systematic and coherent manner. It also offers a number of hypotheses concerning the role that uncertainty plays in this process.

In the domain of mass communication, several functional approaches, as well as the uses and gratifications approach, assert that one important function of media is to provide information that enables people to orient themselves in an uncertain world (Blumler & Katz, 1974). Most of these approaches also recognize, however, that the media serve a number of additional functions such as passing time, entertainment, escape, and companionship (Greenberg, 1974). From the perspective of URT, it is important to note that interacting with mass media can both reduce uncertainties and raise them. Furthermore, research needs to be directed toward the strategies that media consumers employ to gain information from the media. Can persons "de-bias" media information along the lines suggested by Hewes et al. (1985)? A number of research questions concerning media are suggested by URT.

Hewes and Planalp (1982) have asserted that while notions such as uncertainty are useful in communication inquiry, it is important to understand more specific mechanisms available to persons for information processing. I agree strongly with their view. Although the present chapter has not delved into these specifics, I think it has demonstrated the general potential of such an approach for the study of human communication. What could be more basic to the study of communication than the propositions that (1) adaptation is essential for survival (2) adaptation is only possible through the reduction of uncertainty, and (3) uncertainty can be both reduced and produced by communicative activities?

Appendix

CL7 Attributional Confidence Scale (Clatterbuck, 1979)

(1) How confident are you of your general ability to predict how he/she will behave?

(2) How certain are you that he/she likes you?

(3) How accurate are you at predicting the values he/she holds?

(4) How accurate are you at predicting his/her attitudes?

(5) How well can you predict his/her feelings and emotions?

(6) How much can you empathize with (share) the way he/she feels about himself/herself?

(7) How well do you know him/her?

Revised Version of the Attributional Confidence Scale (Gudykunst & Nishida, 1986)

People vary in the degree to which they can predict how other people behave and think. Please answer each of the following questions with respect to your ability to predict selected aspects of the behavior of the person you answered the previous question about. Answer each question using a scale from zero (0) to one hundred (100). If you would have to make a total guess about the person's behavior or feelings you should answer "0"; if you have total certainty about the other person's behavior you should answer "100." Feel free to use any number between 0 and 100.

(1) How confident are you in your general ability to predict how he/she will behave?

(2) How confident are you that he/she likes you?

(3) How accurate are you at predicting his/her attitudes?

(4) How accurate are you at predicting the values he/she holds?

(5) How well can you predict his/her feelings?

(6) How much can you empathize with (share) the way he/she feels about him/herself?

(7) How well do you know him/her?

(8) How certain are you of his/her background?

(9) How certain are you that he/she will behave in a socially appropriate way when this is important?

(10) How certain are you that he/she can understand your feelings when you do not verbally express them?

(11) How certain are you that you understand what this person means when you communicate?

(12) How confident are you that this person will make allowances for you when you communicate?

Consider this . . .

- In his article, "Communicating Under Certainty," Berger argues that communication and uncertainty are inextricably intertwined. What does Berger mean by this statement? Give an example to illustrate.
- While Uncertainty Reduction Theory (URT) focuses on the innate human desire to reduce uncertainty, do humans ever strategically choose to create uncertainty and ambiguity in their personal relationships? If so, why? Give an example to illustrate.
- Using Berger's three-strategy typology as the basis for your discussion, describe a specific strategy you have used to reduce uncertainty in a personal relationship. How effective was the strategy in reducing uncertainty? What other strategies might you have used to reduce uncertainty in this situation?
- How might relational context affect your choice of strategy to reduce uncertainty in a personal relationship? Give an example to illustrate.
- How might cultural context affect your choice of strategy to reduce uncertainty in a personal relationship? Give an example to illustrate.
- How might social context be used to reduce uncertainty in a personal relationship? Describe a situation where information embedded in the social context might actually increase uncertainty. Give an example to illustrate.

References

Abelson, R. (1981). Psychological status of the script concept. American Psychologist, 36, 715-129.

Albrecht, T. L., & Adelman, M. B. (1984). Social support and life stress: New directions for communication research. Human Communication Research, 11, 3-32.

A. M. Best Inc. (1984a). Best aggregates and averages: Property and casuality. New York: Author.

A. M. Best Inc. (1984b). Best industry composite of life and health companies. New York: Author.

Ayres, J. (1979). Uncertainty and social penetration theory expectations about relationship communication: A comparative test. Western Journal of Speech Communication, 43, 192-200.

Baxter, L. A., & Wilmot, W. W. (1984). "Secret tests": Social strategies for acquiring information about the state of the relationship. Human Communication Research, 11, 171-201.

Berger, C. R. (1975). Proactive and retroactive attribution processes in interpersonal communication. Human Communication Research, 2, 33-50.

Berger, C. R. (1979). Beyond initial interaction: Uncertainty, understanding, and the development of interpersonal relationships. In H. Giles & R. St. Clair (Eds.), Language and social psychology (pp. 122-144). Oxford: Blackwell.

Berger, C. R., & Bradac, J. J. (1982). Language and social knowledge: Uncertainty in interpersonal relations. London: E. E. Arnold.

Berger, C. R., & Calabrese, R. J. (1975). Some explorations in initial interaction and beyond: Toward a developmental theory of interpersonal communication. Human Communication Research, 1. 99-112.

Berger, C. R., & Douglas, W. (1981). Studies in interpersonal epistemology III: Anticipated interaction, self-monitoring and observational context selection. Communication Monographs, 48, 183-196.

Berger, C. R., & Kellermann, K. A. (1983). To ask or not to ask: Is that a question? In R. N. Bostrom (Ed.), Communication yearbook 7 (pp. 342-368). Newbury Park, CA: Sage.

Berger, C. R., & Kellermann, K. A. (1985). Personal opacity and social information gathering: Seek, but ye may not find. Paper presented at the annual convention of the International Communication Association, Honolulu, HI.

Berger, C. R., & Perkins, J. (1978). Studies in interpersonal epistemology I: Situational attributes in observational context selection. In B. Ruben (Ed.), Communication yearbook 2 (pp. 171-194). New Brunswick, NJ: Transaction Books.

Berger. C. R., & Perkins, J. (1979). Studies in interpersonal epistemology II: Self-monitoring, involvement, facial affect, similarity and observational context selection. Paper presented at the annual convention of the Speech Communication Association, San Antonio, TX.

Berger, C. R., Gardner, R. R., Parks, M. L., Schulman, L. W., & Miller, G. R. (1976). Interpersonal epistemology and interpersonal communication. In G. R. Miller (Ed.), Explorations in interpersonal communication (pp. 149-171). Newbury Park, CA: Sage.

Berio, D. K. (1960). The process of communication. New York: Holt, Rinehart & Winston.

Berlyne, D. (1960). Conflict, arousal, and curiosity. New York: McGraw-Hill.

Blumler, J. G., & Katz, E. (Eds.). (1974). The uses of mass communication: Current perspectives on gratifications research. Newbury Park, CA: Sage.

Cantor, N., & Mischel, W. (1977). Traits as prototypes: Effects on recognition memory. Journal of Personality and Social Psychology, 35. 38-48.

Clatterbuck, G. W. (1979). Attributional confidence and uncertainty in initial interaction. Human Communication Research, 5, 147-157.

Galbraith, J. K. (1977). The age of uncertainty. Boston: Houghton-Mifflin.

Goffman, E. (1969). Strategic interaction. Philadelphia: University of Pennsylvania Press.

Greenberg, B. S. (1974). Gratifications of television viewing and their correlates for British children. In E. Katz & J. Blumler (Eds.), The uses of mass communications. Newbury Park, CA: Sage.

Gudykunst, W. B. (1983). Uncertainty reduction and predictability of behavior in low- and high-context cultures: An exploratory study. Communication Quarterly, 31, 49-65.

Gudykunst, W. B., & Kim, Y. Y. (1984). Communicating with strangers. Reading, MA: Addison-Wesley.

Gudykunst, W. B., & Nishida, T. (1984). Individual and cultural influences on uncertainty reduction. Communication Monographs, 51, 23-36.

Gudykunst, W. B., & Nishida, T. (1986) Attributional confidence in low- and high-context cultures. Human Communication Research, 12, 525-549.

Gudykunst, W. B., Yang, S. M., & Nishida, T. (1985). A cross-cultural test of uncertainty reduction theory: Comparisons of acquaintances, friends, and dating relationships in Japan, Korea, and the United States. Human Communication Research, 11, 407-455.

Hall, E. T. (1976). Beyond culture. Garden City, NY: Doubleday.

Harvey, J. H., Wells, G. L., & Alvarez, M. D. (1978). Attribution in the context of conflict and separation in close relationships. In J. H. Harvey, W. J. Ickes, & R. F. Kidd (Eds.), New directions in attributional research (Vol. 2, pp. 235-260). Hillsdale, NJ: Lawrence Erlbaum.

Heider, F. (1958). The psychology of interpersonal relations. New York: John Wiley.

Hewes, D. E. & Planalp, S. C. (1982). There is nothing as useful as a good theory...:The influence of social knowledge on interpersonal communication. In M. E. Roloff & C. R. Berger (Eds.), Social cognition and communication. Newbury Park, CA: Sage.

Hewes, D. E., Graham, M. K., Doelger, J., & Pavitt, C. (1985). "Second guessing": Message interpretation in social networks. Human Communication Research, 11, 299-334.

Hogarth, R. (1980). Judgement and choice: The psychology of decision. New York: John Wiley.

Jablin, F. M., & Krone. K. J. (1987). Organizational assimilation and levels of analysis in organizational communication research. In C. R. Berger & S. H. Chaffee. (Eds.), Handbook of communication science (pp. 711-743). Newbury Park, CA: Sage.

Jones, E. E., & Davis, K. E. (1965). From acts to dispositions: The attribution process in person perception. In L. Berkowitz (Ed.), Advances in experimental social psychology (Vol. 2, pp. 219-216). New York: Academic Press.

Kahneman, D., Slovic. P., & Tversky, A. (Eds.). (1982). Judgment under uncertainty: Heuristics and biases. Cambridge: Cambridge University Press.

Kellermann, K. A., & Berger, C. R. (1984). Affect and the acquisition of social information: Sit back, relax, and tell me about yourself. In R. N. Bostrom (Ed.), Communication yearbook 8 (pp. 412-445). Newbury Park, CA: Sage.

Kelley, H. H. (1967). Attribution theory in social psychology. In D. Levine (Ed.), Nebraska Symposium on Motivation (Vol. 15, pp. 192-237). Lincoln: University of Nebraska Press.

Kelley, H. H. (1971). Attribution in social interaction. Morristown, NJ: General Learning Press.

Kelly, G. A. (1955). The psychology of personal constructs. New York: Norton.

Lalljee, M., & Cook, M. (1973). Uncertainty in first encounters. Journal of Personality and Social Psychology, 26, 137-141.

Lester, R. E. (1987). Organizational culture, uncertainty reduction, and the socialization of new organizational members. In S. Thomas (Ed.), Culture and communication—methodology, behavior, artifacts and institutions (pp. 105-113). Norwood, NJ: Ablex.

Livingston, K. R. (1980). Love as a process of reducing uncertainty—cognitive theory. In K. S. Pope et al. (Eds.), On love and loving (pp. 133-151). San Francisco: Jossey-Bass.

Mehrabian, A., & Wiener, M. (1966). Non-immediacy between communicator and object of communication in a verbal message. Journal of Consulting Psychology, 30, 420-425.

Mehrabian, A., & Williams, M., (1969). Nonverbal concomitants of perceived and intended persuasiveness. Journal of Personality and Social Psychology, 13, 37-58.

Miller, G. R., & Steinberg, M., (1975). Between people: A new analysis of interpersonal communication. Chicago: Science Research Associates.

Nisbett, R. E., & Ross, L. (1980). Human inference: Strategies and shortcomings of social judgement. Englewood Cliffs. NJ: Prentice-Hall.

Orvis, B. R., Kelley, H. H., & Butler, D. (1976). Attributional conflict in young couples. In J. H. Harvey, W. J. Ickes, & R. F. Kidd (Eds.), New directions in attribution research (Vol. 1. pp. 353-386). Hillsdale, NJ: Lawrence Erlbaum.

Parks, M. R., & Adelman, M. B. (1983). Communication networks and the development of romantic relationships: An expansion of uncertainty reduction theory. Human Communication Research. 10, 55-79.

Parks, M. R., Stan, C. M., & Eggert, L. L. (1983). Romantic involvement and social network involvement. Social Psychology Quarterly, 46, 116-131.

Planalp, S., & Honeycutt, J. M. (1985). Events that increase uncertainty in personal relationships. Human Communication Research 11, 593-604.

Roloff, M. E. (1981). Interpersonal communication: The social exchange approach. Newbury Park, CA: Sage.

Rosenfeld, H. M. (1966). Approval-seeking and approval-inducing functions of verbal and non-verbal responses in the dyad. Journal of Personality and Social Psychology, 4, 597-605.

Rubin, R. B. (1977). The role of context in information seeking and impression formation. Communication Monographs, 44, 81-90.

Rubin, R. B. (1979). The effect of context on information seeking across the span of initial interactions. Communication Quarterly, 27, 13-20.

Schank, R. C. (1982). Dynamic memory. Cambridge: Cambridge University Press.

Schank, R. C., & Abelson. R. (1977). Scripts, goals, plans and understanding. Hillsdale, NJ: Lawrence Erlbaum.

Scheidel, T. M. (1977). Evidence varies with phases of inquiry. Western Journal of Speech Communication, 41, 20-31.

Shannon, C., & Weaver. W. (1949). The mathematical theory of communication. Urbana: University of Illinois Press.

Sherblom, J., & Van Rheenen. D. E. (1984). Spoken language indices of uncertainty. Human Communication Research, 11, 221-230.

Simard, L. (1981). Cross-cultural interaction. Journal of Social Psychology, 113, 171-192.

Sunnafrank, M. (1986). Predicted outcome value during initial interactions: A reformulation of uncertainty reduction theory. Human Communication, 13, 3-33.

Thibaut, J. W., & Kelley, H. H. (1959). The social psychology of groups. New York: John Wiley.

Wall Street Week. (1985). Program #1514, October 4, 1985.

Waller, W., & Hill. R. (1951). The family: A dynamic interpretation. New York: Dryden Press.

Winograd, T. (1980). What does it mean to understand language? Cognitive Science, 4, 209-241.

Zajonc, R. B. (1980). Feeling and thinking: Preferences need no inferences. American Psychologist, 35, 151-175.

As previously noted, Chapter 6 of Julia Wood's text, *Relational Communication*, discusses the communication tools we use to "launch" or initiate personal relationships; she discusses elements of attraction, tools for reducing uncertainty, and characteristics of early interaction. While there are a variety of personal relationships we could explore from this developmental perspective, perhaps there is no set of relationships more relevant in a culture of "proliferating family forms" than blended families. As Wood herself explains in the Chapter 5, traditional families represent a family prototype that has increasingly become the exception rather than the rule; blended families are far more likely to represent the family norm at the beginning of the 21st century. Since it is likely that many students in this class have participated in creating a blended family (either as parents or children), it seems appropriate to explore the development of this set of personal relationships.

The article entitled, "Becoming a Family": Developmental Processes Represented in Blended Family Discourse," uses a process orientation to gain insight into how blended family members experience different pathways (trajectories) to become a family. The authors begin their article by discussing the limitations of the traditional developmental stage models often used to describe the creation of blended families; from these limitations, they note that researchers have adopted more of a process view of blended family development. Furthermore, the authors provide a brief overview of issues confronted by blended families. As they conclude, the family (traditional or blended) plays a critical role in shaping our personal identity throughout life.

Based on in-depth interviews of both stepparents and stepchildren during the first four years of blended family development (often identified as a "make or break" time frame for these families), researchers have identified five developmental pathways (trajectories) typically followed by blended families striving to attain FLF (i.e., feeling like a family). Building upon previous research, the authors of this study once again conducted in-depth interviews with blended family members and employed text analysis of these interviews to identify the specific path (trajectory) followed by the blended family as well as processes used by family members to negotiate key issues during each year of development. As you read their findings, note differences among the five trajectories described as well as differences found within each year of the time frame discussed. Discussion of critical incidents (turning points) that signify relational changes over the four-year time frame provide a solid application of Turning Point Theory.

"Becoming a Family": Developmental Processes Represented in Blended Family Discourse

Dawn O. Braithwaite, Loreen N. Olson, Tamara D. Golish,
Charles Soukup, & Paul Turman

ABSTRACT *We adopted a process-focus in order to gain a deeper understanding of how (step) blended family members experiencing different developmental pathways discursively represented their processes of becoming a family. Using a qualitative/interpretive method, we analyzed 980 pages of interview transcripts with stepparents and stepchildren. We studied the first four years of family development. using the five developmental pathways developed by Baxter, Braithwaite, and Nicholson (1999). Three salient issues identified in the family experiences were boundary management, solidarity, and adaptation. While the negotiation of these issues varied across the five trajectories, there were commonalities across family experiences that helped determine whether families had a successful experience of becoming a family. Implications for blended family researchers and practitioners are also discussed.*

As an institution, the American family serves a pivotal role in shaping identity, teaching us who we are in relation to others. Within the past two decades the American family has experienced a metamorphosis (Schneider, 1980; Schwartz, 1988; Stacey, 1990). According to Brubaker and Kimberly (1993), "as American society changes, the structure and functions of American families have been altered" (p. 3). This does not suggest that the family as an institution is disappearing or necessarily deteriorating, but certainly it is changing to reflect the complexity of the personal and occupational circumstances in a postmodern society (Brubaker & Kimberly, 1993; Schwartz, 1988; Stacey, 1990). Due to increased divorce and remarriage rates and other changes in non-marital parental relationships, step- or blended families are becoming a more prevalent family form1 (Olson & DeFrain, 1997). In fact, one out of six children under the age of 18 is currently a stepchild (Stepfamily Association of America, 1998).

The increase in the number of blended families leads to a heightened need to better understand this family form. In addition to the sheer number of blended families, the complexities, both positive and negative, inherent in them warrants attention from communication scholars. Many of these complexities are different from "traditional" or nuclear families and are highly communicative in nature. For instance, blended family members must negotiate many complex issues which are challenging to members of these families, such as defining and redefining communication boundaries between the various blended family subsystems (e.g., Bray & Hetherington, 1993; Papernow, 1994; Whitsett & Land, 1992), managing loyalty conflicts between children and (non)custodial parents (e.g., Burrell, 1995; Cissna, Cox, & Bochner, 1990; Visher & Visher 1993), adjusting to change (e.g., Coleman & Ganong, 1995; Kelley, 1992; Visher & Visher, 1988), and negotiating new, unfamiliar roles within and outside the family (e.g., Anderson & White, 1986; Coleman & Ganong, 1995). The body of existing research has contributed to our understanding of the complexity of blended families by shedding light on some of the unique challenges these families confront. However, few communication researchers have yet studied the blended family and how these groups of people come together to become a family. Because of the increase of blended families in our society, it is important for communication scholars to focus on this family form to expand our understanding of family communication, in general, and, more specifically, to increase our knowledge of the role communication plays in blended family functioning. Moreover, at the root of blended family development are many issues such as boundary management, conflict resolution, and role negotiation, all constituted and enacted communicatively (Goldsmith & Baxter, 1996). Thus, to increase understanding of blended family development, we must focus on how blended family members communicatively manage these issues.

Process Model of Blended Family Development

In addition to a limited amount of research on blended family issues by communication scholars, we know relatively little about how these complexities are negotiated within a larger context of how blended families develop. Family researchers have provided a good starting place, but there is limited insight into the process that blended families follow as they develop (Baxter, Braithwaite, & Nicholson, 1999). The scholars who have examined blended family development have tended to depict "becoming a family process" as a unitary model of chronological stages or phases (Coleman & Ganong, 1995; Ganong & Coleman, 1994; Papernow, 1993). One of the most comprehensive models is Papernow's (1993) seven-stage model of blended family development. First, blended family members progress through a "fantasy stage" in which they hold unrealistic expectations. Second, in the "immersion stage" family members' expectations are shattered due to the realistic challenges of their daily lives. Third, the family members attempt to deal with their uncertainty and confusion in the "awareness stage." The fourth stage, "mobilization," is characterized by expressed conflicts and attempts at negotiation and resolution. The attempts at negotiation result in new agreements providing a firm foundation from which to grow in the fifth stage or the "action stage." Sixth, in the "contact stage" blended family members are able to form positive bonds with each other. Finally, the blended family moves into the "resolution stage" in which it is characterized as a solid, healthy family unit. Papernow (1993) posited that unsuccessful blended families do not reach the latter three stages of this model.

These developmental stage models are limited in three ways. First, they are prescriptive in nature, providing suggestions for how blended families "should" develop (see Baxter, Braithwaite, & Nicholson, 1999 for a critique). Prescriptive models hold value for some blended families as they attempt to become a family.

However, they do not provide depth of descriptive information from the members themselves about how different types of blended families develop. Second, these models have a tendency to oversimplify the complexity inherent in blended family development. The approach of developing a single model that fits all blended families fails to recognize the multiple paths that blended families could take in their development. Finally, stage models are problematic as they often do not capture the dynamic, "up and down" nature of blended family relationships, assuming that families move pregressively forward toward greater closeness (Baxter, Braithwaite, & Nicholson, 1999).

In response to the limitations of stage-based models, Baxter, Braithwaite, and Nicholson (1999) adopted a process view of blended family development. By focusing on process, these researchers were better able to describe the complex nature of blended family development, discovering that blended families do indeed develop in multiple ways. They studied the development of blended families over the first four years of blended family life, interviewing both stepparents and stepchildren. Participants discussed the development of their blended family by describing and graphing their family turning points and levels of feeling like a family (more detail is provided in the methods section of this research report and in greater detail in Baxter, Braithwaite, and Nicholson, 1999). From these data, researchers identified five developmental pathways or trajectories different blended families followed as they become a family: accelerated, prolonged, stagnating, declining, and high-amplitude turbulent (See Figure 1 for a representation of the five trajectories). Their study provided a depiction of the changes in the levels of "feeling like a family" in five different patterns of the first four years of blended family life. The accelerated trajectory reflected a pattern of quick and sustained movement toward higher levels of feeling like a family. The prolonged trajectory progressed to higher levels of feeling like a family over a longer period of time. The declining trajectory began with a high level of feeling like a family, which declined to zero at the end of the four year period. The stagnating trajectory began and ended with relatively low levels of feeling like a family. Last, the high-amplitude turbulent trajectory was characterized by a "roller-coaster" effect with rapid increases and decreases in levels of feeling like a family.

As Baxter, Braithwaite, and Nicholson (1999) demonstrated, a process model of blended family development emphasizes multiple developmental trajectories rather than a single sequence of stages. For instance, not all blended families experience a gradual increase in closeness over time, but the closeness may fluctuate in a series of ups and downs. As can be seen in the Figure 1, the trajectories reach a very different ending point, with some families experiencing high levels of feeling like a family, and others virtually none. The trajectories depict a process perspective that recognizes that relationship development is a complex, sometimes messy, process that may be filled with turbulence (Duck, 1994). In summary, these five blended family trajectories provided us with a more descriptive picture of blended family development than previous stage models by recognizing the multiple courses these families can assume.

While the Baxter, Braithwaite, and Nicholson (1999) study provided a useful map of the five different pathways by which blended families develop, it produced

FIGURE 1
Turning point trajectories

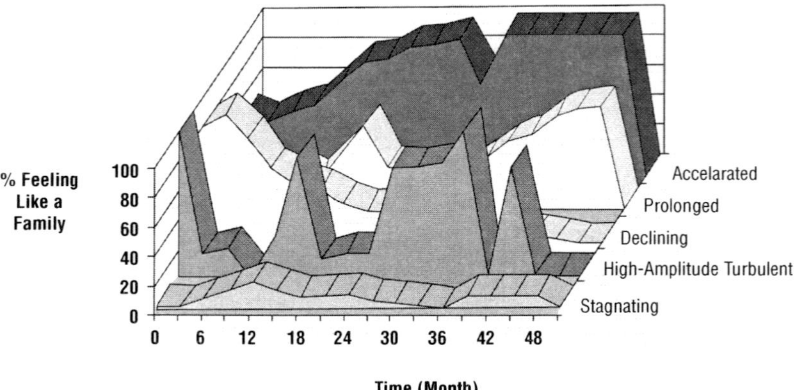

limited insight into what is happening in the families experiencing these different developmental patterns. In other words, their study supplied little detail concerning how families experiencing these five different developmental pathways interact and negotiate complex issues surrounding becoming a family. Therefore, as a follow-up to the Baxter, Braithwaite, and Nicholson (1999) study, the purpose of this present research is to gain a deeper understanding of how the blended family members experiencing the different developmental trajectories discursively represented their processes of becoming a family.

Theoretically, the current study extends our knowledge of the process of blended family development by providing a more in-depth look at what happens within various developmental trajectories. While process models like the one we are using are temporal in nature (see Duck, 1994), they do allow for more variability in the pathways of development than stage models. Braithwaite and Baxter (1995) argued that the focus on process in the turning point analysis is useful as it provides the opportunity to focus on transformative events, positive or negative, that alter the relationship. This form of analysis is still temporal, as it looks at the development of relationships over time, but moves beyond a stage model approach as it captures the dynamic nature of relationships by analyzing events that contribute to change in those relationships and is predicated on the recognition that change is not unidirectional (Baxter & Bullis, 1986; Bullis & Bach, 1989; Siegert & Stamp, 1994). Studying the challenges that move blended families in one direction or another contributes to our understanding of how and why blended families grow, weaken, stagnate, and change with time. In order to understand some of the issues that blended families face as they interact and become a family, we provide a review of the literature on blended family issues that appear central to the process of becoming a family.

Blended Family Issues

The unique challenges that blended family members face influence how these families develop. Therefore, it is important to gain a more complete understanding of these issues. According to Visher and Visher (1988) and Papernow (1994), one of the most critical adjustments for blended families is establishing appropriate boundaries and delineating these boundaries around the various blended family subsystems. In- and out-group membership may result from coalitions formed within the blended family (Fine, 1995; Pasley, Dollahite, & Ihinger-Tallman, 1993). Loyalty conflicts are particularly common and include a child feeling caught between his/her custodial and noncustodial parents (Buchanan, Maccoby, & Dornbusch, 1996; Visher & Visher, 1993) or a noncustodial parent feeling like their parental role has been subsumed by a stepparent (Visher & Visher, 1993). Cissna, Cox, and Bochner (1990) reported that half of the couples they interviewed discussed loyalty conflicts as a significant part of the family restructuring process.

Blended family boundaries also vary in their permeability, or the flexibility and rigidity of family boundaries (Ganong & Coleman, 1994; Kelley, 1992; Visher & Visher, 1988, 1993). The pliancy of blended family boundaries is important to the structural development of the family as well as to members' interpersonal relationships within it. Yet, it is important to note that more flexibility and permeability is not always desired. Researchers have found that boundaries need to be both permeable and firm, depending upon the function they serve; permeable enough to allow access to outside family members and non-kin, but firm enough to protect developing relationships (Ahrons & Rodgers, 1987; Ihinger-Tallmen, 1988; Papernow, 1994).

Blended families also face unique challenges with regard to issues of solidarity. Feelings of closeness and connection take time to develop due to the lack of a common family history, the loss of a previous parent-child bond, the geographical separation from a noncustodial parent, the addition of new children in the household, and the lack of an identifiable legal relationship with the stepparent(s) (Cissna, Cox, & Bochner, 1990; Ihinger-Tallman, 1988). The creation of the blended family can be overshadowed by the children's sense of loss over their parents' marriage, contact with a non-custodial parent, and the old family form (Bray & Harvey, 1995; Giles-Sims & Crosbie-Burnett, 1989). In addition, there is pressure to accept the members of the new entity as "family," which can add to the grief and anger over the losses already experienced (Ganong & Coleman, 1994). Each of these challenges can affect all members of the blended family, as well as family subsystems. For example, feelings of jealousy and resentment may occur between stepsiblings as all strive to adjust and find their niche in the new family (Bray & Hetherington, 1988, 1993). The tensions created by these dynamics can put both original partners and stepparents in an awkward position as they strive to make things work in the new family (Bray & Hetherington, 1993; Hetherington & Jodl, 1994).

As a result of these challenges to blended family members' feelings of solidarity, some researchers suggest that blended families are less close or warm than continuously intact families (i.e., Anderson & White, 1986; Bray & Hetherington, 1993; Fine, Voydanoff, & Donnelly, 1993). This may be particularly true for the relationship between the stepparent and stepchild (Bray & Hetherington, 1993; Whitsett & Land, 1992). For example, researchers have found that parents in blended families perceived their relationships with their own children to be closer than the relationship with their stepchildren (Fine, Voydanoff, & Donnelly, 1993; Kurdek & Fine, 1991). These different feelings of closeness have been associated with less emotional well-being of children in blended families (Fine, Voydanoff, & Donnelly, 1993; White, 1994a, 1994b). However, scholars warn that the differences between stepfamilies and original families are not as great as originally thought. Further, children from families experiencing multiple divorces are at a higher risk than those who are in blended families (Coleman, 1994).

Blended family members also must manage issues of adaptability. When individuals enter the blended family, they are often unsure of the expectations for individual and collective behavior and how, if at all, these expectations will differ from their former family. This uncertainty creates ambiguity surrounding newly formed roles and family norms (Burrell, 1995; Cissna, Cox, & Bochner, 1990). When stepparents enter a blended family, they not only gain a spouse, but they gain a child or children, along with extended familial relationships and social networks of the spouse. This plethora of additional relationships brings on additional roles, which are often culturally undefined, and ambiguous (Coleman & Ganong, 1995; Hetherington & Jodl, 1994). Therefore, many blended family members experience role ambiguity as they adjust to all of the different relationships in their new family.

Due to the uncertainty surrounding their new roles, many blended family members may attempt to reenact "traditional" family roles or the roles they enacted in their old family. This can result in what Visher & Visher (1988) called the "myth of instant love." Stepparents may join their blended family expecting it to be similar to a "nuclear family." If an immediate connection and open relationship with the stepchild does not develop, the stepparent may feel guilty and frustrated (Coleman & Ganong, 1995; Ganong & Coleman, 1994; Hines, 1997). As Baxter, Braithwaite, and Nicholson (1999) found, unmet or unrealistic expectations was one of the most frequently experienced turning points in blended family development. This was especially salient for the more problematic family types of declining, stagnating, and high-amplitude turbulent.

In summary, scholars have focused on delineating the process of blended family development and on the unique challenges confronting blended families, such as boundaries, loyalty conflict, solidarity, and adaptation to change. The Baxter, Braithwaite, and Nicholson (1999) study moved that effort forward, adopting a process approach and discovering five different developmental trajectories of blended families. However, what is lacking is an understanding of how the issues facing blended families are embedded within each of these trajectories. Therefore, our intent was to unpack these issues by focusing on how the participants discursively represented the process of blended family development within these five pathways. With that in mind, we posed the following research question to guide our study:

> **RQ:** How do blended family members experiencing different developmental trajectories discursively represent the issues experienced in the process of becoming a family during the first four years of the new family experience?

We believe this research has great potential to assist practitioners, researchers, and blended family members themselves in understanding the different roads blended families may travel and the changes and challenges they may encounter. More specifically, knowledge of the five different developmental experiences may become a useful tool for family therapists to use. They can help blended family members recognize that blended families develop in multiple ways, help them identify what trajectory their own family is experiencing, and perhaps help them identify useful strategies or pitfalls to avoid, as their family becomes blended (Baxter, Braithwaite, & Nicholson, 1999). Understanding that there is no one right way for blended families to develop may help family members overcome feelings of deficiency or inadequacy if their family does not correspond with the protypical model of-family development. Clinicians could also use information from this research as a way to possibly intervene and alter a blended family's destructive path, helping them chart out a more constructive way for their family to progress. Finally, the findings in this study shed light on the issues most salient to a blended family's development and how these issues could alter the nature of their relationships.

Method

The overall design of the study was in the qualitative/interpretive tradition, seeking to describe recurring patterns of behaviors and meanings from the experiences of participants (Creswell, 1998; Leininger, 1994; Strauss & Corbin, 1990). Members of blended families and interviewers participated together in semi-structured, focused interviews that targeted informants' perceptions and experiences of the early years of life in their blended family (Kvale, 1996; McCracken, 1988). Data gathering ceased when recurring patterns were identified and a point of saturation reached (Leininger, 1994).

Participants/Informants

Data for the current study were transcripts from a study previously conducted by Baxter, Braithwaite, and Nicholson (1999). Participants were originally recruited through announcements in university classes and offices at a large midwestern university and a small southwestern university. Interviews were conducted with one member from 53 blended families: 5 biological/adoptive parents, 15 stepparents, and 33 stepchildren. Of the 53 informants who participated in the interviews, 40 were female (M = 27 years) and 13 were male (M = 31 years). At the time of the interview, the mean age of the stepparents and parents was 41, and the mean age of the stepchildren was 20. Although the participants were asked to reflect on the first four years of their blended family's development, they came from blended families of various lengths (M = 62 months; SD = 20 months). Forty-four of the families were complex blended families (both adults brought children into the remarriage), 5 were simple stepfather families (a man parenting his spouse's children), 3 were simple stepmother families (a woman parenting her spouse's children), and 1 was a de facto family unit (a woman with children cohabitating with a man). Thirteen percent of the couples also had biological children together. No compensation was provided for participation in this study.

Procedures

In contrast to the approach used by most of the previous stepfamily researchers, the researchers asked the participants to define for themselves the date the family began, rather than having the research team establish cohabitation or the marriage of the two adults as the beginning point (Baxter, Braithwaite, & Nicholson, 1999). This became important in the analysis, as many of the participants indicated that their family started well before the date of marriage or cohabitation. Interviews focused on the first 48 months of the family's history as researchers have suggested that blended families go through a two- to four-year period of transition, tending to "make or break" at the fourth year (Mills, 1984; Papernow, 1993). Trained interviewers from the two universities participated in interviews with the 53 blended family members. In-depth interviews, conducted in a single session, lasted between 90 and 150 minutes. Informants and interviewers discussed the development of the blended family during its first four years (or less, if the family had a shorter history). Interviewers and participants talked about family development via a discussion of blended family turning points. Participants diagrammed their blended family's development, creating a graph of the individual turning points by approximate date (X axis) and by the percentage of "feeling like a family" (Y axis) from 0% to 100% for each turning point. To provide an anchor point for the graph, the participants were asked to assess what 0% and 100% "feelings like a family" (FLF) meant to them (Baxter, Braithwaite, & Nicholson, 1999). When describing what "100% FLF" meant to them, the respondents used the following descriptors: "support," "openness," "caring," "sharing," and "comfort." In contrast, "0% FLF" was represented by the absence of these qualities. The participants then went on to describe each of their turning points in great detail.

Data Analysis

The interview audiotapes were transcribed verbatim, resulting in approximately 980 single-spaced pages of text-based data for the present analysis (Baxter, Braithwaite, & Nicholson, 1999). The transcripts represented aggregate data, combining stepparent's and stepchildren's perspectives. While we recognize that individual blended family members have unique standpoints concerning their role in their family, the goal of this study was to gather a holistic understanding of blended family development. In addition, smaller sample sizes used in qualitative projects like this one, even though yielding very large amounts of data, discourage dividing the analysis by even smaller groups.

Several steps were taken in the data analysis. First, we prepared data for our analysis by dividing up the interview transcripts into five developmental trajectories: accelerated, prolonged, declining, stagnating, and high-amplitude turbulent. Baxter, Braithwaite, and Nicholson (1999) previously identified these trajectories using hierarchical cluster analysis. These authors also categorized the participants as belonging to one of these trajectories and we used that analysis. Second, since the participants talked about their family development chronologically, we divided each of the interview transcripts into four one-year periods to investigate more specifically each of the four years of blended family development. Our rationale for dividing the analysis by each year was also driven by the desire to provide an accessible way to describe the trends in family development to professionals and laypersons, thus increasing the potential usefulness of the results. Third, we developed comprehensive narrative descriptions of the family development for each trajectory over each of the four-year periods.

The constant comparative method (Glaser & Strauss, 1967; Strauss, 1987) was used to analyze the data. In general, the constant comparative method entails identifying emergent themes while continually comparing them for similarities and differences to existing themes. Each time a new theme emerges, a new category is created (Creswell, 1998). To complete these processes, the data analysis comprised six steps. First, the transcripts were sorted by trajectories and equally distributed between the three members of the analysis team. Each coder received 17 or 18 transcripts from a mixture of the five trajectories. Second, each transcript was read in its entirety two times to garner a holistic understanding of the experiences in the blended families. Third, each analysis team member recorded emergent themes, including descriptions and labels for each. Fourth, the analysis team came together and synthesized the findings and discussed the themes in detail to obtain consensus between members, choosing exemplar quotations for the research report. Fifth, the findings were written together to ensure that the voices and themes of all informants were included in the study. Finally, the transcripts were read again and the entire research team checked the analysis to ensure the accuracy and consistency of the categories, looking for any rival explanations of the findings (Miles & Huberman, 1994).

Results

We present the results of our analysis by trajectory type, divided into four-year periods. We have organized the results to present the "positive" pathways first, in the accelerated and prolonged trajectories, as they represented 56.6% of the families. Next, we present the more "negative" pathways of declining and stagnating, which accounted for 18.9% of the families. We end with the challenging high-amplitude turbulent trajectory, which represented 20.8% of the blended families.

Accelerated

The accelerated trajectory represented the largest number of families in these data, (n = 16, 30.2%), reflecting a pattern of quick movement toward 100% FLF (feeling

FIGURE 2

Accelerated trajectory

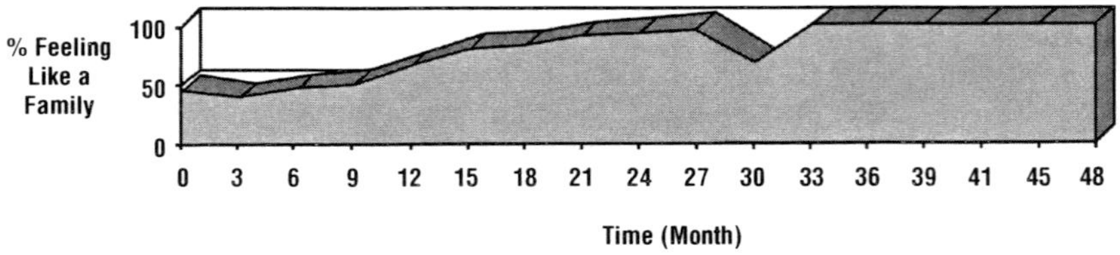

like a family) (Baxter, Braithwaite, & Nicholson, 1999) (See Figure 2). A characterization of the development and "feeling like a family" starts at just below 40% at the beginning of year one, progressing to 60% at the end of the year. In the second year, these families experienced a substantial increase in FLF, rapidly climbing to 92%. Year three was characterized by only a moderate increase of 8%, bringing FLF to 100%, where it stayed through year four as well.

Year 1—"We called her sister from the very beginning." In year one of the accelerated trajectory, family members took on roles comparable to those found within traditional families. These roles helped create the patterns and norms of the family that carried throughout the next three years. Stepparents were often referred to as "mom" and "dad" and played the ascribed roles of parents in "traditional" families. One stepson stated, "He [stepfather] started coming to all of our little league names with our mom and when my mom couldn't make it, he would show up by himself" (53:4, 102-105).3 Clearly, the participants sought to meet the expectations of the traditional family as well. One stepdaughter reflected, "It was Christmas and we just felt we got along ... they all called me 'sister' from the very beginning without making a big deal about me being just a stepsister" (14:1, 28-31). For some participants this transition into new family roles was relatively easy, while for others, the transition was more awkward. A stepfather explained, "I was still kind of hesitant about playing a father role for her children, while she was kind of hesitant about playing the mother role for my children" (26:1, 33-36). At this point, the new roles were somewhat ambiguous for some of the informants.

Year 2—"Still a different set of rules." In year two many of the family members found it relatively easy to adopt the new family roles and norms. In the accelerated trajectory, the second year brought the formation or normalization of family rituals and norms. Family vacations, holiday rituals, and recreation activities were enacted for the families. For example, in one family, members of both the old and new families came together to play football together "for the sake of the children." The parents from both families put their differences aside to combine the families and the football game became a ritual for the family. For other families, the new roles and norms were more difficult to adopt. The strain between biological parents, stepparents, and ex-spouses created conflict in some families in year two. One stepmother expressed, "I felt more comfortable with my role in terms of what to say and what not to say ... but it was still a different set of rules" (4:2, 59-69). Although participants experienced role strain, eventually they were all able to work through their difficulties and awkwardness.

Year 3—"Like a father-son relationship." For the families with difficulties, the role conflicts were more effectively resolved and managed by year three. A positive pattern of interaction continued and familial satisfaction was high. Some blended families had grown so close that family members strove for greater connectedness with other family members. For example, one stepdaughter described that, when she came home from college, her stepbrothers were excited to see her and gave her their undivided attention. But when her sister entered the picture, the stepbrothers shifted the attention onto her, which created some feelings of jealousy, albeit with positive results. She explained,

When just my dad would come to get me from the airport ... the boys would fight over who was going to sit in the back seat with me. And that felt good. But when my sister went with me, they were excited about us coming together ... But I felt jealous because here they wanted to talk to her and were fighting over the backseat and who could sit next to her. (14:5, 148-151)

Year 4—"Feeling very secure." In year four the positive patterns established in the previous years continued. The newly assumed roles were comfortable and satisfying for family members. The relationships had been negotiated and defined in ways that were satisfactory for family members. In addition, conflict and role strains were effectively managed. A stepmother discussed her relationship with her stepdaughter, "We were able to talk a lot more when concerns came up for or things ... that are a part of the family. Responsibilities were easier for her to understand. And if she didn't like it, we could talk about it" (4:3, 121-124).

In summary, blended families experiencing the accelerated pattern developed rather traditional families, families' roles, norms, boundaries, and expectations, resulting in high levels of feeling like a family. These families often entered the first year of their family with the expectation that traditional nuclear family roles and norms would evolve. Similar to other blended family types, these families encountered conflict and adaptation issues, particularly in their second year of formation. However, the primary reason why these families experienced a smooth transition into their new roles and felt a high degree of solidarity was because they were able to put their differences aside and adapt to the changes they confronted. Family members demonstrated a willingness to adapt existing expectations to the uniqueness of the blended family in order to negotiate satisfying family relationships.

Prolonged

The prolonged trajectory represented fourteen (n = 14, 26.4%) of the families in these data and described families that progressed to higher levels of FLF, although not as quickly as the accelerated trajectory (Baxter, Braithwaite, and Nicholson, 1999) (See Figure 3). A characterization of the development and FLF for these families was that they started out low (5%), gradually, increasing to approximately

FIGURE 3

Prolonged trajectory

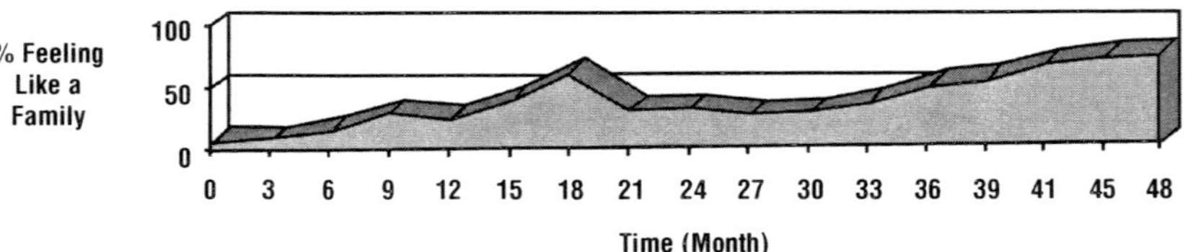

20% at the end of the first year. The second year found FLF peaking at 30% midway through the year, then dropping back down. The third year saw a steady increase from 30%, a slight decrease, and then a gradual climb to 50% FLF. Year four ended with a climb to 70% FLF.

Year 1—"Not dysfunctional, just disjointed." Like other trajectories, in the very beginning, these participants described low levels of solidarity as they began the process of negotiating family boundaries. The newly formed interpersonal relationships created a sense of uneasiness within the blended family. Initially, informants expressed discomfort, awkwardness, and/or a desire to cling to the past. A few stepchildren described experiencing pain and grief over the loss of life they felt forced to leave behind. One stepdaughter told of the difficult transition: "It was like death, because I really felt like our whole past was gone and we were never going to have a future at that house, the family, . . . we were never going to be that again. Also, it was like my mother's last name changed and it was just different" (19: 57-60).

Unlike other trajectories, however, these participants did not compare themselves to a "traditional" family. Rather, they expressed a willingness to allow a new definition of family to emerge for themselves. For example, one stepson discussed his uneasiness with being around his stepmother.

> My dad expected my sister and I to immediately get along with her [stepmother] and it wasn't that easy. He is kind of in La La land. The more we saw her the more we got used to her and talked to her ... started to feel more or less comfortable. (36:6, 166-170)

Importantly, while they remained open-minded about the process of forming a new family, it was still a very uncomfortable transition for the family members.

Year 2—"Getting to know each other stage." Although discomfort and skepticism about the newly formed blended family persisted, in year two there were signs of increased trust, solidarity, and acceptance. Family members had more open communication about their backgrounds, expectations, and roles. As one stepson expressed, "Everyone was in the early stage of relations, of taking it easy, not really boosting their personality to an extreme. Kind of getting to [know each other] stage"

(41:4, 156-158). Even though there was increased communication, the participants recognized that establishing a sense of family and achieving comfort with one another was a process that would take time. By the end of year two, roles became more solidified and blended family members were adjusting to one other. Family rituals such as Christmas celebrations, for example, were adjusted to include other family members. There was a high amount of adjustment needed, but they saw this change as positive, often resulting in higher amounts of feeling like a family.

Year 3—"This was going to stay a family." In year three, participants described more positive communication patterns in the family. Norms and roles became increasingly clear and family solidarity continued to improve. Family roles and communication norms were negotiated and more cooperative and democratic rather than adversarial family relationships were formed. In one family, the stepmother and the divorced mother had developed effective communication strategies by year three, even though they had started out with great animosity and conflict over parenting styles and household rules. The stepmother said that she included her husband's ex-wife in decisions about her stepdaughter, Jessica: "She is Jessica's family. That's something we can't separate, and I don't want to separate her from this family" (4:3, 118-122).

Year 4—"Everyone is comfortable." While each blended family situation was unique, the overall pattern by year four demonstrated a successful negotiation of each of the dimensions of boundaries, solidarity, and adaptation. Even though blended family members' initial expectations for their new family form was rather unrealistic, they were able to adjust to the demands of changing roles, rules, and boundaries. There was an overall sense of satisfaction with their shared family identity. The successful negotiation apparent in this trajectory sets it apart from the negative family types (i.e., stagnating and declining); whereby, the negative types failed to accept the unique quality of the blended family and relied too heavily on preconceived expectations of what it meant to be a family. Also apparent in this trajectory is the subjectivity inherent in what it means to feel like a family. To some blended family members, any positive change since the time of formation may be perceived as a substantial improvement. For example, one stepdaughter described a prolonged pattern, which moved from 0% to 20%, which to her meant that any improvement was significant.

In conclusion, the prolonged trajectory can be described as adaptable, flexible, and relatively satisfying. While families experienced the uncertainties of a new blended family, the participants described a willingness to negotiate family specific roles, norms, boundaries, and expectations. These families started out with low levels of FLF and high amounts of uneasiness. However, unlike the accelerated pattern, these families did not compare themselves to the traditional nuclear family. Rather, they were able to successfully transition into their new family by keeping an open mind and creating their own definition of what it means to be a family. Even though skepticism and conflict continued in their second and third years of formation, these families were open to communication about their roles and expectations.

FIGURE 4
Declining trajectory

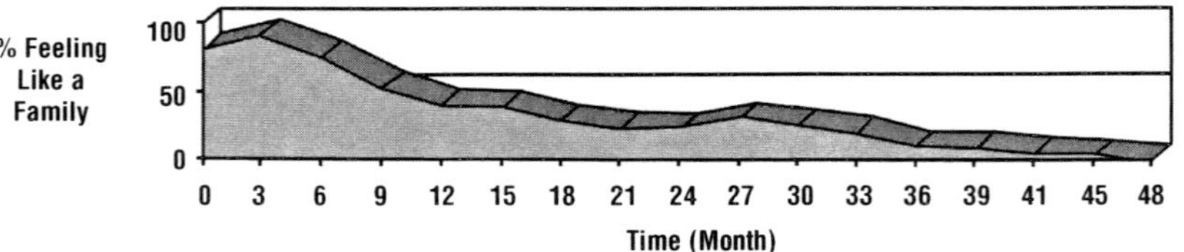

Declining

The declining trajectory represented only three (n = 3, 5.7%) of the families in these data (Baxter, Braithwaite, & Nicholson, 1999) (See Figure 4). Interestingly, these families began with a high level of FLF (80%), which declined to zero at the end of the four-year period. In year one, the FLF score started quite high (80%) and steadily dropped to 40%. Year two brought a gradual decline from 40% to 30% FLF, with no dramatic shifts. Year three saw the level of FLF start at approximately 30 %, take a very small rise to 32 % before dropping dramatically to about 10% at the end of the third year. Year four brought a steady decrease in FLF, beginning the year at 10% and ending with a FLF score of zero within the last three months.

Year 1—"Not the Brady Bunch." In the analysis of the individual years one to four, blended family members expressed high initial expectations for life in this newly formed blended family. One stepmother explained, "First of all my expectations were to have this 'Brady Bunch' family" (10:1, 15-16). These members had high expectations for enacting "traditional" family roles and norms that would be stable and gratifying, thereby increasing family solidarity. Taking part in family rituals, such as Thanksgiving and Christmas, were some of the high points in year one and helped to begin establishing cohesiveness and develop the initial hopefulness that many anticipated.

However, the feeling of solidarity was short-lived as members began to experience family instability even in the first year of formation. One salient problematic dimension involved loyalty conflicts. Boundaries began to emerge, dividing blended family members by bloodlines or generations. For example, one stepdaughter commented that her brother was physically beaten because "he was not my [step]father's child, he was my mother's child, so my [step]father had no kin relation to him" (18:5, 188-191). In another instance, this same stepdaughter did not view her stepmother as a part of her family because she believed her stepmother instigated conflict and blamed the children for family problems.

A second theme that emerged was the family's inability to adapt to changing roles and norms within the adaptation dimension. Participants expressed conflicts over the appropriateness of address terms and behaviors of family members. One stepdaughter recalled that she resented that her stepmother expected she would call her "Mom" when she didn't feel comfortable doing so. She stated

She would always, you know, she would say she wasn't trying to take the place of my mother and she couldn't take the place, but yet she was forcing it on me. I was like forced to call her "Mom." I called her "Mom" out of a guilty conscience. (18:6, 198-201)

Problems with adaptation dramatically altered the new family's sense of solidarity, leaving expectations unfulfilled. The stepmother who had earlier expressed dreams of being like the Brady Bunch, later acknowledged that "it wasn't the Brady Bunch and it was never going to be ... it got worse instead of better" (10:1, 28-29).

Year 2—"Like a Battlefield." A pattern of tension and conflict emerged strongly in the second year. The participants expressed more intense role and loyalty conflicts in their new blended families. For example, one stepmother described the climate in her family, "There was ... a battlefield right there and there I was stuck in the middle" (10:8, 285-286). Membership boundaries of inclusion in the family became more rigid and impermeable. Members were both literally and figuratively separated from one another and members often avoided contact and communication with one another.

Year 3—"It just wasn't there." By year three, the decline was even greater. Participants described their families as fraught with unresolved tensions and conflict. The physical boundaries became so extreme that some family members removed themselves from the household and went to live elsewhere. One mother described the effects of this festering tension and conflict on her new husband, "Bob developed allergies from the tension ... [he] move[d] out partially due to allergies and stress" (24:3, 88-89, 107-108). By the end of year three, the participants described a sense of pending doom for the family's survival: "it just wasn't there, it just really wasn't there" (10:11, 374-375). The optimism and search for traditional family roles and norms of the early years shifted to pessimism in the third year, represented by the drop to 10% FLF at the end of year three.

Year 4—"Bob moves out permanently." Year four was characterized by a complete loss of hope and no sense of family membership or solidarity. By this point, family members had physically or emotionally disengaged from the blended family structure. Patterns of avoidance, alienation, and jealousy became the family norms. Not surprisingly, by the end of year four the percentage of FLF had dropped to 0%.

In summary, the declining trajectory was characterized by loyalty conflicts, ambiguous and strained familial roles, and divisive family boundaries. While they started with high, and perhaps unrealistic, expectations (evidenced by a FLF score of 80%), these quickly diminished and ended at zero, preventing the members from ever forming feelings of solidarity and identity as a family. In particular, these families experienced intense loyalty conflicts, creating impermeable boundaries among family members by bloodlines and generations. The struggles often resulted in avoidance of communication and/or physical removal of family members from the household. What once started out as hopefulness for the future of the family ended in a sense of hopelessness and impending doom by year four.

FIGURE 5

Stagnating trajectory

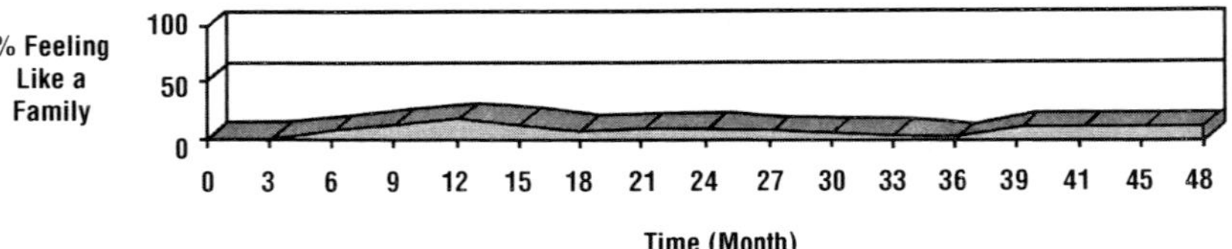

Stagnating

The stagnating trajectory represented seven (n = 7, 13.2%) of the families in these data and described families that "never took off" (Baxter, Braithwaite, & Nicholson, 1999) (See Figure 5). A characterization of the development and FLF scores was that they began and ended with relatively low levels of feeling like a family. Participants reported 10% FLF level in year one, climbing to a high point of only 20%. Year two began at 20%, dropping to 5%, and declining to zero in year three. The fourth year brought very little change, as the FLF scores rose from zero to only 5% at the end of the four-year period.

Year 1—"They just kind of threw us together." Several of the family members experiencing this trajectory described the sense of being in an "instant family" that was thrown together and immediately expected to feel like a family. One stepdaughter described, "They just kind of threw us together and pretended we were one big family and we really weren't" (9:2-3, 142-143). Another stepdaughter recalled her experience with this sudden change, "They ran off and got married and didn't tell my sister and I, and then came home in very nice clothing and told us they were married, and Jess and I were going to have to deal with it" (11:1, 16-19). Participants described a sense of solidarity that was manufactured and felt like a façade erected to meet expectations. They described their experiences as if they were simply "going through the motions" of the family life that now seemed to be expected of them.

Like in the declining trajectory, family members also experienced significant role ambiguity and loyalty conflicts. One stepson described his experience,

> Yeah, 'stepfather,' I didn't know what that meant. I don't think I knew anyone with a 'step.' I probably didn't know how I was supposed to react to him. That was what was scary. I knew I couldn't call him 'Dad.' I didn't know how to deal with it. (37:5, 120-122)

One stepmother also recalled her feelings of tension as a result of her role ambiguity. She talked about her stepdaughter, Beth, whose biological mother had left the family years before they became a blended family. She described how Beth had become "the lady of the house," caring for her father and brother. The stepmother then explained the tension that developed when she entered their family:

> So I came into their lives, and I was there in a very active role, much different than what her mother had been. And I think she felt like, you know, there was a competition there. And, um. . . that she was displaced and she couldn't figure out what her place was. Little did she know that we were both trying to figure that out. (30:4, 140-145)

With the addition of new family members, loyalty conflicts became an issue because of perceived threats to established family relationships. Stepchildren were especially likely to describe difficulties dealing with intrusions upon their parent-child bonds, rituals, and norms from the old family. For example, one stepdaughter resented her stepfather's newly assumed role as her mother's caretaker. She told him, "I know how to take care of her, I know what's best for her, she doesn't need you to help her feel better when she's in a bad mood" (33:3, 71-72). The role ambiguity and loyalty conflicts led to a stagnating pattern of apathy that continued into year two and beyond.

Year 2—"All of this at once." During this year, the participants continued to express problems with issues of adaptability and boundary management. Blended family members struggled to establish trust and to define their roles in this newly-formed family. One stepdaughter related the difficulties of adjusting to all the changes going on:

> This is the first time to be a family. This is the first time that he [stepfather] had his stuff there and my mom had her stuff there ... there is no desensitizing to that point. I wasn't ready for that shock and you just arrive there, plus in a different town, in a different school, and you are start[ing] school yourself. So, it was a very big letdown and to be a family ... all of this at once. (37:9, 234-243)

Family members continued to confront and experience loyalty conflicts. One stepdaughter expressed the struggle she had defining her relationship with her stepmother. "She's not my mother, you know. It's not like my mom is dead" (9:8, 159). Another stepdaughter discussed her resentment toward her stepfather, as she perceived him interfering with her relationship with her mother,

> I always bought my mom my own presents and every holiday he'd ask me, offer me [saying], "I saved up money so you could buy your mom a present." And that's always bothered me because I always bought my mom my own present and he was trying to interfere. (35:4, 108-111)

Finally, at this stage in the blended family's development, the participants expressed a fluctuating sense of solidarity which was reflected in beginning the year at 20% FLF (the highest point these families ever reached) and ending down at 5%. Many of the respondents felt as if important family decisions and roles were being forced upon them and they had little or no input. One stepdaughter gave this example:

> I got along with my stepmom because Dad asked me to. He took me into his room and he asked me, "Please get along with her. Just to like her, talk to her, you know. She tries to be nice to you and she tries to be, you know, like your mother" (9:8, 156-157).

The informants' narratives demonstrated that relationships with blended family members appeared artificial or contrived, forcing members to try and assume roles from "traditional" families.

Years 3 and 4—"Everything was just normal." These two years were collapsed together due to their similarity and represented a pattern of equilibrium, with periodic, but temporary, feelings of solidarity. For example, one stepdaughter described an instance of temporarily high solidarity while her stepmother was undergoing chemotherapy for cancer. Many times prior to this interaction, the stepdaughter felt like an outsider in the blended family. However, during this crisis period, her feelings of group membership increased significantly:

> And I saw her without her wig. And she just looked at me and she looked like she was going to cry. And I said, "It's okay." And she said, "Are you okay with seeing me like this?" And I said, "Yeah." . . . From then on she left it [the wig] off ... right now, I didn't have to ask to do things in the house. If I wanted to make a phone call, I used the phone. If I wanted to go swimming, I used the pool . . .. Everything just felt ... everything was just normal. (9:12, 242-249)

Similar to this stepdaughter's experience, participants in other stagnating families expressed sporadic feelings of solidarity. However, the level of FLF fluctuated little, ranging from only 0% to 5%. Several of the participants helped promote stability, by enacting avoidant patterns of conflict management—choosing not to confront problematic issues in the blended family.

Overall, these participants clearly sought high solidarity and to enact the roles and norms they associated with "a normal family." Ironically, the harder these family members worked toward normalcy, the more change and instability they experienced. We speculate that this was due to unmet expectations, since members did not feel comfortable filling these traditional family roles or having them enacted by others. While the families did not end, the stagnating families did not develop closeness either. By the end of year four, five of the seven participants found life in the blended family "bearable." However, for two of the participants, the blended family was very unsatisfying, resulting in family members emotionally and/or physically distancing themselves from each other. For instance, one stepmother commented, "We just can't do the phony-baloney family get-togethers anymore" (30:15, 592-593).

In summary, stagnating families experienced family life as being "thrown together" and awkwardness concerning familial roles and expectations. While the families sought a "normal" or "traditional" family arrangement, the instability and

FIGURE 6

High-amplitude turbulent trajectory

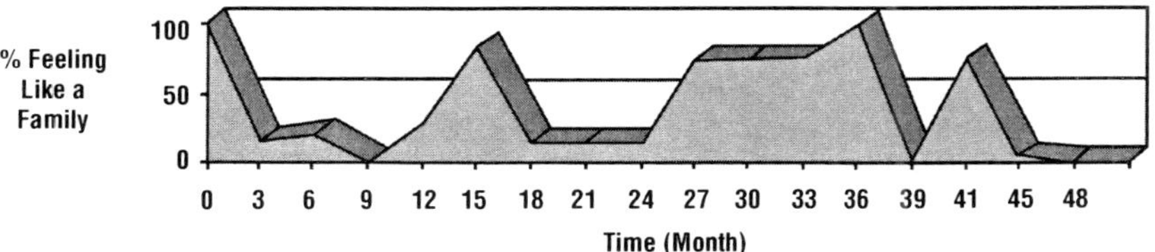

unmet expectations led to consistent feelings of dissatisfaction and artificiality. Family members often felt as if expectations to become an instant family were being forced upon them. The more the family members pushed to become a traditional family, the more resistance they experienced. These family members also encountered loyalty conflicts, which often represented intrusions or threats to pre-existing family relationships. Children in these families also resented their parents and stepparents for not including them in important family decisions, such as an upcoming marriage. As their FLF scores indicated, there was some small fluctuation in feeling like a family, but that fluctuation was small and this stagnating pattern revealed dissatisfaction and apathy toward the blended family.

High-Amplitude Turbulent

The high-amplitude turbulent trajectory represented eleven (n = 11, 20.8%) of the families in these data (Baxter, Braithwaite, and Nicholson, 1999) and was, in essence a blend of both positive and negative family experiences (See Figure 6). Their development and levels of FLF suggested the sense of being on a roller coaster, with dramatic up and down shifts in FLF scores. Year one was characterized by fluctuations of FLF, ranging from 100% to 0%. The second year brought changes from 30%-90%, with a sudden drop to a series of 10%-15% peaks and valleys in FLF. Year three brought with it a leap up to 80%, followed by the same series of peaks and valleys, ending at 100%. Finally year four saw a crash to zero, back up to 80%, and ending at 0%.

Year l—"A major adjustment for me." The turbulent trajectory was difficult to conceptualize. By definition, the trajectory precluded consistency. Nonetheless, the instability of the turbulent trajectory seemed to foster some patterned behavior in the families. A theme that emerged in the first year, which was common to several other trajectories, is that family members experienced the unrealistic expectation of the "instant family." For several of them, this was an extremely difficult transition. One stepdaughter explained,

> In the beginning it was just, "no way," he was nothing to me, a stranger. He was taking away my mother, almost negative. But then he bought me tapes and he started hanging around more ...

> it wasn't like family, it was just some feeling toward someone being there all the time, but not ... a family member. (38:3, 88-92)

For other families, the awkwardness of a new, blended family was compounded by the inability to meet societal expectations of being a member of a "traditional" family. Members experienced tensions between wanting to be part of the family but not knowing how to carry out the new role. Even though several of these participants experienced the discomfort and strain associated with sudden formation of a new family, some individuals still described their relationships as satisfying and positive.

Year 2—"Let-down phase." The second year brought with it increased instability, chaotic household boundaries, and unmet expectations of perceived family roles and norms. For instance, one stepdaughter commented, "I had to get adjusted to my stepfather and stepbrothers and I'd have to say that was another adjustment ... It was real hard to be myself at that point" (21:3, 86-90). Family members began moving in and out of households as a result of conflict. One stepdaughter, for example, ran away from home and moved in with her grandmother because of the high degree of conflict and lack of solidarity in her blended family. Other family members perceived an intense betrayal and had difficulties establishing trust in their new family members. Extreme or inadequate conflict strategies were also implemented among the family members, particularly the couple. Another key issue that continually emerged was the lack of solidarity between the parental couple. Often these couples were unable to create a unified front for the children, but rather competed with one another for the children's attention and love.

Year 3—"This is like the stock market." Perhaps the best way to describe this year is in terms of a "fork in the road" metaphor. Family members either confronted their instability and conflict, which made their road much easier, or continued to avoid them, resulting in escalation of instability and conflict. Those individuals who experienced escalation of negativity continually dealt with their conflict using avoidance tactics. Major issues in their family, such as health problems, alcohol and drug abuse, emotional manipulation, and verbal abuse, were characterized by either passive or aggressive strategies, which, in turn, drove feeling like a family up and down wildly. The issues were either denied, or they exploded in aggressive confrontations. One stepdaughter described her stepsister's passive-aggressive behavior: "My mom has severe allergies. We couldn't use perfume for a while and obviously you couldn't smoke. And Laura would sit downstairs in the basement and smoke" (38:8, 244-247).

The family members who constructively managed the turbulence in their family also initially used avoidance tactics but eventually confronted the conflict, airing differences and unmet expectations. One stepmother stated, "We talked openly about a lot of things, which wasn't our usual type of communication about feeling, about what we perceived, about lying to one another, and it seemed like we were having better communications (7:4, 193-195). As this quotation indicates, confronting family issues finally helped open their lines of communication.

Year 4—"Keeping communication lines open." For those individuals caught in the negative cycle, the conflict perpetuated into year four. One stepmother described her explosive episodes with her new husband:

> I remember yelling at each other ... I remember throwing ... I don't remember who threw it ... throwing a remote control. Got a major dent in my wall ... Hung a picture there so the dent wouldn't show ... I remember I didn't want to talk with anybody. Here we are back in town. I could have talked to my parents, could've talked to Pastor Rich, and just really thinking, you know, screw this whole deal...I made a mistake. I never should've gotten married. I just ... He didn't understand. He was a man and I didn't want anything to do with him. (31:20, 266-272)

Overall, the participants caught in the negative cycle described feelings of hopelessness and a desire to avoid confronting the problems of their families.

On the other hand, families that engaged in a more positive cycle opened the lines of communication. One stepdaughter described her increasing connectedness and relationship with her stepfather, explaining, "At that point, I'd been in the family long enough to really feel more of a bond with my stepdad, and just knew that I belonged there and he belonged there ... I really felt he was my Dad, as opposed to being my stepdad" (32:5, 90-98). Even though FLF would shoot up and down due to conflict, these participants described confronting the conflict, resulting in feelings of higher solidarity.

In general, as the name implies, the turbulent trajectory was characterized as diverse, unstable, and unpredictable. Similar to many of the other family types, unrealistic expectations of forming an instant family was associated with discomfort and strain. Participants often experienced feelings of betrayal and a lack of trust among new family members. A common theme among these families was a lack of solidarity between the couple. The blended family couples were unable to communicate a unified front for the children and demonstrate positive conflict management strategies. The amount of conflict these families experienced reached an impasse in year three. This "fork in the road" was often met with extreme behavioral patterns of avoidance or aggressive confrontation. However, the families that positively confronted the conflict and instability tended to perceive more satisfying family relationships, while the families that avoided the conflict and instability experienced greater dissatisfaction with family relationships.

Discussion

The results of this study underscore the utility of looking at the development of blended families not as a unitary model moving always forward but as a process involving different developmental pathways, each with its own unique pattern of development (Baxter, Braithwaite, & Nicholson, 1999; Coleman & Ganong, 1995). A process perspective emphasizes that individual blended families may experience family development in different ways. Recognizing that blended family development can occur along various trajectories avoids the tendency that researchers, counselors, or blended family members themselves have to prescribe a single pattern for the successful development of blended families. This avoids trying to model the blended family after television's "the Brady Bunch" or a more traditional family form. Unitary perspectives often infer "one right way" for families to develop, making those who do not follow such paths feel inferior or defective. Unlike the chronological, prescriptive stage models, a process model, that allows for variation in blended family development, helps us better understand the complexity inherent in this family form. Accounting for such diversity allows researchers and practitioners to move beyond a unitary approach to one that is more inclusive and, thus, representative of a larger number of blended families. Knowledge of the multiple ways in which blended families develop can be especially useful to mental health professionals and blended family members themselves because they can be cautioned to avoid the assumption that there is only one way to "become a family." Contrary to past work, which has cast blended families as different from or inferior to traditional families, the results of this study also legitimate the blended family as a unique family form capable of success, and demonstrates that success can come via multiple pathways and timeliness

Moreover, the results of this study provide, through reflective discourse, a detailed understanding of how blended family members negotiate their way through the various pathways—some of which are healthy, constructive paths and some of which are destructive ones. By focusing specifically on how blended family members described their first four years of family development, our findings provide researchers and practitioners insights into the lived experiences of this unique family form. The three most salient issues we identified in these data were boundary management, solidarity, and adaptation. While these issues were evident in our analysis, we discovered that how they were negotiated varied by trajectory. More specifically, we found that issues of boundaries, solidarity, and adaptation were central to the enactment of the different pathways of becoming a family. Blended family members in our study frequently discussed how, in their first four years of development, they dealt with family group membership, feelings of closeness, and flexibility to change. From our analysis, we observed that their negotiation of these issues varied across the five trajectories. And yet, there were some commonalties across family experiences as well.

First, in terms of family boundaries, our results revealed that individuals who experienced the more constructive trajectories were more likely to describe successful and flexible boundary management. For many of these families, it meant the ability to negotiate movement of blended family members from one household to another due to shared custodial parental or extended family relationships. For others, it meant a relatively smooth transition to in-group membership within the newly created blended family. Importantly, while the management of these boundaries was not always easy, the accelerated and prolonged trajectories were both characterized by their members being able to eventually negotiate the new boundaries successfully. In contrast, individuals who experienced the declining, stagnating, and high-amplitude turbulent pathways shared an inability to successfully negotiate newly formed family boundaries. In fact, in some of these families, boundaries became extremely rigid and impermeable, demarcating bloodlines and generations. These findings support research by Visher and Visher (1988) and Papernow (1994) who argued that appropriate boundary management is one of the most critical adjustments blended families face. Successful management of newly formed and previously existing family boundaries was indeed critical to our participants' descriptions of their blended family development as well, setting apart the more positive patterns (those who eventually achieved high levels of feeling like a family in the accelerated and prolonged patterns) from the less positive family experiences.

With regard to solidarity, our findings demonstrate that most people enter into blended family situations with at least some sense of optimism, wanting to be part of a family and feel like a family, even though they are often upset about the loss of the old family. Families in each of these trajectories started out with a desire for solidarity, even if short-lived, or even if that sense of solidarity was more of an artifact of what members thought they should feel, rather than what they were actually feeling. In the accelerated and prolonged pathways, the solidarity did develop in these families; most quickly in the accelerated pattern. Happily, these two trajectories represented more than half of the families in the study (56.6%). In the other three pathways, the push for family solidarity seemed to cause more tension and conflict as family members strove to be what they were not. While the declining and stagnating patterns represented families with severe problems that did not achieve high levels of feeling like a family, the high amplitude turbulent pattern, representing 20.8% of the families, did have high levels of feeling like a family at times. What we noted in this pattern was that it appeared to us that those families that were able to constructively confront conflict and deal with the constantly changing nature of the blended family situation seemed to report a more positive experience and were able to cope with the ups and downs of this family type. From our analysis of their discourse, while their road was a rocky one, we noted that these families reported feelings of solidarity if they were able to effectively manage conflict and change.

Third, in terms of adaptability, our results highlight the omnipresent nature of change in blended families (Ganong & Coleman, 1994; Kelley, 1992; Visher & Visher, 1988). This is consistent with previous research. For example Baxter, Braithwaite, and Nicholson (1999) found that change was the turning point reported most often in the first four years of blended family life. Role ambiguity and the reenactment of "traditional" family roles are often key to the amount of change experienced by, and adaptability needed, within blended families. In our analysis, we found that struggles ensued (except in the accelerated pattern) when family members attempted, and perhaps felt pressure to, replicate traditional family roles and norms. With the exception of the accelerated pattern, the expectation of the "instant family" was an unrealistic goal (Ganong & Coleman, 1994). It was clear that blended family identity and roles take time to develop through these periods of great change. Hetherington and Jodl (1994) stressed that blended family roles necessitate "negotiation among all family members, including the children, biological parent, noncustodial parent, and even grandparents" (p. 58). Additionally, blended family members need to be open to developing roles that may be different than ones enacted in other family forms (Kelley, 1992). Hence, understanding and accepting this as part of the process of "becoming a family" will be helpful for immediate blended family members, as well as their extended network of family and friends.

In addition, one element that seemed to add to members' ability to accept change was what happened in the premarital stages of the family. There are strong indications in these data that the adaptation to the new family and the development of solidarity within the family began well before marriage, and in fact, began in the dating period of the parental couple. We agree with Baxter, Braithwaite, and Nicholson (1999) that it is important for researchers to take this premarital period into account and to allow research participants to determine when the family started. Choosing the date of marriage, or even cohabitation, is arbitrary and leaves out important steps in family development. From an applied perspective, adults who believe early on that a new relationship might lead to permanent blending of families should be cognizant that the blended family is taking shape from the earliest interactions. Thus, having realistic expectations, and trying to develop healthy communication patterns, norms, and roles from the start will be useful. How this can be done is beyond the scope of the present study, but is certainly a worthwhile enterprise for researchers and practitioners to take on.

From our results, it appears that families who were patient, expected and accepted change, and understood that it would take some time to feel like a family tended to see closeness develop. Those who fought changes or were not able to "roll with the punches" when it came to boundaries and adaptation of roles and norms experienced great struggle and conflict. Similarly, those who tried to force-fit close relationships from the start experienced disappointment. This reinforces the need to see closeness in most blended family relationships as evolving, and it cautions family members about the importance of having patience and realistic expectations of themselves and others. Our results point to the importance of the family as a whole working through this entire adjustment period, to give the new family the opportunity to develop their own unique and flexible boundaries, feelings of solidarity and closeness, and roles and norms adaptive to the needs of the new family. When family members, especially children, were not given the opportunity to adjust before the marriage of the parents, problems persisted. This premarital stage was also an extremely important time in these families because of the myth of the instant family that was expected by many of the parents in the first year of marriage. The more that family members let themselves take the time and opportunity to grow together, the more positive the experience. In addition, some of the families used direct communication, such as regular family meetings, to air issues surrounding the adjustments to becoming a family.

Moreover, in terms of managing conflict, blended families that were characterized by flexibility, open communication, and constructive conflict management were able to handle almost anything that occurred. In contrast, when individuals or families were unable to develop constructive ways to manage conflict, problems persisted. While all blended families experience some conflict and negative experiences (as do all families), those which were able to remain flexible considered themselves successful (Visher & Visher, 1988). Our results also lead us to agree with other scholars that, while blended families experience challenges, there is no reason to conclude that all blended families are problematic and inferior to other family forms (Coleman, 1994; Kelley, 1992; Kurdek, 1994). Instead, scholars should glean the success stories from blended families and spend more time identifying what successful blended families do.

While our study sheds light on some of the nuances of blended family development and the unique issues that affect development, it also has several limitations. First, only one member from a blended family took part in the interviews. Even though it may be more difficult to do, we suggest that researchers solicit the perspectives of multiple family members from a given family. In addition, a larger number of participants will better allow us to compare the experiences of parents, stepparents, and stepchildren, to see how they are similar and different. We also suggest that researchers include the perspectives of families from different cultural backgrounds. Finally, we are aware that, like all families, blended families are part of larger social networks. Like many researchers before us, we have so largely ignored the influence and perspective of extended family members, such as grandparents, parents and siblings of the couple, friends, and fictive kin.

Taking these limitations into account, we do believe that these findings provide new insight into, and extend our theoretical understanding of, these blended family developmental issues by recognizing that not all families experience them in the same way. In fact, we are convinced that it is absolutely essential that scholars and practitioners need to stress that there is no singular "right" way for blended families to develop and that feeling like a family is a process that takes time. Rather than generalizing and essentializing the blended family experience, our results suggest that the negotiation of these issues varies by developmental pathway. More specifically, as reflected in their discourse, the blended family members' successful or unsuccessful management of these issues coincided with the type of trajectory they experienced. Individuals experiencing the constructive pathways described being able to more successfully manage the issues of boundaries, solidarity, and adaptation In contrast, blended family members who had experienced the less healthy trajectories described an inability or difficulty in managing these same issues. As communication researchers, we are also keenly aware that there is much more work to be done to identify the specific communication messages and behaviors that will lead families to develop flexible boundaries, feelings of solidarity, and the ability to adapt and find workable expectations and roles within different developmental pathways.

In addition, our findings have important implications to practitioners working with members of blended families. First, because of the reflective nature of discourse, our findings suggest that a practitioner could gain insight into the developmental course a particular blended family has charted by listening to how she or he describes these issues. Second, by recognizing that the issues are experienced differently by trajectory, the practitioner could then use the discussion of the issues as an intervention tool and help change the way the blended family negotiates these issues and, thus, chart a different developmental path. If these trajectories are to be a useful tool for professionals and family members, we need to examine their applicability in applied settings. Some of our research team are involved in a new study where research participants are shown the five trajectories and asked to identify which represents their blended family experience. If they are able to do so, this will give an indication that the tool that would be possible for professionals and family members to use. By "translating scholarship into practice" (Petronio, 1999), we hope that our work will encourage practitioners and applied communication scholars to "transport" the findings to their professional interactions with members of blended families. Functioning as "transporters" of scholarship, those working with and living in blended families can use this information to help identify families heading into the declining, stagnating and turbulent trajectories and facilitate their move toward more positive, adaptive, and successful pathways.

Endnotes

1. As communication scholars, we are sensitive to the labels used to describe families. We recognized the emotional loading of the term "stepfamily" (Ganong, Coleman, & Kennedy, 1990; Preston, 1984), and found "remarried" family (e.g., Ganong & Coleman, 1994) to be inadequate, as it assumes all the couples heading blended families are married, and, more importantly, it views the family from the perspective of the parents' marital status alone. Therefore, we adopted the term "blended" family (e.g. Arliss, 1993; Preston, 1984).
2. We also struggled with how to refer to the "original" or "old" family and the "new" blended family. Most scholars refer to the "original," "biological," "natural," or "family of origin" (e.g., Ganong & Coleman, 1994). Again, we recognized both the emotional loading and the inaccuracy of those labels, for example, blended families may contain some or all non-biological children. We use "old" family to refer to the family(ies) from which members of the blended come and blended or "new" families to refer to the present family configuration in which members live.
3. These numbers refer to interview number, page number, and line numbers in the transcripts. Hence, (53:4, 102-105) refers to interview #53, page #4, and lines 102-105.

Consider this . . .

- How do developmental stage models differ from a process view of blended family development? What are the advantages and disadvantages of each developmental perspective?
- Of the unique challenges blended family members confront, which challenge do you consider the most difficult to overcome? Why?
- Using the five trajectories as the basis for your discussion, briefly describe the processes blended family members used while striving to acquire FLF

(feeling like a family). How accurately do these trajectories and processes reflect your knowledge of blended families?

- Briefly describe some critical turning points that typically occur along the four-year time frame within each of the five trajectories. How accurately do these turning points reflect your knowledge of blended families?
- Given the results of this study, what findings do you believe are most valuable for blended families striving to acquire FLF (feeling like a family)? Why?

References

Ahrons, C. R., & Rodgers, R. H. (1987). The remarriage transition. In C. R. Ahrons & R. H. Rodgers (Eds.), *Divorced families: A multidisciplinary development* (pp. 185-200). Beverly Hills, CA: W. W. Norton.

Anderson, J. Z., & White, G. D. (1986). An empirical investigation of interaction and relationship patterns in functional and dysfunctional nuclear families and stepfamilies. *Family Process, 25,* 407-422.

Arliss, L. P. (1993). *Contemporary family communication: Messages and meanings.* New York: St. Martin's Press.

Baxter, L. A., & Bullis, C. (1986). Turning points in developing romantic relationships. *Human Communication Research, 12,* 469-493.

Baxter, L. A., Braithwaite, D. O., & Nicholson, J. (1999). Turning points in the development of blended family relationships. *Journal of Social and Personal Relationships, 16(3),* 291-313.

Braithwaite, D. O., & Baxter, L. A. (1995). The role of rituals in the management of the dialectical tensions of "old" and "new" in blended families. *Communication Studies, 49,* 101-121.

Bray, J. H., & Harvey, D. M. (1995). Adolescents in blended families: Developmental family interventions. *Psychotherapy, 32,* 122-130.

Bray, J. H., & Hetherington, E. M. (1988). Families in transition: Introduction and overview. *Journal of Family Psychology, 7,* 3-24.

Bray, J. H., & Hetherington, E. M. (1993). Development issues in blended families research project: Family relationships and parent-child interactions. *Journal of Family Psychology, 7,* 76 -90.

Brubaker, T. H., & Kimberly, J. A. (1993). In Brubaker, T. H. (Ed.), *Family relations: Challenges for the future* (pp. 3-16). Newbury Park, CA: Sage.

Buchanan, C. M., Maccoby, E. E., & Dornbusch, S. M. (1996). *Adolescents after divorce.* Cambridge: Harvard Press.

Bullis, C., & Bach, B. W. (1989). Are mentor relationships helping organizations? An exploration of developing mentee-mentor organizational identification using turning point analysis. *Communication Quarterly, 37,* 199-214.

Burrell, N. A. (1995). Communication patterns in stepfamilies: Redefining family roles, themes, and conflict styles. In M. Fitzpatrick & A. Vangelisti (Eds.). *Explaining family interactions* (pp. 290-309). Thousand Oaks, CA: Sage.

Cissna, K. N., Cox, D. E., & Bochner, A. P. (1990). The dialectic of marital and parental relationships within the blended family. *Communication Monographs, 37,* 44-61.

Coleman, M. (1994). Stepfamilies in the United States: Challenging biased assumptions. In A. Booth & J. Dunn (Eds.), *Stepfamilies: Who benefits? Who does not?* (pp. 29-235). Hillsdale, NJ: Erlbaum.

Coleman, M., & Ganong, L. H. (1995). Family reconfiguring following divorce. In S. Duck & J. Wood (Eds.), *Confronting relationship challenges* (pp. 73-108). Thousand Oaks, CA: Sage.

Creswell, J. W. (1998). *Qualitative inquiry and research design: Choosing among five traditions.* Thousand Oaks, CA: Sage.

Duck, S. (1994). *Meaningful relationships: Talking, sense, and relating.* Thousand Oaks, CA: Sage.

Fine, M. A. (1995). The clarity and content of the stepparent role: A review of the literature. *Journal of Divorce and Remarriage, 24,* 19 -34.

Fine, M. A., Voydanoff, P., & Donnelly, B. W. (1993). Relations between parental control and warmth and child well-being in blended families. *Family Psychology, 2*, 222-232.

Ganong, L. H., & Coleman, M. (1994). *Remarried family relationships.* Thousand Oaks, CA: Sage.

Ganong, L. H., Coleman, M., & Kennedy, G. (1990). The effects of using alternate labels in denoting stepparent or stepfamily status. *Journal of Social Behavior and Personality, 5*, 453-463.

Giles-Sims, J., & Crosbie-Bumett, M. (1989). Stepfamily research: Implications for policy, clinical interventions, and further research. *Family Relations, 38*, 19-23.

Glaser, B. G., & Strauss, A. L. (1967). *The discovery of grounded theory. Strategies for qualitative research.* New York: Aldine de Gruyter.

Goldsmith, D. J., & Baxter, L. A. (1996). Constituting relationships in talk: A taxonomy of speech events in social and personal relationships. *Human Communication Theory, 1*, 106-127.

Hetherington, E. M., & Jodl, K. M. (1994). Stepfamilies as settings for child development. In A. Booth & J. Dunn (Eds.), *Stepfamilies: Who benefits? Who does not?* (pp. 55-79). Hillsdale, NJ: Erlbaum.

Hines, A. M. (1997). Divorce-related transitions, adolescent development, and the role of the parent-child relationship: A review of the literature. *Journal of Marriage and the Family, 59*, 375-388.

Ihinger-Tallman, M. (1988). Research on stepfamilies. *Annual Review of Sociology, 14*, 25-48.

Kelley, P. (1992). Healthy stepfamily functioning. *Families in Society: The Journal of Contemporary Human Services, 73*, 529-587.

Kurdek, L. A. (1994). Remarriages and stepfamilies are not inherently problematic. In A. Booth, & J. Dunn (Eds.), *Stepfamilies: Who benefits? Who does not?* (pp. 37-44). Hillsdale, NJ: Erlbaum.

Kurdek, L. A., & Fine, M. A. (1991). Cognitive correlates of satisfaction for mothers and stepfathers in stepfather families. *Journal of Marriage and the Family, 53*, 565-572.

Kvale, S. (1996). *InterViews: An introduction of qualitative research interviewing.* Thousand Oaks, CA: Sage.

Leininger, M. (1994). Evaluation criteria and critique of qualitative research studies. In J. M. Morse (Ed.), *Critical issues in qualitative research methods* (pp. 95-115). Thousand Oaks, CA: Sage.

McCracken, D. (1988). *The long interview.* Newbury Park, CA: Sage.

Miles, M. B., & Huberman, A. M. (1994). *Qualitative data analysis* (2nd ed.). Thousand Oaks, CA: Sage.

Mills, D. (1984). A model for blended family development. *Family Relations, 33*, 365-372.

Olson, D. H., & DeFrain, J. (1997). *Marriage and the family: Diversity and strengths* (2nd Ed.). Mountain View: Mayfield.

Papernow, P. L. (1993). *Becoming a blended family. Patterns of development in remarried families.* San Francisco: Jossey-Bass.

Papernow, P. L. (1994). *What is effective stepparenting?* San Francisco: Jossey-Bass.

Pasley, K., Dollahite, D. C., & Ihinger-Tallman, M. (1993). Clinical applications of research findings on the spouse and stepparent roles in remarriage. *Family Relations, 42*, 315-322.

Petronio, S. (1999). "Translating scholarship into practice": An alternative metaphor. *Journal of Applied Communication Research, 27*, 87-91.

Preston, G. (1984). Structural problems in the formation and function of blended families. *Australian Journal of Family Therapy, 5*, 17-26.

Schneider, D. M. (1980). *American kinship: A cultural account* (2nd ed.). Chicago, IL: The University of Chicago Press.

Schwartz, P. (1988). The family as a changing institution. *Journal of Family Issues, 8*, 455-459.

Siegart, J. R., & Stamp, G. H. (1994). "Our first big fight" as a milestone in the development of close relationships. *Communication Monographs, 61*, 345-371.

Stacey, J. (1990). *Brave new families.* NY: Basic Books.

Strauss, A. (1987). *Qualitative analysis for social scientists.* New York: Cambridge University Press.

Strauss, A., & Corbin, J. (1990). *Basics of qualitative research: Grounded theory procedures and techniques.* Newbury Park, CA: Sage.

Stepfamily Association of America (1998). *National statistics on stepfamilies.* Available: www.stepfam.org.

Visher, E. B., & Visher, J. S. (1988). *Old loyalties, new ties.* New York: Brunner/Mazel.

Visher, E. B., & Visher, J. S. (1993). Remarriage families and stepparenting. In F. Walsh (Ed.), *Normal family processes* (2nd ed., pp. 235-253). New York: Guilford.

White, L. (1994a). Growing up with single parents and stepparents: Long-term effects on family solidarity. *Journal of Marriage and the Family, 56*, 935-948.

White, L. (1994b). Blended families over the life course: Social support. In A. Booth & J. Dunn (Eds.), *Blended families: Who benefits? Who does not?* (pp. 109-137). Hillsdale, NJ: Lawrence Erlbaum.

Whitsett, D., & Land, H. (1992). Role strain, coping and marital satisfaction of stepparents. *Families in Society, 73*, 79-92.

Received August 19, 1999

Accepted December 12, 2000

CHAPTER 7

COMMITTING TO PERSONAL RELATIONSHIPS

In Chapter 7 of her text, *Relational Communication*, Julia Wood discusses commitment as a conscious choice participants make to create a relational culture for the present as well as the future. As we seek intimacy in our personal relationships, Wood writes of the difference between passion and love in a committed relationship; she then explains how various styles of loving shape both our expectations and experiences in personal relationships. Finally, Wood explores the communication processes that occur when we commit to our personal relationships. She concludes that intimacy involves both love (a feeling) and commitment (a choice) in our personal relationships.

Communication scholars John H. Harvey (University of Iowa) and Ann L. Weber (University of North Carolina at Asheville) have established distinguished careers in writing about intimate relationships. In their book chapter entitled, "Love and Commitment," they provide valuable insight into the study of intimate, committed relationships. They begin their chapter by providing an historical perspective on the study of love; they then review both definitions of love as well as various typologies often used to examine love. Perhaps most interesting is their use of Social Exchange Theory and Attachment Theory, both discussed earlier in this course, to explain and predict love in personal relationships.

While love is often viewed only as a positive feeling or emotion, Harvey and Weber also explore the destructive aspects of love. They provide powerful examples of obsessive love; furthermore, they discuss the destructive situations that can arise when infatuation is mistaken for love or when love is created out of need or the desire to control. As you read about this "dark side" of love, consider your own experience with personal relationships that may reflect some of these destructive aspects of love.

Finally, Harvey and Weber conclude their chapter with an extensive discussion of commitment as it relates to love. An extension of material presented in the Wood text, the authors of this chapter provide a solid overview of literature that explores both the process of committing as well as the process of building trust to create intimacy in our personal relationships. Harvey and Weber conclude their chapter by noting the complexity of this powerful emotion known as love and the conscious choice to commit to such intimacy.

Love and Commitment

John H. Harvey and Ann L. Weber

> *There is hardly any activity, any enterprise, which is started with such tremendous hopes and expectations and yet, which fails so regularly as love.*
>
> -Eric Fromm (1956)

> *Love is such a tissue of paradoxes, and exists in such an endless variety of forms and shades, that you may say almost anything about it that you please, and it is likely to be correct.*
>
> (In Berscheid & Walster, 1978, p. 105; original quote taken from H. T. Finck's Romantic Love and Personal Beauty, 1891, Macmillan, London)

> *Love may not make the world go round but I must admit it makes the ride worthwhile.*
>
> -Sean Connery

On Valentine's Day (February 14) 2000, USA TODAY ran a "USA Snapshot" on adults who believe in love at first sight. Amazingly, there was consensus across all age groups on the preponderance of respondents believing in love at first sight ages 18-29, 60%; ages 30-49, 56%; ages 50-64, 45%; and 65 and older, 41%. Hence, it may be concluded that we are a culture that strongly values love and believes that it can be instantly recognized. Although the literature may suggest pause about how quickly true love can be perceived, these beliefs appear to be deeply ingrained in most of us even if we have had mixed personal experiences with love.

Sternberg (1998) argues that love is a social construction, meaning that there is no one particular reality of love—rather there are many constructed by all of us in the course of our careers of loving many others. The quotes that open this chapter speak to diversity of ideas about love, from the great disappointment that sometimes attends love to the intricacies of the feeling of love to the excitement that we feel in pursuing love.

This chapter is about love, the central concept in the whole field of close relationships. The chapter also links love to the idea of commitment in close relationships.

The Difficult Journey to Study Love

The historical back-drop for the study of love is similar to that for the study of sexuality, which is briefly reviewed in chapter 4. For present purposes, it is important to note that the study of the social psychology of love is a 20th century phenomenon. Until the end of the Victorian Period of the late 19th century in the United States, human love usually was unequivocally linked with obeying of God's will in marriage. There was little recognition of passionate love (which is similar to romantic love). Passionate love did not have an accepted place in the intimate lives of people in the. Puritan or Victorian eras, that took up much of the first 3 centuries in this country.

In fact, other than early work by sociologists on love within the context of the family, the first systematic study of love by psychologists did not begin until the 1960s. Pioneers such as Ellen Berscheid, Elaine (Walster) Hatfield, Keith Davis, George Levinger, and Bernard Murstein began to develop this topic in the 1960s and 1970s. However, they encountered much criticism from the mainstream psychology fields and from grant review committees, who often wrote their work off as common sense, or "too soft" (meaning not well-grounded in theory and clear-cut empirical operations). Berscheid and Hatfield's work on love, which probably involved the most influential and ground-breaking early research, was singled out in the 1970s by Senator William Proxmire of Wisconsin for one of his "Golden Fleece Awards" that he gave to people receiving federal grants and whose work he found to be so wanting that they were "fleecing the government." Proxmire suggested that we as scholars should not dig into some sacrosanct topics—yet, ironically, at the same point in time, Proxmire was engaged in his own difficult divorce! Here is what Berscheid and Walster (1978) quoted Proxmire as saying in 1975 in his criticism of their work:

> I believe that 200 million other Americans want to leave some, things in life a mystery, and right at the top of things we don't want to know is why a man falls in love with a woman and vice versa.... So National Science Foundation—get out of the love racket. Leave that to Elizabeth Barrett Browning and Irving Berlin. Here, if anywhere, Alexander Pope was right when he observed, "If ignorance is bliss, 'tis folly to be wise." (p. 150)

As millions of Americans' book-buying tendencies, interests in relationship counseling, and subscription to college relationships courses indicate, Proxmire was dead wrong! People want to try to know about any mystery, especially one so fundamental to the human condition as what love is and why it occurs. Gladly, Proxmire's view did not prevail. In fact, it may have indirectly speeded along some scholars' quest to learn about love.

There also is a lot to be learned from common sense, as another pioneering psychologist Fritz Heider showed in his seminal (1958) work *The Psychology of Interpersonal Relations*. The scholars who built this area of scholarship in psychology deserve great praise. They endured an onslaught of criticism and persevered, such that today the topic is fairly common in psychology (e.g., see Berscheid, 1988, p. 360). In the 1980s and 1990s, several federal research grants were awarded to study topics directly related to love.

Definitions

Love. What is "love"? As implied in the beginning paragraph, love is one of the most difficult concepts to define in the close relationships field. As an illustration, in one of the most useful analyses of love, Susan and Clyde Hendrick (Romantic Love,

1992) avoided a definitive definition and simply said: "We choose not to provide a formal definition of love, but rather to let the context of the entire book engage in the defining process (p. 6). The context of their book provides many rich connotations of love, such as their provocative work on different loving styles that will be discussed next.

Yet, is there no simple definition we can offer at the outset in the way of a general definition? No, there is no such simple definition. We can do some general outlining of the concept and bring in what other scholars have said. One general idea is that love is an emotion, that is positive in valence and may be directed toward other and/or self. In this same vein, love has been construed as an attitude involving positive feeling toward self and/or other. People frequently make a distinction between "loving someone" and "being in love." The latter usually is reserved for a special romantically oriented relationship, whereas the former may be said to apply to a number of others including relatives and friends.

In her last book *Courage My Love*, written before dying an untimely death, Merle Shain (1989) wrote engagingly about love in a chapter she called "What is this thing called love?" She defined love as involving stages: First, there is the "some enchanted evening," or bell-ringing, highly romantic stage that she suggested is short-lived, lasting usually around 6 weeks. It should be noted that many other theorists believe that romantic love may last a lot longer. These other theorists, though, typically are referring to love in a general and positive way and not defined mainly by idealization of other, feeling a loss of personal control, and other such illusory qualities. Shain suggested that after this early highly romantic period, a more substantial stage, involving much less idealization of other, usually occurs if the couple continues to be engaged in a close relationship. In this more advanced stage, respect (which Shain referred to as "love in plain clothes"), acceptance, understanding, and mutual self-disclosure—to a high degree—represent love. If love matures to this more advanced stage, it involves also self-love. Shain quoted the theologian Martin Buber who contended that there cannot be a "we" until there is an "I" to keep company with the "thou." In this context Shain (1989) said: "And while it's often easier to flesh someone out with your own creativity and fall in love with what you've made, the real joy is in understanding and accepting and loving what you find" (p. 31).

Aaron Beck (1988) wrote a useful book entitled *Love Is Never Enough*, which is discussed in more detail in the chapter on maintenance. He, too, did not define love in any direct way. The title of this book is an appropriate one, since the book makes explicit that whatever love is, it is not enough to sustain a relationship over an extended period.

Bernard Murstein was a pioneer in the study of love, sex, and marriage (see his 1974 entitled *Love, Sex, and Marriage*), but he also has deferred trying to define love in a simple way. In a definitional piece on love (1988), he reviewed a number of other analysts' deffintions, including:

> Love is the triumph of imagination over intelligence. -H. L. Mencken (in Murstein, 1988, p. 14)

> Love is a substitute for another desire, for the struggle toward self-fulfillment, for the vain urge to reach one's ego-ideal. -Theodore Reik (same reference)
>
> Aim-inhibited sex. -Sigmund Freud (same reference)

Interestingly, Murstein, after reviewing work on different types of love, said, "My taxonomy of love did not lead to the conclusion that there is a useful single definition" (p. 34). Now, are we more enlightened? I doubt it. These definitions cloud further our attempt to provide at least one short definition that can hold up against many qualifications.

As noted previously, Ellen Berscheid was one of the major shapers of the early literature on liking and loving. Her commentary in Sternberg and Barnes' (1988) book *The Psychology of Love* is one of the most cogent statements on the multifaceted nature of love. She said:

> ... love is not a single distinct behavioral phenomenon with clearly recognizable outlines and boundaries. Rather, the genus love is a huge and motley collection of many different behavioral events whose only commonalities are that they take place in a relationship with another person (in that they are caused by and/or affect the behavior of another ...). (p. 362)

The value of Berscheid's point is its emphasis on behavioral events. Too often, scholars who try to define and work with love do not readily operationalize love as involving clear-cut behavior. How can we know about another's love for us lest we have behavioral evidence?

Beyond the contextual and behavioral emphases of the foregoing analyses, the following simple definition by Seymour Epstein's (1993) is compelling: "To love is to derive satisfaction from observing the welfare and fulfillment of the love one.... I know I love you because it makes me happy to see you happy" (p. 109). Implied in this definition is that idea that the lover acts toward the loved one in a way that enhances this satisfaction and happiness.

A final point to consider in defining love is conveyed by Oscar Wilde's famous line that we always hurt the one we love. What does that mean. Coleman (1984) interpreted this line to suggest that love involves a special vulnerability on the part of the lover. We invariably are hurt most by people whom we love. Interestingly, we may be primed for them to hurt us due to a personal history that has involved disillusionment in love, perceived rejection, and lessened hope for the future.

Friend, Lover, and Sexual Partner

Are liking and loving points along a continuum concerning how intensely we feel about another person? Not necessarily. In pioneering work on this distinction, Zick Rubin (1973) provided the seed for later work on typologies of love by trying to distinguish between liking and loving. As an illustration of Rubin's interest in a component analysis of love, he suggested that love was composed of attachment (involving passion and possessiveness), caring (involving giving to other), and intimacy (reciprocal sharing between two people).

Rubin and his colleagues created different scales to measure liking and loving (Hill, Rubin, & Peplau, 1976). An example from their liking scale was: "My partner is one of the most likable people I know." An example from their loving scale was: "I feel I can confide in my partner about virtually everything." In their research, it was found that, as expected, there was a very high correlation (around .80) for responses to items within each scale—suggesting that the items within scales were reliably similar. On the other hand, the correlations between the liking and loving scale items was quite a bit lower—0.36 for females and 0.56 for males. Why were the correlations less similar for females and more similar for males? One argument is that females make clearer distinctions between liking and loving than do males. Although one may develop various reasons to support this difference between females and males, this finding has not been pursued enough in subsequent work and remains quite tentative. A related finding from a study conducted in Australia by Cunningham and Antill (1981) did show positive relationships among liking, love, and a personality trait called romanticism. Again, males showed higher associations among these qualities than did females, augmenting the position that females may be more differentiating among the various states of liking and loving.

Subsequent research on Rubin's liking and loving scales led to some qualifications regarding when they differ. Dion and Dion (1976) asked people in different types of relationships to fill out the liking and loving scales. They found that only casual daters clearly differentiated between liking and loving. Exclusive daters, engaged couples, and married couples revealed less differentiation. This finding makes sense. The more positively involved people become, the more likely they are to report both high degrees of liking (e.g., "he also is my best friend") and loving (e.g., "I don't know what I would do without his love").

Liking versus loving is a dilemma for most people. We want to be liked by and be friends with our lovers. An implicit theory many of us entertain is that we must first like one another and be close friends in order to develop a close relationship. After we become lovers, we hope that our friendship endures and that both it and the love we have together grow in depth and breadth over the course of our lives together. In her (1992) book, *A Book of Self-Esteem: Revolution from Within*, Gloria Steinem suggested the importance in her life of the sequence of friendship to lover:

> The only problem was that, having got this man to fall in love with an inauthentic me, I had to keep on not being myself..... Having for the first time in my life made a lover out of man who wasn't a friend first—my mistake, not his, since I was the one being untrue to myself ... (p. 265)

Many times people are unsure, however, about whether they should cross the line between liking and loving, or between being a friend versus being a lover (the classic question posed in the movie "When Harry Met Sally"). Thus, in these cases, we may preserve a friendship-liking relationship and never know if it could have been successfully turned into love. Some people do cross the line from friendship to being lovers and then successfully return to being "just friends." Indeed, to have at least a few people whom we have liked for an extended period and who have liked us and who are good friends is a great blessing. It may be as much a blessing in terms of social support as to have one good, long-term lover.

What if we become lovers with a person, and yet we are not sexually excited by this person? That too is a fairly common dilemma. It also is a matter that now the judiciary system has addressed. In April, 1993, a California court jury awarded an ex-husband $242,000 in a civil suit against his ex-wife because she never told him in their 11-year marriage that she was not attracted to him sexually—even though she loved him!

Language of Love

In a fascinating study, Meyers and Berscheid (1997) provided empirical evidence on the commonly used distinction between loving another person and being "in love" with that person. It was hypothesized that the number of others in respondents "love" category would be much greater than the number of others in respondents "in love" category. As Meyers and Berscheid note, the language of love matters in our daily interactions. What are the cognitive categories into which we organize people and entities in our world? Neisser (1987) suggests that such categories emerge from the demands of social life and the need to make distinctions in order to communicate coherently. Certainly, most of us have learned in the "game of love" (see further discussion of this idea at end of chapter) that words matter. Meyers and Berscheid had put their finger on the culturally common idea that being "in love" is different than loving others—which so many people blithely attach to various pieces of communication with semi-strangers in their lives.

Meyers and Berscheid's (1997) procedure involved asking 388 students at the University of Minnesota to list all persons in their social worlds whom they believed in the "love," "in love," and "sexual attraction/desire" categories. The evidence collected showed the general predicted effect. Both men and women named significantly more persons as members of the love category than as members of the in love category. The sexual attraction/desire category was in-between these the [sic] former categories in size. Meyers and Berscheid found gender effects with these findings: Women loved more of the people they sexually desired than did men. Women also sexually desired even fewer of the people they loved than did men. Men included fewer people in the love category than did women. What about overlap among categories? The principal type of overlap found by Meyers and Berscheid was that the in-love category refers to people who are both loved and sexually desired. The in love and sexual attraction categories are nested within the larger love category.

Typologies and Styles of Love

As we will see in the following discussions, several typologies of love have been proposed in the last 3 decades. Common concern about these typologies is how well they reflect the processes of loving, and how well they capture changes across time and different relationships in any one person's type/style of loving.

Companionate Love versus Passionate Love

Walster and Walster (1978) and Berscheid and Walster (1978) first explored the idea of companionate love and distinguished it from passionate love. They contended that companionate love involves friendship and desire to be together as its core features. Companionate love becomes very common as people age and as they have experienced different relationships in their relationship careers. Companionate love is theorized to involve a low-keyed set of emotions.

Passionate love, unlike companionate love, is theorized to have a large component of physiological arousal (or feelings of "chemistry"). Couples may combine companionate and passionate love or may emphasize one component more than the other. Passionate love, like romantic love, is theorized to be especially likely to occur early in a relationship. Later, as a couple grows together in their relationship, they may have a solid base of companionate love, but also enough continuing spark to have periods of passionate love as well.

Although for most of us, simple companionship may not do, we nonetheless would be well-advised to carefully consider the value of a mixture of romance, passion, companionship, and friendship in our close relationships. Such a mixture coupled with the dose of reality that comes with experience and careful thinking about relating may offer a great antidote to disillusionment about love that is common when a couple has experienced only romantic or passionate love. Tennov (1979), who has engaged in detailed studies of limerant-romantic love argued that companionate love likely is a far more lasting form of love than are passionate or romantic love.

Passionate love and romantic love often are treated as synonymous in the literature. Table 5.1 provides Hatfield and Sprecher's (1986) listing of the primary components of romantic love, as well as example items from their "Passionate Love Scale:'

TABLE 5.1

Primary Components of Romantic Love

Cognitive Components

1. Preoccupation with the one you love.
2. Idealization of the other.
3. Desire to know and be known by the other.

(continued)

Emotional Components

1. Attraction, especially sexual attraction, to the other.
2. Positive feelings when things go wrong.
3. Negative feelings when things go awry.
4. Longing for reciprocity. (Passionate lovers love and want to be loved in return.)
5. Desire for a complete and permanent union.
6. Physiological arousal.

Behavioral Components

1. Attempting to determine the other's feelings.
2. Studying the other person.
3. Assisting the other.
4. Maintaining physical closeness.

Example Items from Hatfield and Sprecher's (1986) Passionate Love Scale

1. I would feel deep despair if ________ left me.
2. I yearn to know all about ________.
3. I have endless appetite for affection from _____.
4. ______ always seems to be on my mind.
5. I get extremely depressed when things don't go right in my relationship with _______.

Adapted from Hatfield & Sprecher, 1986.

Styles of Love

The sociologist John Lee (1975) was the first investigator to argue that there are styles of love that are analogous to colors (with primaries—eros, ludus, and storge; and secondaries—pragma, mania, and agape). Lee developed this approach based on his research in which he asked people to sort through a large set of cards describing relationships and select the ones that fit their relationship.

Lee's original work has been extended into a major conceptual approach and body of evidence by the Hendricks (1986, 1989, 1992). They have conducted over a decade of work on love styles and how such styles are associated with close relationship events including sexuality. A general assumption is that people do exhibit personality-like styles in their loving behavior. Hendricks developed a love attitudes scale to measure styles of loving. Briefly, these six types of love posited in Lee's work and amplified on in the Hendricks' work are defined in Table 5.2.

TABLE 5.2

Hendricks' Conception of Six Love Styles

1. Eros—This style is characterized by strong sexual desire and intense emotional attachment.
2. Storge—This style is comparable to what is called companionate love (see later) and involves a slow, affection-oriented pace of relating, emphasizing the development of frienship [sic] before love; mutual need fulfillment also is embraced.
3. Ludus—This style is characterized by the term that means "game" in Latin; it is a nonpossessive type of love that typically does not lead to marriage; another focus is on the conquest of a number of sexual partners.
4. Mania—This is an obsessive, jealous, possessive, and dependent style of loving. It is highly stressful and involves many peaks and valleys in emotion (see Tennov's limerant love described later).
5. Pragma—This style is characterized by keen awareness of one's market value and comparison level. Love is maintained for practical reasons.
6. Agape—This style embraces altruism, or unselfish concern for other (see discussion of communal love later). Love is freely given without expecting anything in return; also, this style may involve a spiritual component that focuses on communion and other nonphysical aspects of relating.

Adapted from Hendrick & Hendrick, 1992.

As might be expected, the Hendricks have found that relationships often involve mixtures of these styles of loving. Their work has increasingly moved from love styles in dating relationships to love styles in more advanced, long-term close relationships. Some of their more interesting findings using this approach include:

1. Males report themselves to be more ludic than do females. Why? Maybe it is simply because many males buy into the stereotype about them to be game-players in relationships?
2. Women report themselves to be more storgic, pragmatic, and manic than do men. The Hendricks suggested that women have been socialized to marry both a love partner and someone who can provide economically for them.
3. Men and women score similarly on eros; that is, both females and males believe they are passionate in their close relationships.
4. Eros lovers have been found to be more disclosing to their partners and able to elicit self-disclosure. Eros lovers appear to be sensitive to the important role of communication in sexuality and relating.
5. Ludic lovers score relatively quite high in desire for excitement and novelty. Ludic lovers also have been found to be more extroverted in their behavior.

6. Manic lovers were found to be sensitive and emotionally expressive, but they also showed higher defensiveness, aggressiveness, and neurotic tendencies.

7. For ongoing close relationships, partners have been shown to have considerable similarity on their storge, mania, ludus, and agape scores. Also, in terms of relationship satisfaction, men appear to favor women who are high in eros and agape; whereas, women's satisfaction was unrelated to their partner's scores on eros and agape.

This body of work on love styles has been quite stimulating for research and theory on how people love one another in relatively durable ways. What we do not know at present, however, is how well the ideas would apply to people at quite disparate points along life's continuum. If and when research is conducted with a senior population, will we find, for example, that there are 88-year-old men who still are "erotic" lovers to the day they die? Let's hope so!

Triangular Theory of Love

Robert Sternberg's (1986, 1988) previously mentioned triangular theory of love suggests that there are three major components—intimacy, passion, and decision or commitment—that are arranged at the apexes of a triangle. Intimacy includes sharing emotions and stories with other—it is enhanced by self-disclosure; passion involves erotic interest in other; decision or commitment involves making a decision to stay with other and to defer this type of relationship with others. When all three are present, consummate love exists. That hardly ever happens according to Stemberg. Most of the time, each member of a couple emphasizes one or more of the elements, while the other may emphasize a slightly different combination. To the extent that they emphasize quite divergent positions, the couple may experience problems in relating. For example, it often is argued that men emphasize what Sternberg calls passion, whereas women emphasize what he calls intimacy. If so, either they will converge over time in what they really seek and exhibit, or they likely will have conflict.

Other types of love in Sternberg's conception were: infatuated love (involving high passion but low intimacy and commitment); romantic love (involving high intimacy and passion, but low commitment); empty love (involving high commitment, but low intimacy and passion); companionate love (involving high intimacy and commitment, but low passion); and fatuous love (involving high passion and commitment, but low intimacy).

Sternberg's component analysis has been well-received by close relationships scholars. This conception still requires further empirical attention to determine how partners sharing or not sharing the different love emphases may contribute to satisfaction in their relationships. Fortunately, Sternberg (1986, 1997) has created a triangular love scale that has been shown to be effective in its ability to demarcate the intimacy, passion, and decision components (Acker & Davis, 1992).

Communal Love

This position on love was developed by Judson Mills and Margaret Clark (Clark & Mills, 1979; Mills & Clark, 1982) as an alternative to the idea that equity usually guides interactions among family members and friends. Equity basically means that people in a relationship believe that they are getting from the relationship exactly what they deserve, given their contributions to the relationship (Walster, Walster, & Berscheid, 1978). Mills and Clark perceptively asked, however, why do people in close relationships often remove the price tag from gifts they buy one another? Their answer is that people in communal relationships (as with kin, close nommarital, and close marital) do not always follow the principles of equity in their resource exchanges. Rather, they follow the law of intent and good faith motivation. Mills and Clark argued that in a noncommunal exchange relationship, people give to others with the expectation that their giving will be reciprocated. Not so in a communal relationship. In such a relationship, members assume that each is concerned about the welfare of the other. Each person has a positive attitude toward benefiting the other especially when the other has a need for such a benefit. Members are following what Pruitt (1972) referred as the norm of mutual responsiveness. Mills and Clark further contended that participants in communal relationships are seldom guided by traditional laws of exchange or equity in their feelings for one another. These researchers have developed an impressive body of evidence to support their conception and establish the idea of communal love.

It appears that in many close relationships, communal love is the norm and a chief basis for the satisfaction of the participants. We should not, however, conclude that all close relationships, by definition, are communal in nature. As has been implied in other chapters, a couple may have what in principle is a close relationship without any love or sexual intimacy being exchanged at all; in such a case, indeed they may give to one another on the basis of quid pro quo—giving something of like value in return for an original gift from other. Still another likely scenario in many close relationships is a mixture of communal and quid pro quo exchange. It might be postulated that when a close relationship is highly satisfying to both parties, a lot of communal love in how the relationship is implemented will be displayed in the behavior of both parties.

Exchange Theory and Love

One interesting theory involving love as an exchange approach was developed by Foa and Foa (1974) that emphasizes the "societal structures of the mind." According to the Foas, as part of the socialization process, people learn what is acceptable to give to (or take away from) one another in various types of relationships. Their approach is unique in that it focuses on the content of exchanges. In their view, people give one another status, love, services, goods, money, and information. These resources are seen as ordered on the dimensions of particularism and concreteness. Love, for example, is the most particular resource; it matters a great deal from whom we receive love. Money, on the other hand, is the least particularistic and most concrete resource. The resources of status and services are less particularistic than is love. With regard to our understanding of love, the Foas suggest that people learn that concrete resources such as money should not be given in order to get love. To get love from others, one must give love, or possibly status—which the Foas have shown to be close to love in people's mental maps of relations among interpersonal resources. An intriguing proposition of the Foas' analysis is that when one gives love to other, one receives in return love from the very act of giving, supporting the biblical saying "It is more blessed to give than receive."

Attachment Styles and Types of Love

The last theory of love to be discussed has produced the most research of any approach in the 1990s. It is the simple notion that what happens early in our socialization especially with parents and key caregivers has a reverberating impact on our adult close relationships. The exact nature of this relationship is not clear. However, attachment processes represent one of the most active research areas in the close relationships field entering the 21st century.

Cindy Hazan and Philip Shaver (1987, 1994) developed the provocative idea that people's adult style of close relationship or love is premised on their early attachment experiences with one's parents. "Romantic love" clearly was part of the phenomenon initially conceptualized by Hazan and Shaver. These scholars also suggested that attachment theory may serve as an organizing framework for the close relationships field (Hazan & Shaver, 1994). Their first paper (Hazan & Shaver, 1987) was entitled "Romantic love conceptualized as an attachment process." They proposed that the formation of adult romantic relationships is a biosocial attachment process analogous to the development of child-caregiver bonds during infancy (Bowlby, 1969, 1973). Just as infants can be described as having a secure, anxious/ambivalent, or avoidant attachment to a primary caregiver (Ainsworth, Blehar, Waters, & Wall, 1978), adults can be similarly depicted in their typical approaches to close relationships.

According to Hazan and Shaver's (1987) definition of the adult attachment styles, secure individuals feel comfortable becoming close to and depending on others; avoidant individuals feel uncomfortable becoming close to or depending on others; and anxious/ambivalent individuals have a strong quest to get close others coupled with a fear of abandonment or rejection.

In their early work, Hazan and Shaver (1987) asked people to select the one attachment style that best described their feelings and experiences. About 50% selected the secure style of attachment (i.e., "I find it relatively easy to get close to others and am comfortable depending on them and having them depend on me."). Approximately 25% chose the avoidant style (i.e., "I am somewhat uncomfortable being close to others; I find it difficult to trust them completely, difficult to allow myself to depend on them. I am nervous when anyone gets too close . . ."). Finally, another approximate 20% selected the anxious or ambivalent style (i.e., "I find that others are reluctant to get as close as I would like. I often worry that my partner doesn't really love me or won't want to stay with me.").

In terms of the original ideas and method for studying attachment and close relationships, Bartholomew (1990) and Bartholomew and Horowitz (1991) developed finer distinctions of attachment types and a questionnaire approach to assessing attachment type. Their proposed attachment styles were: secure (generally positive feelings about self and others); dismissing (positive feelings about self but not toward others); preoccupied (anxiety about self but valuing of others); and fearful (negative feelings about self and others). Bartholomew and Horowitz referred to their questionnaire as the "Relationship Questionnaire." Later research testing the value of this questionnaire against other methods for assessing attachment styles is reported by Crowell, Treboux, and Waters (1999).

Since the original work by Hazan and Shaver, whole research programs have been developed based on these attachment theory of love ideas. It has been found that secure individuals experience greater satisfaction in close relationships and tend to report more positive love experiences than do either avoidant or anxious/ambivalent individuals (Fraley & Shaver, 1999). Tucker & Anders (1999) reported that anxiously attached men in close relationships showed consistently lower accuracy in perceiving their partner's feelings. However, this pattern was not found for avoidant individuals.

Fraley and Shaver (1999) report one of their studies in which the attachment styles of couples separating in a public airport were assessed. They found that anxious women were more likely to express distress prior to such separations. Women who had avoidant styles tended to pull away from their partners when separation was imminent. Secure women showed much less of these distress tendencies. Simpson, Ickes, and Grich (1999) reported that highly anxious/ambivalent individuals were more empathically accurate about the thoughts and feelings harbored by their romantic partners than were secure or avoidant individuals. They also reported that 4 months later, more anxious/ambivalent men's relationships had ended relative to relationships for all other groups.

This qualifying work in the late 1990s is stretching the reach of attachment theory and showing many tentacles of association with other variables and processes. Obviously, the theory has been quite stimulating for the relationship field. However, it remains to be seen whether further theory will elaborate successfully aspects of attachment processes both from infancy to adulthood and after people become adult. For example, do early adult attachments also have major impacts on people's later types of love relationships? One piece of evidence was a 4-year longitudinal study by Kirkpatrick and Hazan (1994) that showed that secure respondents who experienced breakups were less likely to remain secure in the future. On the other hand, avoidant respondents who initiated new relationships after breakups were less likely to remain avoidant than were those who did not initiate new relationships.

Perhaps the most daunting continuing challenge for attachment-close relationship work is the question of whether attachment style changes over time (and different relationship partners). To date, there is conflicting evidence on this question. Baldwin & Fehr (1995) reported that approximately 30% of their respondents changed their attachment style classification over a period of time from 1 week to several months; especially likely to change were the anxious/ambivalent respondents. They argue that there may be variability in the underlying construct rather than in the measurement instrument, and that style may depend on relational schema activated for the moment. Davila, Burge, and Hammen (1997) reported that change in attachment style may reflect an individual difference tendency. They found that some women (particularly those similar to women with consistently insecure attachments) were more prone to attachment fluctuations, possibly reflecting earlier adverse experiences.

A related type of challenge is that people apparently remember past adult attachment patterns as similar to their current attachment pattern (Scharfe & Bartholomew, 1998). This finding may reflect the general tendency of people to reconstruct past experiences to be consistent with present experiences (Ross, 1989).

Hazan and Shaver's personality-developmental approach to close relationships is fascinating. One of the major difficulties with the approach, however, is how to establish strongly the link between early experiences with parents and later experiences with adult lovers. Because of its great difficulty in terms of feasibility, thus far longitudinal research has not been conducted that follows people over a significant part of their life course to evaluate links between their early attachment experiences with parents and caregivers and later, adult relationship experiences.

Destructive Aspects of Love

Love is not always a positive human state or emotion. M. Scott Peck, in his well-known 1978 book, *The Road Less Traveled*, argued persuasively that people who love and respect themselves are most capable of loving and giving respect to others. He also suggested that constructive love is not so much something you feel as something you do. How can we expect for others to know that we love them if our actions are not consistent with that sentiment? The following types of love are problematic both for self and other.

Obsessive Love

Tennov (1979) conceived a type of love she called limerance that often involved a high degree of obsession with other. She believed that some people were more limerant than others. According to Tennov, to be more limerant is to be more subject to romantic and obsessive love. Certainly not all romantic people are obsessed with love. It is only when a devotion to romance and a high degree of obsession regarding other converge that the stage is set for destructiveness.

At the heart of obsession is projection, the belief that other entertains the same viewpoint that you do about how much you care for and love other. The sociologist William Goode (1959) made the following statement about this type of projection in love:

> Love is the most projective of drives; only with great difficulty can the attracted person believe that the object ... does not and will not reciprocate the feeling at all. Thus the person may carry the action quite far, before accepting a rejection as genuine. (p. 38)

The following is an excerpted account taken from Tennov's (1979) report of the conclusion of a love affair between a man and the respondent, an obsessed young woman:

> When I found Danny's letter in the mail box, I actually staggered. I was afraid to read it; my premonition was strong. My hands literally shook as I opened it ... It was just one short sentence saying, "Let's call it quits because it's really over for me." It was total, final, the end.
>
> I don't remember how I made it upstairs except that I was in a state of true shock.... I hardly breathed. It was as if, if I remained absolutely. motionless, it would in some magical way not be true.... Then I considered actions ... like going after Barbara (the woman toward whom Danny's interest had shifted) with a knife or throwing myself out the window (p. 147)

Indeed, one of the most hazardous situations involving romantic love is when excessive obsession enters the picture. When a lover is obsessed (as in the movie "Fatal Attraction"), there is a feeling of helplessness and of losing oneself within the other. This latter abandonment of self may occur even when the loved one does not reciprocate and, in fact, is trying to get rid of the obsessed party. Such obsession is not unusual, but it also is one of the most self-destructive tendencies encountered in the close relationship world. It essentially renounces and degrades self and cannot produce a happy outcome for either party. Further, until the obsessed one moves off of this petard of undue regard for other, the individual cannot be a contributing person to the world at large. In some measure, obsessive, romantic love is narcissistic love. In one such scenario, we spend so much time thinking about, directing affective energy toward, and slavishly acting around the loved one that we feel miserable and let everyone know it to an incessant degree.

Tennov (1979) said as much eloquently regarding the obsessive limerent: "Tbe limerant endures painfully intense suffering as daydreams smash against the rocks of events, until hope can only be built from the rubble through interpretation" (p. 61).

Love as Infatuation, Need, and Control

Epstein (1993) analyzed the destructive situations involving infatuation masquerading as love and love as need and control. Just as they sometimes become obsessed with other, people also become infatuated and believe that they are in love. Epstein argued that this form of loving is related to automatic thoughts that often are irrational. It is as if you have just encountered the person whom you have always longed—the person of your dreams. Thus, as in the typical romantic love scenario, you begin to idealize other, and it may be some time before the "real other" is clear to you. Along the way, you convince yourself that you are "in love," whether or not that sentiment is being reciprocated by other and whether or not it is a well-considered decision on your part.

Love as need and control are similarly irrational in their nature. Love as need refers to the frequent belief on the part of the love that he or she cannot do without the other. The other makes you complete. You may feel you cannot live without the other. This state is that of the quintessential form of destructive romantic love. As Epstein perceptively suggested, one cannot attain a secure love relationship if one is not secure enough to relinquish the relationship.

Love as control is the flip side of love as need. In love as control, one expresses his or her insecurity by not being able to love other without trying to control other's thoughts and actions. Domination by one person in the relationship represents a frequent pattern when love as control is being played out. In truth, the person who must be in control is exhibiting anxiety about his or her vulnerabilities in personality or background or some other important domain.

Epstein also noted the control through guilt strategy of some individuals. In this situation, the person tries to keep other bound to him or her through a sense of obligation or guilt. "If you are the right kind of person, you will take care of me and never leave." "Can't you see how much I care about you [which involves the subtext, "You should be ashamed that you cannot appreciate more my care for you."]

As should be clear, love as infatuation or love as need and as control hardly represent love as a positive state of human affairs. Usually, too, these forms of "love" are doomed in that people (most often the persons who serve as objects of the love) will in time try to extricate themselves from the situation, leaving the "needy one" with the task of finding a new object.

Commitment and Love

There has been valuable work directed toward distinguishing commitment and love. Following an influential theoretical analysis of commitment and love by Harold Kelley (1983), Beverley Fehr (1988, 1994) conducted a series of studies designed to probe how commitment and love are similar versus how they differ. One of her studies, for example, asked respondents to list characteristics of these two states. There was some overlap in the characteristics, but there also were key differences. Characteristics that were associated with love centered around the experience of positive affect and emphasized the qualities of caring and intimacy. Characteristics associated with commitment centered around the experience of making a decision and emphasized the qualities of loyalty and responsibility.

Turning to the "real world," we might wonder what writers who give advice about love have to say about how love and commitment are related. In one such commentary, *Chicago Sun-Times* writer Diane Crowley told a writer to her "Dear Diane" column that "Without a commitment, there may be no love." Crowley was responding to a 40-year-old woman's plight of having been dating and relating to a man for 2.5 years with no sign of marriage in sight. Crowley responded:

> What seems to be spooking Ben [the woman's lover] is commitment, which is the next step when you are "in love." Your undemanding relationship has stayed spectacular because you and Ben have maintained a certain distance from each other. Now you want more closeness, but Ben feels squeezed. He wants

> to continue the no-strings-attached arrangement—more than friendship, but less than marriage....
>
> If commitment has become a must-have for you, tell Ben how you feel.
>
> If it's clear that what you've seen is what you're gonna get, it may be time to seek true love elsewhere. (Tuesday, March 9, 1993, Section 2, p. 1)

Crowley's advice is interesting in that it suggests that commitment naturally follows love, and that without such a progression, the lover desiring more perhaps should move on. But how often do people maintain a close relationship and yet desire no marriage-type commitment? In the 1990s, frequently. These same people, however, often indicate that they are making a commitment to one another through their love and other forms of committing behavior (e.g., living together, being known as a "couple"), and that a formal commitment such as marriage is unnecessary.

Commitment

What is commitment? It is a quality that people regularly associate with ideal intimate partners (Fletcher, Simpson, Thomas, & Giles, 1999). In terms of definition, Kelley (1983) suggested that commitment pertains to a person's attitudinal and behavioral indication that he or she will continue in a relationship (as the sayings go, "through thick and thin," "for better or for worse"). However unorthodox a close relationship may be, it would be surprising to encounter many such relationships that did not depend upon perceived commitment for sustenance. Perceived commitment likely depends on various types of behavioral evidence in order for the relationship's participants to believe they are a couple (Beach & Tesser, 1988). As Caryl Rusbult's important work in the 1980s and 1990s (e.g., Rusbult, 1983; Rusbult, Bissonnette, Arriaga, & Cox, 1998) has shown, investments of time and resources contribute to a person's perception of his or her partner's commitment. An engagement ring may symbolize a commitment, but more important to a person in a relationship may be more subtle indications that other's thoughts reflect a committed state.

According to Rusbult's (1980, 1983) formulations on commitment, it may be proposed that feelings of commitment arise from forces that make an individual desire the relationship (i.e., satisfaction), and forces that "lock" the individual into the relationship (i.e., alternatives and investments). Thus, commitment = satisfaction - alternatives + investments.

Fehr (1988, 1999) has conducted one of the most definitive research programs on commitment. She has asked many respondents to generate features of commitment. The prototype features include: loyalty, responsibility, living up to one's word, faithfulness, and trust. She has found that people have elaborate cognitive structures regarding commitment and differentiate commitment in romantic relationships versus commitment in friendships.

Hinde (1979) wrote of the "private pledge" as one process by which commitment develops. This pledge may be an explicit act, such as a promise of fidelity. More often, however, these pledges are part of the implicit unfolding of understanding between the individuals; they are signs of intention to act in certain ways and continue the relationship. Frequently, people look for evidence that their partner will be exclusive sexually and in terms of closeness and will spurn other romantic, close relationship possibilities. Although it seems essential, this criterion may be one for which people often become uncertain as they evaluate their close relationships. Ambivalence may develop about whether, after further review, one's partner is the best one available, or whether one's partner is being faithful. If not worked through in one's thinking and feeling satisfactorily, such considerations can eventually erode a close relationship.

Thus, perceived commitment is a very critical ingredient as most of us conduct our close relationships. What determines perceived commitment? Rusbult (1983) found that global satisfaction with a relationship is one determinant. That may sound circular, because satisfaction should be influenced greatly and positively by perceived commitment. And in nature, these powerful factors likely do have mutual influences on one another. The circularity, if such mutuality deserves that term, is part of the complicated set of rules and processes we must learn to appreciate and seek to understand better.

In a longitudinal study of commitment over a 4-year period, Sprecher (1999) found that unmarried romantic partners who continued their relationships over this period perceived their love, commitment, and satisfaction to increase over time. Sprecher also found that for those whose relationships dissolved, perceived commitment decreased before the breakup; interestingly, respondents did not perceive their love to decrease prior to breakup.

Trust

Trust is vital to a close relationship. Trust is essential for commitments to be made in close relationships. Trust also is necessary for people to engage in what Altman and Taylor (1973) referred to as social penetration. In the process of social penetration, people get to know one another through self-disclosures that increase in depth over time and that tend to be reciprocated by one's partner. Trust, as Kelley and Thibaut (1978) have suggested, is the exchange of actions or messages that over time reduces uncertainty and increases mutual assurance that the close relationship will endure. In one of the most impressive analyses of trust in close relationships, Holmes and his colleagues have examined the dynamics of trust in close relationships and in so doing have developed the concept of trust as a dispositional quality that people have to certain degrees. Rempel, Holmes, and Zanna (1985) developed an 18-item trust scale that covers a range of trust-related experiences. This scale measures a person's perceptions of his or her partner's predictability, dependability, and faith in the future of the relationship.

One finding emerging from this work and reported by Holmes and Rempel (1989) is that high-trusting couples tend to be more positive in their attributions and feelings about their partner's behavior in past conflictual situations than did couples who were low in trust. Holmes and Rempel suggested that high-trusting couples take a more extended perspective on their partner's behavior and do not judge particular actions (e.g., that may be negative for the relationship) out of that extended, and generally positive, context.

Holmes and Rempel also analyzed the typical course of the development of trust in a close relationship. They argued that initially "trust is often little more than a naive expression of hope" (1989, p. 192). Later, however, the extent of trust in the relationship becomes part of its defining fabric. Couples may have a little or a lot. Couples may need regular reassurances regarding their trust, or they may proceed without much continued scrutiny. Couples may test one another on occasion to evaluate the trustworthiness of one another.

We frequently wonder about how to evaluate the commitment of our relationship partners. As an illustration of how to evaluate the trustworthiness of a partner, knowing a partner's past love history may be essential to become trusting and committed. If the potential lover admits that he or she had affairs while married or committed to someone else, does it not follow that you can expect the same thing if you become involved with this person? Such reasoning has some merit, although possibly we often become involved anyway because we believe the excuse offered. "The marriage was over anyway" is a frequent excuse that, if we can buy into it, we then may be able to develop enough trust in other to become significantly involved—although deep in our minds we may continue to mull over the diagnostic likelihood that we too may become victims to other's deceitful behavior.

Of course, often both lovers and their partners are experienced in the "games of love" and each plays a set of cards over the course of the relationship in how they try to influence one another's perceptions. Consider Tereza, Tomas' lover in Milan Kundera's (1984) profound love novel *The Unbearable Lightness of Being* (see also discussion of Kundera's ideas in the sexuality chapter). Tereza recently has had sexual relations with someone other than Tomas and is left with the following quandary over the possibility that she will be blackmailed with a picture of her and the other person in intimate embrace:

> What would happen if Tomas were to receive such a picture? Would he throw her out? Perhaps not. Probably not. But the fragile edifice of their love would certainly come tumbling down. For that edifice rested on the single column of her fidelity, and loves are like empires: when the idea they are founded on crumbles, they, too, fade away. (p. 169)

So much of what we know as both trust and commitment in close relationships may boil down to the "maturity" of the couple. George Levinger (1983) said as much quite well describing the middles of close relationships, as opposed to the beginnings:

> Beginnings of relationships are marked by the partners' experiences of novelty, ambiguity, and arousal. In contrast, middles are accompanied by familiarity, predictability, and the reduction of cognitive and emotional tension. The smoother the

> functioning of a marriage, the less will be the partners' self-consciousness of their ambivalence. (p. 336)

Conclusions

The Hendricks' (1992) final conclusions about love apply well to the foregoing discussion:

> It seems clear that no one volume or theory or research program can capture love and transform it into a controlled bit of knowledge. Love is too complex for that, and even simple questions such as the relation of love to sexuality, cannot be given simple answers.... An ultimate purpose in research on love is to help enrich the vocabulary of love such that everybody will have a more variegated, yet integrated conception of love than has existed in past eras.... If, by promoting the growth of knowledge about love, people can increase the precision of their understanding of love and its meaning within relationships, the opportunity is provided for them to develop and live out more satisfying love relationships.
>
> Romantic love may not be essential to life, but it may be essential to joy. Life without love would be for many people like a black-and-white movie-full of events and activities but without the color that gives it vibrancy and provides a sense of celebration. (p. 117)

We would argue that love for others that is well-conceived and communicated is one of the major positive ways a person can contribute to and connect with other human lives (which is an imposing proposition as we will see throughout this book). Martin Luther King spoke of such a type of love when he said, "Love is the only force capable of transforming an enemy into a friend." This reasoning is similar to another poignant conclusion offered by the Hendricks:

> When we love and are loved in return, we are somehow 'more' than we were before. . . When we are loved in the bestowal sense, without rules or conditions, loved for exactly who we are at this moment in time, then we are somehow free to become closer to what we might ideally wish to be. (p. 117)

> In real love you want the other person's good. In romantic love you want the other person.
>
> *-Margaret Anderson*

Consider this . . .

- As you consider the definitions of love provided in this article as well as the text chapter, what aspect of love do you find most interesting? Why?
- Using the typologies and styles of love discussed in this article as well as the text chapter, identify three intimate relationships in your life that reflect three different types or styles of love. What specific characteristics distinguish these relationships from one another?
- How does Social Exchange Theory provide valuable insight into the study of love and intimacy?
- How does Attachment Theory provide valuable insight into the study of love and intimacy?
- Using the destructive aspects of love discussed in the article as the basis for your analysis, describe a personal relationship in your life that reflected this "dark side" of love. What specific behaviors became destructive to this relationship?

In Chapter 7 of her text, *Relational Communication*, Julia Wood provides an extensive discussion of intimacy in our personal relationships that involves both love (a feeling) and commitment (a choice). Though Wood has no problem discussing the powerful emotion of love, theories that explain and predict intimacy in close relationships often omit a discussion of the specific emotions that create such intimacy. Theory-building often lends itself to explain and predict observable, measurable behaviors; however, feelings are subjective and not easily observed or measured.

In her article entitled, "The Unacknowledged Role of Emotion in Theories of Close Relationships: How Do Theories Feel?", communication scholar Sally Planalp (University of Utah) argues that several theories often used to explore close relationships give little attention to the role of emotions. After making the argument that most emotions can be measured and observed, Planalp writes that it is critical for applications of these theories to incorporate the critical role emotions play in close relationships. Specifically, she explores the use of emotions in the applications of Social Exchange Theory, Dialectical Theory, and Stage Development Theory.

In exploring the application of Social Exchange Theory, Planalp endorses the value of the economic metaphor as a framework for assessing costs and rewards in close relationships. However, she goes on to note the limitations of the theory when personal definitions of these costs and rewards offer little discussion of the emotions that drive our assessments. Since she believes the theory's infrastructure lends itself to a discussion of emotions, as they relate to costs, reward, comparison levels, and comparison of alternatives, Planalp provides valuable insight into how emotions can be incorporated into all aspects of this theory's application.

In exploring the application of Dialectical Theory, Planalp once again confirms the value of this theory to explore the inherent tensions participants negotiate as they seek to develop close relationships. From her initial observation, however, she posits that the theory could be strengthened if it incorporated attention to how feelings move participants toward one pole and away from the other pole of a dialectical tension as well as the simultaneous emotional push and pull between dialectical tensions. Once again, she makes a compelling argument for placing emotions at the forefront of this relational theory.

Finally, Planalp addresses the use of emotions in a variety of models and theories known as Stage Development Theory; these theories often identify specific behaviors that indicate early stages of relationship formation, stages of relationship development and maturity, and stages of relationship deterioration. Once again, Planalp believes that a discussion of how emotions drive participants from one stage to the next, as well as a discussion of powerful emotions typically found within each stage, is critical if we are to understand the development of close relationships.

The Unacknowledged Role of Emotion In Theories of Close Relationships: How Do Theories Feel?

Sally Planalp

Emotion clearly plays a leading role in close relationships and may even direct their development, durability, and dissolution. In theories of close relationships, however, emotion is often given only a supporting role. Recent research in the study of emotion suggests several ways in which existing theories might be enriched by letting emotion into the limelight. Social exchange theory could become more intuitively appealing by incorporating recent research on the role of emotion in decision making. Dialectical theories could be enriched by incorporating emotions that provide feelings of dialectical tension and drive movement between poles. Stage theories of relational development could be elaborated by including how feelings change as relationships develop and deteriorate.

Emotion conceives, develops, and nurtures marriage, and emotion is the only thing that can kill it. (Johnson & Greenberg, 1994, p. 126)

It is the plague of theory and research on close relationships that people use their own subjective experience to peer over our work and keep nagging us to get it right. As a group, scholars have mixed feelings about subjective experience. Some think it is a touchstone for good theory; others think it is a distraction from studying what is truly important objective phenomena. Anyone who does believe that theories must account for people's experience, as well as for researchers' observations, cannot ignore emotion because the overwhelming lived experience of close relationships is that we feel them.

In fact, feeling may be more central than behavior is to what most people mean by relationship. Acting close without feeling close seems more of a travesty of intimacy than feeling close without acting close. Civility leads us to treat our enemies with respect even though we might hate them, but it is the hate that defines the relationship more than the civility, at least to the participants. Interdependence is another well-established hallmark of relationships, but being connected seems to be less important than feeling connected. People who work together on highly coordinated tasks day in and day out but care not one whit for one another (if that is possible) would probably say they do not have a close relationship. Two long-married partners who take each other for granted emotionally have a close relationship, not just because their lives are coordinated, but also because the potential for emotion is immense, ready to be triggered if the routine is disrupted (Berscheid, 1983). If they could walk away from each other without pain and regret, perhaps they weren't really close after all.

It seems that emotion should always have played a prominent role in theories of close relationships, but theories are influenced by the general cultural and scholarly milieu in which they grow up. In 1987 Berscheid claimed that "What is now not known about the role emotion plays in interpersonal communication will someday fill books" (p. 77). The books are beginning to fill. Nowadays emotion is recognized not only as important to scholars (e.g., Andersen & Guerrero, 1998; Lewis & Haviland-Jones, 2000), but also as downright trendy even beyond academics and the literati (Goleman, 1995; Moore, 1992). Some theories give emotion a prominent role, but even those that give emotion a bit part might be enlivened and expanded by introducing more feeling.

There are excellent role models. Attachment theory, for example, integrates emotional, cognitive, social, developmental, and other perspectives on close relationships. Emotion, especially anxiety, plays a key role as the mechanism by which interaction patterns affect individuals and individuals later generate further interaction patterns (e.g., Feeney, 1999; Lopez et al., 1997). Recent work also places emotional understanding and empathy at the heart of marital therapy (Christensen & Jacobsen, 2000). With those models in mind, it may be useful to go back to theories that were developed before emotion research began to prosper and to rethink them in light of what we know about emotion today.

What Is an Emotion?

What are these things—emotions-that we might add to theories? The answer is both intuitively obvious and conceptually arduous. People can easily think of examples of emotions—love, anger, hate, depression, fear, jealousy, happiness, and the list goes on (Shaver, Schwartz, Kirson, & O'Connor; 1987). When the list goes on too far, gray areas start to muddle distinctions between emotion and its cousins—attitude, disposition, physical drive, and the like. The fact that fuzzy boundaries are common (e.g., XXY chromosomes) is small comfort if you want to know what counts as emotion and what does not.

A common solution is to give up on clear boundaries and adopt the prototype approach, which identifies ideal characteristics of members of a category while recognizing that many cases will match the ideal only partially. Prototypes of basic emotions have been described (Shaver et al., 1987), and they have similar components: precipitating events, appraisal processes, physiological changes, action tendencies, expressions or actions, and regulation processes (for review, see Planalp, 1999). A prototypic emotion like anger has all components, but less prototypic emotions like loneliness may not have precipitating events or physiological changes. The two essential components are appraisal—at minimum, positive and negative—and action tendencies, especially approach avoidance (Frijda, Kuipers, & ter Schure, 1989). Together they prepare the organism to assess the environment and act in ways that enhance wellbeing, such as running from danger, approaching sexual partners, or overcoming obstacles (Lazarus, 1991). Theorists differ on precise definitions, but most agree that emotions are evaluative and move people to action (or inaction in the case of depression).

Social Exchange and the Emotional Ledger

The common currency that underlies all of our decisions, and indeed all of our transactions, is not money at all; it is hedonic tone. (Johnston, 1999, p. 172)

To many of us, social exchange theory has always seemed right on and yet never quite right. One source of discomfort is that the monetary metaphor makes us all seem so crass, mercenary, and unfeeling. As Oscar Wilde (1891/1974) said, "Nowadays people know the price of everything and the value of nothing." The same might be said for social exchange theory; it helps us understand the rewards and costs of relationships but not their value. Even Blau, one of the founders of social exchange theory (1964, p. 89), wrote, "People do things for fear of other men or for fear of God or for fear of their conscience, and nothing is gained by trying to force such action into a conceptual framework of exchange." How about the other way around? What would happen if we made feeling or emotion the currency of social exchange rather than, or in addition to, rewards and costs? How would it transform social exchange theory?

With feelings as currency, people would not audit the relational books; they would register the feelings they get from other people. Relationships would not be assessed by computing rewards, like goods or services, and costs, like wasted time and physical discomfort, but rather they would result from experiencing things that promote or detract from well-being, resulting in positive or negative emotions. Some of those experiences might come from commodities, to be sure—tasty goods like cheesecake, enjoyable services like backrubs, but others are less obvious and do not fit the commodity model well. For example, love can be a reward received from another, but it is more fundamentally a feeling that one gets from being with another. Blau agrees: "It is not what lovers do together but their doing it together that is the distinctive source of their special satisfaction" (1964, p. 15). The actual gift is the beloved's mere presence and the love that it engenders—not the love received from the other as a gift.

Although love received from another tends to make the other more attractive, it is not enough. If it were, Jodi Foster would have loved David Hinckley, and there would be no unrequited love (Baumeister & Wotman, 1992). To use a less menacing example, parents do not get much of any useful commodity, much less love, from a newborn child. What they get are good feelings. The physiological substrate of those feelings, neural chemicals such as oxytocin (Taylor, 2002), may be the engines of generalized exchange from one generation to the next (where A gives to B, B gives to C, etc.).

Social exchange theorists recognize, of course, that feelings are related to rewards in some way—either resulting from them, serving as a stand-in for them, or perhaps even being defined in terms of them (if it feels good, it's a reward; if it feels bad, it's a cost). Thibaut and Kelley refer to rewards as pleasures, satisfactions, and gratifications that the person enjoys, and costs include embarrassment or anxiety (1959, pp. 12-13). In a study of interpersonal exchange and sexual satisfaction, for example, common rewards for men were feeling comfortable with your partner, feeling good about yourself (for men), having fun (for men), and among the greatest costs were having sex when your partner is not in the mood (for men) and when you are not in the mood (for women; Lawrance & Byers, 1995, pp. 280-281). In many cases it may be possible to view social phenomena through either the emotional or the social exchange lens (as in the faces-vases illusion), but the emotional framework offers several advantages (Lawler & Thye, 1999).

Feelings Underlie Decisions, Especially Social Ones

Damasio (1999, pp. 43-47) reports a fascinating case of a brain-impaired patient, "David," who had virtually none of the high-level cognitive functioning that would be necessary to compute social exchange outcomes. David could not learn any new fact at all, and he was unable to recognize any new person or remember any event that occurred between himself and that person. Nevertheless, he showed clear preferences for people who treated him well, which Damasio documented in a simple experiment. Damasio arranged for three people to have specific types of interactions with David: One person was pleasant, welcoming, and rewarding; one was neutral; and the third treated David in a brusque manner, denied him any request, and engaged him in boring tasks. When asked to choose "someone you think is your friend," David consistently chose the picture of the "good guy" and avoided the "bad guy" despite having no recollection whatsoever of ever having met any of them. He also showed a brief emotional response (wince and hesitation) when he was being taken to meet with the "bad guy," even though he said nothing was the matter. In other words, David reacted in a way that exemplified social exchange theory, but his reactions stemmed, in Damasio's words, from "the biological machinery underlying emotion [that] is not dependent on consciousness" (p. 43). It seems that costs and rewards register emotionally, presumably not just for David but for everyone (see also, Monahan, 1998).

Feelings Ring True to Experience

We marry people not because we find them rewarding but because we love them. The most common rewards of romantic relationships are companionship, happiness, and mutual love, according to Sedikides, Oliver, and Campbell (1994). We avoid people, not because they are more costly than rewarding, but because they sometimes make us laugh but mostly irritate us. People stay with abusive spouses, not because the rewards outweigh the costs or are better than the alternatives, but because he loves her, because she would be lonely without him, or because one or both are afraid to leave. Few couples, even worldwide, tolerate arranged marriages these days, presumably not because they think the rewards and costs are miscalculated, but because they prefer passionate love (Hatfield, 1999).

Sometimes people do things on impulse, driven by passion, not rational calculation, and sometimes we even admire them for it. Frank (1988, 2002) argues that specific emotions serve as solutions to commitment problems. He offers the example of a thief being tempted to steal a briefcase from someone on a business trip. If the thief could count on the traveler to act out of self-interest, he would know that finding the briefcase would not be worth calling the police, missing a flight, returning to testify, and all the other hassles. If, however, the thief could not count on the traveler to be rational, but instead expected the traveler to get very angry and track him down, the thief might be deterred. Just as anger serves as a commitment to justice beyond self-interest, passionate love serves as a commitment to the investment required to raise a family, even though it might be in one's self-interest to philander. Frank concludes that "on purely theoretical grounds, the commitment model suggests that the moving force behind moral behavior lies not in rational analysis but in the emotions" (2002, p. 196).

Social Exchange Infrastructure Looks Emotional

The key concepts that make social exchange theory work seem to bear a striking resemblance to basic assumptions or concepts in emotion theory. One of the persistent problems of social exchange theory is how to define rewards and costs. Conceptual definitions are hard enough; operational ones seem impossible. Rewards are in the eye of the beholder, and so are emotions. Nothing has inherent value, either in social exchange terms or emotionally, although general trends are apparent. Kindly acts, for example, tend to be considered rewarding or pleasurable, but if they are seen as manipulative or attempts to incur obligations, they are costly and unpleasant. What you feel depends on how you assess or appraise the situation, as a number of theories indicate (Omdahl, 1995; Scherer, Schorr, & Johnstone, 2001). For example, the most basic distinction is between positive and negative appraisals, resulting in positive or negative feelings (i.e., happiness vs. sadness, love vs. hate, or, in SE terms, rewards vs. costs). Unlike social exchange theory, however, emotion theories go on to make distinctions based on intensity (love vs. fondness), control (anger vs. sadness), agency (pride vs. gratitude), urgency (anxiety vs. terror), and a number of other judgments.

Thibaut and Kelley (1959) posit that satisfaction or dissatisfaction with an outcome depends on the comparison level, or the expected level of reward. Similarly, emotions are evoked by violations of expectations (e.g., Mandler, 1984) as a way of alerting the organism to changes that might require attention and action. Yet, emotions save energy by ignoring common patterns. Specifically, positive emotions occur when things go better than expected ("I got three gumballs when I was expecting two!"), negative emotions occur when things go worse than expected ("Drat! Only one gumball!), and little if any emotion occurs when things go as expected ("Okay, two gumballs").

Habituation or adaptation (Berscheid, 1983; Frijda, 1988) occurs when people become accustomed to a situation that would normally produce strong feelings in others, but to them it is emotionally neutral because it is recurrent, such as taking a rewarding spouse for granted or becoming habituated to conflict or even violence. Homans (1974) referred to essentially the same phenomenon as the "deprivation-satiation proposition": The more often one receives a reward the less valuable it becomes (cited in Roloff, 1981, p. 37).

Thibaut and Kelley (1959) also refer to the comparison level for alternatives to explain why one relationship would be chosen over another (see also Chadwick-Jones, 1976, chap. 5). Translated into terms of emotion, your comparison level for alternatives refers to your feelings toward an alternative—a person or your life with that person—including anticipated feelings. You love one more than another, you imagine feeling guilty about leaving the one for the other, you find yourself trying to avoid one but not the other. You may not even make a conscious direct comparison, but instead just gravitate toward one rather than the other without knowing or caring why.

Other key concepts in social exchange theory are interdependence and investment (Blau, 1964; Thibaut & Kelley, 1959). From an emotion perspective, interdependence makes most sense when viewed as how people's emotions (especially their emotional well-being) depend on each other compared to other things in life, such as children, work, or other activities. If two people would be miserable without being together, they would be considered emotionally interdependent even if their behaviors seldom intersect. Similarly, investments in a relationship can be thought of as emotional. People not only tie up resources such as time and energy in relationships, they tie up feelings in the sense that their pleasures and pains over the years have been shared with the other in ways that are irreplaceable. It is not as joyful to reminisce about your child's first steps with a former spouse as it is with a current one. Some investments produce a different and irreplaceable quality of feeling. A new house may not be a home, with all the emotional attachment that the word implies. You are unlikely to be as emotionally open and connected with new friends as you are with old friends. If home and friends must be sacrificed to exidt a relationship, those emotional losses are likely to be anticipated as well. On the other hand, anticipated feelings might pale by comparison to the joys experienced with a newfound guru. The question is whether the decision is made by calculating rewards or by imagining and feeling emotions.

Feelings Spotlight Concerns, Especially Fairness

The evolutionary perspective has been used as an accessory to social exchange theory, adding some biological credibility. Emotion adds even more if we think of emotions as biologically prepared "omens" of life and death (Johnston, 1999, p. 75). Emotions evolved to give us their best guesses about what is good for us, to prepare the body to take appropriate action, and yet to leave enough flexibility to use culture and learning as additional guides. The emotional element also makes social exchange and evolutionary theories feel better. In Johnston's words (p. 88), "These cold biological facts are clothed in the warmth of tender, powerful, and persistent emotional feeling," to which I might add, "These warm biological facts can be chilled by hatred, fury, and the desire for vengeance."

Emotions put the spotlight of attention on concerns that are essential for survival and perhaps even bias our responses to certain perilous situations. For example, emotion theorists talk about "prepared fears," or susceptibilities to fears of a certain kind (Dozier, 1998). It is easy to make people afraid of snakes, large mammals, and closed spaces, presumably because they were real threats in our evolutionary past and may still be today. It is much more difficult to make people fear flowers, smiling faces, and cuddly objects. Like prepared fears, it seems to be easy to make someone love their own child, but hard to make someone love their lover's lover or a stranger. In fact, social relationships may receive more emotional attention than any other aspect of human life because they are absolutely crucial to survival (e.g., see Leary, 2000).

In particular, we seem to be tuned to fairness (Cosmides & Tooby, 1992), as is consistent with social exchange theories (Chadwick-Jones, 1976, chap. 11; Walster,

Walster, & Berscheid, 1978). We respond with strong feelings when fair play is violated, even to the point of self-destructive acts of vengeance (Frijda, 1994). Evolutionary theory would suggest that fairness is so vital to human relations that our emotions have evolved as beacons to help us keep an eye on it. There is too much to lose by being taken advantage of and even by taking advantage, assuming that lack of reciprocity undermines long-term cooperation and even connection (Buunk & Prins, 1998).

Another vital issue is blame. Personal experience tells us that blame packs intense emotional force, but additional evidence comes from an unlikely source. Hupka, Lenton, and Hutchison (1999) analyzed a sample of the world's languages and found that some basic emotion words were found in nearly all languages whereas others were found only in languages with large emotional vocabularies. What were the basic emotions? Anger and guilt. Who is to blame—you or I?

It Is Hard to Ignore Compassionate Altruism

Unselfish acts have always been the Achilles heel of social exchange theory. Social exchange can accommodate altruism only by resorting to the reward value of doing good, but sometimes people take on other people's pain out of compassion (Batson & Oleson, 1991; Eisenberg, 2002). People offer comfort to those who are grieving, not to relieve their own pain, but to try to relieve the pain of others, at least in some cases. It is certainly more rewarding to ignore others' pain, unless we anticipate costs coming later in the form of negative feelings, but that is guilt and we are back to feelings. It is hard to write off Mother Teresa as motivated by the meager rewards she got from alleviating the suffering of others. Surely deep-seated awareness of their suffering (empathy) must be more costly than the self-satisfaction of relieving a bit of it temporarily.

Feelings Are Not Lost When Exchanged

If you take the exchange metaphor seriously, nothing comes without a price. When someone gains, the other loses. With feelings, however, one person may gain while the other loses, but mostly both gain and both lose. In fact, people seem to be naturally so attuned to one another. Newborns transmit distress to one another by crying, and people continue to infect each other with emotions throughout their lives (Hatfield, Cacioppo, & Rapson, 1994). Depressed people bring others down (Segrin, 1998). Laughter can be contagious. Misery loves company (Clark, 1997). Even if we are not susceptible to others' emotional expressions, empathizing with others by imagining their situations seems to be another universal mechanism for sharing feelings (Eisenberg & Strayer, 1987). Shared emotions emerging from interaction seem to be more the rule than the exception.

Discrepancies don't feel right, and we have bad words for those feelings. If we want the pleasure that others have, we call it envy. If we don't want others to have the intimacy we deserve, we call it jealousy. If we don't want others to feel bad when we feel good, we call it sympathy. If we don't want others to feel good if we feel bad, we seek vengeance. Frijda (1994, p. 274) calls it the "law of comparative feeling."

Pleasures and pains are not absolute, but relative. It is more painful when "he walks in pleasure and I in suffering" than when we suffer together. We try to overcome discrepancies with comfort (helping the other feel as good as you do) or revenge (helping the other feel as bad as you do).

Emotion Adds Necessary Complications

One place to find emotion in social exchange theory is when people believe their outcomes are unjust. The simple answer is that if they feel underbenefited they feel angry, and if they feel overbenefited they feel guilty. But is it really that simple? Being underbenefited can result in anger, to be sure, but also in depression, hate, hurt, and resentment (Sprecher, 1986, p. 317; 2001, pp. 490-491) or burnout (Ybema, Kuijer, Hagedoorn, & Buunk, 2002). Being overbenefited can result in guilt if the self is blamed, in hubris if the self is given credit, gratitude if others are responsible, or sympathy if we reflect on others' scarcity. Injustice may result in no feelings at all if it is taken for granted or if it comes to be expected in cases of long-term oppression (Gaventa, 1980). Fairness is not at all simple, and it is very emotional (Solomon, 1994).

Emotion theory also introduces more complications into determining the degree of distress felt when fairness is violated. Again, the simple answer is that the greater the inequity, the more distress is felt and the harder people will try to restore justice (Sprecher, 1998). There seems to be more to it than that, however. We do not see fathers taking over care of newborns for 9 months to compensate for mothers' pregnancies; some inequities are inevitable and therefore do not arouse ire. Other inequities are about concerns that are too trivial to provoke much anger or guilt. In fact, unfairness can be found anywhere; the question is where to spend one's energy. That is where emotion theory can tell us that unfairness will provoke more intense emotions when important concerns are at stake (Frijda, 1986). An emotional charge surrounds housework because on average 1 month per year is at stake—not to mention social identities (Hochschild, 1989). In effect, emotion does triage to elevate important concerns to awareness and keep up the pressure for resolution in a way that social exchange theories cannot explain well.

Clark's distinction between communal and exchange relationships offers either a friendly amendment or a major challenge to social exchange theory depending on how it is interpreted. Acts of reciprocity such as offering a fellow student money in payment for a ride home might be interpreted as either appropriate or insulting depending on how the relationship is defined. Paybacks can backfire if the relationship has moved from "you look out for you and I look out for me" to "we look out for each other" (Clark & Mills, 1979). Emotion seems to play a more prominent role in communal relationships compared to exchange relationships because it signals needs (e.g., expressions of distress) and felt responsibility for those needs (e.g., expression of sympathy; for review see Clark, Fitness, & Brisette, 2001).

One important question is what the mechanism is for an exchange relationship to be transformed into a communal one or vice versa. Clearly there is some way in which the individual ceases being the unit of exchange and the dyad takes over. Self is willing to ignore or even suffer costs if the other or the pair benefit. Why? One possibility is that a large enough reservoir of good feeling has accumulated so that there is no fear of it running dry. Another is that enough trust has been built to alleviate fears of being taken advantage of. Another possibility is that each person has developed empathy for the other so that feelings are shared, not guarded. There is evidence that cooperative situations generate empathy whereas competitive ones generate counterempathy, even schadenfreude (Lanzetta & Englis, 1989). Empathy seems to explain better why helping others improved the moods of people in communal relationships but not those in exchange relationships—it improved the other's mood, hence one's own (Williamson & Clark, 1989)—and why emotion talk was more appropriate in communal than exchange relationships, if the relationship was built on shared feelings (Clark & Taraban, 1991). Still, all three explanations seem plausible.

Dialectical Theory—Torn Between Feelings

In a video on animal emotion (Fleischerfilm, 1999), there is a scene in which an elephant calf is born unable to walk. His mother stays behind with him while the rest of the herd moves on in search of the food that they must have to survive. What is most interesting, however, is that the calf's elder sister, Enid, is in a dilemma. First she stays, then she starts to go off to join the herd, then the calf cries out, and you see Enid spin around and return. She is torn between connectedness with her mother and brother and the autonomy she needs to survive, or perhaps connectedness with the rest of the herd. Her brother's cry seems to tip the balance toward connection. Enid is moved by emotional forces and emotional expressions, not by dialectical abstractions. Her dilemma is not philosophical or cognitive; it is gut-wrenching, even to onlookers.

Dialectical theories could benefit from considering how emotions move people toward one pole, away from the other, and how they experience the simultaneous pull and push in both directions of mixed emotions (VanLear, 1998; Weigert, 1991). The basic social dialectic is between autonomy and connectedness, as Enid's struggle illustrates. We humans have labels for the emotional forces that move us toward connectedness or toward separation and autonomy. In American English, for example, we have proconnection affection, compassion, love, warmth, lust, and loneliness, and anticonnection hostility, hate, shame, hurt, resentment, to name but a few. We also have feelings that do not have convenient labels—relational claustrophobia, social overload, love of being alone, or, in the words of one of Baxter and Erbert's interviewees, "feeling smothered" (1999, p. 562). Fear of intimacy is a good umbrella term for such emotions as fears of exposure, abandonment, angry attacks, loss of control, one's own destructive impulses, or being engulfed (Hatfield, 1984) or "fear of what we might be missing out on because we had been together" (Baxter & Erbert, 1999, p. 563). Comfort with or anxiety over closeness are underlying dimensions of secure, preoccupied, dismissing, and fearful attachment styles (Feeney, 1999).

Theorists have noted that stable cultural orientations toward connection or toward autonomy are reflected in or perhaps operate through emotional orientations and vocabularies. Baumeister and Leary (1995) argued for the need to belong (i.e., connectedness) as a "powerful, fundamental, and extremely pervasive motivation" (p. 497) using evidence from positive, connective emotions (love, joy) but also from negative emotions that result when connections are threatened or broken (anxiety, grief, loneliness, jealousy, guilt; pp. 505-508). Markus and Kitayama (1994) focused on differences between cultures in whether the self was defined as connected to others (interdependent selves) or autonomous from others (independent selves), tracing the implications for emotional orientations. They argue that interdependent cultures foster the more social emotions such as guilt and selfless love, whereas independent cultures foster more individualistic feelings such as pride and anger.

Emotions also move us along other dialectical dimensions that have been studied (Baxter, 1988, Baxter & Montgomery, 1996; Rawlins, 1992). Boredom moves us to seek novelty and excitement, which enhance relationship quality, especially after the initial thrill or the honeymoon is over (Aron, Norman, Aron, McKenna, & Heyman, 2000). There is such a thing as too much excitement as well, but no single word in American English captures the desire for *predictability*—perhaps stress, overload, confusion, or uneasiness. The Ifaluk have a basic emotion category, translated as "the emotions of inability," that occur in situations such as "when the teacher puts an assignment on the board at school, you look at it and feel all three[:] *nguch* [sick and tired, bored], *saumawal* [confused] and *waires* [worried/conflicted]" (Lutz, 1986, p. 274). Uncertainty moves people at least to seek information (Berger & Bradac, 1982), though the driving force is primarily cognitive and does not pack much of an emotional wallop, theoretically speaking.

We move toward openness and expressiveness when we feel curious and excited; we move toward closeness and protectiveness when we feel anxious or threatened. Kennedy-Moore and Watson (1999) discussed at length the emotional forces that underlie tensions between expressing and not expressing feelings. Suppression of strong feeling seems to require effortful control of physiological arousal that can take its toll, but so does active and productive engagement of feelings, and extreme or misguided expression can intensify and prolong arousal (Kennedy-Moore & Watson, 1999, p. 298; Pennebaker, 1997). Believing that feelings are dangerous, wrong, or shameful can lead to nonexpression (Kennedy-Moore & Watson, 1999, p. 208; Rimé, Finkenauer, Luminet, Zech, & Philippot, 1998), but believing that feelings are safe, inherently good, or always right can lead to inappropriate expression, which itself can be dangerous, wrong, or shameful (Planalp, 1999, pp. 116-133).

Interviews with people about their relationships have revealed a number of emotional forces at work. "You feel a lot better just to tell somebody" (Rawlins, 1992, p. 83). "She depended on me—it made me feel good but also made me feel resentful" (p. 126). "He was an obvious choice for that longing or that lack in my life" (Goldsmith, 1990, p. 542). "We had an agreement [to see others] but it was still hard.... I felt guilty" (p. 543). "After we got back he told me he had slept with her and that really blew me away! ... that's when I started feeling threatened" (p. 544). Tracy's interviewees (1994) reported feeling suffocated (p. 8), jealous and threatened (by a rival; p. 10), depressed, angry, resentful (p. 12), fearful of being hurt (p. 14), and on "an exciting emotional roller coaster" (p. 22). Of course, the underlying metaphor describing the push and pull of dialectic forces is "tension," and the tension seems to be not just metaphorical but truly emotional.

Dialectic theory and various theories of emotion also share underpinnings in adaptation level theory, which assumes a point of equilibrium, but a floating, shifting equilibrium that can be reset when circumstances change (Altman, Vinsel, & Brown, 1981, pp. 132-138). Dialectical tensions occur when equilibrium is thrown off, and so do emotions. Frijda (1988, p. 353) articulates the "law of change: Emotions are elicited not so much by the presence of favorable or unfavorable conditions, but by actual or expected changes in favorable or unfavorable conditions" and the "law of habituation: Continued pleasures wear off, continued hardships lose their poignancy."

Emotional forces are not simple, but they are undeniable. Emotional tensions and mixed feelings are undeniable as well, characterized (or perhaps caricatured) by scenarios such as the reluctant groom at the altar, the secret that you want both to reveal and to withhold, the simultaneous excitement and anxiety of a first date. How dilemmas get resolved may depend, not on reflective analysis of tradeoffs, but on which feeling dominates at the time that action needs to be taken. A cry of distress from one's brother, a well-timed question, a reassuring smile can make all the difference.

Stage Theories: Rising Emotional Expectations

Like social exchange theory, stage theories are hard to live with and hard to live without. No one questions that there are fundamental differences among the beginning stages of relationships, their mature and developed forms, and the stages of deterioration, any more than people question the differences between infants, adults, and the elderly. What is arguable is what, if any, natural breaks divide stages, what dynamics move people between stages, what interaction patterns characterize stages, and what makes stages relational instead of individual.

How can emotion help? Emotion probably tells us nothing about whether there are natural breaks between stages except that emotional dynamics tend to be gradual rather than abrupt, arguing against step changes. Emotional forces drive movement among stages, in direct parallel to the ways they drive relational dynamics from social exchange and dialectical points of view. Loneliness, for example, may move people to enter the initiation stage, increase the reward value of interaction, or move toward the connection pole of the dialectic, depending on your theoretical point of view.

It seems unlikely that any single dimension of emotion is sufficient in itself to explain relationship stages (Guerrero & Andersen, 2000), although valence would be the most obvious candidate (Shaver, Schwartz, Kirson, & O'Connor, 1987). Stages of coming together tend to be positive and those of coming apart tend to be negative, but earlier stages of romantic love involve more unalloyed positive feelings (perhaps delusionally so) than more balanced and mature love. During break-ups, feelings are probably more purely negative at the height of disruption than they are when more detachment has been achieved. Similarly, one might expect intensity to follow the same course—increasing monotonically with closeness, but clearly it does not. If it did, we would burn out emotionally after 50 years of marriage. Indeed, emotions are often more intense in shallow and unstable relationships than they are in solidly close ones. We might hold out some hope for mutual emotional involvement, except that long-married couples are able to ignore or avoid each other's most dramatic emotions whereas early daters may hang on every smile or touch. We also know that feelings bounce around as different sorts of turning points produce passion, jealousy, or a host of other strong feelings (Baxter & Bullis, 1986).

Perhaps the bottom line is that as relationships develop, stabilize, and deteriorate, partners recognize that their long-term emotional well-being depends on being connected with or disconnected from the other. Early in a relationship, all that is at stake emotionally is the pleasantness of the encounter, so negative feelings are managed carefully (Aune, Buller, & Aune, 1996); later, being with (or absent from) the other takes on more emotional force. Bonding recognizes that each person's emotional well-being is dependent on an enduring connection with the other; deterioration seems to involve an increasing recognition that they were wrong, that in fact, well-being is enhanced by being separate, most often in increments (circumscribing, avoiding) or perhaps suddenly (abrupt termination). Similarly, emotional effects become more long-lasting at each stage. A promising date might thrill or upset you for a weekend, depending on how it goes, but a promising marriage might thrill or upset you for a lifetime, depending on how it goes.

A central aspect of stage theories such as that of Knapp and Vangelisti (2000) is self-disclosure, although self-disclosure can live independently, theoretically speaking (Petronio, 2000). Emotion generally gets little attention, though it clearly plays a role in guiding disclosure from topics likely to provoke mildly positive feelings, if any at all, to topics with strong emotional potential, especially for negative feelings. High on the list are topics that are deeply personal and potentially controversial (religion and money) and those that reveal personal defects (for example, being a drug addict) and are likely to produce shame, arguably the most toxic of all emotions. The purpose, one supposes, is to build up positive emotional reserves before taking a risk on depleting them, presuming one cares how the other feels at all.

Emotion itself is also a topic of self-disclosure that, on the surface, seems to have some inherent intimacy. Saarni (1999, p. 249) writes that "mature intimacy is in part defined by mutual or reciprocal sharing of genuine emotions." What she probably means are deep emotions, or threatening emotions, or emotions about one's partner. Sharing feelings about colors of paints, or love of ice cream, or dislike of the Secretary of State is probably not a hallmark of mature intimacy. Sharing feelings about your life goals, your greatest sin, or how angry you were when she accused you of not being a good father probably is. In some families, any emotional expressions may be thought to come from the devil (Gottman, Katz, & Hooven, 1997), but surely that is rare. To probe deeper, we might suppose that understanding the emotional dynamics that guide one's own and one's partner's reactions to important events or issues in a close relationship may be vital to mature intimacy in ways that we are just now beginning to understand (Christensen & Jacobson, 2000). Highly developed mutual emotional sensitivity, attunement, empathy, and adaptation do seem to characterize mature personal relationships (Saarni, 1999, p. 267).

An especially interesting issue for stage theories is what makes stages relational rather than individual. Why is it that we can write about friends being in the intensifying stage or romantic partners bonding without asking, "Are they both there?" One obvious answer is that if we are looking only at patterns of dialogue, it will be impossible to separate the two partners' contribution, especially if we use the dyad as the unit of analysis (e.g., Planalp, 1993). A second obvious answer is that often they both are not there. Unrequited love is quite common (Baumeister, Wotman, & Stillwell, 1993), and discrepancies between stages surely are not rare. Nevertheless, discrepancies seem to be the exception rather than the rule. Why?

Emotional discrepancies do not feel good, as argued earlier, and so people coordinate emotionally, both automatically and deliberately. Saarni (1999, p. 259), for example, wrote about the spiral of mutual liking during which one person's expressions of liking are both contagious and reassuring to the other, promoting responses in kind, onward and upward. Downward spirals of mutual disliking no doubt work in the same way in the opposite direction. Conversely, failure to respond in kind emotionally can put a damper on the process in either direction. Beyond primitive reciprocity of expressions, one relational partner may also deliberately play hard to get until love is reciprocated or play "you can't fire me, I quit" when it is not. Unrequited love is hard for the rejected party, to be sure, but also surprisingly hard for the rejecter, whose negative feelings may be more enduring (Baumeister & Wotman, 1992, p. 67).

Partners or potential partners in relationships also seek out or orchestrate shared activities and experiences as a basis for creating shared feelings. Planalp (1999, pp. 61-62) calls this "emotional coincidence" because on the surface each partner appears to be responding independently to a shared experience, but similar feelings are not just coincidental when two people talk over a movie and decide it was disappointing or when one person points out a lovely sunset. Jakobs, Fischer, and Manstead (1997) found that when people imagined experiencing an emotionally evocative situation together with a friend, the feelings they anticipated depended in part on the friend's reaction. If the friend was disappointed in a lottery win, for example, the respondents believed it would dampen their own enjoyment.

People share positive experiences when they can get them, but powerful negative feelings can be relational catalysts as well. Personal crises, natural disasters, and war are notorious for breaking down barriers and creating social bonds as people share feelings and try to cope together. Combat can make a dyad leap from the initiating stage to a lifelong bond in ways that years of sitting at desks side by side can never do. Profound emotional experiences seem to make people jump into the deep waters of emotion and create bonds that come much more quickly and can be as durable as those created by easing in, testing the waters carefully at each step.

Advantages of Giving Emotion a Leading Role in all Three Theories

Emotional processes offer several advantages for theory in general and so apply to all three theories addressed in this article. Adding emotion enhances our ability to test and develop theories and make links to other theories and phenomena they might explain.

Independent Evidence

When emotional processes are incorporated into relational theories, we strengthen the theory by positing a theoretical entity for which we can seek independent evidence. Evolutionary theory was solidified by positing the existence of genes because then it was possible to search for, find, and understand the functioning of DNA separate from the larger processes of reproduction and natural selection. I am not claiming that emotions have the same status in verifiable reality as DNA, but only that a theory is strengthened when important components can be studied and understood separate from the theory for which they were posited originally. There is less risk of finding only what you are looking for or building your theory on an abstract entity that does not exist.

In addition, studying a theoretical mechanism in one domain often yields insights that apply to a new domain. Learning how environmental forces impact DNA, for example, might explain rates of mutation and even lead to better understanding of cancer. In the case of emotion, we might ask why people do things that seem to be so clearly out of character and against their own best interests. No rational computation would lead someone to throw away the long-term, dependable, stable, and diverse satisfactions of wife and family for a "blond bimbo." Then why do people do it? Because the reward value has changed? Maybe. Because other rewards have become more salient? Maybe. Because one is overcome by feelings? Very likely. Thinking is affected by feelings, including selective memory for mood-consistent events and mental lapses due to shame. Similarly, a deeper understanding of how mixed feelings are managed or resolved might also help us to understand how dialectical tensions are managed or resolved, and vice versa.

Influence of External Forces

Emotion also provides a general mechanism by which experiences external to the dyadic relationship influence the relational dynamics explained by the theory. In dialectical theory, for example, emotional processes provide a basis for explaining movement between dialectical poles, but also a mechanism by which external forces can influence dialectical forces within the relationship. A couple may have achieved a comfortable level of autonomy and connectedness, then their children leave home and they are drawn together. Why? Because the loneliness from the loss of the children produces an emotional dynamic that can carry over to the marital relationship. Conversely, being moved from a private office at work to an open office with little privacy might influence relations at home in the opposite way. Someone might gravitate away from connection and toward separation (in dialectical terms) or devalue the usual end-of-the-day discussions with her husband (in social exchange terms). Why? She is feeling a lot more overwhelmed socially and a lot less lonely.

Attachment theory, again, serves as a good role model. In attachment theory, emotional dispositions formed through early childhood experiences provide the mechanism by which later attachment patterns are realized in adulthood (Zeifman

& Hazan, 1997). Emotion serves as the connection between past and future, just as emotion serves as a connection between inside and outside the dyad with social exchange, dialectic, and stage theories.

Generalizability

Emotional processes can be thought of as the common currency of social exchange theory, regardless of the type of rewards and costs—all have affective value. Emotional processes apply to different kinds of economies—not just exchange economies but more communal economies based on needs (Lutz, 1988) and gifts (Hyde, 1979). The economic metaphor is not only limited in its cultural applicability, but it is often blatantly offensive to those who believe that the economic metaphor is applied too widely, even in capitalist economies (Kohn, 1995). It seems to have special offensive capabilities when applied to close relationships.

Emotional processes can also be thought of as the common force moving people between poles of dialectics, regardless of the type of dialectic. Emotions like loneliness and love move people along the continuum of connection-separation, emotions like boredom or anxiety move them along the continuum of novelty-predictability, and so on. Even dialectical tensions such as instrumental-expressiveness might be seen as governed, at least in part, by the presence or absence of emotion. We do not need a new mechanism for each new dialectical tension, although we do need new emotions. Nevertheless, the same emotional infrastructure applies reasonably well to all emotions, even those with no convenient labels (e.g., see Frijda, 1986).

Emotions seem to work in many cultures as ways of understanding close relationships, at least as translated through the concepts of Western anthropologists (Briggs, 1970; Lutz, 1988; Wikan, 1990). They apply to practically the whole domain of human experience, not just close relationships. They apply to other species, as the elephant example given earlier illustrates (see also Masson & McCarthy, 1995).

Emotion as Motivation

Another way that emotion adds to these three theories is to make the link between interpretation and action. It is the hallmark of emotions, in contrast to beliefs, judgments, or thoughts, that they link interpretation to action tendencies (or tendencies not to act). Anger links believing that you have been treated unjustly with tendencies to yell, stomp your feet, and perhaps even attack someone. Thankfully, those action tendencies are not always followed, but usually they are felt. With emotion added to the equation, we know that someone who is underbenefited and angry is likely to take action, whereas someone who is underbenefited and depressed is likely to retreat. From a dialectical perspective, we might add that loneliness can move someone to seek connection in a way that rational awareness of dialectical tensions cannot.

Emotion as Empirical, Interpretive, and Critical

One final theoretical advantage of emotions is that their characteristics are consistent with the basic premises of empirical, interpretive, and critical theory. Expressive and physiological manifestations of emotion can be observed on videotape or with instrumentation, thus providing a solid basis for theory building from an empirical perspective. Emotions are often felt, sometimes quite vividly, and can be reported in varying degrees of detail, thus providing ample evidence for interpretive theories. Finally, and less obviously, as powerful forces for social action, emotions can play an important role in critical theories directed toward social justice (Solomon, 1989) and human well-being (Lane, 2000).

The role of emotion is so essential to social life that it is hard to imagine that the theorists who originated and developed the theories reviewed here meant to give it such a minor role. The larger point, however, is that emotion should be pulled out of the theoretical backstage and put in the limelight in order to enrich our understanding of the entire social drama.

Author

Sally Planalp is a professor in the Department of Communication, University of Utah, USA, and adjunct professor in the Department of Management Communication, University of Waikato, New Zealand. An earlier version of this paper was presented as a part of the symposium on Emotions in Relationships at the International Conference on Personal Relationships, Brisbane, Australia, June-July 2000. Correspondence concerning this article should be addressed to Sally Planalp, Department of Communication, 255 S. Central Campus Drive, Room 2400, University of Utah, Salt Lake City, Utah 84112, USA.

Consider this . . .

- What emotions do you believe are most powerful in the creation of close relationships?
- How do you believe emotions play a vital role in the application of Social Exchange Theory to understand the development of close relationships? Give a specific example to illustrate.
- How do you believe emotions play a vital role in the application of Dialectical Theory to understand the development of close relationships? Give a specific example to illustrate.
- How do you believe emotions play a vital role in the application of Stage Development Theory to understand the development of close relationships? Give a specific example to illustrate.
- Of the three theories addressed by Planalp in her article, which theory do you believe would most benefit from a stronger emphasis on the emotions of close relationships?

References

Altman, I., Vinsel, A., & Brown, B. B. (1981). Dialectic conceptions in social psychology: An application to social penetration and privacy regulation. In L. Berkowitz (Ed.), *Advances in experimental social psychology* (Vol. 14, pp. 107-150). New York: Academic Press.

Andersen, P. A., & Guerrero, L. K. (Eds.). (1998). *The handbook of communication and emotion.* San Diego, CA: Academic Press.

Aron, A., Norman, C. C., Aron, E. N., McKenna, C., & Heyman, R. E. (2000). Couples' shared participation in novel and arousing activities and experienced relationship quality. *Journal of Personality and Social Psychology, 78,* 273-284.

Anne, K. S., Buller, D. B., & Aune, R. K. (1996). Display rule development in romantic relationships: Emotion management and perceived appropriateness of emotions across relationship stages. *Human Communication Research, 23,* 115-146.

Batson, C. D., & Oleson, K. C. (1991). Current status of the empathy-altruism hypothesis. In M. S. Clark (Ed.), *Prosocial behavior* (pp. 62-85). Newbury Park, CA: Sage.

Baumeister, R. F., & Leary, M. R. (1995). The need to belong: Desire for interpersonal attachments as a fundamental human motivation. *Psychological Bulletin, 117,* 497-529.

Baumeister, R. F, & Wotman, S. R. (1992). *Breaking hearts: The two sides of unrequited love.* New York: Guilford Press.

Baumeister, R. F, Wotman, S. R., & Stillwell, A. M. (1993). Unrequited love: On heartbreak, anger, guilt, scriptlessness, and humiliation. *Journal of Personality and Social Psychology, 64,* 377-394.

Baxter, L. A. (1988). A dialectical perspective on communication strategies in relationship development. In S. W. Duck (Ed.), *A handbook of personal relationships* (pp. 257-273). New York: Whiley

Baxter, L. A., & Bullis, C. (1986). Turning points in developing romantic relationships. *Human Communication Research, 12,* 469-493.

Baxter, L. A., & Erbert, L. A. (1999). Perceptions of dialectical contradictions in turning points of development in heterosexual romantic relationships. *Journal of Social and Personal Relationships, 16,* 547-569.

Baxter, L. A., & Montgomery, B. M. (1996). Relating: Dialogues and dialects. New York: Guilford Press. Berger, C. R., & Bradac, J. J. (1982). *Language and social knowledge.* London: Arnold.

Berscheid, E. (1983). Emotion. In H. H. Kelley, E. Berscheid, A. Christensen, J. H. Harvey, T. L. Huston, G. Levinger, et al. (Eds.), *Close relationships* (pp. 110-168). New York: Freeman.

Berscheid, E. (1987). Emotion and interpersonal communication. In M. E. Roloff & G. R. Miller (Eds.), *Interpersonal processes: New directions in communication research* (pp. 77-88). Newbury Park, CA: Sage.

Blau, P. M. (1964). *Exchange and power in social life.* New York: Wiley.

Briggs, J. L. (1970). *Never in anger.* Cambridge, MA: Harvard University Press.

Buunk, B. P., & Prins, K. S. (1998). Loneliness, exchange orientation, and reciprocity in friendships. *Personal Relationships, 5,* 1-14.

Chadwick-Jones, J. K. (1976). *Social exchange theory.* New York: Academic Press.

Christensen, A. S., & Jacobson, N. S. (2000). *Reconcilable differences.* New York: Guilford Press.

Clark, C. (1997). *Misery and company.* Chicago: University of Chicago Press.

Clark, M. S., Fitness, J., & Brissette, I. (2001). Understanding people's perceptions of relationships is crucial to understanding their emotional lives. In G. Fletcher & M. S. Clark (Eds.), Blackwell handbook of social psychology: Vol. 2. *Interpersonal processes* (pp. 253-278). Oxford, UK: Blackwell.

Clark, M. S., & Mills, J. (1979). Interpersonal attraction in exchange and communal relationships. *Journal of Personality and Social Psychology, 37,* 12-24.

Clark, M. S., & Taraban, C. (1991). Reactions to and willingness to express emotion in communal and exchange relationships. *Journal of Experimental Social Psychology, 27,* 324-336.

Cosmides, J., & Tooby, J. (1992). Cognitive adaptations for social exchange. In J. H. Barlow, L. Cosmides, & J. Tooby (Eds.), *The adapted mind: Evolutionary psychology and the generation of culture* (pp. 163-228). New York: Oxford University Press.

Damasio, A. (1999). *The feeling of what happens.* New York: Harcourt Brace.

Dozier, R., Jr. (1998). *Fear itself.* New York: St. Martin's Press.

Eisenberg, N. (2002). Empathy-related emotional responses, altruism, and their socialization. In R. J. Davidson & A. Harrington (Eds.), *Visions of compassion: Western scientists and Tibetan Buddhists examine human nature* (pp. 131-164). New York: Oxford University Press.

Eisenberg, N., & Strayer, J. (Eds.). (1987). *Empathy and its development.* Cambridge, UK: Cambridge University Press.

Feeney, J. A. (1999). Adult attachment, emotional control, and marital satisfaction. *Personal Relationships, 6,* 169-185.

Fleisherfilm, Inc. (Producer). (1999). *Why dogs smile and chimpanzees cry* [videorecording]. (Available from Discovery Channel, 1-800-475-6636 or www.discovery.com).

Frank, R. H. (1988). *Passions within reason: The strategic role of the emotions.* New York: Norton.

Frank, R. H. (2002). Altruism in competitive environments. In R. J. Davidson & A. Harrington (Eds.), *Visions of compassion* (pp. 182-211). New York: Oxford University Press.

Frijda, N. H. (1988). The laws of emotion. *American Psychologist, 43,* 349-3S8.

Friida, N. H. (1986). *The emotions.* Cambridge, UK- Cambridge University Press.

Frijda, N. H. (1994). The lex talionis: On vengeance. In S. H. M. van Goozen, N. E. van de Poll, & J. A. Sergeant (Eds.), *Emotions: Essays on emotion theory* (pp. 263-289). Hillsdale, NJ: Erlbaum.

Frijda, N. H., Kuipers, P., & ter Schure, E. (1989). Relations among emotion, appraisal, and emotional action readiness. *Journal of Personality and Social Psychology, 57,* 212-228.

Gaventa, J. (1980). *Power and powerlessness.* Urbana: University of Illinois Press.

Goldsmith, D. (1990). A dialectic perspective on the expression of autonomy and connection in romantic relationships. *Western Journal of Speech Communication, 54,* 537-556.

Goleman, D. (1995). *Emotional intelligence.* New York: Bantam Books.

Gottman, J. M., Katz, L. F., & Hooven, C. (1997). *Meta-emotion: How families communicate emotionally.* Mahwah, NJ: Erlbaum.

Guerrero, L. K., & Andersen, P. A. (2000). Emotion in close relationships. In C. Hendrick & S. S. Hendrick (Eds.), *Close relationships: A sourcebook* (pp. 171-183). Thousand Oaks, CA: Sage.

Hatfield, E. (1984). The dangers of intimacy. In V. J. Derlega (Ed.), *Communication, intimacy, and close relationships* (pp. 207-220). New York: Academic Press.

Hatfield, E. (1999). Applied affect science. *Emotion Researcher, 13,* pp. 1, 7.

Hatfield, E., Cacioppo, J. T., & Rapson, R. L. (1994). *Emotional contagion.* Cambridge, UK: Cambridge University Press.

Hochschild, A. R. (with Machung, A.). (1989). *The second shift: Working parents and the revolution at home.* New York: Viking.

Homans, G. (1974). *Social behavior. Its elementary forms* (rev. ed.). New York: Harcourt, Brace, Jovanovich.

Hupka, R. B., Lenton, A. P., & Hutchison, K. A. (1999). Universal development of emotion categories in natural language. *Journal of Personality and Social Psychology, 77,* 247-278.

Hyde, L. (1979). *The gift.* New York: Random House.

Jakobs, E., Fischer, A. H., & Manstead, A. S. R. (1997). Emotional experience as a function of social context: The role of the other. *Journal of Nonverbal Behavior, 21,* 103-130.

Johnson, S. M., & Greenberg, L S. (1994). *The heart of the matter: Perspectives on emotion in marital therapy.* New York: Brunner/Mazel.

Johnston, V. S. (1999). *Why we feel. Reading,* MA: Perseus Books.

Kennedy-Moore, E., & Watson, J. C. (1999). *Expressing emotion: Myths, realities, and therapeutic strategies.* New York: Guilford Press.

Knapp, M. L., & Vangelisti, A L. (2000). *Interpersonal communication and human relationships* (4th ed.). Boston: Allyn & Bacon.

Kohn, A. (1995). *Punished by rewards.* New York: Houghton Mifflin.

Lane, R E. (2000). *The loss of happiness in market demcracies.* New Haven, CT: Yale University Press.

Lanzetta, J. T., & Englis, B. G. (1989). Expectations of cooperation and competition and their effects on observers' vicarious emotional responses. *Journal of Personality and Social Psychology, 56,* 543-554.

Lawler, E. J., & Thye, S. R. (1999). Bringing emotions into social exchange theory. *Annual Review of Sociology 25,* 217-144.

Lawrance, K.-A., & Byers, E. S. (1995). Sexual satisfaction in long-term heterosexual relationships: The interpersonal exchange model of sexual satisfaction. *Personal Relationships, 2,* 267-28S.

Lazarus, R. S. (1991). *Emotion and adaptation.* New York: Oxford University Press.

Leary, M. R. (2000). Affect, cognition, and the social emotions. In J. P. Forgas (Ed.), *Feeling and thinking: The role of affect in social cognition* (pp. 331-356). New York: Cambridge University Press.

Lewis, M., & Haviland-Jones, J. M. (2000). *Handbook of emotions* (2nd ed.). New York: Guilford Press.

Lopez, F. G., Gover, M. R., Leskela, J., Sauer, E. M., Schirmer, L., & Wyssmann, J. (1997). Attachment styles, shame, guilt, and collaborative problem-solving orientation. *Personal Relationships, 4,* 187-199.

Lutz, C. (1986). The domain of emotion words in Ifaluk. In R. Harré (Ed.), *The social construction of emotions* (pp. 267-288). Oxford, UK: Blackwell.

Lutz, C. A. (1988). *Unnatural emotions.* Chicago: University of Chicago Press.

Mandier, G. (1984). *Mind and body.* New York: Norton.

Markus, H. R., & Kitayama, S. (1994). The cultural construction of self and emotion: Implications for social behavior. In S. Kitayama & H. R. Markus (Eds.), *Emotion and culture* (pp. 89-130). Washington, DC: American Psychological Association.

Masson, J. M., & McCarthy, S. (1995). *When elephants weep: The emotional lives of animals.* New York: Delacorte Press.

Monahan, J. L. (1998). I don't know it but I like you. *Human Communication Research, 24,* 480-500.

Moore, T. (1992). *The care of the soul.* New York: HarperCollins.

Omdahl B. L. (1995). *Cognitive appraisal, emotion, and empathy.* Mahwah, NJ: Erlbaum.

Pennebaker, J. W. (1997). *Opening up: The healing power of expressing emotions.* (rev. ed.). New York: Guilford Press.

Petronio, S. (Ed.). (2000). *Self-disclosure.* Mahwah, NJ: Erlbaum.

Planalp, S. (1993). Friends' and acquaintances' conversations II: Coded differences. *Journal of Social and Personal Relationships, 10,* 339-354.

Planalp, S. (1999). *Communicating emotion: Social, moral, and cultural processes.* New York: Cambridge University Press.

Rawlins, W. K. (1992). *Friendship matters: Communication, dialectics, and the life course.* New York: Aldine de Gruyter.

Rimé, B., Finkenauer, C., Luminet, O., Zech, E., & Philippot, P. (1998). Social sharing of emotion: New evidence and new questions. In W. Stroebe & M. Hewstone (Eds.), *European review of social psychology* (Vol. 9, pp. 145-189). Chichester, UK: Wiley.

Roloff, M. E. (1981). *Interpersonal communication: The social exchange approach,* Beverly Hills, CA: Sage.

Saarni, C. (1999). *The development of emotional competence.* New York: Guilford Press.

Scherer, K. R., Schorr, A., & Johnstone, T. (Eds.). (2001). *Appraisal processes in emotion.* New York: Oxford University Press.

Sedikides, C., Oliver, M. B., & Campbell, W. K. (1994). Perceived benefits and costs of romantic relationships for woman and men: Implications for Exchange Theory. *Personal Relationships 1,* 5-21.

Segrin, C. (1998). Interpersonal communication problems associated with depression and loneliness. In P. A. Andersen & L. K. Guerrero (Eds.), *Communication and emotion: Theory, research, and applications* (pp. 215-242). San Diego, CA: Academic Press.

Shaver, P., Schwartz, J., Kirson, D., & O'Connor; C. (1987). Emotion knowledge: Further explorations of a prototype approach. *Journal of Personality and Social Psychology, 52,* 1061-1086.

Solomon, R. C. (1989). The emotions of justice. *Social Justice Research, 3,* 345-374.

Solomon, R. C. (1994). Sympathy and vengeance: The role of the emotions in justice. In S. H. M. van Goozen, N. E. van de Poll, & J. A. Sergeant (Eds.), *Emotions: Essays and emotion theory* (pp. 291-31 1). Hillsdale, NJ: Erlbaum.

Sprecher, S. (1986). The relation between inequity and emotions in close relationships. *Social Psychology Quarterly, 49,* 309-321.

Sprecher, S. (1998). Social exchange theory and sexuality. *Journal of Sex Research, 35,* 32-44.

Sprecher, S. (2001). A comparison of emotional consequences of and change in equity over time using global and domain-specific measures of equity. *Journal of Social and Personal Relationships, 18,* 477-501.

Taylor, S. E. (2002). *The tending instinct.* New York: Henry Holt.

Thibaut, J. W., & Kelley, H. H. (1959). *The social psychology of groups.* New York: Wiley.

Tracy, S. J. (1994). *Towards an emotionality of dialectics.* Unpublished paper for graduate seminar on communication and emotion, University of Colorado, Boulder.

VanLear, C. A. (1998). Dialectical empiricism: Science and relationship metaphors. In B. M. Montgomery & L. A. Baxter (Eds.), *Dialectical approaches to studying personal relationships* (pp. 109-136). Mahwah, NJ: Erlbaum.

Walster, E., Walster, G., & Berscheid, E. (1978). *Equity. Theory and research.* Boston: Allyn & Bacon

Weigert, A. J. (1991). *Mixed emotions.* Albany: State University of New York Press.

Wikan, U. (1990). *Managing turbulent hearts.* Chicago: University of Chicago Press.

Wilde, O. (1974). *The picture of Dorian Gray.* London: Oxford University Press. (Original work published 1891).

Williamson, G. M., & Clark, M. S. (1989). Providing help and desired relationship type as determinants of changes in moods and self-evaluations. *Journal of Personality and Social Psychology, 56,* 722-734.

Ybema, J. F., Kuijer, R. G., Hagedoorn, M., & Buunk, B. P. (2002). Caregiver burnout among intimate partners of patients with a severe illness: An equity perspective. *Personal Relationships, 9,* 73-88.

Zeifman, D., & Hazan, C. (1997). A process model of adult attachment formation. In S. Duck (Ed.), *Handbook of personal relationships* (pp. 179-195). New York: Wiley.

CHAPTER 8

MAINTAINING AND REPAIRING PERSONAL RELATIONSHIPS

In Chapter 8 of her text, *Relational Communication*, Julia Wood emphasizes that personal relationships are a "work in progress." Even the most stable personal relationships are continually changing and evolving; as Wood notes, they are "ongoing creations." Because maintaining relationships involves continual negotiation of relational change, this chapter discusses the importance of five everyday processes that help us link our lives to one another: 1) routines for contact, 2) common involvements, 3) patterns of interaction, 4) everyday talk, and 5) reflection. Exploration of these processes only serves to reinforce the conclusion that day-to-day communication in personal relationships provides the critical thread that creates the fabric of our personal relationships.

In her article entitled, "The Everyday Accomplishment of Work and Family: Exploring Practical Actions in Daily Routines," communication scholar Caryn E. Medved (Ohio University) explores the challenges of managing both work and family in our daily lives. Specifically, her study provides concrete examples of the daily interactions that negotiate the divide between balance and conflict related to work and family in our personal relationships. As you read her discussion of these interactions, relate them to the five processes Wood discusses in Chapter 8.

Medved's article begins with a review of literature focused on two primary areas of study that has been explored by researchers over the past three decades — dual-career couples and workplace interactions. From this discussion of communication-based literature, Medved justifies exploring the process of managing work and family responsibilities by viewing communication as a set of practical actions used in the management process. Focusing specifically on the practical actions used by women as they manage work and family responsibilities, she generates two broad research questions: 1) How do women account for the accomplishment of daily work and family routines in terms of practical actions and interactions? and 2) What commonsense rules do women use to account for practical actions and interactions shaping work and family routines?

Using data gathered from interviews with women managing both work and family responsibilities, Medved identifies four practical actions that become "routine" in this process – connecting, alternating, prepping, and reciprocating. In addition, she identifies three practical actions that are "improvised" in this process – requesting assistance, trading off, and evading. To illustrate each of these practical actions, the article provides specific examples of excerpts from the interviews themselves. Finally, Medved discusses the processes of deliberation and negotiation used to restructure practical actions when a new set of behavioral routines. Discussion of these processes provides valuable insight for both men and women as they negotiate both work and family issues in their personal relationships.

The Everyday Accomplishment of Work and Family: Exploring Practical Actions in Daily Routines

Caryn E. Medved

Research investigating the challenges of managing work and family responsibilities has been rife across many social science disciplines over the past 30 years. The following study contributes to the growing body of communication scholarship by problematizing the everyday routine; in doing so, it explores the micro-practices of navigating work and family life. Through the analysis of 35 women's accounts of their daily work and family routines and conflict scenarios, results are reported including the detailing of three superordinate practical action clusters: routinizing, improvising, and restructuring, along with related commonsense rules. Results are then discussed in terms of the relational nature of work. Findings argue for examining how work and family balance and conflict get played out in daily practice. Finally, limitations and future directions a discussed.

Social science research investigating the challenges of managing work and family has been extensive over the past 30 years. Recently, scholars have examined work and family issues from a number of communication perspectives (for a review see Kirby, Golden, Medved, Jorgenson, & Buzzanell, 2003). This study contributes to the growing body of communication scholarship by problematizing everyday work and family routines. In doing so, it richly explores the micro-practices of navigating and negotiating daily work and family life. The purpose of this study is to delineate the actions and interactions embedded in and constitutive of work and family routines at the level of daily practice. This study allows us to see the taken-for-granted daily activities so intimately connected to, indeed constructive of our experiences of balance and conflict. It is argued that meticulous investigation of everyday actions and interactions is essential to communication studies of work and family because it allows for an examination of the relational work embedded in such routines. Further, it demonstrates the fundamentally communicative nature of managing work and family.

First, a review of communication scholarship on work and family issues is presented to situate and provide further rationale for the present investigation. Next, a brief explanation of practical action and commonsense rules per Garfinkel (1967) is presented as sensitizing concepts that guide this study. Results are reported from a study of 34 women's accounts of their daily work and family routines and conflict situations including the detailing of three superordinate practical action clusters. Finally, a discussion of these findings is provided along with study limitations and future research directions.

Literature Review

Two areas of communication scholarship both inform and provide the point of departure for this study: the dual-career couple communication research and investigations of workplace interactions related to work and family issues. Although this review focuses primarily on scholarship published in the field of communication, key sources from the broader work and family studies literature will also be integrated. The review of literature below demonstrates there is a convincing need to explore work and family routines at the level of daily practice and thus, to examine how we carry out the taken-for-granted nature of managing work and family.

Dual-career couples. Communication researchers have created empirically-based typologies of dual career marriages (Rosenfeld, Bowen, & Richman, 1995), explored their decision making patterns (Kruger, 1986), argued that limited research with a communication focus exists across the dual-career literature (Heacock & Spicer, 1986), and speculated about the role of internal structuring in the maintenance of dual-career marriages (Wood, 1986). Levels of self-disclosure (Rosenfeld & Welsh, 1985), along with influence strategy use in dual career couples have also been studied (Steil & Weltman, 1992). Alternatively, Golden (2000) takes a discourse-oriented approach and empirically explores dual career couples' work and family arrangements through interview data. Through an analysis of interpretive repertoires, Golden concludes that participants' accounts contain a noticeable absence of structural rather than personal explanations for work and parenting arrangements. Thus, her findings compel researchers to consider the differential meanings or ideologies underlying work and family accommodations to better inform organizational policy makers.

While this body of research reports that dual career couples engage in various patterns of interaction and that their discourse is revealing of important underlying assumptions, it does not extend our focus to the everyday interactions of dual career couples that comprise daily work and family routines. It also fails to fully explore the nature of such interactions. In other words, we need to examine not just how a particular type of interaction leads to a given outcome or is indicative of particular assumptions, but *how* interaction can also be explored as constitutive of daily work and family routines, as well as revealing of constructs such as gender and emotion.

Hochschild's (1989) exploration of dual career couples in the *Second Shift* provides additional insight, particularly in relation to gender. Hochschild argues that gender strategies or "plan(s) of action through which a person tries to solve a problem at hand, given the cultural notions of gender at play" (p. 15) are partly predicated on our gender ideologies or beliefs and values for gender roles in society. Such gender ideologies are complexly played out in dual career couple interactions.[1] Indeed, women and men in Hochschild's study, at times, articulated a contradiction between their gender ideology and how they actually felt about their enacted marital roles. Thus, shifting ways of making sense in relation to gendered beliefs and perceived options are embedded in a complex process of on-going interaction and sensemaking by dual career couples. That is, "doing" work and family is "doing gender" (West & Zimmerman, 1987). Risman (1998) extends Hochschild's work by arguing that the interactional level of gender "bears heavy responsibility for continuing gender inequity in American family life" (p. 6). As such, it is important to explore interaction in dual career couples as producing and reproducing gendered structures, gendered relations, and gendered work (Rakow 1992). Riseman's (1998) own work, however, treats interaction more so as a context or a set of role expectations rather than as ongoing communicative behaviors or meanings constructed through interaction.

Finally, Buzzanell (1997) also suggests that these relationships are excellent sites for exploring the emotion work embedded in the daily balancing of work and family. She argues from a feminist perspective "that greater attention to emotional labor and emotion work would promote the kind of understanding about women's (and men's) dual career lives that is conducive to fundamental change" (p. 40).

Workplace interactions. In another context, Kirby (2000) explores workplace communication among organizational members regarding policy implementation. Kirby's interpretive study finds that "mixed messages" were often sent by supervisors about the potential use of work and family policies; thus, necessitating personal judgment calls by employers. In addition, Jorgenson (2000) explores how women engineers frame work and family practices. While some frames demonstrated maintenance of the separate spheres ideology, these women's accounts also provided evidence for "frame bending" (p. 11) or other ways of slowly creating social change. Medved and Heisler (2002) explore critical interactions in the university workplace between faculty and students managing work, family, and school responsibilities and found that childcare concerns most often triggered students to initiate negotiations with faculty members, informational support was often lacking on how to manage such negotiations, and faculty members not granting student requests often relied on rules-based or fairness rationales.

Farley-Lucas (2000) investigated women's motherhood talk in the workplace and found that employees perceived talk with co-workers about children as highly valuable. Such talk, Farley-Lucas argues, can enhance support networks and organizational loyalty. Moreover, supervisors who were perceived as supportive by employees allowed "motherhood talk" in the organization. Self-surveillance was also described by participants as operating in contexts where supervisors were viewed as non-supportive or when "subtle or overt discrimination [may] have been enacted in the workplace" (p. 16-17). Interestingly, women recalled editing their own interactions when they perceived that co-workers might judge children's behavior as undesirable.

Finally, two additional studies by scholars outside the field of communication can also offer important insight for this project. More recent work by Hochschild (1997) argues that for some employees, organizational relationships have become a haven from the stresses and instabilities of the family. She argues that what is needed is a "time revolution" where we reconsider the taken-for-granted assumption that "time is money" causing workplace time and relationships to be privileged over family. In addition, Nippert-Eng (1995) examines how our cognitive categories for home and work translate into particular behaviors, including communicative behaviors. It is through these behaviors that we continually negotiate the boundaries between work and home in our everyday lives. Through ethnographic methods,

Nippert-Eng, constructs a continuum of "integrating" to "segmenting" to explain different ways employees enact the boundaries between their work and family lives. For example, one difference between integrating and segmenting was "cross-realm talk" and "style of talk." Integraters were more apt to talk about work at home and vice versa as well as engage in a similar interaction style in both realms.

Research on workplace interaction explores specific messages and types of talk, along with their connections to our understandings of work and family roles. These researchers place communication central to the notions of work and family; yet, we need to purposively examine the nature of everyday actions and interactions that comprise daily routines. Such actions and interactions or micro-practices should be the focus of investigation in and of themselves, not merely as data to explain higher order constructs but as constitutive of the daily accomplishment work and family. It is these daily practices that reveal how navigating and negotiating work and family happens.

Thus, this study situates communication as action embedded in the process of managing work and family responsibilities (i.e., negotiating with a spouse to alter how childcare responsibilities are divided). Interaction is also explored as a regular part of everyday work and family routines; it can be seen as partly constitutive of the routines themselves (i.e., a caregiver is called daily to "check on" a child's needs). Borrowing from the framework of ethnomethodology (Garfinkel, 1967), this investigation strives to make a contribution by exploring the everyday practical actions, including interactions, of daily work and family routines. This investigation is specifically informed by Garfinkel's (1967) concepts of accounting, practical action, and commonsense rules.

This study explores participants' accounts[2] of *practical actions* or those that individuals take "for practical purposes," "in light of this situation," or "given the nature of actual circumstances" (Garfinkel, 1967, p.77). Moreover, "[Slpeaking is one form of action" (Feldman, 1995, p. 11); thus, interaction is one form of practical action key to understanding the accomplishment of daily work and family routines. Finally, commonsense rules are schemes of interpretation or ways of explaining particular actions based on our commonsense knowledge or institutionalized understandings of the world. It must be noted that rules, according to ethnomethodology, are not preexistent, culturally determined norms that are mechanically followed, but "what people use to interpret and chose action" (Feldman, 1995, p. 10).

Thus, given the gaps identified in the literature reviewed above and the guidance provided by the sensitizing concepts of practical action and commonsense rules, two broad questions will guide this effort: How do women account for the accomplishment of daily work and family routines in terms of practical actions and interactions? What commonsense rules do women use to account for practical actions and interactions shaping work and family routines?

Method

Participants

Purposive, network sampling was used to solicit 34 participants from daycare facilities as well as from the researcher's personal networks in two university communities and one large metropolitan area in the Midwest. Participants were all female, married, had at least one child under the age of five, and worked a minimum of 30 hours per week in paid employment outside the home. The average number of children reported by interview participants was 1.74 (range 1 to 4) and the average age of children was 4.43 years (range 6 months to 12 years). Racially, this sample was homogeneous, with only one non-Caucasian participant. The average salary for the women participating in this study was $36,000 annually while the average combined spousal income was $74,500. Participants can be seen to reflect a broad range of organizational experiences, however, given the criteria for hours worked, this sample is not inclusive of women only able to secure part-time, intermittent paid employment, or unemployed. Over 43% of these women worked in jobs traditionally classified as hourly or non-exempt positions, i.e., administrative assistants, hourly supervisors, technicians. Another 47% of the sample worked in jobs traditionally classified as professional or managerial, i.e., doctor, lawyer, manager, professor.

Interviewing Procedures

Interviews for this study were semi-structured and questions asked women to describe a "typical day" of balancing work and family in a time-ordered sequence, including: morning routines, evening routines, division of household labor and childcare responsibilities. In addition, participants were asked to describe a situation when they had difficulty balancing work and family. Interviews were conducted at either participants' homes or offices and were carried out in a casual, informal style. Interviews lasted between 45 and 90 minutes, averaging around 60 minutes.

Analysis Procedures

Interviews were transcribed verbatim with the cumulative length of transcript data totaling over 600 pages.[3] Transcripts were reviewed for accuracy by comparing audiotapes to segments of transcripts. Transcripts were first read with a broad understanding of the concept of practical actions and with particular attention to interaction in daily routines and conflict scenarios. Preliminary inductive categories of practical actions were developed through early readings. Then, as categories developed, transcripts were more specifically coded for particular practical actions and interactions (Miles & Huberman, 1984; Patton, 1990).

In the course of inductively developing specific categories, logical ways of grouping or organizing these particular micro-practices emerged out of this analytic process. Women talked about the nature of their actions and interactions in relation to time, not just a given day or week, but over the course of years as punctuated by particular life events such as different work situations or family structures. It was this temporal language that provided insight into the data leading to the construction of three superordinate clusters of practical actions and interactions[4]: (a) routinizing (constitutive of daily routines), (b) improvising (constitutive of ways of managing interruptions to these routines), and (c) restructuring (the process of reorganizing existing routines into new "ways of doing" work and family) (see Table 1). It should be noted that the categories of routinizing and improvising, respectively, include actions and interactions that constitute an identifiable, ongoing "routine" or, at times, a fleeting but recognizable "improvisation" to this daily routine. Restructuring, alternatively, constitutes a process, thus interactions embedded in sequences of (restructuring daily routines are illustrated through subcategories.

Descriptions of particular actions and interactions within each superordinate cluster were further explored for commonsense rules or schemes of interpretation that participants used to justify enacting particular micro-practices. Commonsense rules often took the form of implicit and explicit "cause-effect" statements about actions justifying why, for example, a particular spouse always picked up the children after daycare. For coherence of reporting results, rules are discussed in relation to particular subcategories of practical actions and interactions. Women provided different commonsense rules for enacting similar practical actions. An attempt is made through this analysis to illustrate this variety and maintain the fragmentation in these data.

Coding Assumptions. This analysis illustrates one possible representation of these data (Bochner, 1985; Reissman, 1995). Alternative readings of these transcripts, indeed alternative categories, could be produced. These categories were not constructed to be exhaustive or mutually exclusive, but representations of how these women make sense out of their everyday lives through the process of interviewing. Replicability is not an assumption of this analysis.5 "Facts and interpretations require and shape one another" (Steivers, 1993, p. 421). The validity of this analysis should be judged by its usefulness, plausibility, truthfulness (not "truth"; see Feldman, 1995), and unique contribution to communication research on work and family issues.

TABLE I

PRACTICAL ACTIONS AND INTERACTIONS OF WORK AND FAmiLy ROUTINES

Routinizing Actions	***Definition***
1. Connecting	A daily interaction between spouses or with a caregiver to "check in" on the daily routine or inquire about care.
2. Alternating	Spousal actions and interactions to trade off performing particular childcare behaviors on a routine basis.
3. Prepping	A nightly action that serves the purpose of getting ready for the morning routine the night before, i.e., packing lunches or setting children's clothing out.

(continued)

4. Reciprocating	Actions and interactions exchanging childcare services with family members or friends on a routine basis.
Improvising Actions	***Definition***
1. Requesting Assistance	Asking for help or social support on a temporary or short-term basis.
2. Trading Off	Actions and interactions spouses engage in alternating who takes off work during a childcare emergency.
3. Evading	Interactions altering or withholding information from a work colleague or spouse to manage an interruption.
(Re) Structuring Actions	***Definition***
1. Negotiating	Interactions where one party perceives an incompatibility of goals thus offers particular proposals in an attempt to restructure a routine.
2. Deliberating	Interactions consisting of a conscious process of weighing alternatives, considering options, and making decisions in an attempt to restructure a routine.

Results

Routinizing Practical Actions

First, routininzing practical actions are those that are a part of carrying out daily or reoccurring household, paid work, and childcare duties. Repetition of these actions and interactions constitutes a particular daily routine. Routines were articulated as quasi-permanent instantiations or ways of doing work and family for a given period of time; reoccurring social practices. Four key routinizing practical actions were identified:

- connecting
- alternating
- prepping
- reciprocating

Connecting. Connecting was explained as an interaction that checked in on or coordinated childcare activities. Connecting was accounted for across a number of different relational contexts and sites for interaction. For example, Peggy, a communications coordinator with one son who worked for a large retailer, explained that she and her husband regularly communicated from the workplace late in the afternoon to coordinate daycare pick up responsibilities. "We usually make arrangements to talk to each other about 4:00." Connecting was described as a phone call and even as face-to-face interactions. Deanna, a tray line supervisor and mother of two explained:

Excerpt 1:

R: He [her husband] stopped in [to her workplace] and said, hey, I'll be off by 3:00 so I'll grab the kids.

I: He came into work and told you this?

R: Yea, he stopped at my work ... so he picked up the kids and when I got off at 4, I called and made sure he was there. Called my parents, Chris there? Yep, just walking in the door. I said, okay, I'll talk to him at home, just wanted to make sure the kids got picked up.

Deanna's language depicts the web of relationships that maintains the structure of her work and family routine. The coordination of tasks through connecting was how women often described orchestrating everyday activities and support (Hochschild, 1989).

In addition to connecting as a way to manage or monitor children's "drops offs" and "pick ups," women also talked about connecting with caregivers during the day or at the start or end of the day to "check in" on childcare. Annie, a production scheduler and mother of one child explained, "[I] call throughout the day [from work]. I call twice a day; once in the morning, once in the afternoon to see how she's doing." Annie explains her connecting was a strategy for ensuring her child's needs are met during the day. Samantha, a research consultant and mother of one also described herself as being conscious of the process of spending time talking with her in-home daycare provider each day when she drops off her son. Samantha justified her action in terms of a direct tie between the relationship she had with her care provider and the quality of childcare:

Excerpt 2:

R: and I have made it a point to get to know Kelly and her children, because my thinking is, I want them to like my son more than any other kid there.

Through Samantha's language we can also see how she tries to manage her identity during the interview. Later, she acknowledges that her logic may be negatively perceived or as she explains, "may sound crass," but then provides an alternative explanation for her behavior in that she has genuine fondness for her caregiver.

Alternating. Alternating responsibility for particular childcare activities on a routine basis in the home is the second category of practical action that emerged through women's accounts. Language such as "we alternate," "we take turns," and "we switch around" was used to describe the nature of sharing of childcare activities in the relational context of marriage. Jeny, a nurse and mother of two, explained how they alternated performing particular childcare tasks through emotional and pragmatic the commonsense rules:

Excerpt 3:

R: Well and a way it is part of the partnership thing again, you know, we both love the kids and we both have things we need to do and so one of us will do a little project for a little while and the other one will watch the kids and then we'll switch. And you know, take turns and ...

Tracy, a lawyer and mother of two, explained that evening baths and bedtime routines were alternated each night and, interestingly, the routine was even maintained through interaction with their children, "The kids are fully aware of it and they'll say, well, it's dad's turn 'cause you did it last night." At times, husbands' participation in alternating childcare was attributed to the "exceptional" personal qualities of men. Tracy explained her husband's willingness to alternate by justifying that he was "just more evolved" than other husbands. Other participants used language such as "better than your typical husband" or that he was "really a partner."

Prepping. Preparing for the next day's activities the night before was another essential practical action also accounted for by women (e.g., packing lunches, setting children's clothing out). Peggy's language is characteristic of this practical action: "Well a typical day actually begins the night before and I find that it is critical for me to know what I am going to wear the next day...." This action occurred alone at home, not in concert with a relational partner or care provider. Prepping was often explained or justified as a way to make the morning "easier" for women and for their husbands. Betsy, a budget specialist and mother of two explained:

Excerpt 4:

R: But what I find most important in the morning is everything is all laid out. Before I go, before my husband and I are down everything is out. The kid's clothes are out. Their backpacks are packed, what they need in there. I find that if I don't I don't have that extra time in the morning so I'm in big trouble.... We just have to, he flips on the coffemaker and that's going while he's getting ready.

Hochschild's (1989) work might alternatively explain that women at times attempt to "protect" spouses from the stress inherent in daily routines by adapting their own schedules or doing gendered work (Rakow, 1992). Natalie, a medical sales representative with two children, however, explains a different reason for doing the same practical action. Natalie describes her "prepping" through a gendered commonsense rule:

Excerpt 5:

R: [During] the night time I will usually have the kids clothes laid out because he just doesn't like getting things coordinated. And, I want her looking pretty, so that's my job.

In Natalie's explanation, we see how her assumptions about appropriate gender roles become explicit in her explanations of everyday actions.

Reciprocating. The practical action of exchanging childcare services on a periodic basis with friends and extended family members was another important component of some participants' work and family routines. This action was predicated on the other individual being in the position to "return the favor" in a similar manner. This practical action was described as "swapping" or "trading" childcare services. Bethany, a program coordinator and mother of two explained that the way her and her husband find time alone is to "swap" childcare with friends:

Excerpt 6:

R: we do go out on date nights, we swap with our friends.... To swap a couple of times with our friends umm and unfortunately we can't go out with those friends cause we're always swapping with them.

Bethany's language reveals the tension between having friendships that allow for the reciprocation of childcare, but the challenge of maintaining these relationships given the nature of this support. Tia, a church education director and mother of one also explains that they share childcare with mothers of their son's friends, "we trust these women a lot and so we trade around with them quite a bit ... sometimes we'll watch their son and vise versa." Tia uses the language of "trust" in her explanation for reciprocating childcare. These friendships allows [sic] for a comfortable and acceptable form of sharing of childcare responsibilities.

Improvising Practical Actions

Improvising practical actions are those that participants accounted for when perceived short-term interruptions to a routine occurred. Improvisations were temporary "ways of doing" daily routines made necessary to solve an immediate conflict, but previously established patterns of routinizing actions were assumed to return. The actions below constituted an improvisation lasting for only an afternoon, a day (daycare closed for holiday) or might have spanned as long as a week or even a period of months (daycare provider on vacation for a week or kids out for summer).

Women explained that particular interruptions beget improvising actions, for example: sick children not able to attend school or childcare, temporary loss of daycare arrangements (closed instutionalized daycare due to bad weather conditions or home daycare provider not available), personal emergencies (sick parent), and occasional last minute changes in work scheduling. Events may have been anticipated, thus allowing for time to set up an improvisation or may have been an unanticipated event requiring last minute arrangements. Three improvising practical actions emerged from this analysis: requesting assistance, trading off, and evading.

Requesting assistance. Interactions that ask for assistance or social support on a temporary or short-term basis were coded as "requesting assistance." Requesting assistance was often accomplished through asking for temporary help from supervisors and co-workers for work accommodation and from family members and friends for childcare assistance. Different than reciprocating, requesting assistance did not presuppose the regular exchange of services or even the potential for exchange. Betsy explained requesting assistance for time off from her boss:

Excerpt 7:

R: I can say, look. This is what I have on my plate right now. Next week my mom is going on vacation. You know she watches Jamie and I don't have anybody to take, you know, my husband would not get paid if he took it off and so we decided it would be best for me, and she's like, no problem ...

She further explained feeling comfortable making such a request because of the perceived similarity between her and her supervisor. Betsy's boss also had children, she explained, "so she understands." This relational commonsense rule was often found in women's accounts of requesting assistance from supervisors or co-workers when the need for an improvisation arose. Ironically, one supervisor's unsupportive behavior was described as inexplicable and confusing because, as one participant explained "although she is a working mom herself doesn't seem very sympathetic to those things."

Many women also accounted for requesting assistance from individuals from within their family and personal networks. Grandmothers, in particular, were often asked for assistance. Peggy, for example, explained that when she had to work late, she would call her mother and ask her to pick up her son and start dinner. Peggy explained, "its kind of sneaky" but requesting assistance in this manner was a way to manage her spouse's expectations. In another example, Janice, an administrative assistant and mother of one, realized one evening that she would not able [sic] to stay home from work if her son remained sick the following morning. She explained that she asked her mother for assistance first and found that she could only take care of her son in the afternoon, she continues:

Excerpt 8:

R: So, I called my mother in law, can you watch my kids until 1:00? Then, my mother can pick them up at 1:00 and she'll take them to my house, but they have to be there, I'll have to bring them to you at quarter to 7 because I have to be at Shop Rite at 7:15 and Dennis can't do it cause he's got a job to do, he doesn't get sick time in his job. . .

Janice needed to make multiple requests for assistance. She explained her practical actions through her relational commonsense rule. She also justifies her action because of her spouse's lack of "paid sick time." Financial considerations as commonsense rules were often used to justify both requesting practical actions and the trading off practical actions that are explored below.

Trading off. In addition to requesting assistance from work colleagues and family members, the practical action of "trading off" was also often described in women's accounts. Different from requesting as described above, this practical action took place in the relational context of marriage when spouses took turns staying home from work to manage childcare needs. Often, these interactions were recalled as brief and relatively easy ways to coordinate emergency care. At times, however, trading off was also explained as a more tension-filled, even argumentative interaction. Regardless of the nature of the interaction, trading off was most often explained in relation to childcare emergencies.

Carey, a VP of Finance and mother of two described quick interactions to coordinate emergency care. She justified the trading off with her spouse as a function of levels of flexibility in their two jobs and an attempt to "balance":

Excerpt 9:

R: You know, he's a little more flexible I guess as far as taking days off... He probably takes a few more off. We try to balance it out. You know, if he took when they're sick then I'll take the next one if I can.

Thus, implicit or explicit agreements to go back-and-forth when emergency situations arose were evoked in women's talk about trading off. Women also explained and justified choices again through financial considerations. "If I don't work, I don't get paid" explained Christine, a beauty salon owner and mother of two. If Christine were to solely shoulder the responsibility of emergency childcare, it would result in financial loss to the family.

Linda's account of trading off begins to describe the potential challenges that may come with this improvision. Linda, an HR Generalist and a relatively new mother at the time of the interview described:

Excerpt 10:

R: Probably the biggest piece that's hard to balance is when she's sick and can't go to daycare. Then it's, there's horrible tension of whose turn is it. Who went last time. Who's going to take her to the doctor. We know we want to stay home with her but we both have things at work that we know we can't just drop suddenly ...

While Linda's account of trading off hints at the difficulty of managing temporary childcare responsibilities, Cali's description captures how trading off can be tension filled and problematic. Her mother normally provided full time daycare for Cali's young daughter while she worked as a budget specialist at a local university, but was unavailable for care one week during the summer:

Excerpt 11:

R: This was the time we had to call friends at 10:30 at night and that was hard. We got into an argument at 10:30 at night saying, I'm just going to stay home. No, I'll stay home. Call the neighbor. No! I'm not calling the neighbor. Go over to the neighbors. No! So, that was kind of, trying to find a babysitter.

At times, interactions described with language of anger and negative emotions were reported triggered by unanticipated changes in established routines. Focusing on emotion in the context of dual career couples, even negative interactions, furthers our understanding of dual career couple's work and family experiences (Buzzanell, 1997).

Evading. Finally, the practical action of evading in a particular situation was also accounted for as one type of improvisation. Evasions, in these data, took the form of altering or withholding particular types of information. Although perhaps not perceived of as a constructive communicative behavior, participants described this action as [sic] practical way of managing their work and family routines at certain times.

Linda explained that in a previous discussion with her supervisor, she was honest about her use [sic] a personal day for the care of her one-year-old daughter. She described that her boss, in response to her request, had questioned her need to take the whole day off and reminded her that they "were very busy." Similar to Farley-Lucas's (2000) work on self surveillance, Linda felt betrayed by her boss's comment and explained future plans to evade:

Excerpt 12:

R: And in terms of a strategy I thought next time I'm either just gonna tell her or I hate to say this, I'm just gonna lie and I know a lot of people do it because they don't like the hassle and, you know, you hate to make something up but if I'm going to get a hassle then ... I'll just call in sick that day, how's that, you know.

Peggy also described her use of "strategic ambiguity" (Eisenberg, 1984). If she needed to stay at work late, her husband routinely asked exactly what time she would be home. She explained, "I always say I don't know. Because if I tell him two hours, he expects me to be home in two hours ... I say, I don't know." Peggy made sense out of her own deceptive behavior as a way to manage her spouse's expectations when temporary alterations to their routine became necessary.

Restructuring Practical Actions

The superordinate clusters of routinizing and improvising were elaborated upon through the provision of subcategories of actions and interactions that constituted either an identifiable, ongoing routine or, at times, a fleeting but recognizable improvisation to a daily routine. Restructuring practical actions are categorically different. Restructuring actions constitute a process[6] leading to a new set of routinizing behaviors. Thus, we focus our attention on interactions that are embedded in this process, not necessarily constitutive of a particular structure.

The process of restructuring was explained in these data to be triggered by perceived "permanent" changes in daycare arrangements, changes in work situations (loss of employment, change of schedule, change of job), children's changing developmental needs, or the birth of a new child. Events triggering the process of restructuring routines could be interpreted as relational/family turning points per Baxter and Bullis (1986). Participants described multiple iterations or various times where their regular routines for work and family dissolved through the process of restructuring then eventually re-emerged as a different set of routinizing behaviors. Through the process of accounting, participants' attempt to make their own reorganizing of routines overtime appear ordered and logical. As Natalie described, "well, we've had three different situations." Two restructuring practical actions that participants accounted for were deliberating and negotiating.

Deliberating. When describing the process of reconstructing ways of doing work and family routines, some women talked about a series of steps taken in the decision-making process. Deliberating practical actions were accounted for as a conscious process of weighing alternatives, considering options, and making decisions. Ellen, a VP of Operations and mother of two, recalled the process of restructuring triggered by her frustrations upon returning to work immediately after her first son was born. She explained:

Excerpt 13:

R: And, so we sat and talked about it. We actually got up at 3 in the morning one morning ... so, we actually went downstairs and powered up the PC and went through a decision support process and said, okay, what are all

> the alternatives ... I could drop out of the workforce, you could drop out of the workforce. I could go part-time, you could go part-time.

Ellen's description of practical actions clearly demonstrates a process of deliberation over alternatives. They attempted to rationalize a process of decision making by laying out potential options. Ironically, Ellen explains further that although their rational decision making criteria led them to one decision, they chose another option. She explained: "What's real interesting is, you know, your feelings, your gut feel and everything was completely different than what the quantitative data showed and I can't explain that to this day."

Betsy also described a situation where she and her husband sat down to weigh alternative courses of action. After Betsy's husband bad been laid off from his job, he stayed at home full time with their daughter but the birth of their new son trigged a period of restructuring by deliberation. She explained:

Excerpt 14:

> R: It took some thought and planning between my husband and I. My husband stayed home a year and a half with our son because we were so concerned about the daycare issue and the cost and how this was gonna work. Was he just going to be working for the daycare and things ... so we, we really had to sit down and think about how we were going to do this and if it was cost-effective to put 'em both in daycare and things.

Betsy and her husband, she further explains, weighed issues of daycare cost, her husband's need to work, and opportunities for social interaction for their children.

Negotiating. Another restructuring practical action described in women's accounts of work and family routines was that of negotiating. At times of restructuring, women may have perceived an incompatibility of goals arise in interaction. Negotiating was the described as offering proposal or alternatives as ways of coming to a shared solution. Ellen explained a situation where she negotiated with her spouse about their roles. Her husband had quit his job and was at home with their two children during a weather emergency. He was unable to contact her at work, she recounts:

Excerpt 15:

> R: We have this new infant son, you know, and um, he called and called and couldn't get a hold of me ... And you know, he was fuming ... I said. . I can't be in the demands of this job and I can't be in your demands too. So, I'm willing to go to my manager and tell him I want a lesser job ... [but] we need to talk about how much of a pay cut I can take as a result of that, but if this is your role, this is and if I need to stay in this position because we want to keep the income, then we can't have this where you get upset because you can't get a hold of me.

While Ellen and her husband negotiated broad sets of behaviors, other participants described more informal, regular negotiations that occurred during a period of restructuring. Linda explained how their daily routine was restructured after the birth of their daughter:

Excerpt 16:

R: We, almost every night we would say whose turn is it?

I: Kinda check in there.

R: Yeah, and then we would joke and say, I'll pay you $5,000 if you take care of her tonight.

I: Right.

R: So we tend to just remind ourselves, you know, who's on schedule and we sometimes do get into scorekeeping though like I gave her a bath two nights in a row and so then we try to talk about it again and rebalance.

Deliberating and negotiating both represent micro-practices or practical actions and interactions that constitute the process of restructuring work and family routines.

Discussion

Calling a spouse at the end of the workday, stopping to have a conversation with a daycare provider in the morning, or setting out a child's clothing at night are all inconspicuous activities and interactions too mundane for social inquiry, one might argue. These taken-for-granted micro-practices, however, were accounted for by the participants of this study as ways they navigated the everyday accomplishment of their work and family lives. It is through these everyday actions and interactions that we get a glimpse of the practices that constitute work and family balance, or alternatively conflict. Detailing these practical actions and organizing them into the clusters of routinizing, improvising, and restructuring provides two important insights for communication scholarship: (a) relational work as practical action and (b) reframing key concepts through practical action.

Relational Work as Practical Work and Family Action

These women connected, reciprocated, requested, prepped, and even evaded in the ongoing maintenance or improvisation of work and family routines. They deliberated and negotiated when establishing new routines. Doing work and family must also be explained as doing relationships, not just taken-for-granted as a function of time management or organizational policies.

Hochschild (1997) discusses the concept of the "third shift" or what she labels as the relational work performed during early mornings or late evening hours with tired children often resistant to their parent's scheduled use of time. These data, however, demonstrate other types of relational work also central to maintaining of the "first" and "second" shifts. Connecting, for example, was articulated as the everyday relational work though [sic] which women orchestrated daily routines or attempted to ensure quality care. Reciprocating was explained as fostering relationships that would allow for the exchange of childcare services. Indeed, the relational work that goes into maintaining social support is persuasively illustrated in these data. Although past work has explored how the existence of social support can have psychological benefits as well as positive outcomes for physical and mental health (see Shinn, Wong, & Oritz-Torres, 1989 for a review), these data demonstrate the relational work needed maintain [sic] social support as well as relational stress that may result from not having support.

Gender and relational work. Above, the argument is put forth that the accomplishment of daily work and family management can be richly understood through investigating the relational work embedded in daily routines. In a parallel manner, West and Zimmerman (1987) put forth a definition of gender as "a routine accomplishment embedded in everyday interactions" (p. 125). Thus, we can also examine how these participants are "doing gender" through the practical actions and commonsense rules. Although the research questions of this study did not set out to explore the gendered nature of practical actions we would be remiss to not acknowledge gender in this discussion.

Connecting, for example, could be interpreted as a way for women to perform the gendered role of childcare even in their absence, similar to the outsourcing role that working mothers often play (Hochschild, 1997). Furthermore, Ruddick's (1989) work on maternal thinking argues that mothers often engage in the connecting work that binds key relationships in a child's life. Here we see this gendered relational concept in action in daily practice. Fletcher (1999) also talks about gender, power, and relational practices in the workplace, one of which is preserving or "activities intended to preserve the life and well-being of the project by taking on tasks that would protect it from harm" (p. 49). One way that women in Fletcher's study engaged in preserving activities was to connect with other project team members thus, acknowledging that relationships were essential to the project's success. Similar to Samantha's recognition that her relationship with her caregiver was important to her child's well-being, women in the paid labor force also connect with others for various emotional and instrumental reasons. Interestingly, Fletcher laments the lack of value placed on such relational work in the organization. That is, women are paradoxically expected to provide this type of relational work while simultaneously devaluing or "disappearing" it in the organization. By extension, the devaluing of domestic work shapes how we assess the worth of routine domestic work or care labor such as connecting, reciprocating, and prepping (see Medved & Kirby, 2002).

Emotion and relational work. In addition to the embeddedness of gender in practical actions, hints of emotion and emotion work in participants' accounts also must be noted. Buzzanell (1997) tells us that while emotional labor refers to the management of feeling in the workplace for pay, emotion work in the private context shapes how dual career couples also experience and make decisions surrounding work and family (see Hochschild, 1983; Goffman, 1959). Emotion has not often been explored as key to understanding work and family experiences. In the descriptions of these participant's practical actions, however, we see glimpses of the emotion filled interactions of work and family.

Connecting, for example, can be interpreted as an example of how emotional responsibility gets enacted as a part of daily routines or is a part of the experience of managing interruptions (DeValut, 1991; Hochschild, 1997; Hood, 1986). Stressful, tension-filled interactions, in particular trading off or negotiation interactions were recalled by participants that provide clear illustrations of the emotion embedded in, or arguably constructed through (Harré, 1986) the relational process of managing work and family. Cali recalls a heated argument while Linda remembers a moment of "horrible tension." While vivid examples of negative emotions were culled from these data, women also described positive emotions such as love and caring.

Reframing Key Constructs

Oftentimes the extant work and family research uses the terms conflict and balance in a broad, even ambiguous manner. For example, with the exception of the marital division of labor research (see Pleck, 1985; Crouter, et al., 1987), ironically, work and family conflict is often not explored in relation to interaction. Intra-psychic definitions of conflict are often relied upon (see Kirby et al., 2003); for example, we experience a feeling of conflict because of time, emotion, or behavioral constrains (Greenhaus & Beutell, 1985) or events such as a sick child are labeled the cause of conflict. While psychologically-based definitions of conflict and balance are useful, the findings of this study would argue for further examination of how these concepts get played out, indeed constructed and reconstructed in the micro-practices of daily work and family routines. Concepts such as balance and conflict must be conceptualized as everyday accomplishments and investigated at the level of daily practice.

Furthermore, the categories of routinizing, improvising, and restructuring reveal that both conflict and balance are dynamic. Routines get established through repeated actions and interactions, interruptions to routines occur thus creating the need for an improvisation, and eventually, through a process of restrucuturing new routines get re-established. A trigger such as job loss, promotion, or a new child might beget the process of restructuring or, alternatively, repeated improvising might also provide the impetus for deliberating or negotiating. The process is not always smooth, linear, nor necessarily purposive; however, it is surely one of ongoing action, interaction and sensemaking.

Limitations and Future Directions

In closing, limitations of this study must be carefully outlined. Shortcomings of this analysis are explored in relation to the nature of the sample and the type of data collected for this project. These limitations will be explicated below then further developed as points of departure for future research.

The nature of the actions and interactions outlined here as comprising the daily accomplishment of work and family, even the commonsense rules used to justify these practices are clearly a function of the women who participated in this study. All participants were married, primarily white women with access to full-time employment. For example, the very existence of a practical action such as trading off is only made possible by through [sic] marriage. Requesting assistance is predicated on the existence of family or friends available as social support. The nature of work and family routines for single mothers, for example, would certainly reflect a different set of practical actions and interactions. Smith (1993) argues for moving away from the Standard North American Family (SNAF) model and incorporating diverse voices in work and family research.

Future research needs to explore micro-practices that would constitute the routines of single mothers, single fathers, divorced parents, and more broadly incorporating the lives of people of color, gay and lesbian individuals, and the working poor. Furthermore, this study inadvertently perpetuates the equation of family equals children. Individuals balancing work and responsibilities for elders, close friends, or partners should also be the focus of the study. Future research needs to explore more fully parents' interactions with children surrounding work (see Galinsky, 1999; Ritchie, 1997). While broadening study samples is important, the very concepts of balance and conflict need to be further critiqued from the positions of class and race (see Wilson, 1996).

In addition to exploring a more diverse population of women, these data are also limited in the lack of inclusion of men in this study. A discussion of gender in relation to work and family routines is severely limited without knowing how men would account for routines or explain their actions through commonsense rules. Most certainly, having comparable data from men would provide a richer set of data for investigating the gendered nature of work and family routines. Perlow's (1997) work provides a framework for future research in relation to this limitation. In daily diaries produced [sic] both male and female employees, Perlow demonstrates the ways in which women's days are shaped more significantly than men's by duties outside of work. Thus, if men were included in the present study, what types of practical actions would they describe? For example, would "connecting" be a part of their daily routine?

In addition to exploring data from other voices, future research also needs to use additional methods of data collections such as participant observation, shadowing, diaries, or focus groups to explore the nature of daily routines from other perspectives (see Hoschschild 1989; 1997; Fletcher, 1999; Nippert-Eng, 1997; Perlow, 1997 for examples of more ethnographic work and family research). Interview data provides valuable recollections and sensemaking of past and current work and family routines but it does not elicit the descriptive data of that, for example, structured observation could provide. Fletcher (1999) shadows organizational members throughout the work day recording action and interactions then brings her observations back to participants and focus groups for explication. This combination of methods could be used to study parents managing work and family for further development of the micro-practices and commonsense rules brought forth in this study. In addition, such methods should also incorporate longitudinal designs. Admittedly, not an easy task, but diary methods, overtime participant observation and interviewing can all contribute data for continuing analysis of work and family routines.

Finally, while beyond the scope and framing of this analysis, these data could surely be reinterpreted through feminist frameworks on gender, emotion, and power. Fletcher's (1999) poststructuralist feminist framework could be adopted to examine power through routinizing, improvising, and restructuring and potentially reveal "how what we think of as commonsense definitions or natural self-evident truths are actually reflections of dominant cultural assumptions" (p. 5) about work and family routines.

Notes

1 Communication in marital couples has been extensively studied by scholar Mary Anne Fitzpatrick (1998). Her typology of marital couples is based on three dimensions: interdependence, communication, and ideology. Based on these three dimensions, individuals are then placed into relational categories: traditional, independent, and separate. Different types of couples, for example, may enact conflict in their relationships differently. Although this qualitative study does not utilize Fitzpatrick's Relational Dimensions Instrument (RDI), future research could explore practical actions in relation to couple type per this categorization scheme.

2 The present exploration of work and family borrows concepts from Garfinkel's (1967) framework of enthnomethodology as a routine to understanding how women construct order or make "account-able" their daily work and family routines. This study does not, however, claim to be conducted following the strict or traditionally "radically descriptive" assumptions of this paradigm per the "documentary method of analysis." Rather, this study employs interview data to explore the accounting process in which knowledgeable actors engage in articulating and justifying their activities.

3 Extended versions of the excerpts included in this manuscript can be viewed at: www.class.uh.edu/comm/commstudies/index.html.

4 This analysis does not assume Husserl's standards of "objectivity" or undifferentiated experience; there is no attempt here to directly describe experiences. Instead, the act of accounting in these interviews takes participants outside the flow of discrete experience. The interview process, in this way, fosters attention and recollection necessary to the turning of acts into "meaningful experiences" (see Schutz, 1967, especially chapter 2).

5 This study explores currently existing work and family routines. While it would be useful to explore, this study does not focus on how initial routines come into existence.

6 Interestingly, participant's accounts also described "failed attempts" at restructuring of routines. For example, a number of women described trying to reorganize their routines to regularly include a spousal "date night" or one late work night each week, but were unsuccessful in consistently establishing this routine action.

Consider this . . .

- As you reflect on the literature review presented in this article, what do you consider to be some critical issues that individuals confront as they negotiate both work and family?
- From your own experience negotiating work and family responsibilities, discuss a specific example to illustrate a practical action that has become routine for you. How do these processes relate to those discussed by Wood in Chapter 8?
- From your own experience negotiating work and family responsibilities, discuss a specific example to illustrate a practical action that you improvised. How do these processes relate to those discussed by Wood in Chapter 8?
- From your own experience, discuss a specific example to illustrate the process you used to restructure a routine typically used to negotiate both work and family responsibilities. How successful was your restructuring process?

- How does Medved's discussion about the routines of practical actions used to address work and family responsibilities relate to Rules Theory?

References

Baxter, L. A., & Bullis, C. (1986). Turning points in developing romantic relationships. *Human Communicatio Research, 12,* 469-493.

Bochner, A. P. (1985). Perspectives on inquiry: Representation, conversation, and reflection. In M.L. Knapp & G. R. Miller (Eds.), *Handbook of Interpersonal Communication* (pp. 27-58). Beverly Hills, CA: Sage.

Bogdan, R., & Taylor, S. J. (1975). *Introduction to qualitative research methods: A phenomenological approach to the social sciences.* New York: Wiley.

Buzzanell, P. M. (1997). Toward an emotion-based feminist framework for research on dual career couples. *Women and Language, 20,* 40 - 48.

Crouter, A. C., Perry-jenkins, M., Huston, T. L., & McHale, S. M. (1987). Processes underlying father involvement in dual-earner and single-earner families. *Developmental Psychology, 23,* 431-440.

DeVault, M. L. (1991). *Feeding the Family: The social organization of caring as gendered work.* Chicago: University of Chicago Press.

Eisenberg, E. M. (1984). Ambiguity as strategy in organizational communication. *Communication Monographs, 51,* 227-242.

Farley-Lucas, B. (2000). Communicating the (in)visibility of motherhood: Family talk and the ties to motherhood with/in the workplace. *The Electronic Journal of Communication/La revue Electronique de Communication, 10* (3). Available http://www.cios.org/ejcrec2.htm

Feldman, M. S. (1995). *Strategies for interpreting qualitative data.* Thousand Oaks, CA: Sage.

Fitzpatrick, M.A. (1988). *Between husbands and wives: communication in marriage*, Newbury Park, CA: Sage.

Fletcher, J. K (1999). *Disappearing acts: Gender, power, and relational practice at work.* Cambridge, MA: The MIT Press.

Galinsky, E. (1999). *Ask the children: What america's children really think about working parents.* New York: Morrow.

Garfinkel, H. (1967). *Studies in ethnomethodology.* Oxford, UK: Polity Press.

Goffman, E. (1959). *The presentation of self in everyday life.* New York: Anchor Books.

Golden, A. (2000). What we talk about when we talk about work and family: A discourse analysis of parental accounts. *The Electronic Journal of Communication/La revue Electronique de Communication, 10* (3). Retrieved April 7, 2003, from http://www.cios.org/www/ejcrec2.htm.

Greenhaus, J. H. & Beutell, N. J. (1985) Sources of conflict between work and family roles. *Academy of Management Review, 10,* 76-88.

Harré, R. (Ed.) (1986). *The social construction of emotions*, New York: Blackwell.

Heacock, D. & Spicer, C. H. (1986). Communication and the dual career: A literature assessment. *Southern Speech Communication Journal, 51(3),* 260-266.

Hochschild, A. R. (1983). *The managed heart: The commercialization of human feeling.* Berkley, CA: University of California Press.

Hochschild, A. R. (1989). *The second shift.* New York: Avon Books.

Hochschild, A. R. (1997). *The time bind: When work becomes home and home becomes work.* New York: Metropolitan Books.

Hood, J. C. (1986). The provider role: Its meaning and measurement. *Journal of Marriage and the Family, 48,* 349-359.

Jorgenson, J. (2000). Interpreting the intersections of work and family: Frame conflicts in women's work. *The Electronic Journal of Communication/La revue Electronique de Communication, 10 (3).* Retrieved April 7, 2003, from http://www.cios.org/www/ejcrec2.htm.

Kirby, E. L. (2000). Should I do as you say, or do as you do? Mixed messages about work and family. *The Electronic Journal of Communication/La revue Electronique de Communication, 10 (3).* Retrieved April 7, 2003, from http://www.cios.org/www/ejcrec2.htm.

Kirby, E. L. Golden, A., Medved, C. E., Jorgenson, J. & Buzzanell, P. M. (2003). Exploring organizational communication problematics for empowerment: Challenging and revisioning the discourse of work and family research. P. Kalbfleish (Ed.), *Communication Yearbook, 27,* 1-44.

Krueger, D. L. (1986). Communication strategies and patterns in dual-career couples. *Southern Speech Communication Journal, 51(3),* 274-281.

Medved, C. E., & Heisler, J. (2002). A negotiated order exploration of critical student-faculty interactions: Student-parents manage multiple roles. *Communication Education, 51,* 105-120.

Medved, C. E., & Kirby (2002). *From having the "most important job in the world" to being a "Family CEO": A contradiction-centered postmodern feminist analysis of the corporate framing of stay-at-home mothering.* Paper presented at the National Communication Association Convention, New Orleans, LA.

Miles, M. B., & Huberman, M. (1984). *Qualitative data analysis: A sourcebook of new methods.* Beverly Hills, CA: Sage.

Nippert-Eng, C. E. (1995). *Home and work: Negotiating boundaries through everyday life.* Chicago, IL: University of Chicago Press.

Patton, M. Q (1990). *Qualitative evaluation and research methods, second edition.* Newbury Park, CA: Sage.

Pleck (1985). *Working wives/working husbands.* Newbury Park, CA: Sage.

Rakow, L. F. (1992). *Gender on the line: Women, the telephone, and community life.* Urbana, IL: University of Illinois Press.

Risman, B. J. (1998). *Gender vertigo: American families in transition.* New Haven, CT: Yale University Press.

Reissman, C. K. (1993). *Narrative analysis.* Newbury Park, CA: Sage.

Ritchie, L. D. (1997). Parent's workplace experiences and family communication patterns. *Communication Research, 24,* 175-187.

Rosenfeld, L. B., Bowen, G. L., & Richman, J. M. (1995). Communication in three types of dual-career marriages. In M. A. Fitzpatrick & A. L. Vangelisti (Eds.), *Explaining family interactions* (pp. 257-289). Thousand Oaks, CA: Sage.

Rosenfeld, L. B., & Welsh, S. M. (1985). Differences in self-disclosure in dual career and single-career marriages. *Communication Monographs, 52,* 253-263.

Ruddick, S. (1989). *Maternal thinking: Toward a politics of peace.* Boston, MA: Beacon Press.

Schutz, A. (1967). *The phenomenology of the social world.* Evanston, IL: Northwestern University Press.

Shinn, M., Wong, N., Smiko, P. A., & Oritiz-Torres (1989). Promoting the well-being of working-patents: Coping, social support, and flexible job schedules. *American Journal of Community Psychology, 17,* 31-55.

Smith, D. E. (I 993) The standard north american family: SNAF as an ideological code. *Journal of Family Issues, 14,* 5065-5085.

Steil, J. M., & Weltman, K. (1992). Influence strategies at home and at work: A study of sixty dual career couples. *Journal of Social and Personal Relationships, 9,* 65-88.

Steivers, C. (1993). Reflections on the role of personal narrative in social science. Signs: *Journal of Women in Culture and Society, 78,* 408-425.

Thompson, A. J., & Walker, A. J. (1989). Gender in families: Women and men in marriage, work and parenthood. *Journal of Marriage and the Family, 57,* 845-871.

West, C., & Zimmerman, D. (1987). Doing gender. *Gender & Society, 1,* 125-151.

Wilson, J. W. (1996). *When work disappears: The world of the new urban poor.* New York: Vintage.

Wood, J. T. (1986). Maintaining dual-career bonds: Communicative dimensions of internally structured relationships. *Southern Speech Communication Journal, 57,* 267-273.

In Chapter 8 of her text, *Relational Communication*, Julia Wood discusses the importance of both maintaining and repairing our personal relationships. While the prior reading focused on processes used to maintain relationships, this reading focuses on relationship repair after a major transgression – the breaking of a relational value or rule. As Wood notes, when participants in a personal relationship encounter such an abrupt disruption, they must first decide whether they will repair the relationship; if they decide to repair, then they must decide how to repair.

In her reading entitled, "When Partners Falter: Repair After a Transgression," communication scholar Tara M. Emmers-Sommer (University of Arizona) begins with a discussion of both relational maintenance and repair. From this initial discussion, she focuses her discussion exclusively on relational repair. Emmers-Sommer identifies two types of transgressions (social and relational) that prompt relational repair; she then discusses these transgressions as a single event or a series of events that occur over time. Finally, Emmers-Sommer explores the feelings of embarrassment, guilt, and shame often experienced by the offender since these feelings may impact the repair process.

After providing an understanding of transgressions, Emmers-Sommer then moves her discussion to relational repair strategies. Specifically, she identifies various types of repair strategies, explores factors that influence their selection, and assesses the impact of their use. From this extensive discussion, Emmers-Sommer offers concrete suggestions about how to approach the process of relational repair following a major transgression.

Finally, Emmers-Sommer concludes her reading by discussing two specific directions for future research about relationship maintenance and repair. First, since relationships develop over time, she suggests that more attention be given to strategies that are most effective during specific stages of relationship development. For example, what repair strategies are most effective during the early stages of relationship development and what repair strategies are most effective during the later stages of relationship development? Second, with the proliferation of online relationships, Emmers-Sommer suggests that this new relationship genre provides fertile ground for exploration of all aspects of relationship maintenance and repair. If online relationships develop differently, Emmers-Sommer suggests that we may need to explore different maintenance and repair processes as well.

When Partners Falter: Repair After A Transgression

Tara M. Emmers-Sommer
University of Arizona

Maintenance and Repair

One might wonder why a chapter addressing relational repair exists in a book on maintenance in close relationships. Indeed, a close relationship with an intimate partner is something that many people strive for as it brings fulfillment to their lives (Duck, 1988). Similarly, many theories and models of relational development address closeness as a desired product in our relationships (e.g., Altman & Taylor, 1973). In a word, individuals value and cherish their close, personal relationships. It seems to follow, then, that examining the maintenance of such valued relationships is in order. And, it is necessary to examine relational repair within those very same close, personal relationships. In fact, it might be somewhat more necessary to examine repair in close relationships, in part because people tend to treat close relational partners more poorly than they treat complete strangers (e.g., Birchler, Weiss, & Vincent, 1975). Thus, a seeming paradox exists: If we value and cherish our close relationships, why would we threaten their maintenance?

According to Miller (1997), several sources of ammunition exist that influence individuals' engagement in undesirable, adverse behavior toward their relational partners. These sources of ammunition, if you will, include use of intimate information against the partner, learning undesirable information about the partner, the erosion of illusion about the partner, the loss of novelty, reduction of maintenance strategies in the relationship, interdependence, loss of gains from the relational developmental period, and exclusion. Miller (1997) furthered that additional elements can fuel negative behavior in close relationships. For example, the interjection of culture might affect behavior adversely if partners hail from different cultures with different cultural values and goals. If opposing goals exist, conflict is likely to ensue. Similarly, individual differences such as differences in personality reflected through varied levels of assertiveness, aggressiveness, or self-esteem (to name a few) between the partners can affect behaviors negatively. Given that partners do not always treat one another well, the focus of this chapter is the processes of relational maintenance and repair in close, personal relationships.

As the truism states, "if it ain't broke, don't fix it." Indeed, within ongoing close relationships, the process of maintaining is often not so clearly recognized as when partners are not maintaining, when aspects of the relationship are broken, distressed, challenged, or the like than when the relationship is stable. This truism, however, implies that relationships are self-sustaining and effortless, and that effort is not necessary until a problem arises. This assumption is problematic, as lack of effort to maintain a relationship will inevitably result in the need for repair at some point in time (Duck, 1988; Guerrero, Eloy, & Wabnik, 1993). For this reason, it is nearly impossible to think of maintenance without considering repair. Although both maintenance and repair are separate constructs, they nevertheless exist within the context of the other. Relational repair can, in fact, be conceptualized as a type of relational maintenance. For instance, Dindia (1994) labeled relational repair as "corrective maintenance" (p. 100). The coexistence notion of maintenance and repair is further elaborated later in the chapter.

The purpose of this chapter is to examine: (a) the notions of relationship maintenance and repair and how the constructs are brought together by the presence of a relational transgression; (b) assumptions regarding relational repair in close relationships; (c) communication strategies used to repair close relationships; (d) conclusions drawn from the extant literature; and (e) directions for future research. To begin, the constructs of relational maintenance and repair are addressed within a definitional framework. This definitional framework is to be considered for the remainder of this chapter as issues regarding relational transgressions and repair are addressed.

A variety of definitions of relational maintenance and relational repair exists. Whereas relational maintenance is often conceptualized as attempts to preserve the relationship in its current state (e.g., Baxter, 1994; Canary & Stafford, 1992; Dindia & Baxter, 1987; Stafford & Canary, 1991), relational repair involves partners engaging in behaviors to restore the relationship to its former condition, which assumes that something has disrupted the relationship (e.g., Aune, Metts, & Ebesu Hubbard, 1998; Davis, 1973; Dindia & Baxter, 1987). Repair has been approached in the literature from both individual and dyadic standpoints (e.g., Duck, 1984; Roloff & Cloven, 1994) as well as from a position of social networks and the role they play in enabling the couple repair their relationship (Duck, 1984). For the purposes of this chapter, relational maintenance and repair is later addressed with a focus on the relational partners. This focus does not imply that social networks do not and cannot play a salient role in the repair of a couple's relationship. Indeed, they can and do. However, this chapter conceptualizes the partners comprising the couple as the primary unit and the social network as a source of support secondary to that primary relationship. Given this focus, Roloff and Cloven's (1994) definition of relational maintenance (and repair) is most appropriate for the direction of this chapter. Specifically, this chapter focuses on the partners in the close, personal relationship and their efforts, both individually or dyadically, to maintain or repair their close relationship. Second, and as argued earlier, this chapter conceptualizes maintenance and repair as coexisting entities. That is, it is necessary to consider repair within the context of maintenance and vice versa. Roloff and Cloven's definition of relational maintenance best suits the direction of this chapter because it melds the constructs of relational maintenance and repair, and it recognizes and addresses the constructs similarly. Further, Roloff and Cloven's definition of maintenance focuses on individuals in intimate relationships and identifies maintenance as an individual or joint activity. Second, Roloff and Cloven's definition of maintenance acknowledges the role of relational transgressions as disrupting relational maintenance and recognizes the actions an intimate partner or partners take in an effort to repair a close relationship that has been threatened by a transgression or series of transgressions. Specifically, Roloff and Cloven defined relational maintenance as, "the individual or joint approaches intimates take to limit the relational harm that may prior or future conflicts and transgressions" (p. 27). Their conceptualization of relational maintenance is adopted because it involves efforts to correct past problems as well as engage in preventative measures to keep the relationship going as smoothly as possible. This framing of relational maintenance closely aligns with Dindia and Baxter's (1987) research maintenance and repair, which crafted relational maintenance strategies as composing of corrective strategies (i.e., repair) and preventative strategies. In essence, preventative maintenance strategies are affected by prior relational repair episodes. With this framework in mind, the following section examines a phenomenon that can conjoin the constructs of maintenance and repair, relational transgressions.

Transgressions

This section of the chapter addresses three aspects of relational transgressions. First, a higher order discussion of transgressions is presented. It is argued that transgressions can be incidental or incremental. That is, a transgression can comprise a single incident or episode or reflect a cumulative process. Second, specific types of transgressions are presented. Third, responses to transgressions are addressed. To begin, the various forms of transgressions are presented.

Transgressions can take the form of a social transgression or a relational transgression (Metts, 1994). Social transgressions involve the violation of some socially accepted rule, convention, or practice. For example, not accepting someone's hand to shake when it is extended in a greeting represents a social transgression. Relational transgressions, on the other hand, involve the violation of relational rules and expectancies (e.g., Emmers & Canary, 1996; Metts, 1994; Roloff & Cloven, 1994). Examples of these rules and expectancies might be explicit or implicit (Metts, 1994). Although certain rules exist that generalize to most close, romantic relationships (e.g., monogamy), other rules can be negotiated between relational partners that are relationship specific. For example, many couples in close relationships accept and practice monogamy as rule in their relationships. Beyond those implicit rules and expectancies, partners can negotiate rules and expectancies that are specific to their relationship. Examples of such rules and understandings might include not discussing past partners or relationships, not discussing in-laws, not going to bed angry, or not discussing relational problems with friends or co-workers. Interestingly, what can be drawn from the definitions of what constitutes a relational transgression is that an act or series of acts that might qualify as a transgression need not necessarily be negative, Indeed, a positive act or event might nonetheless violate a relational rule and represent a transgression. Research by Afifi and Metts (1998), for example, examined relational expectancy violations and responses to such violations. The authors argued and found that relational expectancy violations can be positive or negative in valence. They created a nine-category typology of violations that included both positive and negative expectancy violations. One category of Afifi and Metts' typology involved relational transgressions. The authors noted that their conceptualization of relational transgressions involved "behaviors that involve a clear violation of taken-for-granted relational rules" (p. 377). Yet, this author contends that a positive expectancy violation can constitute a relational transgression. An illustration of this argument might involve a couple that has negotiated a relational rule to keep things "out in the open" and to "not have any surprises." Yet, one partner organizes a surprise party for the other to celebrate a landmark birthday. Whereas many would perceive such a gesture as kind and generous, the partner on the receiving end of this gesture might interpret the surprise party as violating the couple's no-surprises rule. This notion is further addressed in a latter section on transgression types.

Relational Transgression as Incident or Increment

As previously identified, transgressions can take on a variety of forms. It must also be recognized that transgressions can take the form of a single incident or represent a cumulative process. Duck (1994), for instance, argued that events can represent ongoing relational processes constituted in everyday talk. Emmers (1995) found that both positive and negative events in romantic relationships took the form of either an isolated incident or a process that evolved over time (see Table 9.1 for a listing of events). Thus, the violation of a relational rule could occur in the form on an instantaneous behavior (e.g., an act of infidelity). Alternately, a relational rule could slowly be chipped away over time. For example, assume that a couple has negotiated the rule to be open and honest with one another. Over time, this rule slowly erodes as disclosures become more infrequent and less detailed; this erosion would constitute a relational transgression. Similarly, research on responses to troubled relationships also suggests that behavior can be instantaneous or cumulative. Baxter's (1984, 1985) research on termination strategies, for example, illustrates that termination behaviors can be long in the coming (e.g., cost escalation) or instantaneous (e.g., fait accompli). Cost escalation involves an individual making the relationship costly over time for the partner. For example, the individual might become increasingly distant or difficult toward the partner. Fait accompli, on the other hand, involves ending the relationship in an abrupt manner. In sum, what can be concluded from the literature on what instantly affects relationships adversely or what slowly erodes at relational maintenance is that transgressions can be framed as either an incident or as an incremental process.

In addition to the violation of relational rules, it is important to note that the culmination of everyday interaction in close relationships can also be trying because the interactions are often adverse in some respect (e.g., Miller, 1997). Similarly, Afifi and Metts (1998) concurred that relational expectancy violations need not necessarily constitute a single event. Miller contended that the everyday interaction between intimates, although not intentional, can be fraught with unexpected "hassles, frustrations, nuisances, and disappointments that relational partners impose on one another" (p. 14).

TABLE 9.1

Supraordinate and Subordinate Categories of Positive and Negative Events and Processes

Positive Events	Negative Events
1. Commitment	1. Substance Abuse
Cohabiting	Illicit drugs
Future together	Alcohol
Loss of virginity	2. Deceptive Practices
Commit to each other	Unfaithfulness
Propose/plan marriage	Infidelity
2. Physical Separation	Lying
Can manage "ex's"	Flirting
Partner is "Mr./Ms. Right"	3. Distance
Managed dating others	Physical separation
Balanced relationship, work, school	Psychological separation
Abstinence	(avoidance, ignoring, break up)
Managed third parties	Psychological separation
3. Realize Relationship is Temporary	(fear of intimacy)
Partner is not "Mr./Ms. Right"	4. Deviant Behavior
4. Expression of Feelings	Sexual practices
Expressed feelings	Personal past
Expressed love	5. Inhibiting emotions
5. Acceptance from Network	Jealousy
Family/friends were accepting	Suspicion/lack of trust
6. Break Up/Trial Separation	Worries
Broke up	Stress
7. Trial separation	Lack of motivation
Unfaithfulness/Infidelity	Possessiveness
Unfaithfulness	6. Aggression
Infidelity	Violence
	Attitude
	7. Third Party
	Third party
	Others
	8. Miscellaneous
	Rekindling
	No identity
	Pornography
	Rape
	Boredom
	Stealing
	Pet died

Over time, these oversights and unintentional behaviors can challenge the preservation of a close relationship. Indeed, it could be argued that everyday irritants and hassles provide strong fodder for a transgression to erupt. Similarly, everyday nuisances could evolve into a transgression.

Types of Relational Transgressions

Within the context of personal relationships, a variety of relational transgression types have been identified. Transgressions have been described using an abundance of terminologies, including uncertainty arousing events (e.g., Emmers & Canary, 1996; Planalp & Honeycutt, 1985; Planalp, Rutherford & Honeycutt, 1988), negative events (e.g., Emmers-Sommer, 1999), negative relational turning points (e.g., Baxter & Bullis, 1986), betrayals (Jones, Moore, Schratter, & Negel, 2000), face threats (e.g., Metts, 1997), relational expectancy violations (Afifi & Metts, 1998), and problematic events (e.g., Samp & Solomon, 1998), to name a few. Although various forms of relational transgressions exist, the literature is consistent in identifying infidelity and unfaithfulness as the most frequently reported relational transgressions in close, romantic relationships (Metts, 1994).

Indeed, a variety of messages conveyed in our close relationships are perceived as hurtful (Vangelisti, 1994). In particular, individuals experience hurt when a person close to the [sic] communicates a message that reflects a devaluation of the relationship (Leary, Springer, Negel, Ansell, & Evans, 1998). Both intentional and unintentional messages hurt, but intentional messages have more of a distancing effect on the relationship (Vangelisti & Young, 2000). Research examining intentional versus unintentional transgressions indicates that intentional transgressions are perceived more negatively (e.g., Manstead & Semin, 1981). The fact that offenders experience less guilt when their transgression is intentional (vs. accidental) likely adds to the violated partner's sting (McGraw, 1987). Overall, such behavior contributes to relational breakdown and the need for reparation.

Responses to Relational Transgressions

Duck (1984) offers two key questions regarding the situations that correspond with relational breakdown and the processes by which individuals rebuild the relationship: "What breaks down when a relationship breaks down? How does the answer to that question help to define the corresponding goals of repair interventions?" (p. 163). These issues are important when considering responses to a transgression. Specifically, who or what broke down the relationship in some respect affects one's goals regarding repair interventions (Samp & Solomon, 1998). Similarly, emotional response to the transgression might affect how reparation might be approached.

As noted earlier, transgressions can take a social form or a relational form (Metts, 1994). Emotional responses to the transgression also vary, depending on whether the transgression was social or relational in nature. Specifically, in the event of a transgression, an individual could feel embarrassed, could experience guilt or shame, or not really care at all. It is likely that an individual's emotional experience in light of a transgression will relate to how he or she responds to it in terms of reparation.

In a phenomenological examination of guilt and shame, Tangney (1998) observed the two emotions to be distinct such that shame involved a focus on the self, and guilt resulted in a focus on particular behaviors. Tangney also found that motivations in interpersonal relationships differed due to experiencing either of these emotions, with guilt leading to more adaptation in response to transgressions. In an empirical study, Tangney (1992) found that guilt was typically aroused by moral transgressions whereas shame was aroused by both moral (e.g., engaging in deception) and nonmoral transgressions (e.g., personal failure in a performance situation). Although both shame and guilt aroused offender's concern about how this might affect the partner, only shame was related to concern about the partner's evaluation of the offender. This conclusion makes sense given that someone who committed a moral transgression was not being sensitive to the partner's feelings in the first place, thus the offender is likely not concerned with the partner's evaluation of him or her. On the other hand, if an individual commits a nonmoral transgression (e.g., being late in attending an important occasion for the partner) the individual is likely ashamed for his or her tardiness and is concerned that the partner will think less of him or her for the lack of consideration.

In an empirical investigation examining embarrassment, guilt, and shame, Keltner and Buswell (1996) found results similar to Tangney's (1992). Specifically, the authors found that embarrassment was most often associated with transgressions involving social rules and conventions that guide public interaction. Guilt most often occurred when the transgression involved behaviors that violated responsibilities or behaviors that harmed others. Similarly, Jones, Kugler, and Adams (1995) found that guilt was associated with relational transgressions but not nonrelational transgressions. Finally, shame resulted when the transgression involved a failure to meet salient personal standards (e.g., being reliable, being prompt; Keltner & Buswell, 1996). Other research also suggests that associating shame with personal failure is consistent across individualistic (i.e., values individual goals over group goals) and collectivistic (i.e., values group goals over individual goals) cultures (Stipek, 1998).

Overall, the emotions experienced by the offender could affect the repair strategies enacted. It appears that experience of shame or embarrassment most often results in the repair of the self. That is, shame results from a personal failure and embarrassment results from the failure to adhere to a social convention. Accordingly, personal adjustments must be made so as not to embarrass or shame oneself. The experience of guilt, however, reflects a situation whereas reparation to the partner and repair of the relationship are in order as guilt is typically experienced due to harm inflicted on others, also, guilt feelings are abated when the transgression is intentional (McGraw, 1987).

Overall, of the three emotions aroused due a [sic] transgression, guilt is most tied to a relational transgression, although various emotions are experienced depending on the type of transgression committed. Below, various repair strategies enacted in response to a relational transgression are reviewed.

Relational Repair Strategies

This section focuses on several aspects of repair. First, a variety of relational repair strategies will be offered. Second, the relationship between the form of relational transgression committed and repair strategy chosen to manage the transgression is addressed. Finally, the efficacy of relational repair strategies enacted is reviewed.

Research suggests that if there was ever a relationship type in which partners need to possess a vast repertoire of repair strategies, close romantic relationships certainly qualify. Specifically, the research is clear that close relational partners do not treat each other well (Birchler et al., 1975; Miller, 1991, 1997). Specifically, close relational partners often engage in behaviors toward one another that they would make a conscious effort not to engage in when in the company of nonintimates (e.g., being impolite, insensitive, irresponsible, unreliable). And, despite the obvious need for relational repair strategies, the research indicates that partners possess a greater array of relational maintenance than relational repair strategies (Dindia & Baxter, 1987).

Types of Relational Repair Strategies

Little exists on relational repair in terms of typologies of relational repair (Dindia, 1994). Dindia argued that her and Baxter's work (Dindia & Baxter, 1987) as well as Davis' (1973) work examined maintenance and repair in the same breath. "Both Davis (1973) and Dindia and Baxter (1987) defined relational maintenance to include both strategies to maintain the relationship (preventative maintenance) and strategies to repair the relationship (corrective maintenance)" (Dindia, 1994, p. 100). Dindia and Baxter's (1987) work rendered 11 supraordinate categories of maintenance and repair strategies: changing the external environment, communication, metacommunication (e.g., relational talk), avoid metacommunication, antisocial strategies, prosocial strategies, ceremonies, antirituals/spontaneity, seeking/allowing autonomy, and seeking outside help. Of these strategy types, prosocial, ceremonial, communication and togetherness strategies were used most. However, metacommunication strategies were used more when partners wanted to repair the relationship, whereas spontaneity was more prevalent when the partners' desire is to maintain the relationship.

Although not labeled relational repair strategies per se, Rusbult's (e.g., 1980a, 1980b) work examined responses to periodic episodes of decline in close relationships. Inspired by interdependence theory, Rusbult argued in her investment model of responses to relational decline that partners choose responses depending on the levels of investment and satisfaction in their close relationships as well as quality of alternatives to their close relationship. Collectively, Rusbult argued that these indicators affect an individual's level of commitment to their partner and relationship. In turn, level of commitment affects an individual's response to periodic relational decline. Specifically, in the event of relational decline, a partner can choose to: (a) voice his or her dissatisfaction, (b) remain loyal to the partner and relationship, (c) approach the partner and relationship in a neglectful manner, or (d) engage in exit behaviors, which involve actually leaving the partner and relationship or threatening to do so. Rusbult argued that each response falls onto a constructive-destructive axis and a passive-active axis at they relate to the preservation of the relationship. In a word, voice involves an active response that is constructive to the preservation of the relationship. Loyalty entails a passive response that is also constructive to the preservation of the relationship. On the other hand, neglect reflects a passive response that is destructive to the preservation of the relationship and exit involves an active response that is destructive to the preservation of the relationship. It is important to note that the notions of constructive and destructive within the context of Rusbult's model refer only to the preservation of a relationship. Indeed, in the event of a dysfunctional relationship, exiting might be the most constructive behavior one could enact in terms of personal well-being. Nevertheless, the action of exiting is destructive to the preservation of the relationship.

Relational Repair Strategy Selection

A variety of issues affect response choices when a relational transgression occurs. For example, attributions for the transgression and severity of the offense are considered when examining response options to a transgression (Metts, 1994). Similarly, individuals' goals after a transgression vary and such goals affect response (e.g., Samp & Solomon, 1998). Specifically, Samp and Solomon found that responses to a problematic event in close relationships included maintaining the relationship, accepting fault for the event, managing positive face, addressing the event, managing the conversation, managing emotion, and restoring negative face. Accepting fault for the event was the most frequent goal in both friendships and dating relationships. The authors also found that the goal to accept fault for the event was intense and frequent, whereas the goal to avoid addressing the event was not frequent.

As mentioned earlier, Rusbult (e.g., 1980a, 1980b, 1983) and Rusbult and others (e.g., Rusbult, Drigotas, & Verette, 1994; Rusbult, Johnson, & Morrow, 1986a; Rusbult & Verette, 1991) clearly demonstrated that factors such as relational commitment, satisfaction, and alternatives to the relationship affect choices partners make in response to a transgression. Specifically, Rusbult (1987) indicated that partners who experience low satisfaction, low investment, and a high quality of alternatives are inclined to respond to dissatisfaction with the response of exit. Partners who experience low satisfaction, low investment, but a poor quality of alternatives are inclined to respond with neglect. Conversely, partners who experience high satisfaction, high investment, and a poor quality of alternatives are likely to respond to dissatisfaction with loyalty. Finally, partners who experience high satisfaction with their close relationship, high investment, and high quality of alternatives are likely to respond to relational dissatisfaction with voice. It is important to note, however, that the relationship between quality of alternatives and the responses of voice or neglect are weak at best (Rusbult, 1987).

Finally, aspects of an individual's, personality, such as levels of self-esteem, affect repair strategies (Rusbult, 1987). For example, assertive individuals are more likely than responsive individuals to assume control and exercise optimistic strategies when trying to repair a relationship. Assertive partners were less likely to use sensitivity strategies, whereas responsive partners were more likely to engage in listening strategies (Patterson & Beckett, 1995).

Strategies for managing relational problems can also vary by relationship type (e.g., Canary & Stafford, 1994). For example, Emmers-Sommer (1999) found that individuals were most likely to use integrative strategies, as opposed to distributive or avoidance (i.e., passive and indirect) strategies, when their goal was to repair their closest relationship after a negative event. Integrative strategies involve partners discussing the matter in a constructive manner, not seeking concessions, and offering a neutral evaluation of the partner. Distributive strategies involve engaging in destructive behaviors that do seek concessions from the partner and can involve behaviors such as negative attributions or threats. Finally, avoidance strategies involve not discussing the issue. Sillars (1980a, 1980b), however, found that individuals in less close relationships (i.e., college roommates) were more inclined to use avoidance or distributive strategies than integrative strategies in response to conflict. Thus, the type of relationship one is engaged in as well as the importance of that relationship affect relational repair choices. Specifically, one can choose to begin dissolving the relationship (e.g., Duck, 1984; Rusbuit, 1983), to break off the relationship (e.g., Baxter, 1984, 1985), or to repair the relationship (e.g., Dindia & Baxter, 1987; Duck, 1984).

Aune et al. (1998) examined a variety of relationship types varying in closeness and found that repair strategies exercised varied by closeness. Specifically, in a study of responses to the transgression of deception, Aune et al. found that close partners (e.g., marrieds) were more likely to engage in behaviors that communicated the positive aspects of their relationship in an attempt to repair than were less close relational partners (e.g., coworkers). Other research also demonstrates that deception is managed differently according to relationship type (e.g., Metts, 1989).

Relational Repair Strategy Efficacy

Research on relational repair strategies indicates that partners do not perceive all strategies equally and that some strategies are more effective than others in remedying the ill brought about by a relational transgression. For example, research indicates that voicing feelings in a constructive manner to be beneficial to the preservation of close relationships (e.g., Gottman, 1994). For example, Gottman clearly demonstrated that partners who respond to relational dissatisfaction and conflict in a constructive manner experience more satisfactory relationships. Constructive conflict management behaviors include refraining from the use of behaviors such as defensiveness, criticism, contempt, avoiding the issue, mindreading, or making negative attributions toward the partner. Instead, Gottman argued the benefits of engaging in voicing dissatisfaction without blaming, paraphrasing a partner's feelings to ensure accurate understanding of the partner's perspective, and focusing on behaviors rather than the individual (e.g., avoiding negative personal attacks).

Other research findings concur that discussing the issues and the relationship in a constructive manner are beneficial to the preservation of the relationship. Guided by an uncertainty reduction perspective, Emmers and Canary (1996) examined what uncertainty reduction strategies (passive, active, and interactive) were enacted by couples in an effort to repair their relationship. Interactive strategies involve directly talking to the partner; active strategies involve seeking information from the partner from a knowing third party or manipulating the environment to observe how the partner reacts; finally, passive strategies involve observing the partner. The authors added a fourth strategy category, assumed acceptance, for those individuals who seemingly accepted the uncertainty arousing event and made no efforts to reduce uncertainty. The authors found that romantic couples most often engaged in the interactive communication strategy of relational talk when the couples' goal was to repair the relationship after experiencing a negative event. This finding is similar to Dindia and Baxter's (1987) finding that couples most often engage in relational talk strategies when their goal is to repair the relationship. Similarly, Guerrero, Andersen, Jorgensen, Spitzberg, and Eloy (1995) found that individuals' use of integrative strategies to communicate jealousy resulted in more satisfying relationships. Finally, Courtright, Millar, Rogers, and Bagarozzi (1990) examined eight couples undergoing counseling due to their distressed marriages. Following the 6-week counseling sessions and three taped marital discussions, these researchers found that the spouses who engaged in direct communication and negotiation behaviors repaired their marriage. However, the couples that engaged in avoidant, indirect, and decreased involvement behaviors terminated their marriages.

Partners' use of apologies, excuses, or justifications used in response to a transgression has also been examined in the literature. Apologies entail the offender admitting fault and expressing regret for the wrongdoing (Hunter, 1984). Excuses involve the offender admitting that the offense occurred, but not accepting responsibility for the offense. Finally, justifications involve the offender admitting responsibility for the act, but denying that the act was an offense (Hunter, 1984; Scott & Lymon, 1968). Hupka, Jung, and Silverthorn (1987), for example, found that apologies (e.g., "I am sorry I was insensitive") were the preferred response to a transgression, regardless of intent. Excuses were perceived as weak accounts to a transgression (e.g., "I've been under a lot of stress"). Interestingly, justifications (e.g., "Everyone loses their temper sometimes and is insensitive, I'm no different") were rated the most negatively when the intent was to maintain the relationship. However, justifications were rated more highly than excuses when the intent was to terminate the relationship. Transgressors appraised justifications and apologies higher than the violated partners. Hupka et al.'s study only examined intent to maintain or terminate the relationship, however, and did not examine when the intent was to repair the relationship.

Overall, the prescription appears simple: Be nice to your partner to maintain your relationship, and if you transgress, engage in prosocial, communicative behaviors to repair the relationship. Indeed, the research evidence overwhelmingly suggests that engaging in some type of prosocial behavior (e.g., being positive, talking about the relationship positively) and engaging in direct, metacommunicative behavior strongly affects close relationship repair (and maintenance) positively (e.g., Aune et al., 1998; Canary & Stafford, 1992; Dindia, 1989; Dindia & Baxter, 1997; Emmers-Sommer, 1999; Emmers & Canary, 1996; Samp & Solomon, 1998; Stafford &Canary, 1991) Yet, we are well aware that relationships are complex and are constantly evolving. Thus, a simple elixir to relational problems is nonexistent. Nevertheless, the aforementioned findings do suggest that certain reparations are more effective than others.

Conclusion

The purpose of this chapter is to examine aspects of relational transgressions and relational repair strategies. In doing so, evidence from the extant research was presented and some extending arguments were offered. The purpose of this section is to briefly offer conclusions from what was reviewed and presented in this chapter.

First, both relational transgressions and reparation strategies are prevalent in close, personal relationships. As argued in this chapter, it is necessary to perceive maintenance and repair in a coexistent fashion as repair is corrective maintenance and maintenance strategies represent preventative strategies such that the need for repair is lessened. Despite many individuals' quest to find a close, intimate partner, they nonetheless often treat that close partner adversely or insensitively. This negative treatment often involves one or both partners' engagement in relational transgressions. Second, what constitutes a relational transgression can be implicit or explicit in nature. That is, a transgression can involve the violation of an implicit relational rule or expectancy such as monogamy or an explicit, negotiated relational rule or expectancy (e.g., to not keep secrets from one another, to not go to bed angry). Third, and related, a transgression can constitute a single incident or an incremental process. That is, a single event might (e.g., an act of infidelity) represent a transgression. On the other hand, a transgression might represent the cumulative or incremental process of actions and interactions. For example, the negotiated rule and expectancy to remain open and honest with one another erodes over time. Fourth, a transgression can be positive or negative in valence. That is, an act that might be perceived as positive in nature might nevertheless violate a relational rule or expectancy and thus constitute a transgression. Fifth, varied emotional reactions to the transgressions can be experienced depending on the nature of the transgression. Specifically, embarrassment is often experienced due to a social transgression, whereas shame is often experienced due to a relational transgression due to a personal incompetence and guilt is often experienced when a relational transgression affects the partner adversely. Sixth, perceptions of the transgression within the context of the importance of the relationship affect repair strategies enacted. That is, individuals in close relationships who value and want to preserve their relationships often engage in constructive, prosocial, metacommunicative strategies when relational reparation is the goal. Finally, and related, the efficacy of relational repair strategies varies. Specifically, partners' admission of fault and willingness to be open in discussing the problem and the relationship is more efficacious than not taking responsibility for a transgression and avoiding discussing the situation. In sum, it is evident that communication plays a central role in the maintenance and repair processes of close relationships.

Future Directions

Dindia (1994) argued that numerous relational strategies are multiphasic in nature. That is, certain strategies (e.g., relational talk) are useful during various stages of relational development (e.g., initiation, development, maintenance, repair). This contention assumes a phase or stage approach to relationships. Yet, because relationships do not occur in a vacuum, there is also movement within stages. Within the context of relational transgressions in close relationships, one future direction of research might want to examine how relational rules are negotiated and renegotiated over the course of a relationship. Specifically, this chapter addresses how transgressions occur when a relational rule or expectancy is violated by one or both relational partners. Given the evolution of relationships, what might have qualified as a transgression during one phase of a close relationship might not qualify at a later phase of the relationship. For example, partners might have negotiated "not talking about past partners" as a relational rule early in their relationship. However, as the relationship develops and strengthens, a topic that might have been perceived as a threat is no longer perceived in that fashion. In fact, partners might eventually refer to past relationships openly in their present relationship. Future research should examine the negotiation and renegotiation of relational rules and how that process affects perceptions of transgressions.

Another area worthy of consideration involves the burgeoning area of new technologies and the onset of online relationships (see Rabby & Walther, chap. 7, this volume). This new area in the interpersonal literature provides fertile ground for researchers to test existing interpersonal theories, models, and typologies in an online environment. Several possible questions exist that are worthy of exploration. For example, how do online relational partners negotiate relational rules? How do online partners identify and manage a transgression? Also, how do individuals in primary, face-to-face relationships perceive a partner's "involvement" with someone online? Research suggests that whereas some individuals perceive online relationships as real (e.g., Parks & Roberts, 1998), others perceive them as nonreal (e.g., Walther, 1996). Depending on the nature of the face-to-face relationship, then, the perception of whether or not a transgression has been committed in the primary relationship due to a partner's actions in the online relationship will vary. Overall, the development, maintenance, and repair of online relationships are fast-growing aspects of society and provide a new environment (i.e., the online domain) in which to examine relational processes.

Consider this . . .

- As you consider transgressions in terms of whether they are social or relational and incremental or a single incident, what type of transgressions do you believe are most difficult to repair? Why?
- What role do you believe the feelings of the offender play in the repair process? What feelings may inhibit or enhance the repair process? Why?

- What relational repair strategies do you believe are most effective to repair relationships? Give a specific example to illustrate how these strategies have proved to be effective in relationship repair.
- How might relational repair strategies differ in different stages of relationship development? For example, how might repair strategies differ in a relatively new relationship compared to a more established relationship?
- How might relationship repair differ in online relationships? What transgressions might warrant repair in these relationships? What repair strategies might be most appropriate to use in these relationships?

References

Afifi, W. A., & Metts, S. (I 998). Characteristics and consequences of expectation violations in close relationships. *Journal of Social and Personal Relationships, 15,* 365-392.

Altman, I., & Taylor, D. A. (1973). *Social penetration.* New York: Holt, Rinehart, & Winston.

Aune, R. K., Metts, S., & Ebesu Hubbard, A. S. (1998). Managing outcomes of discovered deception. *The Journal of Social Psychology, 138,* 677-689.

Baxter, L. A. (1984). Trajectories of relationship disengagement. *Journal of Social and Personal Relationships, 1,* 29-48.

Baxter, L. A. (1985). Accomplishing relationship disengagement. In S. Duck & D. Perlman (Eds.), *Understanding personal relationships: An interdisciplinary approach* (pp. 243-265). Beverly Hills, CA: Sage.

Baxter, L. A. (1986). Gender differences in the heterosexual relationship rules embedded in breakup accounts. *Journal of Social and Personal Relationships, 3,* 289-306.

Baxter, L. A. (I 994). A dialogic approach to relational maintenance. In D. J. Canary & L. Stafford (Eds.), *Communication and relational maintenance* (pp. 233-254). San Diego, CA: Academic Press.

Baxter, L. A., & Bullis, C. (I 986). Turning points in developing romantic relationships. *Human Communication Research, 12,* 469-493.

Birchler, G. R., Weiss, R. L., & Vincent, J. P (1975). Multimethod analysis of social reinforcement exchange between martially distressed and nondistressed spouse and stranger dyads. *Journal of Personality and Social Psychology, 31,* 349-360.

Canary, D. J., & Stafford, L. (1992). Relational maintenance strategies and equity in marriage. *Communication Monographs, 59,* 239-267.

Canary, D. J., & Stafford, L. (1994). Maintaining relationships through strategic and routine interaction. In D. J. Canary & L. Stafford (Eds.), *Communication and relational maintenance* (pp. 3-22). San Diego, CA: Academic Press.

Courtright, J. A., Millar, F. E., Rogers, L. E., & Bagarozzi, D. (1990). Interaction dynamics of relational negotiation: Reconciliation versus termination of distressed relationships. *Western Journal of Speech Communication, 54,* 429-453.

Davis, M. S. (1973). *Intimate relations.* New York: The Free Press.

Dindia, K. (I 994). A multiphasic view of relationship maintenance strategies. In D. J. Canary & L. Stafford (Eds.), *Communication and relational maintenance* (pp. 99-112). San Diego, CA: Academic Press.

Dindia, K., & Baxter, L. A. (1987) Strategies for maintaining and repairing marital relationships. *Journal of Social and Personal Relationships, 4,* 143-158.

Duck, S. W (1994). *Meaningful relationships: Talking, sense, and relating.* Thousand Oaks, CA: Sage.

Duck, S. W (1984). A perspective on the repair of personal relationships: Repair of what, when? In S. W Duck (Ed.), *Personal relationships 5: Repairing personal relationships* (pp. 163-184). London: Academic Press.

Duck, S. W (1988). *Relating to others.* Monterey, CA: Brooks/Cole.

Emmers, T. M. (1995). *The prevalence of uncertainty in romantic relationships: Examining individuals' instrumentality in the uncertainty reduction process.* Unpublished doctoral dissertation, Ohio University.

Emmers, T. M., & Canary, D. J. (1996). The effect of uncertainty reducing strategies on young couples' relational repair and intimacy. *Communication Quarterly, 44,* 166-182.

Emmers-Sommer, T. M. (1999). Negative relational events and event responses across relationship-type: Examining and comparing the impact of conflict strategy-use on intimacy in same-sex friendships, opposite-sex friendships, and romantic relationships. *Communication Research Reports, 16,* 286-295.

Gottman, J. M. (1994). What predicts divorce? Hillsdale, NJ: Lawrence Erlbaum Associates.

Guerrero, L. K., Eloy, S. V, & Wabnik, A. L. (1993). Linking maintenance strategies to relationship development and disengagement: A reconceptualization. *Journal of Social and Personal Relationships, 10,* 273-283.

Guerrero, L. K., Andersen, P A., Jorgensen, P F., Spitzberg, B. H., & Eloy, S. V (1995). Coping with the green-eyed monster: Conceptualizing and measuring communicative responses to romantic jealousy. *Western Journal of Communication, 59,* 270-304.

Hunter, C. H. (1984). Aligning actions: Types and social distribution. Symbolic Interaction, 7, 155-174.

Hupka, R. B., Jung, J., & Silverthorn, K. (1987). Perceived acceptability of apologies, excuses, and justifications in jealousy predicaments. *Journal of Behavior and Personality, 2,* 303-313.

Jones, W H., Kugler, K., & Adams, P. (1995). You always hurt the ones you love: Guilt and transgressions against relational partners. In J. R Tangney & K. W. Fischer (Eds.), *Self-conscious emotions: The psychology of shame, guilt, embarrassment, and pride* (pp. 301-321). New York: Guilford.

Jones, W. H., Moore, D. S., Schratter, A., & Negel, L. A. (2001). Interpersonal transgressions and betrayals. In R. M. Kowalski (Ed.), *Behaving badly: Aversive behaviors in interpersonal relationships* (pp. 233-256). Washington, DC: American Psychological Association.

Keltner, D., & Buswell, B. N. (1996). Evidence for the distinctiveness of embarrassment, shame, and guilt: A study of recalled antecedents and facial expressions of emotion. *Cognition & Emotion, 10,* 155-171.

Leary, M. R., Springer, C., Negel, L., Ansell, E., & Evans, K. (1998). The causes, phenomenology, and consequences of hurt feelings. *Journal of Personality and Social Psychology, 74,* 1225-1237.

Manstead, A. S., & Semin, G. R. (1981). Social transgressions, social perspectives, and social emotionality. *Motivation and Emotion, 5,* 249-261.

McGraw, K. M. (1987). Guilt following transgression: An attribution of responsibility approach *Journal of Personality and Social Psychology, 53,* 247-256.

Metts, S. (1989). An exploratory investigation of deception in close relationships. *Journal of Social and Personal Relationships, 6,* 159-179.

Metts, S. (1994). Relational transgressions. In W. R. Cupach & B. H. Spitzberg (Eds.), *The dark side of interpersonal communication* (pp. 217-239). Hillsdale, NJ: Lawrence Erlbaum Associates.

Metts, S. (1997). Face and facework: Implications for the study of personal relationships. In S. W Duck (Ed.), *Handbook of personal relationships: Theory, research and interventions* (2nd ed., pp. 373-390). Chichester, England: Wiley.

Miller, R. S. (1991). On decorum in close relationships: Why aren't we polite to those we love? *Contemporary Social Psychology, 13,* 74-76.

Miller, R. S. (1997). We always hurt the ones we love: Aversive interactions in close relationships. In R. W. Kowalski (Ed.), *Aversive interpersonal behaviors* (pp. 11-29). New York: Plenum Press.

Parks, M. R., & Roberts, L. D. (1998). "Making MOOsic": The development of personal relationships on line and a comparison to their off-line counterparts. *Journal of Social and Personal Relationships, 15,* 517-537.

Patterson, B. R., & Beckett, C. S. (1995). A re-examination of relational repair and reconciliation: Impact of socio-communicative style on strategy selection. *Communication Research Reports, 12,* 235-240.

Planalp, S., & Honeycutt, J. M. (1985). Events that increase uncertainty in personal relationships. *Human Communication Research, 11,* 593-604.

Planalp, S., Rutherford, D. K., & Honeycutt, J. M. (1988). Events that increase uncertainty in personal relationships II: Replication and extension. *Human Communication Research, 14,* 516-547.

Roloff, M. E., & Cloven, D. H. (1994). When partners transgress: Maintaining violated relationships. In D. J. Canary & L. Stafford (Eds.), *Communication and relational maintenance* (pp. 23-43). San Diego, CA: Academic Press.

Rusbult, C. E. (1980a). Commitment and satisfaction in romantic associations: A test of the investment model. *Journal of Experimental Social Psychology, 16,* 172-186.

Rusbult, C. E. (1980b). Satisfaction and commitment in friendships. *Representative Research in Social Psychology, 11,* 96-105.

Rusbult, C. E. (1983). A longitudinal test of the investment model: The development (and deterioration) of satisfaction and commitment in heterosexual involvements. *Journal of Personality and Social Psychology, 45,* 101-117.

Rusbult, C. E. (1987). Responses to dissatisfaction in close relationships: The exit-voice-loyalty-neglect model. In D. Perlman & S. Duck (Eds.), *Intimate relationships: Development, dynamics, and deterioration* (pp. 209-237). Thousand Oaks, CA: Sage.

Rusbult, C. E., Drigotas, S. M., & Verette, J. (1994). The investment model: An interdependence analysis of commitment processes and relationship maintenance phenomena. In D. J. Canary & L. Stafford (Eds.), *Communication and relational maintenance* (pp. 115-139). San Diego, CA: Academic Press.

Rusbult, C. E., Johnson, D. J., & Morrow, G. D. (1986). Impact of couple patterns of problem solving on distress and nondistress in dating relationships. *Journal of Personality and Social Psychology, 50,* 744-753.

Rusbult, C. E., & Verette, J. (1991). An interdependence analysis of accommodation processes in close relationships. *Representative Research in Social Psychology, 19,* 3-33.

Samp, J. A., & Solomon, D. H. (1998). Communicative responses to problematic events in close relationships I: The variety and facets of goals. *Communication Research, 25,* 66-95.

Scott, M. B., & Lymon, S. M. (1968). Accounts. *American Sociological Review, 33,* 46-62.

Sillars, A. L. (1980a). The sequential and distributional structure of conflict interactions as a function of attributions concerning the locus of responsibility and stability of conflicts. In D. Nimmo (Ed.), *Communication Yearbook 4* (pp. 217-235). New Brunswick, NJ: Transaction Books.

Sillars, A. L. (1980b). Attributions and communication in roommate conflicts. *Communication Monographs, 47,* 180-200.

Stafford, L., & Canary, D. J. (1991). Maintenance strategies and romantic relationship type, gender and relational characteristics. *Journal of Social and Personal Relationships, 8,* 217-242.

Stipek, D. (1998). Differences between Americans and Chinese in the circumstances of evoking pride, shame, and guilt. *Journal of Cross-Cultural Psychology, 29,* 616-629.

Tangney, J. P. (1992). Situational determinants of shame and guilt in young adulthood. *Personality and Social Psychology Bulletin, 18,* 199-206,

Tangney, J. P (1998). How does guilt and shame differ? In J. Bybee (Ed.), *Guilt and children* (pp. 1-17). San Diego, CA: Academic Press.

Vangelisti, A. L. (1994). Messages that hurt. In W. R. Cupach & B. H. Spitzberg (Eds.), *The dark side of interpersonal communication* (pp. 53-82). Hillsdale, NJ: Lawrence Erlbaum Associates.

Vangelisti, A. L, & Young, S. L. (2000). When words hurt: The effects of perceived intentionality on interpersonal relationships. *Journal of Social and Personal Relationships, 17,* 393-424.

Walther, J. B. (1996). Computer-mediated communication: Impersonal, interpersonal, and hyperpersonal interaction. *Communication Research, 23,* 3-43.

The author wishes to thank Rachel Rainwater McClure for her assistance with this chapter and Dan Canary and Marianne Dainton for their very helpful suggestions on an earlier draft of this chapter.

CHAPTER 9

TRANSFORMING AND ENDING PERSONAL RELATIONSHIPS

In Chapter 9 of her text, *Relational Communication*, Julia Wood addresses the process of deterioration and ending personal relationships. She discusses a model that reflects the process of deterioration; in addition, she explores the symptoms and sources of decline in relationships, including transgressions explored in the last reading. Though Wood discusses several ways to end or redefine personal relationships, she offers little discussion of the grief felt during such loss.

In her reading entitled, "Holding On by Letting Go / Letting Go by Holding On: Approaches in Grief," communication scholar Christine B. Smith (George Mason University) provides valuable insight into the grieving process. Smith begins by clarifying the conceptual distinction between bereavement and grief, two terms that she notes are often used interchangeably. From there, Smith discusses three primary themes that have dominated Western studies of grief during the past century and she notes two traditional models used to approach the study of grief – task-based models and stage-phase models. Smith provides an exceptionally strong review of research that explains these two traditional models and compares both models; throughout her discussion, she also assesses the limitations of these traditional models.

From her overview of the traditional perspectives, approaches, and models, Smith then posits the need for a new paradigm that reflects a more integrative approach to the grief process. As she notes, the dialectical perspective emphasizes the dual process of oscillating between "focus on the loss" and "coping with other stressors that arise from the loss." This Dual Perspective Model (DPM) recognizes that grieving is not an either/or process; instead, it acknowledges that both orientations are necessary. Applying this model, the focus becomes how we navigate between the two orientations and the healthy or unhealthy oscillation between the two dialectics that may result. Perhaps most interesting is Smith's observation that the Dual Perspective Model may allow us to understand how different standpoints (i.e., gender differences) may navigate differently between the two dialectics in the grief process.

Finally, as you read Smith's article, place her discussion of bereavement and grief not only in the context of the death of loved one, but in the greater context of loss that all of us feel in various aspects of our lives; such loss is inevitable and yet often debilitating. For me, it is always comforting to know that others have negotiated such loss with all its challenges, survived the journey, and have even become healthier individuals in their personal relationships. Hopefully, you will find the insight presented in this article helpful in your journey as well.

Holding On by Letting Go/Letting Go by Holding On: Approaches to Grief

Christine B. Smith
George Mason University

To grieve alone is to suffer most.
- Traditional Jewish proverb

Bereavement is a social network crisis (Stylianos & Vachon, 1993). The death of a loved one can be devastating to survivors. The loss itself may bring its own problems, but the effort of coping with the loss, or perceptions of how others are or are not responding (either to the loss or the one bereft), can damage or destroy a social network. Grief, the outcome of bereavement, is a struggle for most of us because grief is pervasive, painful, and because we do not understand it (Kübler-Ross, 1969). When we are grieving, it is easy to get confused by the many conflicting theories and accounts that purport to guide us through the process, to the extent that we may be troubled as much by the confusion as the grief itself.

What is grief? When someone dies, is grief something that happens to us or is it something we do? Is grief a desolate place we journey through or a destination we fight our way back from? Is it the journey itself? Is it the process of giving up something we have already lost? Or is it transforming absence into a new form of presence? Moreover, is grief a "hard-wired" or socially constructed response to loss? Must we simply endure it? Or should we overcome it? Is getting over it the same as learning to live with it? Is there good grief and bad grief? These are not just idle questions framed while perusing the sympathy section of a greeting card store. How we describe grief is instrumental in how we experience it and how we respond to others' grief (Small, 2001). Greater awareness of what grief is, especially its power and variability, should equip us with more effective skills to cope with our losses. Equally important, a broader perspective on loss and its consequences allows us to better understand and support those who are bereft and grieving.

This article will critically examine how grief has been defined and described in selected research and writing on bereavement. The literature I have chosen to review reflects competing models of grief experience that have greatly influenced responses to loss in Western society and continue to do so today. After a brief overview of three primary themes of contradiction in bereavement literature, I will examine the models comprising these themes more closely. From this "old paradigm" I will shift to more integrative approaches that show how a dialectical perspective allows not only greater understanding of the complexity of grief experience, but also explains more of the experiences reported by grievers themselves. Throughout, I will elaborate on areas of weakness and gaps in our understanding that may continue to impede our wellbeing as we struggle to cope with our losses and the losses of others.

First, for clarity and conceptual accuracy, I will distinguish among terms often used interchangeably. While there is no consensus on definitions, some common interpretations are drawn from the literature. Bereavement is a state of loss arising from the death of a relationally significant person (Brabant, 1996; Corr et al., 1997;

Hindmarch, 1993; Stroebe et al., 1997). Grief is the voluntary or involuntary response to the loss, and may be emotional, behavioral, cognitive, and spiritual in its dimensions (Parkes, 1998; Corr et al., 1997). Grief is theoretically complex, in that it may be described as anticipatory, pathological, morbid, chronic, prolonged, delayed, unresolved, complicated, dysfunctional, and exaggerated (Jacobs, 1993; Middleton, Raphael, Martinek, & Misso, 1993). Grief may be also described as marginalized, de-legitimized, stifled, or disenfranchised. Such grief remains hidden, or goes unrecognized or supported due to the circumstances surrounding or the nature of the loss, and results from perceptions that grief is more or less unwarranted, is inappropriately expressed, or has exceeded normative bounds (Doka, 1987; Eyetsemitan, 1998; Farnsworth & Allen, 1996; LaGrand, 1991; Pine, 1990). A few researchers have described the phenomenon of "prohibited" grief, referring specifically to siblings who do not express grief normally in order to protect parents from additional pain (Mahon & Page, 1995; Rosen, 1984-1985).

Some scholars, Rando (1993) in particular, view grief as passive—what one experiences—and mourning as the active processes of coping with bereavement—what one does. Brabant (1996), taking the more common approach, which we will here, argues that mourning is the socially approved, learned aspect of grief, that which tells us the nature of our loss and how it should be expressed. More specifically, mourning consists of those cultural, religious, spiritual, and personal rituals one undertakes, alone or more typically with others, to acknowledge a loss. In some ways, such rituals can be construed as social enactments of grief, geared towards infusing both the death and the loss with personal meaning (Cameron, 1991) and cultural meaning (Currer, 2001; Small, 2001). According to anthropologist Rosenblatt (1997), who with his colleagues has compared accounts of grief and mourning in over 70 societies, the emotional experience of grief, as well as the expression of it, is to some extent culturally constructed. Thus, it is important to note that the following examination is limited to bereavement as experienced and studied in North American and European cultures. This ethnocentric approach has been dominant in bereavement research and literature (Currer, 2001; Walter, 1997). The "new paradigm," however, attempts to take into account cultural variation (Stroebe & Schut, 1999).

Three Primary Themes of Grief

Three primary themes have dominated Western studies of grief in the past century. Each theme reflects divergent models and theories of loss that have significantly shaped clinical, social, and personal perceptions of grief. The first theme is whether grief "recovery" entails breaking or continuing the bonds of attachment with the departed. For example, the early works of Freud (1917) and Bowlby (1980) suggest grief is a process that is incomplete unless one withdraws one's energy from attachment to the deceased, freeing it to invest in another relationship On the other hand, Klass (1997) and his colleagues (Klass, Silverman, & Nickman, 1996; Klass & Walter, 2001; Marwit & Klass, 1995; 1996), claim that grief is a process of finding a way to maintain a relationship with the deceased, or at least to continue the bond. The second theme raises the question of whether grief ends or endures. It contrasts grief as a process of resolution that culminates in satisfactory progression through stages or phases (e.g., Averill, 1968; Engel, 1961; 1964; Horowitz, 1990; Parkes, 1986), and/or the adequate completion of tasks (e.g., Harvey et al., 1995; Parkes & Weiss, 1983; Rando, 1993; Van der Wal, 1989-1990; Worden, 1991), with the opposing view that grief never entirely goes away, and is perhaps only mitigated over time as one learns to live with it (e.g., Klass, 1997; McCabe, 2003; Moules, 1998). The third primary theme is that there is good grief that is adaptive and constructive, provided it culminates in some satisfactory outcome such as letting go and closure or the happy medium of maintaining a psychic relationship with the departed (Pollock, 1961; Silverman, 2000; Stroebe & Schut, 1999; Stroebe & Stroebe, 1991). Furthermore, grief has sometimes been construed as life's defining necessity, the only means whereby people grow (Viorst, 1986). Conversely, there is also bad grief, for example one's inability to move on or the failure to grieve at all (Lindemann, 1944; Rando, 1986; Raphael, 1983).

One's stance within the constellation of these themes drives one's thinking on the fundamental, underlying question of bereavement research and counseling: when does "normal grief" cross over into something else and arouse consternation or demand clinical intervention? The line, if there is one, is by no means clear, but modern approaches to bereavement tend to favor a low pain threshold and rapid recovery. Some reasons for this include vested economic interest in maintaining bereavement support programs that have come into existence and the need to demonstrate "results" (Small & Hockey, 2001; Walter, 1999) and, not surprisingly, the discomfort and concerns of survivors themselves. Feeling helpless and confronting raw, seemingly endless grief, one of the things new survivors usually want to know is, "How long will I suffer like this?" And because more than a little concern attends the question, "Why isn't so-and-so getting over it?" enormous bias exists for the view that grief is painful and should end as quickly as possible. Certainly prolonged, traumatic grief can be debilitating and inconvenient. The difficulty is in defining "prolonged" and "traumatic." There is danger in pathologizing grief, or at least doing so too quickly. But there is equal danger in not supporting people who are "stuck" or overwhelmed and at risk of self-harm or harming others because of their grief. All too frequently, those most in need of help are unaware that help is available or that they need it. Misguided cultural and personal perceptions of what appropriate mourning behavior is, or the heavy cognitive load of dealing with grief itself, may blind survivors to looming crises. Jacobs (1993) estimates that up to a third of those bereft by the death of a spouse or child (regardless of the manner of death) will suffer detrimental mental and/or physical effects. When help is sought, it is most frequently sought from general practitioners who, as Parkes points out, may not be the best equipped to respond adequately:

The consequences of loss are so far reaching that the topic should occupy a large place in the training of health care providers-but this is not the case. One explanation for this omission is the assumption that loss is irreversible and untreatable: there is nothing we can do about it, and the best way of dealing with it is to ignore it. This attitude may help us to live with the fact that, despite modern science, 100% of our patients still die and that before they die many will suffer lasting losses in their lives. Sadly, it means that, just when they need us most, our patients and their grieving relatives find that we back away. (1998b, p. 856)

At the opposite end of the pendulum swing is the view that the pain of coping with relational loss is meaningful, that it brings about positive change and growth and therefore it is a disservice to dull it or ameliorate it through clinical means. From this perspective, grief pain is healing and adaptive rather than symptomatic and medically adverse (Nesse, 1991). Both views have merit, and as we will see, newer approaches to the study of grief look for ways to reframe and transcend the seeming contradictions, and to both increase our understanding and ease our pain, effectively optimizing grief experience. Above all, there is movement away from a one-size-fits-all approach to grief.

If you were to poll your classmates, you would likely find a wide variety of loss experiences. Some may report no losses and yet have firm ideas of what constitutes "good grief" while others may be said to have suffered more than their fair share and remain inarticulate, uncertain, or in denial about the impact. Two students may share a common loss, the death of a mutual friend, and manifest their grief differently: One has "moved on"; the other's grief continues. A single, long ago death may still torment a classmate, while another may speak with some equanimity about a recent personal tragedy. Like relationships, responses to relational loss are unique; however there are discernable patterns of grief and mourning behavior that people characterize as appropriate or inappropriate, problematic or normal. Moreover there are individual, relational, and social factors that influence how people think, feel, and behave when someone dies. Grief is not a simple, straightforward, process with predetermined stages and predictable outcomes. Yet earlier models of bereavement, purposefully or otherwise, have been used to suggest that it should be.

The next section begins with an overview of traditional models of grief. Two theoretically and therapeutically prominent approaches to grief are collectively known as task-based models and stage-phase models. As will be seen, the two views are not necessarily mutually exclusive. The areas of overlap are clearest when examining the work of Sigmund Freud and John Bowlby.

Grief as Work: Freud and Bowlby

In 1917, Sigmund Freud published his book, Mourning and Melancholia, which established a protocol of normal grief recovery. Freud saw relationships as attachments (object relations) formed and held together by energy invested by the individuals within the relationship. When one person died, others who were attached to that individual engaged in ruminating about the person and relationship (repeatedly confronting the reality of the loss) until "the full force of the loss was appreciated" and the bonds were freed/broken and the energy was reinvested elsewhere (Steiner, 1993, p. 34). Theoretically, psychic pain eased as the bonds attaching family and friends to the deceased weakened, and an end to the pain coincided with an end to grieving. This natural process occurred without intervention most of the time. The work of reviewing thoughts and memories of the deceased in order to let them go was deemed critical by Freud, who saw relational energy as finite, and those who failed to withdraw and reinvest it as emotionally stunted. One can imagine this fear in the minds of caring family and friends, who often urge mourners not only to let go, but also to meet new people as a prescription for ending their misery (whose misery is left purposely ambiguous). What we do not learn from Freud's theory is how the energy exchange takes place, i.e., how does thinking about and reviewing the relationship, otherwise known as confronting the reality (Steiner, 1993), result in the bonds slowly relinquishing their hold on us? Steiner (1996) contends that for Freud, the work of mourning meant a slow, iterative process of reclaiming the self from the hold of the deceased—quite literally, those parts of ourselves we had invested in the other person or the relationship. But while almost anyone who has experienced intense grief is familiar with the compulsive need to relive and remember, a connection between doing so and eventually not needing to do so is not made clear by Freud. Even so, Freud's theorizing is obviously the source of later models that entail the tasks of account making and meaning making (e.g., Harvey et al, 1995; Neimeyer, 2001a) which is typically done in interaction with others. Also, while we can see Freud's imprint in later work that describes grief as a "rebuilding" of the self, this highly intrapersonal take on grief does not consider how shared memories can comfort us and help us sustain connections with other mourners as well as with the deceased (Nadeau, 1998).

John Bowlby (1969; 1973; 1980) formed attachment theory based on his observations of infants' behaviors when separated from their caregivers. This theory has since expanded to cover all relationships, contexts, and objects that provide some base of security and thus arouse strong emotions when lost (such as one's job or favorite teddy bear). Bowlby's conception of what grief is—separation anxiety plus—is not that different from Freud's, in that the broken attachment is the source of pain (Shaver & Tancredy, 2001; Stroebe et al., 1996; Stroebe & Schut, 2001b). Unlike Freud, however, Bowlby saw grief as primal attempts to recover the missing bond, or proximity to the missing object. It is a biological response to separation designed to elicit the desired response of reconnection (Holmes, 2001). Ultimately, however, when one is unable to reconnect, one abandons hope, falls into despair and eventually recovers when the bond is fully severed. Both Freud and Bowlby saw grief as natural progression through painful stages, culminating in a state of resolution or reorganization after the survivors cut the ties binding them to the dead. It is critical, at this juncture, to stress that detaching or diverting one's energy is not synonymous with forgetting (Fraley & Shaver, 1999). Even so, the precise nature of a state of detachment is not well defined other than to recognize it as the desirable outcome of grief. The processes whereby one achieves this are called "grief work" (Lindemann, 1944), a metaphor that was to carry bereavement research well into contemporary times, spawning a whole new scholarly and clinical discipline known as thanatology, the study of death and dying (Small, 2001).

Other Stage-Phase Models of Grief

Proponents of stage-phase models see grief as stages or phases that the bereaved encounter and work through towards the goal of completing or resolving their grief.

Stages most often described include numbness, shock/denial, awareness, protest/anguish, mourning/restitution, and resolution (Bowlby, 1973; Bowlby & Parkes, 1970; Kavanaugh, 1972; Lindemann, 1944; Weizman & Kamm, 1985; Zisook & Shuchter, 1991). The strength of descriptive stages is that they serve to normalize the change process for grieving individuals. Regardless of what mourners are experiencing, they can be assured that it is a normal phase and will pass (Wambach, 1985). One of the more prominent stage theorists was George Engel (1964), who likened the mental trauma of grief to physical trauma. His model suggested that grief injury healed in progressive stages over time just as physical injuries did. The further implication is that some injuries might leave no trace whilst others leave an ugly scar or never entirely heal. Because time is a variable but necessary change indicator of any stage model, critics feel these models depict a grief process that is at once too passive and too vulnerable to the imposition of arbitrary time constraints (Attig, 1991, 1996). And like other stage/phase theories of human behavior, this approach does not explain the tendency of many survivors to repeat phases, skip phases, experience them "out of order" or even simultaneously. In actuality, stages and phases of grief do tend to overlap and to be recursive rather than linear and sequential, so this perspective is out of favor with many who work in a support or counseling role with the bereaved. Those who currently maintain a phasic aspect to their approach tend to emphasize the flexibility of movement between phases (Bowlby, 1980; Sanders, 1999; Worden, 2002). The problem is that a too-literal public hears of the "Five Stages of Grief" (in actuality, Kübler-Ross's [1969] stages of dying, but arguably the most frequently encountered model of grief; Kastenbaum, 1993) and other popularized versions of grief theories (Hawkins, 1990) and applies them to their or someone else's grief experience, like a family recipe that will not turn out right if not done "just so."

Strict adherence to stages "necessary" for completion may give rise to more problems than they resolve (Samarel, 1995). But as Walter (1999) and Small (2001) note, it is important to distinguish between the intent of the framers (or theorists) and the (mis)interpretation of the masses. Few scholars of bereavement apply stringent rules to grief (Stroebe, van den Bout, & Schut, 1994). Even so, the leap between theory and practice is sometimes blind and perilous, perhaps more so with more complicated forms of bereavement. Time and resource-strapped counselors and other bereavement support personnel frequently look for the simplest away to describe and facilitate mourners' experience (Archer, 2001a). The lay public is not alone in taking stages or phases too far; counselors are sometimes overly zealous in their interpretation of appropriate grief processes (Corr et al., 1997; Payne, Jarrett, Wiles, & Field, 2002; Samarel, 1995; Worden, 2002). An example of a too-literal application of stage-theory is research reported by Tekavcic-Grad and Zavasnik (1992), who contend that suicide survivors must work through an anger phase which consists of recognizing the deceased as the target of anger and venting that anger or aggression. In fact, they conclude that the grief process is not complete without successful maneuvering through the anger phase. Whether they intend it or not, Tekavcic-Grad and Zavasnik's claim marks survivors who cannot feel anger toward their loved ones as victims of unhealthy or complicated grief. Most stage-phase oriented therapists are not so prescriptive, but more than one survivor has encountered a therapist who has taken Tekavcic-Grad and Zavasnik and other writers too literally (Corr, 1993; Ellis, 2000). As will be shown, task-based approaches can be equally prescriptive with similarly questionable applications.

Task-Based Models of Grief

Freud and Bowlby's work also led to an alternative, but related approach. Proponents of attachment theory tend to think of grief as both evidence of and outcome of loss, and this thinking is clearest in task-based views of grief (e.g., Parkes & Weiss, 1983; Worden, 1991, 2002). Bereavement task models delimit certain necessary tasks that are accomplished in the successful resolution of grief. For example, a consistent theme in bereavement research is the problem of coping with the changed nature of the relationship with the deceased. Task-based approaches address this as a need either to detach from the relationship or to transform it (Silverman & Klass, 1996; Walter, 1999). For example, Worden's (1982) model is frequently cited and summarized:

- acknowledge reality of the loss;
- work through emotional turmoil;
- adjust to deceased person's absence;
- loosen ties to deceased and reinvest energy elsewhere.

Although some experimental animal research supports the notion that replacing a lost relationship is beneficial to resolving grief (Hofer, 1984), the last task of Worden's list is troublesome and dissonant with many survivors' experience. It is particularly difficult for parents, who have attachments to the past, present, and future through their children, who are irreplaceable extensions of the parents. Although bereft parents may feel like that part of their selves has been amputated, they also continue to feel a strong connection to their deceased children. In a comment on early task models, Rando (1986) noted that the traditional criteria used to specify abnormal grief were normative components of parental grief. Klass and Marwit (1997; 1995, 1996) observed that bereaved parents reformed an inner relationship with a dead child's "psychic double" to replace the physical child who is lost in the parent's inner and social world. Subsequently, this observation recurred across loss types as scholars, clinicians, and writers scrutinized people's experience more closely and over longer periods (Archer, 1999). Thus "successful" grief process, for many investigators, has come to mean a continuation of the relationship with the deceased, or with an inner representation of the deceased, rather than the disengagement stressed in earlier conceptualizations (Boerner & Heckhausen, 2003; Datson & Marwit, 1997; Klass, 1988; Klass, Silverman, & Nickman, 1996; Marwit & Klass, 1995, 1996; Rubin, 1985, 1993; Shuchter & Zisook, 1988; Stroebe et al., 1992, 1996).

Acknowledging that healthy mourners do maintain bonds with departed loved ones, Worden's current (2002) version of the four-task model of grief work has changed the fourth task, "loosen ties to the deceased and reinvest energy elsewhere," to "emotionally relocate the deceased and move on with life" instead (p. 35, emphasis added). Still, the value placed on relational continuance is somewhat mixed, and is tempered by religious and spiritual practices and beliefs. One of the most enduring, powerful, and comforting beliefs about death is that it does not really exist. This is typically a spiritual concept involving some form of individual survival on a non-physical, non-earthly plane of existence. Death is not final; separation from loved ones is merely temporary. The world's major religions all support, if not demand, some form of this belief on the part of their adherents. Yet to some bereavement counselors, relying on a belief that the departed live on still represents a failure on some level. In a study of how parents cope with the death of a child, Knapp (1986) lumps this potent and effective coping mechanism with denial of the reality of the death along with the operant fiction employed by some parents that the child is merely "away from home." While conceding that this "myth" of continued existence, in whatever form, does "seem to bring comfort to them in their mourning" (p. 84), Knapp maintains that perpetuating the myth only delays an inevitable confrontation with the reality of the separation on an emotional level. Like many other bereavement scholars, Knapp implies that any delay in the process, beyond some arbitrary grace period defined as somewhere in the neighborhood of two weeks to two months, also represents complicating the process in an unhealthy manner (Rando, 1993).

Strategic or not, relational maintenance is not always voluntary or mindful on the part of the survivor. Shuchter and Zisook (1988) described several forms of relational maintenance used by widows they studied. These include dreams and "hallucinatory" encounters with their dead husbands (now called "after death communications" or "ADCs"); prayer about or to the deceased, along with other verbal communication with the deceased; memories; identification through children of the union; and participating in social and cultural rituals. Shuchter and Zisook's clinical approach assumed these experiences can lead to pathological idealization and fixation on the deceased. Consequently, they attempted to counter potential or real idealization of the deceased by getting widows to focus on negative aspects of the relationship along with the positive. Similarly, one facilitator of a widows group insisted members must assume the role of "abandoned victim" in order to generate enough negativity to counter idealization of the deceased (Francis, 1997). Clearly, the process of "letting go" can be far more complex than simply cutting emotional ties. One must figure out what to let go of, when to let go of it, and how to let it go.

The fine lines between pathological denial, idealization and fixation, and salutary relational continuance are difficult to draw. Despite those therapists who demand a more "realistic" view of the dead (which appears to emphasize negative appraisals), most bereaved people who continue a relationship with the deceased tend to do so with a highly positive inner representation of the dead person (Marwit & Klass, 1995). However, some deaths are ambiguous and continuance is problematic, particularly if the relationship with the deceased was highly negative or, at best, ambiguous (Reed, 1993, 1998; Reed & Greenwald, 1991). The bonds of the relationship are often perceived in a more negative fashion if the survivor feels rejected, betrayed, abandoned or unloved. So for these survivors, there is often the need for transformation or even building an altogether new relationship rather than continuation of the old as described by Datson and Marwit (1997). For some writers, any death of a close relational partner is traumatic. It shatters the "assumptive world" of the survivor and entails rebuilding one's inner world and one's relationships (Attig, 1991; Janoff-Bulman, 1989, 1993) or reconciling one's inner reality with external reality (Horowitz, Bonanno, & Holen, 1993; Parkes, 1988). Theoretically, the more fundamental the assumption violated (such as "children outlive their parents") or, alternatively, the greater the discrepancy between one's inner world and one's reality ("we had so many things left to do"), the more traumatic the loss and the more intense or difficult the subsequent grief and the "grief work" required resolve it (Archer, 2001a, 2001b).

Unlike stage-phase models which evoke, however inaccurately, images of passively riding out the throes of grief, task-based models appear to present a somewhat more active view, behaviorally, emotionally, and cognitively, of the grief process. Rando's (1993) six "R" processes reflect a task-centered approach that is more active than passive: (a) recognize the loss, (b) react to the separation it represents, (c) recollect and reexperience the relationship, (d) relinquish old attachments and the old assumptive world they represent, (e) readjust to function adaptively in the new world, and (f) reinvest (p. 45). As this model and Worden's (2002) revised model shows, task-based views are also better than stages or phases at describing actual processes undertaken by the bereaved. This is also apparent in the tasks described by Parkes and Weiss (1983):

- acknowledging and explaining the loss;
- emotionally accepting the loss;
- assuming a new identity.

The strength of Parkes and Weiss' perspective is in its recognition of how death requires a search for meaning and may fundamentally change a survivor. Other writers also have noted the importance of shaping a new self-identity in the wake of significant relational loss (Dunn & Morrish-Vidners, 1987; Neimeyer, 2001a; Neimeyer, Prigerson, & Davies, 2002; Van der Wal, 1989-90). Bowlby (1982) termed this a "cognitive act" of redefining the self and the situation. Forging a new identity, a necessity especially for bereaved spouses who must often assume new roles and functions (Lopata, 1975; Parkes, 1986; Sanders, 1999; Worden, 1982), is another form of breaking the bonds or achieving independence from the deceased.

While community library shelves hold a treasure trove of anecdotal accounts of survivors finding meaning, recovering their sense of self, adjusting to absence, and generally "coming to terms with" profound loss, there is little systematic information available on how these tasks are accomplished. Ethnographic and narrative studies of parents reconstructing and maintaining relationships with their deceased children (e.g., Klass, 1993a, 1993b, 1996; Riches & Dawson, 1998; 2000; Rosenblatt, 2000; Talbot, 2002) are notably few exceptions. Even so, the tasks of finding meaning and making sense of the loss continually appear in both the lay and professional literature. Like most conceptions of what occurs during grief, there is some confusion regarding these tasks. Some writers say that the bereaved attempt to find meaning in the death (e.g., Murphy, 1996; Murphy et al., 2003a, 2003b), or need to make sense of it because death is unfamiliar (Staudacher, 1987); others say that one must find new meaning in life (e.g., Shuchter, 1986; Wheeler, 1993-1994).

Some say making sense of the loss means understanding what has occurred and its impact on one's life (e.g., Van der Wal, 1989-1990). Others write that making sense of the loss means understanding why the death has occurred (e.g., Wortman & Silver, 1990). For others, it is not so much making sense of the loss but constructing a story that makes sense that is key to recovery (Harvey, 1996; Harvey et al., 1992; 1995), or integrating the loss within one's ongoing life narrative and sharing it (Neimeyer, 1999; 2001a,b,c). All of these tasks might be viewed as essential, but they are also highly subjective and, as Stroebe (1992-1993) points out, hardly measurable.

Easily measurable, however, is time, and it is one of the most scrutinized dimensions of grief recovery. There is not a clear standard of how long a phase should last or how long a task should take, nor is there consensus on how long the recovery process should take. Arbitrary time constraints on grieving have been shown to be problematic, yet persist because of the notion that time heals all wounds (Engel, 1964). One model of bereavement response that has gained some attention is Wortman and Silver's (1989) temporal model of grief distress. They observe that grievers fall into one of three common temporal patterns following a loss: overall progression from high to low distress over time (a.k.a. "recovery" or "working through"), persistent low distress, and persistent high distress that does not ease with time. A fault of this model is that it fails to allow for the frequent, wide-ranging, and often-cyclic shifts in distress levels reported by some bereaved people. At the least, there should be some acknowledgement of those whose distress tends to rise over time, such as that of many suicide survivors (for a review, see Stillion, 1996). In addition, the nature of grief distress is not well articulated in their model; for example, the construct is confounded by failure to control for possible sources of distress other than grief, such as depression and coping with the distress of other survivors.

In another recent approach to grief, Moules (1998) argues that while time is the least accurate parameter of grief process, it is probably the most commonly invoked diagnostic as a determination of whether grief requires medical intervention or should invoke social opprobrium. For Moules, grief is a lifelong process of adaptation, of integrating and assimilating loss into our lives. She takes issue with the idea that resolution or finding "closure," a byword recently enshrined in our cultural lexicon, is even possible. Efforts to find therapeutic ways of helping people end their grief may only compound feelings of inadequacy and failure. For Moules and others, it is the integration of and adaptation to grief (e.g., Klass, 1997; Riches & Dawson, 1998, 2000; Stroebe et al., 1993; Walter, 1996, 1997, 1999), not the end of grief, which is the goal.

Still, the bulk of research reflects long-standing psychological, behavioral, clinical, palliative, and even ecumenical perspectives that grief is, above all, a process of resolution. Theories that seek resolution tend to be prescriptive rather than explanatory, adaptive, transformational, or creative. Grief is understood to be a response to painful relational loss, and an end to grief is manifested as an end to the pain and dysfunction associated with the loss (Corr et al., 1997). Not surprisingly, most of the lay literature on grief follows this pattern also. Grief has become the "stranger at our door" in postmodern times, and people require how-to manuals to recover from the process (Staudacher, 1987). Many funeral homes now distribute comprehensive books on grief to their customers. So alien is grief to our experience that Parkes (1998b) observed that people often need permission to stop grieving as much as they need permission to grieve.

What stage-phase and task-based explanations do rather well is offer a heuristically simple framework for the somewhat chaotic experience of grief. It is this very simplicity that probably helped purely descriptive efforts make the "shift from insight into prescription" and from observation to orthodoxy that can "shape both popular applications and professional practice" (Small, 2001, pp.31-32). Aside from prescriptive misuses (Samarel, 1995), stage-phases do have descriptive uses, but tend to retain strong connotations of linearity, unidirectionality, and exclusivity which, when applied to recursive grief experience, seem wholly arbitrary (Archer, 2001; van der Wal, 1989-1990). Additionally, in a rigid stage construction there is no room for outside influences on the process (Wortman & Silver, 1992). Above all, they imply a desirable end point that simply does not exist for many grievers (Corr et al., 1997). Yet stages and phases of grief echo progressive experiences familiar to anyone who has suffered and "recovered from" a significant loss.

Task-based models suggest a more strategic process on the part of the bereaved, but offer conflicting ideas about what specific tasks are required. Evaluative criteria for task performance is sketchy. Furthermore, so much emphasis has been placed on identifying tasks that no clear guidelines exist for how people achieve tasks. However, to discard the task-based model entirely is to ignore compelling research demonstrating that bereaved people do engage in many similar tasks as they grieve (Rando, 1993; Worden, 2002). Clearly, there are tasks that must be performed and problems to be addressed in any process of grief.

While there appears to be no consensus on the nature and extent of grief across a variety of loss circumstances and conditions, the fact that grief is work has seemed indisputable. Research on grief tasks suggests that grief work is arduous and may take up quite a lot of time and effort on the part of the survivor. It must be "pained through" (Lindemann, 1979, p.234). To avoid the emotional turmoil, or to deny it by expressing positive emotions instead, is to run the risk of one's grief being labeled "pathological" (Sanders, 1993). Yet because grief can be so debilitating, avoidance and distraction may be just what a mourner needs to progress beyond the most acute aspects of grief (Bonanno, 2001; Bonanno & Keltner, 1997; Bonanno et al., 1995; Stroebe & Stroebe, 1991). Stroebe and Stroebe (1987) and Wortman and Silver (1989) were the first to challenge the notion that grief work, whether as phases or tasks, constitutes an inevitable and necessary component of bereavement.

A New Paradigm: Alternative Approaches to Grief Work

What if "working through" grief is detrimental to one's well being? This is the perspective offered by Bonanno and Kaltman (1999, 2001). Alternative approaches to grief work suggest grief has become problematic partly because of the "myth" that it is a negative but necessary response to a negative event (Wortman & Silver, 1989).

Supporting Wortman and Silver's challenge to the grief work hypothesis, Bonanno and Kaltman's (1999) review of bereavement research found that those who avoided their grief and "put a happy face on it" later fared better on typical post-bereavement measures of mental and emotional functioning than those who seemed to dwell in their grief and express strong emotion earlier on. Bonanno and his colleagues (Bonanno, Keltner, Holen, & Horowitz, 1995; Bonanno & Kaltman, 1999; Bonanno & Keltner, 1997, Bonanno et al., 1998) suggest that, in part, people who avoid, defer, or minimize emotional processing of their grief are better able to maintain function, thus preventing stress; and to maintain their social network ties, thus garnering more social support and minimizing loneliness and depression.

This, of course, is a departure from even the "gentlest" of grief theories, ones that allow one to continue the bonds (Klass, 1997; Riches & Dawson, 1998, 2000) and dwell in one's grief until it becomes a part of the newly integrated self (Harvey, 1996; Moules, 1998; Pennebaker & Keough, 1999). It is a far cry from the more wrenching ones that suggest a new identity is forged along with a whole new assumptive world after one's reality is shattered (Attig, 1996; Janoff-Bulman, 1989, 1993; Janoff-Bulman & Berg, 1998; Parkes, 1996), or those that suggest one should find a replacement relationship. It is an even more radical departure from the models that predicted complications would arise from delayed, denied, or suppressed grief (Doka, 1987, 1989; Jacobs, 1993; Parkes & Weiss, 1995; Rando, 1993; Sanders, 1993). It also raises all sorts of frightening possibilities like grievers being told to avoid grieving at all costs, governments and other sponsoring organizations cutting bereavement support programs, and people feeling guilty or crazy when they cannot simply ignore it or "get over it." It also reprises the dilemma of precisely what to tell the bereaved.

In effect, competing models exist regarding the value of engaging in grief work or de-emphasizing the emotional impact of a relational loss. So drastic are the implications that the opposing approaches necessarily pit one response against another in a good grief-bad grief dichotomy. On the one hand, long held traditions suggest the importance and cathartic effects of feeling and letting out the pain so as to overcome it more quickly and completely. On the other hand, compelling research by Bonanno and his colleagues undermines this; survivors who focus on anything but the pain tend to score better on certain measures of post-bereavement adaptation (Bauer & Bonanno, 2001; Bonanno, 1998, 2004; Bonanno & Field, 2001; Bonanno & Kaltman, 2001; Bonanno & Keltner, 1997; Bonanno, Keltner, Holen & Horowitz, 1995; Bonanno et al., 1998; Bonanno et al., 2002; Field, Gal-Oz, & Bonanno, 2003; Keltner & Bonanno, 1997). If nothing else, this surprising research underscores the need for a new paradigm.

A new paradigm need not be radical or revolutionary (Kuhn, 1970). A middle ground is emerging between these two competing models of bereavement, a view of grief that allows both working through and minimizing negative emotional experience. For it seems clear that much confusion about grief, and confused experience of grief, stems from the two radically opposing schools of thought and their application to (and by) bereaved people. Longitudinal investigations conducted by Lindstrøm and her colleague (Qvarnstrøm & Lindstrøm, 1982; cf. Lindstrøm, 2002) suggest that it has been the "forced" behavior of attempting either extreme, i.e., struggling to face it or to resist facing it, according to prevailing social and medical dictates (e.g., Small's notion of bereavement "orthodoxy", 2001), that results in physical, emotional, and social problems associated with relational loss. In other words, attempts to help might cause the very problems that we hope to prevent. On the one hand, Lindstrøm is against continuing to advocate traditional grief work, an outdated and scientifically unsupported approach to bereavement support, however venerable and intuitive it may seem. On the other, she poignantly reminds us that grief work (as opposed to avoidance) has its benefits, too:

> I have experienced a unique awareness of what really is meaningful and valuable in my life during periods of grief—an awareness usually hidden behind the trivialities of everyday life. These experiences have changed and enriched my life. If I had completely repressed, sedated, and diverted my grief away, I am afraid these moments of clarity would not have happened. (Lindstrøm, 2002, p. 20)

Stroebe and Schut's (1999; Stroebe, Schut, & Stroebe, 2005) Dual Process Model (DPM) of coping with bereavement is a promising perspective that views grief as a dual process of oscillating between focusing on the loss and coping with other stressors arising from the loss. This approach arose out of recognition that death presents survivors with multiple and diverse stressors that require coping efforts that reflect either a loss orientation or a recovery orientation (Servaty-Seib, 2004). In essence, focusing on the loss is the equivalent of fixating on what one cannot fix, whereas facing other challenges is perceived to be restorative. A loss orientation involves all the traditional "grief work" of feeling one's emotions and expressing them, ruminating, severing ties or maintaining them, finding meaning, constructing a narrative and so on. A recovery orientation, on the other hand, means looking forward, also severing ties or maintaining them, staying busy, seeking other outlets for one's energy, suppressing negative emotions, gaining other sources of support and so on, i.e., working hard to not focus on one's grief.

The point of DPM is that both orientations are necessary, and both inclinations should be present in the course of normal grief. In other words, to paraphrase Parkes (1998b), one should give oneself permission to grieve and permission not to grieve. DPM renders moot the question of whether grief ends or endures; one is either in a loss orientation cycle or recovery orientation cycle, or one is oscillating somewhere in between the two. Because oscillation itself is the core adaptive process, natural grief involves steady oscillation between the orientations, with a shift toward recovery or restorative focus over time (Stroebe & Schut, 2001b). Presumably, this occurs as one gains progressively greater control over the process, with less rapid and unexpected cycling between extremes. Perhaps this is best described as a gradual falling toward the mean as one regains some sense of control over events, cognitions, and emotions. The mean in this case is not interpreted as some overall statistic, but rather one's normal personal tendency; for example, whether it is toward constructive or destructive behaviors, positive or negative emotions, and internal or external locus of control. Other research seems to resonate with this. In comparing DPM to Gestalt theory (think "yin and yang" as two necessary opposites creating a whole), Servaty-Seib (2004) observes that Gestalt theorists have described grief as a process of mastering an alternating rhythm of facing and avoiding the pain (Sabar, 2000), and, alternatively, connecting (with life and others) and separating (focusing on death) (Clark, 1982).

From the standpoint of Stroebe and Schut's DPM model (1999; 2001b), it becomes easier to distinguish good grief from bad. One need merely ask if a person is focusing too much on one orientation at the expense of the other. Chronic grief, for example, would involve too much emphasis on loss, whereas too little focus on loss indicates repressed, delayed, or absent grief. The model is less prescriptive than earlier ones, and it is recognized that what constitutes a loss focus in one case (or culture) may mean a recovery orientation in another. Early research shows that collectivistic and individualistic societies do tend to favor one orientation over another (cf. Stroebe, Schut, & Stroebe, 2005). Similarly, research in gender differences in the efficacy of grief counseling suggests masculine and feminine genders will orient differently. A tendency to avoid loss and its emotional work is likely to be both more typical and problematic among men, whereas women may find themselves indulging too greatly in their emotions and unable to engage in restorative activities (Schut et al., 1997).

Ashes to Ashes: Further Integrating the New with the Old

According to Silverman and Klass (1996), models of grief based on continuing bonds entail sustained emotional interdependence between the living and the dead. In other words, constructing an "inner representation" of the deceased, and remaining involved with and connected to the dead, is part of the normal grieving process. More traditional models of grief specify cutting emotional ties as part of successful grief work. In such conceptualizations, the retention of emotional bonds with the deceased, beyond the initial period of bereavement, is considered detrimental to the grief process and well being of the survivor. Like the problem of expressing or stifling grief, the question of whether to cut, to continue, or simply even to modify relational bonds, leads to conflicting approaches to grief support. As one can imagine, the problem of whether one is "doing it right" can only add to the pain of having to grieve at all.

DPM has been linked to attachment theory and thus incorporates the psychoanalytic notion of working through one's grief (Stroebe, Schut, & Stroebe, 2005), but transcends the need to value detaching from or maintaining relational bonds. Hence, that stressor is listed under both loss and recovery orientations above. Whether one does or does not continue the bond, and whether or not doing so is adaptive or detrimental, is dependent on the nature of the relationship and the attachment style of the bereaved (Noppe, 2000; Stroebe, Schut, & Stroebe, 2005). Ironically, insecurely attached individuals are often most in need of letting go (and need help doing so), but securely attached individuals are likely to both hold on and let go, in a sense "relocating" the deceased so they can go on to other things, as suggested by Worden's (2002) task model.

Stroebe et al. (2005) suggest the pre-loss attachment style and qualities of the relationship are influential factors in the degree of continuing connection with the deceased. However, I also argue that the aspects of the death itself, and other contextual variables unique to that situation, time, and relationship, could significantly alter one's perception of a "lost" relationship. Some deaths involve issues of trust, security, and abandonment, and therefore it is possible that attachment styles could shift from secure to insecure and vice versa as a result of a death, so pre-death attachment style should be interpreted with caution as a predictor of post-loss connection and its value to the bereaved. A significant change in one's model of attachment could explain unexpected patterns of oscillation and the use of certain behavioral and cognitive coping strategies to maintain or favor a particular orientation toward loss or recovery. More complicated grief issues suggest more inner and social conflict between loss and recovery processes; in other words, greater effort is required to manage the more chaotic and dissonant oscillations.

Contradictory yet compelling impulses such as holding on and letting go, experiencing the loss and looking toward recovery, are strongly evocative of the dialectics managed and negotiated more or less successfully by partners in ongoing relationships (Baxter, 1993; Baxter & Montgomery, 1996). While the "negotiating" aspect becomes effectively one-sided after death, I argue that grief is a form of negotiation with one's memories and "inner representation" of the deceased loved one. Invoking both Freud (1917) and Klass and Walter (2001), in a dialogic sense (Mikhail Bakhtin, cf. Holquist, 1990), people are already constantly negotiating contradictory impulses and navigating changes in reality via a sort of ongoing internal dialogue with the self or some imagined other. Grief is just another form of self-dialogue, of negotiated reality, as one learns to reframe and integrate the loss experience. McCabe (2003) has tried to articulate this same argument in an auto-ethnographic report of her grief experience after her mother's death. McCabe's effort has yielded insight into what she calls the relational nature of grief. Other scholars have examined specific dialectics encountered by grieving individuals that seem to fit well with the loss/recovery orientation model. Baxter, Braithwaite, Golish, and Olson (2002) found that wives of men with Alzheimer's experienced a form of anticipatory bereavement wherein many took comfort in their husband's continued physical presence (recovery orientation) while mourning the mental and emotional absence brought on by the disease (loss orientation). Toller (2005) studied bereaved parents and reports that they experienced a strong contradiction between a desire to be open about their loss and to mourn in private (construed here as a recovery focus because it suggests quelling public expression of grief). I anticipate that further research on grief dialectics will continue to elaborate on the constant negotiating between contradictory needs and desires on the part of survivors.

Conclusion

The DPM is not the only new, integrative model in the thanatology landscape. Other theorists are doing important work that continues to lead us away from simplistic and formulaic approaches to grief toward richer and more complex insights that more accurately reflect the depth and diversity of human experience. Integrating diverse realms such as attachment theory and animal grief, Archer (1999) takes an evolutionary perspective that examines how biology informs grief research and experience. Walter's (1996) sociocultural approach explores the connections among grief, memory, and culture. With compelling evidence gleaned via rigorous methods, Bonanno and his colleagues continue to challenge some of our most cherished and ingrained beliefs about how we grieve and how we should grieve (Bonanno, Moskowitz, Papa, & Folkman, 2005; Bonanno, & Papa, in press; Bonanno et al., 2005; Bonanno, Papa, & O'Neill, in press; Bonanno & Wortman, in press). Harvey, Neimeyer, and associates are still probing the importance of finding meaning and constructing narratives as ways to reconstruct lives devastated by loss and trauma (Barnes & Harvey, 2000; Harvey, 1998, 2000; Harvey et al., 2001; Neimeyer, 1999, 2000, 2001a,b,c; Neimeyer & Anderson, 2001; Neimeyer & Arvay, 2004; Neimeyer & Tschudi, 2003). For over twenty years, Pennebaker and his colleagues have assessed how sharing the most painful stories, and even the struggles to complete them, may strengthen those who struggle most (Pennebaker, 1997, 2002; Pennebaker & Keough, 1999; Pennebaker & Suedfeld, 1997; Pennebaker & Susman, 1988; Smyth, 1998).

Grief is an intensely personal response to devastating loss. But it occurs in a social context that is either compassionate and supportive, or lonely and isolating, or some ambiguous mixture of both (Neimeyer, 1999; 2000; Walter, 1996). Consequently, grief has the capacity to be an even more daunting and devastating process beyond coping with the loss itself. Part of the influence on the social and personal context of grief has been how we, collectively and independently, define and value our experience. For as painful as it is, there is value in grief:

To be able to think in terms of past, present, and future, to love and to grieve, is part of the human existential plight and dignity. Grief may add meaning and perspective to one's life just as shadows give depth to a landscape. (Lindstrom, 2002, p. 20)

Consider this . . .

- As you reflect on grief you've experienced in your life, what feelings or themes come to mind about your experience?
- Briefly describe what you consider to be strengths and weaknesses of Stage-Phase Models of Grief. Give an example to illustrate.
- Briefly describe what you consider to be strengths and weaknesses of Task-Based Models of Grief. Give an example to illustrate.
- Briefly describe what you consider to be strengths and weaknesses of the Dual Perspective Model of Grief. Give an example to illustrate.
- Smith observes that the Dual Perspective Model (DPM) may provide the opportunity to assess the grieving process from different standpoint. How might Standpoint Theory be useful in applying this model?

References

Attig T. (1991). The importance of conceiving of grief as an active process. *Death Studies, 15(4),* 385-393.

Attig, T. (1996). *How we grieve: Relearning the world.* New York: Oxford University Press.

Archer, J. (1999). *The nature of grief: The evolution and psychology of reactions to loss.* New York: Routledge.

Archer, J. (2001a). Broad and narrow perspectives on grief: Comment on Bonanno and Kaltman (1999). *Psychological Bulletin, 127(4),* 554–560.

Archer, J. (2001b). Grief from an evolutionary perspective. In M. S. Stroebe, W. Stroebe, R. O. Hansson, & H. Schut (Eds.), *Handbook of bereavement research: Consequences, coping and care* (pp. 263–283). Washington, DC: American Psychological Association.

Averill, J. (1968). Grief: Its nature and significance. *Psychological Bulletin, 70,* 721-748

Barnes, C., & Harvey, J. H. (2000) Comparison of Narratives of Loss Experiences of World War II and Vietnam Combat Veterans. In J. H. Harvey & B. G. Pauwels (Eds.), Posttraumatic Stress Theory, Research and Application. Philadelphia: Brunner/Mazel, and in Special Issue of the *Journal of Personal & Interpersonal Loss, 5,* 167-182.

Bauer, J. J., & Bonanno, G. A. (2001). Doing and being well (for the most part): Adaptive patterns of narrative self-evaluation during bereavement. *Journal of Personality, 69,* 451-482.

Baxter, L. A. (1993). The social side of personal relationships: A Dialectical perspective. In S. Duck (Ed.), *Social context and relationships* (pp. 139-165). Newbury Park, CA: Sage

Baxter, L. A., & Montgomery, B. M. (1996). *Relating: Dialogues and dialectics.* New York: Guilford Press.

Baxter, L. A., Braithwaite, D. O., Golish, T .D., & Olson, L. N. (2002). Contradictions of interaction for wives of husbands with adult dementia. *Journal of Applied Communication Research, 29,* 221-247.

Boerner, K., & Heckhausen, J. (2003). To have and have not: adaptive bereavement by transforming mental ties to the deceased. *Death Studies, 27(3)*:199-226.

Bonanno, G. A. (1998). The concept of "working through" loss: A critical evaluation of the cultural, historical, and empirical evidence. In A. Maercker, M. Schuetzwohl, & Z. Solomon (Eds.), *Posttraumatic stress disorder: Vulnerability and resilience in the life-span* (pp. 221–247). Göttingen, Germany: Hogrefe & Huber.

Bonanno, G. A. (2001). Grief and emotion: A social-functional perspective. In M. Stroebe, R. O. Hansson, W. Stroebe, & H. Schut (Eds.), *Handbook of bereavement research: Consequences, coping, and care* (pp. 493–515). Washington, DC: American Psychological Association.

Bonanno, G. A. (2004). Loss, trauma, and human resilience: Have we underestimated the human capacity to thrive after extremely aversive events? *American Psychologist, 59,* 20–28.

Bonanno, G.A., & Field, N. P. (2001). Evaluating the delayed grief hypothesis across 5 years of bereavement. *American Behavioral Scientist, 44,* 798–816.

Bonanno, G. A., & Kaltman, S. (1999). Toward an integrative perspective on bereavement. *Psychological Bulletin, 125,* 760–776.

Bonanno, G. A., & Kaltman, S. (2001). The varieties of grief experience. *Clinical Psychology Review, 20,* 1–30.

Bonanno, G. A., & Keltner, D. (1997). Facial expressions of emotion and the course of bereavement. *Journal of Abnormal Psychology, 106,* 126–137.

Bonanno, G. A., Keltner, D., Holen, A., & Horowitz, M. J. (1995). When avoiding unpleasant emotion might not be such a bad thing: Verbal-autonomic response dissociation and midlife conjugal bereavement. *Journal of Personality and Social Psychology, 46,* 975–989.

Bonanno, G. A., Moskowitz, J. T., Papa, A., & Folkman, S. (2005). Resilience to loss in bereaved spouses, bereaved parents, and bereaved gay men. *Journal of Personality and Social Psychology, 88(5),* 827–843.

Bonanno, G. A., Notarius, C. I., Gunzerath, L., Keltner, D., & Horowitz, M. J. (1998). Interpersonal ambivalence, perceived dyadic adjustment, and conjugal loss. *Journal of Consulting and Clinical Psychology, 66,* 1012–1022.

Bonanno, G. A., & Papa, A. (in press). *The social and functional aspects of emotional expression during bereavement.* In P. Phillipot, E. J. Coats, & R. S. Feldman (Eds.), Nonverbal behavior in clinical settings. Cambridge, England: Cambridge University Press.

Bonanno, G. A., Papa, A., Lalande, K., Zhang, N., & Noll, J. G. (2005). Grief Processing and Deliberate Grief Avoidance: A Prospective Comparison of Bereaved Spouses and Parents in the United States and the People's Republic of China. *Journal of Consulting and Clinical Psychology, 73(1),* 86-98.

Bonanno, G. A., Papa, A., & O'Neill, K. (in press). *Loss and human resilience.* Applied and Preventative Psychology.

Bonanno, G. A., & Wortman, C. (in press). Tracking the extremes of bereavement: Chronic grief, absent grief, and their pre-bereavement predictors. *Journal of Personality and Social Psychology.*

Bonanno, G. A., Wortman, C. B., Lehman, D. R., Tweed, R. G., Haring, M., Sonnega, J. Carr, D., & Nesse, R. M. (2002). Resilience to loss and chronic grief: A prospective study from preloss to 18-months postloss. *Journal of Personality and Social Psychology, 83(5),* 1150-1164.

Bonanno, G. A., Wortman, C. B., & Nesse, R. M. (2004). Prospective patterns of resilience and maladjustment during widowhood. *Psychology and Aging, 19,* 260–271.

Bowlby, J. (1969). *Attachment and loss: Vol. 1. Attachment.* New York: Basic Books.

Bowlby, J. (1973). *Attachment and loss: Vol. 2. Separation.* New York: Basic Books.

Bowlby, J. (1980). *Attachment and loss: Vol. 3. Loss: Sadness and depression.* New York: Basic Books.

Bowlby, J. (1982). Attachment and loss: Retrospect and prospect. *American Journal of Orthopsychiatry, 52,* 664-677.

Bowlby, J., & Parke, C.M. (1970). Separation and Loss within the Family. In E. J. Anthony (Ed.), *The child in his family* (pp. 197-216). New York: Whiley.

Brabant, S. (1996). *Mending the torn fabric.* Amityville, NY: Baywood.

Cameron, E. C. (1991). Creative ritual: Bridge between mastery and meaning. *Pastoral Psychology, 40(1),* 3-13.

Clark, A. (1982). Grief and gestalt therapy. *The Gestalt Journal, 5,* 49-63.

Corr, C. A. (1993) Coping with dying: lessons that we should and should not learn from the work of Elisabeth Kubler-Ross. *Death Studies, 17,* 1, 69-83.

Corr, C. A., Nabe, C. M., & Corr, D. M. (1997). *Death and dying, life and living,* 2nd ed. Pacific Grove, CA: Brooks/Cole.

Currer, C. (2001). Is grief an illness? Issues of theory in relation to cultural diversity and the grieving process. In J. Hockey, J. Katz, & N. Small (Eds.), *Grief, mourning, and death ritual* (pp. 49-60). Philadelphia: Open University Press.

Datson, S. L., Marwit, S. J. (1997). Personality constructs and perceived presence of deceased loved ones. *Death Studies, 21(2),* 131-146.

Doka, K. J. (Ed.). (1987). *Disenfranchised grief: Recognizing hidden loss.* Lexington, MA: Lexington Books.

Doka, K. J. (Ed.). (1989). *Disenfranchised grief: Recognizing hidden sorrow.* Lexington, MA: Lexington Books.

Dunn, R. G., & Morrish-Vidners, D. (1987). The psychological and social experience of suicide survivors. *Omega, 18,* 175-215.

Ellis, A. (2000). Rational emotive behavior therapy. In R. J. Corsini & D. Wedding (Eds.), *Current psychotherapies* (6th ed., pp. 168-204). Itasca, IL: Peacock.

Engel, G. L. (1961). Is grief a disease? *Psychosomatic Medicine. 23,* 1, 18-22.

Engel, G. L. (1964). Grief and grieving. *American Journal of Nursing, 64,* 93-98.

Eyetsemitan, F. (1998). Stifled grief in the workplace. *Death Studies, 22(5),* 469-479.

Farnsworth, E. B, & Allen, K. R. (1996). Mothers' bereavement: Experiences of marginalization, stories of change. *Family Relations, 45(4),* 360-367.

Field, N. P., Gal-Oz, E., & Bonanno, G. A. (2003). Continuing bonds and adjustment at 5 years after the death of a spouse. *Journal of Consulting and Clinical Psychology, 71,* 110–117.

Fraley, R. C., & Shaver, P. R. (1999). Loss and bereavement: Bowlby's theory and recent controversies concerning "grief work" and the nature of detachment. In J. Cassidy & P. R. Shaver (Eds.), *Handbook of attachment theory and research: Theory, research, and clinical applications* (pp. 735–759). New York: Guilford Press.

Francis, L. E. (1997). Ideology and interpersonal emotion management: Redefining identity in two support groups. *Social Psychology Quarterly, 60(2),* 153-171.

Freud, S. (1917, 1957). Mourning and melancholia. In J. Strachey (Ed. and Trans.), *The standard edition of complete psychological works of Sigmund Freud* (Vol. 14). London: Hogarth Press. (Original work published 1917)

Harvey, J. H. (1996). *Embracing their memory: Loss and the social psychology of storytelling.* Needham Heights, MA: Allyn & Bacon.

Harvey, J. H. (2000). *Give sorrow words: perspectives on loss and trauma.* Philadelphia: Brunner/Mazel.

Harvey, J. H., Barnes, M. K., Carlson, H. R., & Haig, J. (1995). Held captive by their memories. In S. Duck & J. Wood (Eds.), *Relationship challenges* (pp. 210-233). Newbury Park, CA: Sage.

Harvey, J.H., Carlson, H.R., Huff, T.M., & Green, M.A. (2001). Embracing their memory: The construction of accounts. In R. A. Neimeyer (Ed.), *Meaning reconstruction and the experience of loss* (pp. 213-230). Washington, D.C.: American Psychological Association.

Harvey, J. H., Orbuch, T. L., Weber, A.L., Merbach, N., & Alt, R. (1992), House of pain and hope: Accounts of loss. *Death Studies, 16,* 99-124.

Hawkins, A. H. (1990). Constructing death: Three pathologies about dying. *Omega, 22,* 301-317.

Hindmarch, C. (1993) *On the Death of a Child.* Oxford: Radcliffe Medical Press Ltd.

Hofer, M. A. (1984). *Relationships as regulators: A psychobiological perspective on bereavement. Psychosomatic Medicine, 46,* 183-197.

Holmes, J. (2001). *The search for the secure base: Attachment theory and psychotherapy.* Hove, England: Brunner-Routledge.

Holquist, M. (1990). *Dialogism: Bakhtin and His World.* London: Routledge.

Horowitz, M. J. (1990). A model of mourning: Change in schemas of self and other. *Journal of the American Psychoanalytic Association, 38,* 297–324.

Horowitz, M. J., Bonanno, G. A., & Holen, A. (1993). Pathological grief: Diagnosis and explanation. *Psychosomatic Medicine, 55,* 260-273.

Jacobs, S. (1993). *Pathologic grief: Maladaptation to loss.* Washington, DC: American Psychiatric Association Press.

Janoff-Bulman, R. (1989). Assumptive worlds and the stress of traumatic events: Applications of the schema construct. *Social Cognition, 7,* 113-136.

Janoff-Bulman, R. (1993). *Shattered assumptions: Towards a new psychology of trauma.* New York: Free Press.

Janoff-Bulman, R., & Berg, M. (1998). Disillusionment and the creation of value: From traumatic losses to existential gains. In J. H. Harvey (Ed.), Pers*pectives on loss: A sourcebook* (pp. 35–47). Philadelphia: Taylor & Francis.

Kastenbaum, R. (1993). Reconstructing death in postmodern society. *Omega, 27,* 75-89.

Kavanaugh, R. (1972). *Facing death.* Los Angeles: Nash Publishing.

Keltner, D., & Bonanno, G. A. (1997). A study of laughter and dissociation: Distinct correlates of laughter and smiling during bereavement. *Journal of Personality and Social Psychology, 73,* 687–702.

Klass, D. (1988). *Parental grief. Solace and resolution.* New York: Springer.

Klass, D. (1993a) Solace and Immortality: bereaved parents' continuing bond with their children. *Death Studies 17,* 343–368.

Klass, D. (1993b). The inner representation of the dead child and the world views of bereaved parents. *Omega, 26,* 255-272.

Klass, D. (1996). The deceased child in the psychic and social worlds of bereaved parents during the resolution of grief. In D. Klass, P. R. Silverman, & S. L. Nickman (Eds.), *Continuing bonds* (pp. 199-215). Washington/DC: Taylor & Francis.

Klass, D. (1997). The deceased child in the psychic and social worlds of bereaved parents during the resolution of grief. *Death Studies, 21(2),* 147-175.

Klass, D., Silverman, P. R., & Nickman, S. L. (Eds.). (1996). *Continuing bonds: New understandings of grief.* Washington, DC: Taylor & Francis.

Klass, D., & Walter, T. (2001). Processes of grieving: How bonds are continued. In M. S. Stroebe, R. O. Hansson, W. Stroebe, & H. Schut (Eds.), *Handbook of bereavement research* (pp. 431-448). Washington, DC: American Psychological Association.

Knapp, R. J. (1986). *Beyond endurance: When a child dies.* New York: Schocken Books.

Kübler-Ross, E. (1969). *On death and dying.* New York: Collier.

Kuhn, T. S. (1970). *The Structure of Scientific Revolutions.* Chicago: University of Chicago Press.

LaGrand, L. E. (1991). United we cope: Support groups for the dying and bereaved. *Death Studies, 15,* 207-230.

Lindemann, E. (1944). The symptomatology and management of acute grief. *American Journal of Psychiatry, 101,* 141-148.

Lindemann, E. (1979). *Beyond grief: Studies in crisis intervention.* New York: Aronson.

Lindstrøm, T. C. (2002). "It Ain't Necessarily So"...Challenging mainstream thinking about bereavement. *Family and Community Health, 25,* 11-21.

Lopata, H. (1975). On widowhood: Grief work and identity reconstruction. *Journal of Geriatric Psychiatry, 8,* 41–55.

Mahon, M., & Page, M. L. (1995). Childhood bereavement after the death of a sibling. *Holistic Nursing Practice, 9,* 15-26.

Marwit, S. J., & Klass, D. (1995). Grief and the role of the inner representation of the deceased. *Omega: Journal of Death and Dying, 30,* 283-298.

Marwit, S. J., & Klass, D. (1996). Grief and the role of the inner representation of the deceased. In D. Klass, P. R. Silverman, & S. L. Nickman (Eds.), *Continuing bonds: New understandings of grief* (pp. 297-309). Washington, DC: Taylor & Francis.

McCabe, M. (2003). *The paradox of loss: Toward a relational theory of grief.* Westport, CT: Praeger.

Middleton, W., Raphael, B., Martinek, N., & Misso, V. (1993). Pathological grief reactions. In M. S. Stroebe, W Stroebe, & R. O. Hansson (Eds.), *Handbook of bereavement: Theory, research, and intervention* (pp. 44-61). Cambridge: Cambridge University Press.

Moules, N. J. (1998). Legitimizing grief: Challenging beliefs that constrain. *Journal of Family Nursing, 4(2),* 142-166.

Murphy, S. A. (1996). Parent bereavement stress and preventive intervention following the violent deaths of adolescent or young adult children. *Death Studies, 20(5),* 441-452.

Murphy, S. A., Johnson, L. C., & Lohan, J. (2003a). Challenging the myths about Parents' adjustment after the sudden, violent death of a child. *Journal of Nursing Scholarship, 35(4),* 359-364.

Murphy, S. A., Johnson, L. C., Wu, L., Fan, J. J., & Lohan, J. (2003b). Bereaved parents' outcomes 4 to 60 months after their children's deaths by accident, suicide, or homicide: A comparative study demonstrating differences. *Death Studies, 27,* 39-61.

Nadeau, J. W. (1998). *Families making sense of death.* Thousand Oaks, CA: Sage.

Neimeyer, R. A. (1998). *Lessons of loss: A guide to coping.* New York: McGraw-Hill.

Neimeyer, R. A. (1999). Narrative strategies in grief therapy. *Journal of Constructivist Psychology, 12,* 65-85.

Neimeyer, R. A. (2000). Searching for the meaning of meaning: Grief therapy and the process of reconstruction. *Death Studies, 24,* 541-558.

Neimeyer, R. A. (Ed.). (2001a). *Meaning reconstruction and the experience of loss.* Washington, DC: American Psychological Association.

Neimeyer, R. A. (2001b). Reauthoring life narratives: Grief therapy as meaning reconstruction. *Israel Journal of Psychiatry and Related Sciences, 38,* 171-183.

Neimeyer, R. A. (2001c). The language of loss: Grief therapy as a process of meaning reconstruction. In R. A. Neimeyer (Ed.), *Meaning reconstruction and the experience of loss* (pp. 26-292). Washington, DC: American Psychological Association.

Neimeyer, R. A., & Anderson, A. S. (2001). Loss, transition and the search for significance. In N. Thompson (Ed.), *Loss and grief: A guide for human services professionals.* Basingstoke, UK & New York: Palgrave.

Neimeyer, R. A. & Arvay, M. J. (2004). Performing the self: Therapeutic enactment and the narrative integration of traumatic loss. In H. Hermans & G. Dimaggio (Eds.), *The dialogical self in psychotherapy.* New York: Brunner Routledge.

Neimeyer, R. A., Prigerson, H. G., & Davies, B. (2002). Mourning and meaning. *American Behavioral Scientist, 46,* 235–251.

Neimeyer, R. A., & Tschudi, F. (2003). Community and coherence: Narrative contributions to a psychology of conflict and loss. In G. Fireman, T. McVay, & O. Flanagan (Eds.), *Narrative and consciousness: Literature, psychology, and the brain.* New York: Oxford.

Nesse, R. M. (1991). What good is feeling bad? The evolutionary benefits of psychic pain. *The Sciences, November/December,* 30-37.

Noppe, I. (2000). Beyond broken bonds and broken hearts: The bonding of theories of attachment and grief. *Developmental Review, 20,* 514-538.

Parkes, C. M. (1986). *Bereavement: Studies of grief in adult life* (2nd American ed.). Madison, CT: International Universities Press.

Parkes, C. M. (1988). Bereavement as a psychosocial transition: Processes of adaptation to change. *Journal of Social Issues, 44,* 53–65.

Parkes, C. M. (1996). *Bereavement: Studies of grief in adult life* (3rd ed.). London: Routledge.

Parkes, C. M. (1998a). *Bereavement: studies of grief in adult life* (3rd ed.). Harmondsworth, UK: Pelican.

Parkes, C. M., (1998b, March 14). Coping with loss: Bereavement in adult life. *British Medical Journal, 316,* 856-859

Parkes, C. M., & Weiss, R. S. (1983). *Recovery from bereavement.* New York: Basic Books.

Parkes, C. M., & Weiss, R. (1995). *Recovery from bereavement* (2nd ed.). Northvale, NJ: Jason Aronson.

Payne, S., Jarrett, N., Wiles, R., & Field, D. (2002). Counselling strategies for bereaved people offered in primary care. *Counselling Psychology Quarterly, 15,* 161-177.

Pennebaker, J.W. (2002). *Emotion, disclosure & health.* Washington, D.C.: American Psychological Association.

Pennebaker, J. W., & Keough, K. A. (1999). Revealing, organizing, and reorganizing the self in response to stress and emotion. In R. J. Contrada & R. D. Ashmore (Eds.), *Self, social identity, and physical health: Interdisciplinary explorations* (pp. 101–121). Oxford, England: Oxford University Press.

Pennebaker, J.W., & Susman, J.R. (1988). Disclosure of traumas and psychosomatic processes. *Social Science and Medicine, 26,* 327-332.

Pennebaker, J.W., & Suedfeld, P. (1997). Health outcomes and cognitive aspects of recalled negative life events. *Psychosomatic Medicine, 59(2),* 172-177.

Pine, V. R. (Ed.). (1990). *Unrecognized and unsanctioned grief: The nature and counseling of unacknowledged loss.* Springfield, IL: Thomas.

Pollock, G. N. (1961). Mourning and adaptation. *International Journal of Psychoanalysis, 43,* 341-361.

Rando, T. A. (1993). *Treatment of complicated mourning.* Champaign, IL: Research Press.

Rando, T. A. (1986). *Parental loss of a child.* Champaign, IL: Research Press.

Raphael, B. (1983). *The anatomy of bereavement.* New York: Basic Books.

Reed, M. D. (1993). Sudden death and bereavement outcomes: The impact of resources on grief symptomatology and detachment. *Suicide and Life Threatening Behavior, 23,* 204-220.

Reed, M. D. (1998). Predicting grief symptomatology among the suddenly bereaved. *Suicide and Life-Threatening Behavior, 28(3),* 285-301.

Reed, M. D., & Greenwald, J. Y (1991). Survivor victim status, attachment, and sudden death bereavement. *Suicide and Life-Threatening Behavior, 21,* 385-401.

Riches G. & Dawson P. (1998) Lost children, living memories: the role of photographs in processes of grief and adjustment among bereaved parents. *Death Studies 22,* 121–140.

Riches G., & Dawson P. (2000) *An Intimate Loneliness: supporting bereaved parents and siblings.* Open University Press, Buckingham.

Rosen, H. (1984-1985). Prohibitions against mourning in childhood sibling loss. *Omega, 15,* 307-316.

Rosenblatt, P. C. (1997). Grief in small-scale societies. In C. M. Parkes, P. Laungani, & B. Young (Eds.), *Death and bereavement across culture* (pp. 34-46). London, Routledge.

Rosenblatt, P. C. (2000). *Parent Grief: Narratives of Loss and Relationship.* Philadelphia, PA: Taylor and Francis.

Rubin, S. (1985). The resolution of bereavement: A clinical focus of the relationship of the deceased. *Psychotherapy, 22,* 231-235.

Rubin, S. (1993). The death of a child is forever. In M. S. Stroebe, W. Stroebe, W. Stroebe, & R. O. Hansson (Eds.), *Handbook of bereavement: Theory, research and intervention* (pp. 28-299). New York: Cambridge University Press.

Sabar, S. (2000). Bereavement, grief, and mourning: A gestalt perspective. *Gestalt Review, 4,* 152-168.

Samarel, N. (1993). The dying process. In H. Wass & R. A. Neimeyer (Eds.), *Dying: Facing the facts* (3rd ed.). Washington, DC: Taylor & Francis.

Sanders, C. M. (1993). Risk factors in bereavement outcome. In M. S. Stroebe, W. Stroebe, & R. O. Hansson, Eds., *Handbook of Bereavement: Theory, Research and Intervention.* Cambridge, UK: Cambridge University Press.

Sanders, C. M. (1999). *Grief, the mourning after: Dealing with adult bereavement* (2nd ed.). New York: Wiley.

Schut, H. A. W., Stroebe, M., de Keijser, J., & van den Bout, J. (1997). Intervention for the bereaved: Gender differences in the efficacy of grief counseling. *British Journal of Clinical Psychology, 36,* 63-72.

Servaty-Seib, H. (2004). Connections between counseling theories and current theories of grief and mourning. *Journal of Mental Health Counseling, 26(2),* 125-145.

Shaver, P. R., & Tancredy, C. M. (2001). Emotion, attachment, and bereavement: A conceptual commentary. In M. Stroebe, R. O. Hansson, W. Stroebe, & H. Schut (Eds.), *Handbook of bereavement research: Consequences, coping, and care* (pp. 63–88). Washington, DC: American Psychological Association.

Shuchter, S. R. (1986). *Dimensions of grief: Adjusting to the death of a spouse.* San Francisco: Jossey-Bass.

Shuchter, S. R., Zisook, S. (1988). Widowhood: The continuing relationship with the dead spouse. *Bulletin of the Menninger Clinic, 52(3),* 269-279.

Silverman, P. R. (2000). *Never too young to know: Death in children's lives.* New York: Oxford.

Silverman, P.R., & Klass, D. (1996) Introduction: what's the problem? In D. Klass, P. R. Silverman, & S. L. Nickman (Eds.), *Continuing Bonds: New Understandings of Grief* (pp. 3-23). Washington, DC: Taylor & Francis.

Silverman, P. R., Nickman, S., & Worden, J. W. (1992). Detachment revisited: The child's reconstruction of a dead parent. *American Journal of Orthopsychiatry, 62,* 494–503

Small, N. (2001). Theories of grief: A critical review. In J. Hockey, J. Katz, & N. Small (Eds.), *Grief, mourning, and death ritual* (pp. 19-48). Philadelphia: Open University Press.

Small, N., & Hockey, J. (2001). Discourse into practice: The production of bereavement care. In J. Hockey, J. Katz, & N. Small (Eds.), *Grief, mourning, and death ritual* (pp. 97-124). Philadelphia: Open University Press.

Smyth, J. M. (1998). Written emotional expression: Effect sizes, outcome types and moderating variables. *Journal of Consulting and Clinical Psychology. 66,* 174 – 184.

Staudacher, C. (1987). *Beyond grief: A guide for recovering from the death of a loved one.* Oakland, CA: New Harbinger Publications.

Steiner, J. (1993). *Psychic retreats.* London: Routledge.

Steiner, J. (1996). The aim of psychoanalysis in theory and practice. *International Journal of Psycho-Analysis, 77(6),* 1073-1083.

Stroebe, M. (1992-1993). Coping with bereavement: A review of the grief work hypothesis. *Omega, 26(1)* 19-42.

Stroebe, M., Gergen, M., Gergen, G., & Stroebe, W. (1992). Broken hearts or broken bonds? *American Psychologist, 47,* 1205-1212.

Stroebe, M., Gergen, M., Gergen, K., & Stroebe, W. (1996) Broken hearts or broken bonds? In D. Klass, P. R. Silverman, & S. L. Nickman (Eds.), *Continuing bonds: New understandings of grief* (pp. 31-43). Philadelphia, PA: Taylor and Francis.

Stroebe, M. S., Hansson, R. O., & Stroebe, W. (1993). Contemporary themes and controversies in bereavement research. In M. S. Stroebe, W. Stroebe, & R. O. Hansson (Eds.), *Handbook of bereavement: Theory, research, and intervention* (pp. 457–476). Cambridge, England: Cambridge University Press.

Stroebe, M., & Schut, H. (1999). The dual-process model of coping with bereavement: Rationale and description. *Death Studies, 23,* 174–184.

Stroebe, M., & Schut, H. A. W. (2001a). Meaning making in the dual process model of coping with bereavement. In R. A. Neimeyer (Ed.), *Meaning reconstruction and the experience of loss* (pp. 55–73). Washington, DC: American Psychological Association.

Stroebe, M., & Schut, H. A. W. (2001b). Models of coping with bereavement: A review. In M. Stroebe, R. O. Hansson, W. Stroebe, & H. Schut (Eds.), *Handbook of bereavement research: Consequences, coping, and care* (pp. 375–403). Washington, DC: American Psychological Association.

Stroebe, M., Schut, H., & Stroebe, W. (2005). Attachment in coping with bereavement: A theoretical integration. *Review of General Psychology, 9(1),* 48-66.

Stroebe, M., & Stroebe, W. (1991). Does "grief work" work? *Journal of Consulting and Clinical Psychology, 59,* 479–482.

Stroebe, M.S., Stroebe, W., & Hansson, R.O. (Eds.) (1997). *Handbook of Bereavement: Theory, Research, and Intervention, 2e.* Cambridge University Press, Cambridge.

Stroebe, M. S., van den Bout, J., & Schut, H. (1994). Myths and misconceptions about bereavement: The opening of a debate. *Omega, 29,* 187-203.

Stroebe, W., & Stroebe, M. S. (1987). *Bereavement and health.* New York: Cambridge University Press.

Stillion, J. M. (1996). Survivors of suicide. In K. J. Doka (Ed), *Living with grief after sudden loss* (pp. 41-51). Washington, DC: Hospice Foundation of America.

Stylianos, S. K., & Vachon, M. L. S. (1993). The role of social support in bereavement. In M. S. Stroebe, W. Stroebe, & R. O. Hansson (Eds.), *Handbook of bereavement: Theory, research, and intervention* (pp.397-410). New York: Cambridge University Press.

Talbot, K. (2002). *What forever means after the death of a Child.* London: Brunner-Routledge.

Tekavcic-Grad, O., Zavasnik, A. (1992). Aggression as a natural part of suicide bereavement. *Crisis, 13(2),* 65-69.

Toller, P. W. (2005). Negotiation of dialectical contradictions by parents who have experienced the death of a child. *Journal of Applied Communication, 33,* 46-66.

Van der Wal, J. (1989-1990). The aftermath of suicide: A review of empirical evidence. *Omega, 20(2),* 149-171.

Viorst, J. (1986). Necessary losses: The loves, illusions, dependencies and impossible expectations that all of us have to give up in order to grow. London: Simon & Schuster.

Walter T. (1996) A new model of grief: bereavement and biography. *Mortality, 1,* 7–26.

Walter, T. (1997). Letting go and keeping hold: A reply to Stroebe. *Mortality, 2(3),* 263-266.

Walter, T. (1999). *On bereavement.* Philadelphia: Open University Press.

Wambach, J. A. (1985). The grief process as a social construct. *Omega, 16,* 201-21[illegible].

Weizman, S., & Kamm, P., (1985). *About mourning: Support and guidance for the bereaved.* New York: Human Science Press.

Wheeler, I. (1993-1994). The role of meaning and purpose in life in bereaved parents associated with a self-help group: Compassionate friends. *Omega, 28(4),* 261-271.

Worden, J. W. (1982). *Grief counseling and grief therapy: A handbook for the mental health practitioner.* New York: Springer.

Worden, J. W. (1991). *Grief counseling and grief therapy: A handbook for the mental health practitioner* (2nd ed.). New York: Springer.

Worden, J. W. (2002). *Grief counseling and grief therapy: A handbook for the mental health practitioner* (3rd ed.). New York: Springer.

Wortman, C. B., & Silver, R. D. (1989). The myths of coping with loss. *Journal of Consulting and Clinical Psychology, 57,* 349-357.

Wortman, C. B., & Silver, R. C. (1990). Successful mastery of bereavement and widowhood: A life course perspective. In P. B. Baltes & V. M. Baltes (Eds.), *Successful aging: Perspectives from the social sciences* (pp. 419-446). New York: Cambridge University Press.

Wortman, C. B. & Silver, S. R. (1992). Reconsidering assumptions about coping with loss: An overview of current research. In L. Montada, S. H. Filipp, & M. J. Lerner (Eds.), *Life crises and experiences of loss in adulthood* (pp. 341-365). Hillsdale, NJ: Erlbaum.

Zisook, S., & Shuchter, S. R. (1991). Early psychological reaction to the stress of widowhood. *Psychiatry 54,* 320-333.

In Chapter 9 of her text, *Relational Communication*, Julia Wood discusses the process of deterioration and ending personal relationships. As noted earlier, however, she offers little discussion of the grief felt during such loss. In the previous reading by Christine Smith, she provides an overview of traditional themes and models for exploring the grief process; however, she also posits the need for a new paradigm that reflects a more integrative approach to the study of grief. As she notes, this dialectical approach would focus on the process of oscillating between "focus on the loss" and "coping with other stressors that arise from the loss."

In her article entitled, "Negotiation of Dialectical Contradictions by Parents who have Experienced the Death of a Child," Paige W. Toller examines how bereaved parents experience communication with individuals in their immediate social network. After providing a brief overview of the literature that serves as a foundation for the study of relational dialectics, Toller notes that the majority of dialectical research has focused primarily on contradictions experienced within the basic dyadic unit; however, she explains that researchers are increasingly interested in exploring the contradictions experienced between the dyad and its social network.

Given the tremendous grief experienced by parents after the loss of a child, Toller believes it is most appropriate to study the communication about the loss between parents and their social network of family and friends. Specifically, Toller posits two important research questions: 1) What, if any, dialectical contradictions do bereaved parents experience when communicating with others about their loss? and 2) How, if at all, do bereaved parents use communication to manage dialectical contradictions in their relationships with others? Using contacts from a national and local support group for bereaved parents, family, and friends, Toller conducted interviews with parents who have experienced the loss of a child. From transcripts of the recorded interviews, she was then able to identify categories and themes related to two primary dialectics these parents experienced.

As you read the article, note the strategies of selection and taking control that parents use to negotiate the openness – closedness dialectic they encounter as well as the rituals and symbols they use to negotiate the presence – absence dialectic they encounter. As Toller discusses how parents address each of these dialectics, she includes concrete examples and specific dialogue from the interviews of these parents; this data clearly indicates that communication plays a key role in how bereaved parents negotiate and manage these dialectical tensions. Though Toller acknowledges limitations to her study, she provides practical applications for bereaved parents, bereavement support groups, helping professionals, and individuals within the bereaved parent's social network. Perhaps you will find these applications useful as you consider the dialectical tensions you may have to navigate in the bereavement process.

Negotiation of Dialectical Contradictions by Parents who have Experienced the Death of a Child

Paige W. Toller

This study examines how bereaved parents experience communicating with individuals in their social network. The bereaved parents in this study experienced two dialectical contradictions: (a) between the physical absence of their child and the continuing presence and emotional bond with their deceased child; and (b) between being open or closed when deciding whether to talk about the deceased child to others. Results describe how parents communicatively negotiated these contradictions. The article concludes by discussing practical applications for bereaved parents, bereavement support groups, helping professionals, and individuals within the bereaved parents' social network-

The death of a child is one of the most devastating and life-altering events that a parent can experience. Parents describe this deeply painful event as cataclysmic or earth-shattering (Oliver, 1999). For parents, the death of a child challenges the natural order of life, while robbing them of their parental status and identity (Hastings, 2000; Riches & Dawson, 1996a, 1996b). Bereaved parents experience a liminal identity as they continue to feel parental responsibilities and emotion towards a deceased child (Romanoff & Terenzio, 1998). The liminal nature of being betwixt and between may result in bereaved individuals feeling like a parent and not like a parent simultaneously—further affecting the bereaved parents' identities (Romanoff & Terenzio, 1998).

In addition to an altered self-identity, many bereaved parents find relationships with family and friends are changed after the death of a child (Rando, 1986). Communication with family and friends is often strained as it is difficult for others to respond to parents' grief. Often this is due to family and friends' uncertainty about what to say or do (Rando, 1986, 1988).

As a result, communicating about their loss to others creates a dilemma for bereaved parents. Parents experience a persistent need to talk about the child's death in order to make sense of the experience (Attig, 1996; Murphy, 1996). However, friends and family members do not readily engage in conversation with bereaved parents or create opportunities for parents to talk about their loss (Rando, 1986, 1988). Friends and family may even criticize a bereaved parent for perpetuating the memory of the child (Hastings, 2000). As a result, bereaved parents may feel stigmatized (Riches & Dawson, 1996a) or socially ostracized (Rando, 1986).

As the literature suggests, bereaved parents' communication about their loss may be hindered by the potential reactions of friends and family members.

Nonetheless, the literature argues that bereaved parents want to communicate with others about their child's death. As such, further examination of how bereaved parents cope with these tensions is warranted. Furthermore, if communication with friends and family members is inhibited how do bereaved parents communicate to others the ongoing relationship they often have with their dead child, even though the child is physically absent? The purpose of this study is to examine how bereaved parents use communication to cope with such tensions after the death of a child. A dialectical perspective, which centers on contradictions of relating, may illuminate these questions more dearly (Baxter & Montgomery, 1996).

Relational Dialectics

Originating from the work of Russian philosopher Mikhail Bahktin (1981, 1984), Baxter and Montgomery (1996) refined a theory of relational dialectics that examines the inherent tensions within relationships. At the heart of relational dialectics is contradiction or "the dynamic interplay of opposing forces" (Baxter & Braithwaite, in press, P. 3). The dynamic interplay of opposing forces indicates that relationships experience ongoing, co-existing forces that are both/and rather than either/or (Baxter & Montgomery, 1997). All dialectic approaches to communication share three basic assumptions: (a) the process of relating involves contradictions; (b) these contradictions inspire relational change; and (c) the contradictions are constructed and enacted through communication (Baxter & Braithwaite, in press).

Baxter and Montgomery (1996) proposed that three main contradictions exist within relationships. The connectedness-autonomy dialectic is the contradiction between wanting to be more intimate and yet needing to maintain individuality. The stability-change dialectic addresses the contradiction between both the need for familiarity within a relationship and the need for a degree of novelty. Finally, the openness-closedness dialectic concerns the need to share information with a relational partner and the need to retain some degree of privacy. These three internal contradictions demonstrate that relationships experience tensions that do not have either/or solutions, which cannot be resolved but instead are managed through communication (Baxter & Montgomery, 1996.)

Currently, a number of scholars are beginning to look at the dialectical tensions that occur in relationships where one person in the relational equation is absent or somehow incapacitated. For example, in a study looking at married widowhood, Baxter, Braithwaite, Golish, and Olson (2002) found that wives of Alzheimer's patients experienced a relational contradiction resulting from their husband's physical presence' and emotional/mental absence. Golish and Powell (2003) argued that parents who experience the birth of a premature baby encounter a dialectic of joy-grief as the parents are happy about the birth but also feel a sense of mourning or loss due to the baby's unexpected birth date. Bryant (2003) found that recognizing the place of a deceased parent created a presence-absence contradiction in stepfamilies formed after the death of a parent.

Although the majority of dialectical research has focused on the contradictions located within the boundaries of the dyad (e.g., Baxter et al., 2002; Baxter & West, 2003), researchers have examined the external contradictions that exist between the boundaries of the dyad and others in the social network (Baxter, 1993), such as the work of Braithwaite and Baxter (1995) on couples publicly renewing their marriage vows. Although not focused on death or dying, these studies illustrate that individuals experience contradictions not only within dyadic boundaries, but also between the dyad and the outside world.

The death of a child is a tremendous loss as bereaved parents struggle with the agony of their child's permanent absence and yet still experience ongoing feelings toward their dead child. In addition, bereaved parents may desire to talk about their feelings of grief to friends and family members and yet are hesitant to do so because of the potentially negative reactions from others. As such, the reviewed literature does support the notion that contradictions can and do exist in relationships that have experienced loss, whether it is a loss of mental functioning by one relational partner (Baxter et al., 2002) or the loss of a parent (Bryant, 2003). Thus, it is plausible that the theoretical framework of relational dialectics will highlight and accent the contradictions that can occur within bereaved families. Therefore, this study sought to answer the following research questions:

RQI: What, if any, dialectical contradictions do bereaved parents experience when communicating with others about their loss?

RQ2: How, if at all, do bereaved parents use communication to manage dialectical contradictions in their relationships with others?

Method

In order to listen to the voices and experiences of individuals who had experienced the phenomenon of interest, this study used a qualitative-interpretive method. After the University's Institutional Review Board granted approval, participants were located by contacting and attending chapter meetings of The Compassionate Friends, a nationwide peer support group, and Community Friends, a local peer support group.

At each meeting, sign-up sheets were left for parents who were interested in participating in the study, which the support group facilitators later mailed to me. Interview times and dates were arranged with interested participants over the telephone. Following this, in-depth, face-to-face interviews were conducted with 16 parents who had experienced the death of a child. Data were collected until recurring patterns appeared and a point of theoretical saturation had been reached (Leininger, 1994; Strauss & Corbin, 1998).

Participants

Of the 16 parents who participated in the study 12 were women, 4 were men, and all were Caucasian. A total of 12 interviews were conducted, eight taking place with mothers only and four as marital dyads. Thirteen participants were currently married to the biological father or mother of their deceased child, one mother was currently married to someone who was not the biological father of the child, and two mothers were currently divorced. All but one parent was currently participating in a bereavement support group.

The time from the child's death to the interview ranged from 6 months to 29 years, with a mean of 8.2 years. The age of the child at the time of death ranged from 5 months to 35 years, with a mean age of 14.1 years of age. Of the 12 interviews conducted, the reported cause of death was as follows: three from illness (25%), four by suicide (33.3%), and five by accidental death (41.7%).

Interviewer Procedure

The semi-structured interview guide (see appendix) consisted of various demographic questions followed by open-ended and hypothetical questions. Similar to the retrospective interview technique, many of the questions encouraged the parents to describe their interaction with friends and family members before and after the death of their child (Huston, Surra, Fitzgerald, & Cate, 1981). Parents were also asked to describe relationships with friends and family in the present.

Of the 12 interviews conducted, 10 took place in the participants' homes, one at a hospital meeting room, and one at a local café. Because participants were assured that their identities would be kept confidential, pseudonyms are used throughout the study. The interviews ranged from 90 minutes to 4 hours, with the average interview lasting about 2 hours.

Data Analysis

Each audio-taped interview was listened to in its entirety and transcribed verbatim as quickly as possible after the interview had taken place. All of the audio-tapes were number coded, and the transcripts were identified with the corresponding number code as well as pseudonyms. Participants' nonverbal communication was also included in the transcription, such as long pauses, crying, loudly emphasized words, and so forth. The transcribed interviews yielded a total of 472 pages of single-spaced data.

A modified version of the constant-comparative analysis was used to identify and develop categories and thematic patterns (Strauss & Corbin, 1998). First, the transcripts were read through in their entirety. While reading through the transcripts, initial impressions were written down in the form of memos, which continued throughout the entire data analysis.

The raw data were then reduced to a more workable size as a way of "selecting, focusing, simplifying, abstracting, and transforming the data that appears in written-up field notes or transcriptions" (Miles & Huberman, 1994, p. 10). According to Miles and Huberman, data reduction occurs before and throughout the data collection process as the researcher decides certain things such as which theoretical framework to use, which data collection process to use, and so forth. The raw data were examined with an eye towards identifying possible dialectical patterns, as a dialectical perspective served as both a sensitizing concept and an organizing framework (Strauss & Corbin, 1998), consequently reducing the raw data to approximately 75 pages of single-spaced transcription.

The reduced data were then subjected to open coding, where whole paragraphs were separated into categories of information (Strauss & Corbin, 1998). Following the example of Baxter, Braithwaite, Bryant, and Wagner (2004), open coding in this study was organized around Spradley's (1979) attribution semantic relationship, where "X is an attribute (characteristic) of Y" (p. 111). An example of a semantic relationship within this study was the nature of communicating or talking to others about the child's death and the nature of not communicating or talking to others about the child's death. The categories were then compared with each other for similarities and differences (Strauss & Corbin, 1998). When differences were found, a new category was added, resulting in 12 open codes. Generally, open coding is repetitious, as coding categories are added, combined, and revised until the coding categories do not require further modification (Baxter et al.). As such, six open codes remained at the conclusion of open coding.

After open coding, axial coding was used. During axial coding "categories are related to their subcategories to form more precise and complete explanations about phenomena" (Strauss & Corbin, 1998, p. 124). In axial coding, categories and subcategories are examined to see if they are linked or related to one another. Axial coding is similar to Spradley's (1979) semantic relationship of strict inclusion, where "X is a kind of Y" (p. 111) and the "Y" represents contradiction. In this case, axial coding involved looking at the bereaved parents' discourse for simultaneous opposites from the categories created during open coding. Organizing the bereaved parents' discourse was done using a modified version of Spradley's domain analysis worksheet. Using the domain analysis worksheet, simultaneous and opposing contradictions were identified as they related to the selected open code. For instance, during open coding, one category identified was "bringing up the child's name during family conversations." During axial coding a subcategory revealed that a simultaneous opposite of this was "not talking about the child with [certain family members]." It appeared that the simultaneous openness and closedness about the child's death was a contradiction, hence the positing of the openness-closedness dialectic. As contradictions were identified during this stage, four categories from open coding that were not dialectical were removed from analysis. The analysis was also rechecked to ensure consistency of the categories and to identify any rival explanations for the findings (Miles & Huberman, 1994).

To illustrate and support each contradiction, exemplars from the data were used. After the initial version of the manuscript was completed, each parent was sent a copy, along with a letter requesting their feedback concerning its findings. Responses from the participants confirmed the findings of the study, which is discussed further in the practical applications section.

Results and Discussion

For the parents in this study, talking about their dead children to others was often a double-edged sword. Parents often desired to share with friends and family members their grief and feelings of loss. At the same time, most of the parents interviewed were hesitant to be open about their feelings as they were afraid of the potentially negative reactions of others. Likewise, these parents found it difficult to articulate to others that although their child was physically gone from them, they continued to feel an emotional bond with their dead child. As such, the analysis of the interviews revealed two primary dialectical contradictions: (a) openness-closedness and (b) presence-absence. To manage contradictions of openness-closedness parents were selective in their communication and also would take control of the communicative interaction. Likewise, bereaved parents used rituals and symbols to help manage the dialectical contradiction of presence-absence.

Openness-Closedness

The decision of whether to talk to others about the death of their child presented an obvious contradiction for these parents. On one hand, many felt the need to talk about their child and their loss, and on the other hand, they perceived the outcome of this as risky, particularly if friends and family members expressed that they should be moving on. One mother said she is open about her child's death:

> I've kind of gotten to the point that I would tell anyone. Not for any reason, but because they need to know that it doesn't go away. I normally don't cry about it like I did now. But you know, when they ask how many kids you have, I'm able to tell them, I don't cover it up. (10: 456-459; numbers denote interview number and the line number(s) of the corresponding transcript)

This mother communicates openly about her daughter's death so that people are aware of the persistent pain that follows the death of a child.

Parents also felt the need to talk about their children because doing so is comforting to them. Several of them emphasized the healing nature of keeping the child's memory alive through talking with others about the child's death. However, many felt they had to assess the comfort level of others before talking about their deceased child. After losing her adult son to a sudden heart attack, one mother commented:

> You know, I'm not going to ask my friends from work and school and all, come over here because I'm having a candle-lighting ceremony, they wouldn't feel comfortable, oh my gosh, what am I going to have say, oh jeez, I don't want be there when she's crying and carrying on. I mean, I don't know what they think is going to happen, but they are just very uneasy and unnerved by that. (1:670-674)

Consequently, some of the parents found themselves remaining silent about their deceased child. As this mother's comment illustrates, parents often placed the comfort of others above their own.

In addition, many parents were aware of potential discomfort and awkwardness for others if the child's name was brought up, or if there were any artifacts or symbols of the child present. For one particular couple, having company over involved having to decide whether to remove pictures of their dead son, because they believed having them up, as they otherwise did, might create an uncomfortable situation for their guests:

> There was one couple that clearly knew, and the other two couples I'm not sure they did, and you know, I wasn't going to bring it up, and Paul kind of said, well, maybe we ought to take the pictures down, because he was afraid they'd ask. And I'm like, if they ask, I'm going to tell them-I'm not going to hide the pictures. But it didn't come up, and that was a relief. And I probably wouldn't have shared a whole lot of it. (4:673-677)

As the quotation indicates, this couple was faced with the contradiction of being closed about their son's death to prevent awkwardness and yet needing to be open to others about what had happened to their son and family.

In addition, some of the parents felt as though sharing their grief would place stress on other family members. One mother asserted:

> I felt like I just put a tremendous burden on them, they've got their burden with their declining health and issues, I can't do this to my parents, I can't unload this on my parents, and so for a while, I really, I didn't call very often, and I didn't have anything to say to them because the only thing that was on my mind was Sally and I didn't want to unload Sally to them. (3:237-241)

In this situation, the emotional and physical state of her own parents resulted in this mother privileging the closedness pole of the contradiction, even though she may have wanted to be open with them about her daughter's death.

As the previous examples illustrated, the parents used discernment when communicating to others about the death of their child, particularly by being selective and by *taking control* of the interaction. By being selective with their disclosure and taking control of the communicative situation, parents were able to manage this contradiction communicatively.

Being selective

Bereaved parents attempted to manage the contradiction of openness-closedness by being selective regarding to who they disclosed. Parents based this selectivity on whether they perceived a person would react negatively to talk about the dead child. For example, a mother whose teenager daughter committed suicide decided to talk to others about her daughter if she felt that the other person was "safe":

> There are some friends that you lose, you know, but then you also find out who your real friends are. And you find out, even more than your friends, I call them safe people, you know, the people that don't go "[surprised noise] she said her name," you know, and have to change the subject right away or act like they really wished they hadn't asked how you were. (8:153-157)

Similarly, another couple whose daughter died in a car accident also said that they based their openness on the reactions of others:

> We know exactly which people, if we are in a social setting with them and friends, that we go out with, that the subject is just taboo, and we just don't bring up Lori, because that's when everything gets all confused. And so rather than do that, we just figure, it's those people's problem—if they can't handle this about Lori, we'll just go on. (6:439-443)

As both of these examples suggest, the reactions of others were indicative of how "safe," that person was, which ultimately determined how open or closed they would be about their child's death with that person.

In addition to determining whether the person was "safe," the parents' selectivity was based on criteria such as the sincerity exhibited by others or the degree of relational investment they had with the particular person(s). In terms of sincerity, some of the parents felt they could "sense" another person's genuineness:

> It depends, I think, on, the person, and I can't tell you what would make it different. Some people I can just feel or see a look in their eyes, like they want to know, but they don't want to ask, or something like that, you know, and so then, I'll just share that, but other ones, you know, you can tell that they really don't want to know. (9:252-255)

Another mother described her selectivity similarly: "When I feel like that someone's really concerned and really sincere, you know, I will answer their questions and I will talk about it. I don't try to avoid the subject" (1:453-454). Each of these comments indicates that these mothers were open about their child's death if they believed that the person was inquiring out of a genuine interest.

Determining people's sincerity also involved assessing whether they might be judged negatively for openly talking about their dead child. One mother said:

> So you know, those kind of people, that's it, you might go home and cry your eyes out for hours after they hurt you the first time, but you will not, eventually, without even knowing it, you will start to avoid them. (8:232-235)

Another father described how he has restricted communication with a friend:

> There is very poor communication because he has strong attitudes about grief and expectations about me, but a lot of it is he wants me to be the same guy I used to be, and I'm not, and so he kind of wants—yeah, I don't share much with him because it only irritates me what he says. (2:677-680)

As both quotations illustrated, openness is restricted when talking about the death resulted in feelings of judgment, which curtailed any future communication.

Bereaved parents' selectivity was also based on whether there was some sort of relationship between the recipient of the disclosure and the parent. If there was little or no relational history, most parents did not openly discuss their loss. This was especially true of small talk or when an individual was a casual acquaintance. If the relational investment was small, or if the conversation was obligatory, the likelihood of revealing this information was minimal. As one mother said:

> I know, I don't readily tell people what has happened, but if it's somebody I like, and seem genuinely interested in me, if it's somebody I'm going to spend time with, you know, in conversations, I will mention it along the way, so they know. (5:319-323)

This mother is open if she perceives that there is potential for a relationship or sustained interaction. Just as the sincerity of others predicated openness, a perceived opportunity to form relationships influences the parents' degree of openness. In addition, the genuineness and sincerity of the inquiring individual likely plays a role in whether any type of relationship will be formed between the parent and the individual.

In all of these exemplars, being selective was a decisive factor in determining just how open or closed parents would be with others. By being selective, parents were able to protect themselves from future judgment and painful comments by others. Being selective gave parents control over the depth of their disclosure with others. Along with being selective, bereaved parents managed the contradiction of openness-closedness by actively monitoring aspects of the interaction. In particular, parents monitored interactions with others by taking control of the communicative situation.

Taking control

Many of the parents expressed a persistent need to talk about their children as way of keeping the child's memory alive; thus, many of them purposefully integrated their deceased child into conversations. One mother commented: "I used to make it come up) you know, in conversation" (3:114-116). Because of her openness, this mother was able to remind others about her dead daughter during various interactions. However, she remarked that she does not bring her daughter into conversations as much anymore because other family members and friends have indicated that it was "time for her to move on" (3:119). Because of the attitudes and comments of others, this mother often finds herself choosing closedness over openness.

Another couple said that they bring their daughter up as much as they can, even though her death occurred nearly seven years ago:

> Well, we bring her, probably more with his mother, but we bring her into the conversation as much as we can. You know if something happens, we have a new little grandson, too, and if something happens in the conversation, you know, "Remember when Lori did this," or 'Lori would have liked this." (6:180-183)

Bringing their daughter into conversation allowed this couple to reflect and remember things about their deceased daughter, such as activities she liked. Furthermore, bringing their daughter into the conversation prompted others to remember the dead child as well.

For many of the parents, being in a support group taught them that it was important to talk about their deceased child, regardless of the reactions of others. After her son's accidental death nearly 30 years ago, one mother commented:

> Well, I learned in The Compassionate Friends—before I went to The Compassionate Friends people would ask me how many children I had, and I would say that I had a son that died, but then I thought I just wouldn't mention his name anymore, except to my very closest friends. But then I learned after going to The Compassionate Friends, that you know, you're the one that's dealing with the death night and day—if they can't handle it, it's too bad. ... I'm very open about Shawn, his death. (7:230-236)

Being in a support group has taught this mother, and other parents, that they will never "get over it" (7:240) and that healing involves learning to integrate their memories of the child into their present lives.

Just as parents practiced openness by actively integrating their deceased children into the conversation, they also took control by erecting boundaries of closedness. They constructed boundaries to indicate what they would or would not be willing to talk about, or if they wanted to talk about the child at all. Although talking about their loss was therapeutic, it was also emotionally draining as well. Consequently, some parents communicated in a manner that indicated whether they wanted to talk about their deceased child. One mother remarked:

> I tell you what, to be truthful, I will respond in a way to let them know [that] I don't want to talk about it—and I will say, I'm doing better—I'll go ahead, and say that—it lets them off the hook, and it lets me off the hook too, because I just can't bear to cry all the time. But if it's somebody I really want to talk with, you know, that's close to me, I can, I can talk to them. (1:179-183)

Communicating to others that she is "doing better" gives this mother control over the interaction, perhaps lessening any tension the involved parties may be experiencing.

Because it was difficult for her friends to know if she wanted to talk about her son's death, another mother said that she would "talk about it when I want to—when I don't, I don't, and I think that makes it easier for them because they are never really quite sure" (1:155-156). Another mother, whose teenage son committed suicide, agreed:

> But I've found with a lot of people it's just easier—if you feel like talking about it, you say something, because they don't know, they don't know if it's going to bother you, they don't want to take that chance, you know. It's uncomfortable for them, but it's not because they aren't thinking about it. (4:507-510)

According to both mothers, it was easier for everyone if they took the initiative and brought up their children when they felt like it. Each mother felt that the silence of others was not necessarily an indication of not caring or ignoring what has happened, but that these individuals were cautious about upsetting them

Many of the parents suggested that because others are uncertain about what to say or do, they often have to take control by teaching others how to communicate with them. One mother commented:

> I play cards with 11 other women, and afterwards, some of those women were there, about two weeks later I got a bunch of roses, and wrote something that must have been divinely inspired because I couldn't have done it myself, and just said this is what I need, you know, thank you for what you did, and here's where I am, and this is what I need, and don't be afraid to be stupid, and I'll be good. That's pretty much where I went and gave them each that note to take home. They've always been supportive—if I ask, they're there. (3:317-321)

Through the letter, this mother took control and communicated to others her needs and how they could meet those needs. Another mother commented that bereaved parents often have to set up communication guidelines:

> You really need to be the one to tell others how to communicate. They don't know—you have to let them know. And yeah, it's hard to do, but you can't expect them to know if they haven't experienced it. And I think you need to be the first one to bring up your child's name, or, like this book said, ask about their children. Because people are like—I'm afraid to talk to them because I'll mention my kids, and they'll be upset. You have to take the steps of saying, "Well, how are your kids doing—what are they up to?" (4:872-877)

By talking about the other person's child, this mother indicated that it is all right for friends and family members to talk about their living children in front of her. In fact, it is what she wants them to do, as it may create an opportunity for her to talk about her own children, both living and dead.

Along with integrating the child into conversation or teaching others how to communicate, some parents would use nonverbal approaches to remind people about their deceased child. For example, many of the parents included the child's name when signing Christmas cards as a way of communicating that the child was still a part of the family. Oftentimes the cards would be signed with "angel" and the child's name. One mother remarked that she always includes her daughter's name on her Christmas cards:

> On my Christmas cards, I always put her name on the Christmas cards at the very bottom, my angel Amy, just because I want her to be remembered, and you know, it's just the only way—if nobody's going to talk about her, I'm just going to put her name on there. (11:380-383)

For this mother, signing her daughter's name at the bottom of the card was her way of intentionally reminding others that although her infant daughter is dead, she still wanted others to remember her. By signing her daughter's name on cards, this mother is also communicating that her child is still present to her, although she had died several years ago. This example also illustrates the next contradiction bereaved parents experience, which is presence-absence.

Presence-Absence

Bereaved parents experience tensions from both the ongoing emotional bond they have with their child, and the physical absence of the child. This tension is seen through the dialectic of presence-absence (Baxter et al., 2002; Bryant, 2003). One mother commented that she enjoyed hearing stories about her son, because "well, it just gives me pleasure to know that he was such a neat guy, of course—a proud parent, you know, and it just keeps him alive to you—you do anything to keep them alive to you" (1:100-103). Similarly, the bond between one father and his daughter was so strong that:

> There's been times—it's less now—but, lots of times, walking through a store, I make room for her beside me, as I'm walking and I share the moment as if she was there. I kind of feel like she's there, so, you know, I make that adaptation. (2:496-499)

Another mother felt the presence of her son when she went into her basement, which was the place where he committed suicide. She remarked that even though it was difficult to be there:

> I still feel dose to Toby when I go downstairs. I feel close to him because I've hung his artwork there. I don't feel, I don't get that, you know, the other side of it and say this is the last place he was—this was his home. I don't color it to the negative side. (5:332-335)

As all of these quotes suggest, the need to keep their children alive to them is a profound and driving need for these parents. This need is at the heart of the presence-absence contradiction as parents must cope with their feelings of connection and simultaneously acknowledge the utter, physical absence of the child.

Unfortunately, many individuals within the parents' social network did not fully understand or honor this need. One mother commented on how frustrating it was when others were unwilling to talk about her dead child and how meaningful it was when people did remember her deceased daughter:

> It's like, you talk about your children that are alive, so why can't you talk about your child that's dead—that child will always be a part of your life, and you wouldn't want it to not be, so when people act like you're supposed to forget them, and stuff, that's real painful. So the people that do the opposite, you know, are just warming my heart, touching my spirit, because you know, they're like, yeah, I remember Jamie. (8:263-267)

When people were not willing to remember her dead child, the physical absence of her daughter was deeply felt by this mother; however, she was encouraged and comforted when others chose to remember her daughter.

Another mother commented how upsetting a counseling session was with a particular therapist, because the therapist told her to terminate the relationship with her dead daughter:

> The one that really irritated me—she told me that I needed to end my relationship with Jessie. That just didn't seem right to me. I know you have to have a different relationship, but you're not going to end it—it's not going to be over with—it's not going to go away. (10:641-645)

From this mother's point of view, ending her relationship with her dead daughter was unthinkable. She acknowledged that although the relationship was now altered it was certainly not over.

Like the previously discussed contradiction of openness-closedness, bereaved parents take an active role in managing this contradiction as well. This occurs mainly through the enactment of rituals and the use of symbols, particularly through jewelry.

Rituals

For bereaved parents, part of reconciling the presence-absence dialect was the performance of rituals that honored the memory of the child. Every parent interviewed in the present study mentioned visiting and decorating the child's gravesite. Often parents decorated the gravesites at holidays or on the anniversary of the death of the child. The gravesites were often decorated to reflect certain characteristics of the child. For instance, one couple always places a nativity set on their son's grave, because he had collected them since he was a small child.

Besides decorating the gravesite, many of the parents enacted holiday rituals of remembrance with their spouses and surviving children. One family gives each other a gift from their deceased daughter on Christmas morning. This gift is signed "From Angel Sally." Another mother said that her daughter had always wanted a Christmas tree decorated only with white lights and Precious Moments figurines, but for financial reasons they were not able to do so. However, since the death of her daughter, the family puts only those two decorations on their Christmas tree.

In addition to specific holiday rituals, many of the parents enacted daily and weekly rituals as a reminder of the child. In some instances, the rituals were used as a way to "talk" with the child (2:360). One father used daily journaling as a way to express his pain and to communicate with his deceased daughter:

> The journals, big parts of them are written to Jane, after she died, and this one in particular, I would, at noon in the office, I would hide in there, and write letters to Jane. I would do that, and I would pray on this side, but these are all letters to Jane. (2:356-359)

For this father, writing letters was a way to maintain a relationship with his deceased daughter and to acknowledge his contradicting feelings of presence and absence. Another couple described how one, or sometimes both of them would spend quiet time in the deceased child's room, sitting in a rocking chair and reflecting upon their day. For them, being in their daughter's room was a way for them to feel close to her. Other daily rituals parents mentioned were the lighting of candles in memory of the child or family prayers that included the deceased child. For one father, creating a weekly get-together with his surviving sons allowed all of them to share and reminisce together about the deceased child.

Although these rituals were generally private, many parents held very public rituals as well—ones that recognized the absence and honored the presence of the deceased child. At least two couples interviewed gave scholarships in memory of their child, with one couple presenting the scholarship to the recipient at a graduation ceremony. Other public acts of remembrance included taking flowers to church in memory of the child or sponsoring a specific radio station for a day in memory of the child.

Many of the parents also held gatherings for family and friends on specific dates, such as the death date of the child. On the anniversary of their daughter's death, one couple hosted a backyard party they called the "celebration of friends":

> We had a party very dose to the anniversary of her death that we called a celebration of friends, and had tons of people in our backyard and we'll do it again this year. . . . I'd like to see that keep going, even if it doesn't stay as big as it was. I'd like to see it keep going, because it's just one way to keep us together, and it's a good way to remember Sally, and everybody did remember Sally, so we know she's not forgotten, and to have a good time at the same time—so kind of celebrating her life too. (3:533-540)

For this couple, the gathering of friends allowed those present to remember their daughter as well as chance for them to celebrate friendships. In another instance, on the anniversary of their son's death, one couple invited family and friends to the gravesite, where the family participated in singing and releasing of doves. Afterwards, the entire family gathered together for a soup dinner.

Because the holiday season can be especially difficult for parents and other family members, some parents enacted rituals specifically to remember the child and possibly to ease tension that other family members might be experiencing. One mother makes and gives Christmas tree ornaments in memory of her daughter to ensure that everyone remembers her little girl. Another mother, because her son died close to Thanksgiving, lights a candle for her deceased son and other deceased family members at both Thanksgiving and Christmas get-togethers:

> What I did the next Thanksgiving was I got a candle for Sam, and I lit the candle in memory of Sam and other people we had lost. That was so helpful, because even though I cried when I did it, once you did it and you lit it, it's like, okay, there's this elephant in the room, and we've all recognized it and now we can go on with our dinner, because otherwise you're trying to ignore that it's there. (4:784-788)

As this mother suggested, it was obvious to everyone that her son was not physically present at holiday gatherings; however, by lighting a candle she communicated to others that he was still very much present in her memory.

Symbols

Besides the performance of rituals to remember the child, many of the parents wear jewelry and other artifacts as a way of communicating their child's emotional and relational presence. The visible wearing of jewelry, such as crosses or angels, was prevalent among the parents included in this study. Often they would wear a piece of jewelry that had belonged to the child. One couple each wears a piece of jewelry that I had belonged to their daughter; the mother wears a bracelet, and the father wears a ring on a chain around his neck. Both of them wear visible angel pins. When asked about the visibility of the pins, the father said that wearing them so openly was somewhat "troubling" to others, particularly at his workplace:

> That's one of things that bothered the people at work, that I wore an angel pin, especially, I was the manager, and it's an automotive type industry it's supposed to have the macho, and here's this here's your regional manager and owner of the company walking around with this angel pin. It bothered them, it really did, and I thought, well that's their problem. (6:558-562)

The highly visible nature of the pin often resulted in questions from customers. In response, he would tell them that his daughter had died in a car accident. Although this parent occasionally received negative responses to this symbol of his daughter, he persisted in wearing the pin.

In similar fashion, another father wears a pendant around his neck that once belonged to his deceased daughter. For him it is second nature to wear this item every day, often without realizing how noticeable it is to others. He claimed that wearing it every day allows him to feel dose to his daughter.

Another mother described how she, her husband, and their two sons each wore an angel charm around their necks as a meaningful way of keeping her daughter close to them. This woman also wears a visible angel pin. After the death of her son, another mother purchased a cross necklace and a cross pinky ring, as a reminder of both her son and her faith.

The visible nature of the jewelry is indicative of one way parents manage the presence-absence contradiction. Not only does the jewelry serve as a way of keeping the child close, but the visibility of the symbols can create opportunities for the parents to talk about the child when others see the jewelry and ask questions.

Parents also used other artifacts to manage the presence-absence dialectic. Every parent interviewed remarked that they still had pictures of their deceased child up in their home, many times hanging up with pictures of their surviving children. One family had planted and named a garden after their child. They also have a shelf in their living room with some of their daughter's toys on it, as a sign of remembrance. Participating in rituals, wearing jewelry and other mementos, and the presence of artifacts, such as pictures, pays homage to continuing bonds parents feel with their deceased children.

From the numerous quotes and exemplars, it is apparent that bereaved parents experience tensions regarding both openness-closedness and presence-absence.

Parents felt a simultaneous need to be open about their deceased child and yet to be closed to protect themselves and others. In this regard, this study parallels the findings of Bryant (2003). Bryant argued that some children, whose stepfamilies formed after the death of a parent, experienced a contradiction of openness-closedness when communicating with their stepparent about their deceased parent.

Likewise, the present study demonstrated that parents who experienced loss often take an active role in reconciling the contradiction of presence-absence. These findings parallels the findings of Bryant (2003), who discovered that children often used artifacts and rituals to communicatively manage the presence-absence tension after the death of a parent.

Conclusion

The results of this study indicate that talking to others about the death of their child was complex and sometimes difficult for bereaved parents. On one hand, parents indicated that being able to talk about their dead child was meaningful to them. On the other hand, talking to others about their dead child resulted in some parents feeling criticized or judged, leaving them wary of future interactions. As a result, many of the parents established criteria for talking to others. Parents' self-imposed criteria served as both a help and a hindrance. Although parents were able to regulate their communication with others, they were not always able to talk openly and freely about their grief.

Parents discussed how they experienced an ongoing relationship with their child, even though the child was deceased. Parents also discussed how rituals and the use of symbols enable them to keep their child's memory alive. Consequently, these rituals and symbols were also a way for parents to communicate to others that their deceased child was and still is a part of the parents' life.

This study found that communication played a key role in how bereaved parents negotiated and managed the dialectical tensions of openness-closedness and presence-absence. This study contributes to dialectical research as it examines a previously unexplored relational context, as well as another context in which the dialectic of presence-absence is applicable (see Baxter et al., 2002; Bryant, 2003).

Limitations and Future Research

Many of the limitations of this study could be remedied with future research. For instance, future studies could involve a larger, more diverse group of participants, as parents who are not actively involved in bereavement support groups may experience different dialectical tensions. Likewise, the perspective of bereaved parents from varying ethnic and racial backgrounds would also lend insight into the experience and management of dialectical tensions, particularly within differing cultural contexts. Future research also needs to examine whether bereaved parents also experience dialectical contradictions when communicating with their spouse, significant other, or surviving children.

Practical Applications

Bereaved Parents

For the parents in this study, ending their relationship with their deceased child was inconceivable. Regardless of the fact that their child was now permanently absent, parents believed that continuing some form of a relationship with their deceased child was necessary. Unfortunately, these parents discovered that talking about this ongoing relationship with others was difficult and at times painful.

For bereaved parents, the implications of this study reside in the communicative value of rituals and symbols. By enacting rituals, these parents were able to honor the bond they have with their deceased child. Moreover, these rituals, when enacted publicly, communicated to others that there was still an ongoing relationship. Likewise, wearing pieces of significant jewelry allowed parents to feel close to their children, as well as facilitate conversations giving parents the chance to talk about their deceased child with others.

By using rituals and symbols parents were able to communicate about their deceased child to others in a more indirect manner. In turn, the indirect form of communication appeared to protect parents somewhat from the outright disapproval and judgment they often experienced when interacting with others. As such, using rituals and symbols may enable bereaved parents to communicate to others about their deceased child in a manner that is less face threatening to the parent. Furthermore, the use of rituals and symbols allows parents not only to honor the memory of their child but also to manage the tensions of presence-absence.

Many of the parents in this study remarked that communicating to others about the felt tensions of presence-absence was often a burdensome task. Bereaved parents may need additional outlets and resources to help them communicate and mange this tension. As such, it is possible that bereavement support groups are a particular resource that could aid parents in this endeavor.

Bereavement Support Groups

Bereavement support groups, such as The Compassionate Friends, could assist bereaved parents by distributing information to friends and family members that describes how some parents may experience emotional connection with the deceased child. Through pamphlets or workshops, bereavement support groups could help others understand that preserving the child's memory is not a sign of unhealthy grieving or attachment, but is a way for parents to deal with this profound loss. Moreover, the articulation of this tension by support groups might encourage family members and friends to bring up the child's name or to participate in meaningful rituals with the parents.

Bereavement support groups could also rely on community resources, such as regional end of life coalitions, to distribute information to healthcare providers and other end of life professionals. Such groups may be able to encourage professionals to talk with friends and family members about bereaved parents' desire to have a continuing relationship with their child, as well as some of the communication difficulties that bereaved parents may face.

Helping Professionals

As one mother's quote indicated, helping professionals may not recognize or validate the contradiction of presence-absence experienced by parents. Instead, counselors and therapists may believe encouraging parents to move on or to let go is more appropriate. Because of their professional training, it may be difficult to convince therapists, clergy, counselors, and other healthcare professionals that some parents desire to somehow hold on to their relationship with their deceased child and this desire to hold on is not necessarily a sign of denial or unhealthy grieving. Fortunately, bereavement research indicates that grief professionals are beginning to reject the notion that severing all attachments with deceased loved ones is the desired way to facilitate healthy grieving (Hagman, 2001).

Like support groups, helping professionals could also inform family members and friends about some of the difficulties bereaved parents face. For instance, professionals might discuss with friends and family members that although talking about the dead child may be uncomfortable for them, it is often healing for the bereaved parent. Professionals can also educate friends and family members on why rituals are an important part of the healing process and encourage them to participate in rituals if the bereaved parent invites them to do so.

Individuals within the Bereaved Parent's Social Network

As the data from this study suggested, many of the bereaved parents' friends and family members were resistant to talking with the parent about the child. Reasons as to why family members and friends are hesitant to talk with bereaved parents may vary from existing Western thought that talk about death is taboo, to personal discomfort with the topic. Regardless of the reason, parents commented that it was extremely comforting and meaningful when friends and family members would actively remember and talk about the child with them.

The implications of this study for friends and family members is simply to be open and willing to talk with the bereaved parent, regardless of the discomfort they may feel. Friends and family members must realize that talking with the parents about their dead children could result in emotional reactions from the parent, but that these emotional reactions do not necessarily indicate that bereaved parents want to avoid this topic. As many of the bereaved parents in this study indicated, their constant feelings of grief and sadness are not necessarily provoked by the comments of others. Rather, their feelings stem from trying to cope with the fact that their child is permanently gone. Thus, when others avoid talking about the death or act as if things are normal, bereaved parents' feelings are further invalidated.

It is also important that friends and family members know that they too can continue to honor the memory of the child in other ways besides talking with the parent. Many of the parents discussed how meaningful it was to receive recognition of their deceased child, such as receiving a written note or card of support or encouragement, and finding flowers on their child's gravesite. These are examples of the ways in which friends and family members can honor the child's memory and support the bereaved parent.

Findings of this study suggest that for friends and family members to avoid or ignore the child's death simply compounds the parents' pain. Talking with the parent, reminiscing together about the child, and communicating support through symbolic gestures are all ways that friends and family can comfort and support parents who have experienced such a devastating loss.

Consider this . . .

- As you consider the bereavement process, how does Dialectical Theory provide insight to various aspects grief and bereavement?
- This study explored two relational dialectics confronted by parents bereaving the loss of a child. Briefly discuss each of these relational dialectics as well as the strategies or processes parents use to negotiate them. Give an example to illustrate each of your answers.
- While this study identified two primary relational dialectics confronted by parents who have experienced the death of a child, what other relational dialectics might occur for those who experience grief? Give an example to illustrate.
- From the applications offered to bereaved parents, bereavement support groups, helping professionals, and individuals within the bereaved parent's social network, which application do you find most valuable? Why?
- Given what new insight you've gained from our discussion of the grief process, what additional advice might you provide for those experiencing loss in their lives?

References

Attig, T. (1996). *How we grieve. re-learning the world.* New York: Oxford University Press.

Bakhtin, M. (1981). In M. M. Bahktin, & M. Holquist (Eds.), *The dialogic imagination: four essays.* Austin: University of Texas Press.

Bakhtin, M. (1984). in C. Emerson (Ed.), *Problems of Dostoevsky's poetics.* Minneapolis: University of Minnesota Press.

Baxter, L.A. (1993). The social side of personal relationships: a dialectical perspective. In S. Duck (Ed.), *Social context and relationships* (pp. 139-165). Newbury Park, CA: Sage.

Baxter, L. A., & Braithwaite, D. O. (in press). Social dialectics: the contradictions of relating. In B. Whaley, & W. Samter (Eds.), *Contemporary communication theories and exemplars.* Mahwah, NJ: Erlbaum.

Baxter, L. A., & Montgomery, B. M. (1996). *Relating. dialogues and dialectics.* New York: Guilford Press.

Baxter, L. A., & Montgomery, B. M. (1997). *Rethinking communication in personal relationships from a dialectic perspective.* In S. Duck (Ed.), Handbook of personal relationships (pp. 328-349). New York: John Wiley.

Baxter, L. A., Braithwaite, D. O., Bryant, L., & Wagner, A. (2004). Stepchildren's perceptions of the contradictions in communication with stepparents. *Journal of Social and Personal Relationships, 21,* 447-468.

Baxter, L. A., Braithwaite, D. O., Bryant, L., & Wagner, A. (in press). Stepchildren's perceptions of the contradictions in communication with stepparents. *Journal of Social and Personal Relationships.*

Baxter, L. A., & West, L. (2003). Couple perceptions of their similarities and differences: A dialectical perspective. *Journal of Social and Personal Relationships, 20,* 491-515.

Braithwaite, D. O., & Baxter, L. A. (1995). I do again: The relational dialectics of renewing marriage vows. *Journal of Social and Personal Relationships, 12,* 177-198.

Bryant, L. E. (2003). Stepchildren's perceptions of the contradictions in communication with stepfamilies formed post bereavement. Unpublished doctoral dissertation, University of Nebraska-Lincoln.

Golish, T. D., & Powell, K. A. (2003). Ambiguous loss: Managing the dialectics of grief associated with premature birth. *Journal of Social and Personal Relationships, 20,* 309-334.

Hagman, G. (2001). Beyond decathexis: Toward a new psychoanalytic understanding and treatment of mouming. In R. A. Neimeyer (Ed.), *Meaning reconstruction and the experience of loss* (pp. 13-31). Washington, DC: American Psychological Association.

Hastings, S. (2000). Self-disclosure and identity management by bereaved parents. *Communication Studies, 51,* 352-371.

Huston, T. L., Surra, C. A., Fitzgerald, N. M., & Cate, R. M. (1981). From courtship to marriage: Mate selection as an interpersonal process. In S. W. Duck, & R. Gilmour (Eds.), *Personal relationships 2: Developing personal relationships* (pp. 53-88). London: Academic Press.

Leininger, M. (1994). Evaluation criteria and critique of qualitative research studies. In J. M. Morse (Ed.), *Critical issues in qualitative research methods* (pp. 95-115). Thousand Oaks, CA: Sage.

Miles, M., & Huberman, A. (1994). *Qualitative data analysis.* Thousand Oaks, CA: Sage.

Murphy, S. A. (1996). Parent bereavement stress and preventive intervention following the violent deaths of adolescent or young adult children. *Death Studies, 20,* 441-452.

Oliver, L. E. (1999). *Effects of a child's death on the marital relationship: A review.* Omega, 39, 197-227.

Rando, T. A. (1986). *Parental loss of a child.* Champaign, IL: Research Press.

Rando, T. A. (1988). *Grieving: How to go on living when someone you love dies.* San Francisco: Jossey Bass.

Riches, G., & Dawson, P. (1996a). Communities of feeling: The culture of bereaved parents. *Mortality, 1,* 143-162.

Riches, G., & Dawson, P. (1996b). An intimate loneliness: Evaluating the impact of a child's death on parental self-identity and marital relationships. *Journal of Family Therapy, 18,* 1-22.

Romanoff, B. D., & Terenzio, M. (1998). Rituals and the grieving process. *Death Studies, 22,* 697-711.

Spradley, J. P. (1979). *The ethnographic interview.* New York: Holt, Rinehart and Winston.

Strauss, A., & Corbin, J. (1998). *Basics of qualitative research: Techniques and procedures for developing grounded theory* (2nd ed.). Thousand Oaks, CA: Sage.

Appendix: Interview Protocol

1. If you feel comfortable, could you tell me a little bit about your child? What were they like?
2. How would you describe your communication with your spouse before died?
   A. How would you describe your communication with your spouse after died?
   B. How would you describe your communication today?
3. How would you describe your communication with your surviving children before died?
   A. How would you describe your communication with your children after died?
   B. How would you describe your communication today?
4. How would you describe your communication with outside family members before died?
   A. How would you describe your communication with your family after died?
   B. How would you describe your communication with your family today?
5. How would you describe your communication with friends before died?
   A. How would you describe your communication with your friends after died?
   B. How would you describe your communication with your friends today?
6. Overall, what were some things people said or did that were helpful at the time you lost your child?
   A. What were some things people said or did that was not helpful at the time you lost your child?
7. How likely are you, today, to communicate about the loss of your child?
   A. To whom do you communicate about your loss most often?
   B. Who are the people you would not share your loss with?
8. What are some of the most difficult things to talk about after losing your child?
   A. What are some things that are easier to communicate about?
9. What, if any, are some rituals or activities that you do to remember your child?
10. If you were to give advice to others who have a friend or family member who loses a child, what if anything would you advise them to do or say?

Received September 22, 2003
Final revision received January 30, 2004
Accepted April 22, 2004